MW01596813

PINDAR:

THE OLYMPIAN AND PYTHIAN ODES,

WITH NOTES EXPLANATORY AND CRITICAL,

INTRODUCTIONS, AND INTRODUCTORY ESSAYS,

BY

C. A. M. FENNELL, M.A.

LATE FELLOW OF JESUS COLLEGE, CAMBRIDGE.

EDITED FOR THE SYNDICS OF THE UNIVERSITY PRESS.

Cambridge:
AT THE UNIVERSITY PRESS.

London: CAMBRIDGE WAREHOUSE, 17, Paternoster Row.
Cambridge: DEIGHTON, BELL, AND CO.
Leipzig: F. A. BROCKHAUS.
1879

PINDAR:

THE OLYMPIAN AND PYTHIAN ODES.

PREFACE.

In preparing this Edition of the Olympian and Pythian Odes I have had two objects in view: namely, to provide sufficient help for students who find Pindar a very difficult subject, and also to contribute to the criticism and interpretation of the author.

I have not often made special acknowledgments of indebtedness in my notes, and therefore here express in general terms my deep obligations to previous editors, especially to C. I. Tycho Mommsen, Böckh, Dissen (Schneidewin's Edition), and to Dr Donaldson, also to Professors Paley and Colvin. I have also to thank Mr B. Benham, B.A., late Scholar of Corpus Christi, for very valuable assistance in revision and many important suggestions. The extremely careful co-operation of the Press readers, &c., demands grateful mention.

In transliterating Greek words into English I have tried to approximate to what I conclude will be the method of the future; but I have not marked the quantity of long *i* and *u* nor of capitals, and seldom of final syllables. Besides these sacrifices of principle to convenience, I have not marked the quantities of abbreviated names, and have made sundry concessions to custom with respect to familiar names.

That I have substituted the etymologies of a newer school for many of those given by Dr Donaldson should be taken as a mark of respect paid to the weight of his authority. On such points I have often referred to Curtius, i.e., to *Grundzüge der griechischen Etymologie von George Curtius*, Third Ed., Leipzig, 1869.

The grammatical references are to *Syntax of the Moods and Tenses of the Greek Verb*, by Prof. W. W. Goodwin, Sixth Ed., London, 1875; and to *Syntax of the Greek Language*, by Dr J. N. Madvig, Edited by T. Kerchever Arnold, Sec. Ed., 1873.

In the occasional translations I have only aimed at reproducing the exact idea of the Greek, not at putting Pindar's sentiments into the most elegant and poetic English prose at my command; as I conceive that the office of interpreter cannot well be thoroughly combined with that of a tasteful translator.

The introduction to and analyses of the several odes are intended to give as clear a view as possible of the design of each poem and the relations of the several parts to each other and the whole. In some instances my explanations are new.

As few take interest in the metre, I have, to save space, placed the metrical schemes all together after the introductory remarks on Pindar's metres.

In executing a most laborious and responsible task I have been animated by the hope of promoting the sympathetic study of a favourite author.

C. A. M. FENNELL.

ΠΙΝΔΑΡΟΥ ΓΕΝΟΣ

διορθωθὲν παρὰ τοῦ σοφωτάτου κυροῦ Θωμᾶ τοῦ Μαγίστρου.

Ex Aldina et Romana.

ΠΙΝΔΑΡΟΣ τὸ μὲν γένος Θηβαῖος, υἱὸς Δαϊφάντου κατὰ τοὺς ἀληθεστέρους· οἱ δὲ Σκοπελίνου φασίν. οἱ δὲ λέγουσι τὸν αὐτὸν Δαΐφαντον καὶ Σκοπελῖνον· οἱ δὲ Παγωνίδου καὶ Μυρτοῦς, ἀπὸ κώμης Κυνοσκεφαλῶν. ἡ δὲ Μυρτὼ ἐγαμήθη Σκοπελίνῳ τῷ αὐλητῇ, ὃς τὴν αὐλητικὴν διδάσκων τὸν Πίνδαρον, ἐπεὶ εἶδε μείζονος ἕξεως ὄντα, παρέδωκε Λάσῳ τῷ Ἑρμιονεῖ μελοποιῷ, παρ' ᾧ τὴν λυρικὴν ἐπαιδεύθη. γέγονε δὲ κατὰ τοὺς χρόνους Αἰσχύλου, καὶ συγγε- γένηται αὐτῷ, καὶ τέθνηκεν ὅτε καὶ τὰ Περσικὰ* ἤκμαζεν. ἔσχε δὲ θυγατέρας δύο, Πολύμητιν καὶ Πρωτομάχην. κατῴκει δὲ τὰς Θήβας, πλησίον τοῦ ἱεροῦ τῆς μητρὸς τῶν θεῶν Ῥέας τὴν οἰκίαν ἔχων. ἐτίμα δὲ τὴν θεὸν σφόδρα ὢν εὐσεβέστατος, καὶ τὸν Πᾶνα, καὶ τὸν Ἀπόλλωνα, εἰς ὃν καὶ πλεῖστα γέγραφε. νεώτερος δὲ ἦν Σιμωνίδου, πρεσβύτερος δὲ Βακχυλίδου. κατὰ δὲ τὴν Ξέρξου κατάβασιν ἤκμαζε τὴν ἡλικίαν. ἐτιμήθη δὲ σφόδρα ὑπὸ πάντων τῶν Ἑλλήνων διὰ τὸ ὑπὸ τοῦ Ἀπόλλωνος οὕτω φιλεῖσθαι, ὡς καὶ μερίδα τῶν προσ- φερομένων τῷ θεῷ λαμβάνειν, καὶ τὸν ἱερέα βοᾶν ἐν ταῖς θυσίαις Πίνδαρον ἐπὶ τὸ δεῖπνον τοῦ θεοῦ. λόγος καὶ τὸν Πᾶνα ὀρχήσασθαί ποτε τὸν αὐτοῦ παιᾶνα καὶ χαίρειν ᾄδοντα τοῦτον ἀεὶ ἐν τοῖς ὄρεσι. φασὶ δὲ καὶ ὅτι ποτὲ Λακεδαιμόνιοι Βοιωτοὺς ἐμπρήσαντες καὶ Θήβας, ἀπέσχοντο μόνης τῆς οἰκίας αὐτοῦ, θεασάμενοι ἐπιγεγραμ- μένον τόνδε τὸν στίχον· "Πινδάρου τοῦ μουσοποιοῦ τὰν στέγαν μὴ

---

* Scribendum est fortasse τὰ Περικλέους.

καίετε." ὅπερ καὶ Ἀλέξανδρον μετὰ ταῦτά φασι πεποιηκέναι. καὶ
γὰρ οὗτος ἐμπρήσας τὰς Θήβας μόνης τῆς ἐκείνου οἰκίας ἐφείσατο.
ἐχθρῶς δὲ διακειμένων τῶν Ἀθηναίων πρὸς τοὺς Θηβαίους, ἐπεὶ εἶπεν
ἐν τοῖς ποιήμασιν, "Ὦ ταλαίπωροι Θῆβαι," καὶ, "Μεγαλοπόλιες
Ἀθᾶναι," ἐζημίωσαν αὐτὸν χρήμασιν οἱ Θηβαῖοι, ἅπερ ὑπὲρ ἐκείνου
ἔτισαν Ἀθηναῖοι. γέγραπται δὲ αὐτῷ ἑπτακαίδεκα βιβλία, ὧν τέσ-
σαρα ἡ λεγομένη Περίοδος, Ὀλυμπιονῖκαι, Πυθιονῖκαι, Νεμεονῖκαι,
Ἰσθμιονῖκαι.

*   *   *   *   *   *   *

Τέθνηκε δὲ ὁ Πίνδαρος ἓξ καὶ ἑξήκοντα ἐτῶν γεγονὼς [ἢ ὥς τινες
ὀγδοήκοντα] ἐπὶ Ἀβίωνος ἄρχοντος κατὰ ἕκτην καὶ ὀγδοηκοστὴν
Ὀλυμπιάδα. ἀκροατὴς δὲ γέγονε Σιμωνίδου. ὁ δὲ ἐπινίκιος οὗ ἡ
ἀρχή, "Ἄριστον μὲν ὕδωρ," προτέτακται ὑπὸ Ἀριστοφάνους τοῦ
συντάξαντος τὰ Πινδαρικὰ διὰ τὸ περιέχειν τοῦ ἀγῶνος ἐγκώμιον καὶ
τὰ περὶ τοῦ Πέλοπος, ὃς πρῶτος ἐν Ἤλιδι ἠγωνίσατο. γέγραπται
δὲ Ἱέρωνι βασιλεῖ Συρακουσίων· αἱ δὲ Συράκουσαι πόλις τῆς Σικε-
λίας· ὃς καὶ κτίστης Αἴτνης ἐγένετο πόλεως, ἀπὸ τοῦ ὄρους αὐτὴν
οὕτως ὀνομάσας. ἀποστείλας γὰρ οὗτος ἵππους εἰς Ὀλυμπίαν
ἐνίκησε κέλητι.

Καὶ ἄλλως ἐκ τῶν Σουΐδα.

Indidem.

Πίνδαρος Θηβαῖος, Σκοπελίνου υἱός, κατὰ δέ τινας Δαϊφάντου,
ὃ καὶ μᾶλλον ἀληθές. ὁ γὰρ Σκοπελίνου ἐστὶν ἀφανέστερος καὶ
προγενὴς Πινδάρου. τινὲς δὲ καὶ Παγωνίδου ἱστόρησαν αὐτόν.
μαθητὴς δὲ Μυρτίδος γυναικός, γεγονὼς κατὰ τὴν ξε΄ Ὀλυμπιάδα,
κατὰ τὴν Ξέρξου στρατείαν ὢν ἐτῶν μ΄. καὶ ἀδελφὸς μὲν ἦν αὐτῷ
ὄνομα Ἐρωτίων, καὶ υἱὸς Δαΐφαντος, θυγατέρες δὲ Εὔμητις καὶ
Πρωτομάχη. συνέβη δὲ αὐτῷ τὸν βίον τελευτῆσαι κατ᾽ εὐχάς.
αἰτήσαντι γὰρ τὸ κάλλιστον αὐτῷ δοθῆναι τῶν ἐν τῷ βίῳ, ἀθρόον
αὐτὸν ἀποθανεῖν ἐν θεάτρῳ ἀνακεκλιμένον εἰς τὰ τοῦ ἐρωμένου αὐτοῦ
Θεοξένου γόνατα, ἐτῶν νέ. ἔγραψε δ᾽ ἐν βιβλίοις ιζ΄ Δωρίδι δια-

λέκτῳ ταῦτα· Ὀλυμπιονίκας, Πυθιονίκας, Νεμεονίκας, Ἰσθμιονίκας, Προσόδια, Παρθένια, Ἐνθρονισμοὺς, Βακχικὰ, Δαφνηφορικὰ, Παιᾶνας, Ὑπορχήματα, Ὕμνους, Διθυράμβους, Σκολιὰ, Ἐγκώμια, Θρήνους, Δράματα τραγικὰ ιζ΄, Ἐπιγράμματα ἐπικὰ, καὶ καταλογάδην Παραινέσεις τοῖς Ἕλλησι καὶ ἄλλα πλεῖστα. Καὶ ἕτερος Πίνδαρος Σκοπελίνου Θηβαῖος, καὶ αὐτὸς λυρικὸς, ἀνεψιὸς τοῦ προτέρου.

Τὰς Θήβας τὴν πόλιν Ἀλέξανδρόν φασιν εἰς ἔδαφος κατασκάψαι, καὶ πλὴν ἱερέων τε καὶ ἱερειῶν τοὺς ἄλλους ἀνδραποδίσαι. καὶ τὴν Πινδάρου δὲ τοῦ ποιητοῦ οἰκίαν καὶ τοὺς ἐκγόνους τοῦ Πινδάρου, φησὶν Ἀρριανὸς ὁ ἱστορικὸς ἐν τῇ πρώτῃ διαβάσει Ἀλεξάνδρου, ἀπαθεῖς ἐφύλαξεν αἰδοῖ τῇ τοῦ Πινδάρου.

*   *   *   *   *   *   *

Γένος Πινδάρου διὰ στίχων ἡρωϊκῶν.

Ex Romana.

Πίνδαρον ὑψαγόρην Καδμηΐος οὐδεῖ Θήβης
κλειδίκη εὐνηθεῖσα μενεπτολέμῳ Δαϊφάντῳ
γείνατο ναιετάουσα Κυνὸς κεφαλῇ παρὰ χώρῳ,
οὐκ οἶόν γ'· ἅμα τῷ καὶ Ἐρείτιμον, εἰδότα θήρην,
5 εἰδότα πυγμαχίην τε παλαισμοσύνην τ' ἀλεγεινήν.
τὸν μὲν ὅτε κνώσσοντα ποτὶ χθόνα κάτθετο μήτηρ
εἰσέτι παιδίον ὄντα, μέλισσά τις ὡς ἐπὶ σίμβλῳ
χείλεσι νηπιάχοισι τιθαιβώσσουσα ποτᾶτο.
τῷ δὲ λιγυφθόγγων ἐπέων μελέων θ' ὑποθήμων
10 ἔπλετο δῖα Κόριννα· θεμείλια δ' ὥπασε μύθων
τοπρῶτον· μετὰ τὴν δ' Ἀγαθοκλέος ἔμμορεν αὐδῆς,
ὅστε ῥά οἱ κατέδειξεν ὁδὸν καὶ μέτρον ἀοιδῆς·
εὖτε δ' Ἀλεξάνδροιο Φιλιππιάδαο μενοινῇ
Καδμείων ἀφίκοντο Μακηδόνες ἄστεα πέρσαι,
15 Πινδαρέων μεγάρων οὐχ ἥψατο θεσπιδαὲς πῦρ.
ἀλλὰ τὸ μὲν μετόπισθεν. ἔτι ζώοντι δ' ἀοιδῷ

F.   b

Φοῖβος ἄναξ ἐκέλευσε πολυχρύσου παρὰ Πυθοῦς
ἤϊα καὶ μέθυ λαρὸν ἀεὶ Θήβηνδε κομίζειν.
καὶ μέλος, ὡς ἐνέπουσιν, ἐν οὔρεσιν ἠύκερως Πὰν
20 Πινδάρου αἰὲν ἄειδε, καὶ οὐκ ἐμέγηρεν ἀείδων.
ἦμος δ' ἐν Μαραθῶνι καὶ ἐν Σαλαμῖνι παρέσταν
αἰναρέται Πέρσαι μετὰ Δάτιδος ἀγριοφώνου,
τῆμος ἔτι ζώεσκεν, ὅτ' Αἰσχύλος ἦν ἐν Ἀθήναις.
τῷ Τιμοξείνη παρελέξατο δῖα γυναικῶν·
25 ἢ τέκεν Εὔμητιν μεγαλήτορα καὶ Δαΐφαντον,
Πρωτομάχην δ' ἐπὶ τοῖσιν· ἔμελψε δὲ κῦδος ἀγώνων
τῶν πισύρων, μακάρων [δέ τε] παίονας [ἐξεδίδαξεν],
καὶ μέλος ὀρχηθμοῖσι, θεῶν τ' ἐρικυδέας ὕμνους,
ἠδὲ μελιφθόγγων μελεδήματα παρθενικάων.
30 τοῖος ἐὼν καὶ τοῖα πορὼν καὶ τόσσα τελέσσας
κάτθανεν ὀγδώκοντα τελειομένων ἐνιαυτῶν.

Περὶ λυρικῶν ποιητῶν.

Concinnatum ex Ald. Rom. Gott. Vrat. D. et lectione et sede
variante.

Λυρικοὶ ποιηταὶ μουσικῶν ᾀσμάτων εἰσὶν ἐννέα. ἐννέα δὲ καὶ
αἱ καθ' ἡμᾶς τῶν θείων ᾀσμάτων ᾠδαί· τὰ δὲ ὀνόματα τῶν προει-
ρημένων ποιητῶν εἰσι τάδε· Ἀλκμὰν, Ἀλκαῖος, Σαπφώ, Στησί-
χορος, Ἴβυκος, Ἀνακρέων, Σιμωνίδης, Βακχυλίδης καὶ Πίνδαρος.
τινὲς δὲ καὶ τὴν Κόρινναν.

Εἰς τοὺς ἐννέα λυρικοὺς ποιητὰς ἡρωελεγεῖον.

Ex Romana.

Ἐννέα τῶν πρώτων λυρικῶν πάτρην γενεήν τε
μάνθανε, καὶ πατέρας καὶ διάλεκτον ἄθρει.

ὧν Μυτιληναῖος μὲν ἔην, γεραρώτερος ἄλλων,
  Ἀλκαῖος πρότερος, κἠχικὸς Αἰολίδος.
5 ἡ δ' ἐπὶ τῷ ξυνὴν πάτρην φωνήν τε δαεῖσα
  Σαπφὼ, Κληΐδος καὶ πατρὸς Εὐρυγύρου.
Στησίχορος Σικελός· πάτρη δέ οἱ Ἱμέρα ἐστίν·
  εὐφήμου πατρὸς, Δωρικὸς ἁρμονίην.
Ἴβυκος Ἰταλὸς αὖ ἐκ Ῥηγίου ἠὲ Μεσήνης,
10   Ἡελίδα πατρὸς, Δωρίδα δ' ἡρμόσατο.
παρθενίου δὲ πατρὸς λιγυρὸς παῖς Ἡετιήου
  ἦν ἄρα μελπόμενος Τήϊος Ἀνακρέων.
Πίνδαρος ἦν Θηβαῖος, ἀτὰρ πατρὸς Σκοπελίνου,
  δώριον αἰνήσας ἁρμονίην ἐπέων.
15 ἠδὲ Σιμωνίδεω Κείου Δωριστὶ λαλοῦντος
  τὸν πατέρ' αἰνήσας ἴσθι Λεωπρέπεα.
ἴσα δαεὶς καὶ Κεῖος ἔην γενεῇ μελοποιός·
  Μείλωνος πατέρος δ' ἔπλετο Βακχυλίδης.
Ἀλκμᾶν ἐν Λυδοῖσι μέγα πρέπει· ἀλλ' Ἀδάμαντος
20   ἐστὶ καὶ ἐκ Σπάρτης, Δωρίδος ἁρμονίης.

Βίος Πινδάρου.

Ex Vratisl. A.

Πίνδαρος ὁ ποιητὴς Θηβαῖος ἦν ἐκ Κυνοσκεφαλῶν· κώμη δέ
ἐστι Θηβαϊκή· υἱὸς Δαϊφάντου, κατὰ δ' ἐνίους Παγώνδα. ἔνιοι
δὲ Σκοπελίνου αὐτὸν γενεαλογοῦσι, τινὲς δὲ τὸν Σκοπελῖνον πα-
τρωῶν αὐτοῦ γενέσθαι καὶ αὐλητὴν ὄντα τὴν τέχνην διδάξαι αὐτόν.
ὑπὸ πολλοῦ καμάτου εἰς ὕπνον κατενεχθῆναι, κοιμωμένου δὲ αὐτοῦ
μέλισσαν τῷ στόματι προσκαθίσασαν κηρία ποιῆσαι, οἱ δέ φασιν
ὅτι ὄναρ εἶδεν ὡς μέλιτος καὶ κηροῦ πλῆρες εἶναι αὐτοῦ τὸ στόμα,
καὶ ἐπὶ ποιητικὴν ἐτράπη. διδάσκαλον δὲ αὐτοῦ Ἀθήνησιν οἱ
μὲν Ἀγαθοκλέα, οἱ δὲ Ἀπολλόδωρον λέγουσιν, ὃν καὶ προϊστά-
μενον κυκλίων χορῶν ἀποδραμοῦντα πιστεῦσαι τὴν διδασκαλίαν
τῷ Πινδάρῳ παιδὶ ὄντι, τὸν δὲ εὖ διακοσμήσαντα διαβόητον γε-
νέσθαι. ἔρεισμα δὲ τῆς Ἑλλάδος εἰπὼν Ἀθήνας ἐζημιώθη ὑπὸ

Θηβαίων χιλίας δραχμάς, ἃς ἐξέτισαν ὑπὲρ αὐτοῦ Ἀθηναῖοι. ἦν
δὲ οὐ μόνον εὐφυὴς ποιητὴς ἀλλὰ καὶ ἄνθρωπος θεοφιλής· ὁ γοῦν
Πὰν ὁ θεὸς ὤφθη μεταξὺ τοῦ Κιθαιρῶνος καὶ τοῦ Ἑλικῶνος ᾄδων
παιᾶνα Πινδάρου· διὸ καὶ ᾆσμα ἐποίησεν εἰς τὸν θεὸν ἐν ᾧ χάριν
ὁμολογεῖ τῆς τιμῆς αὐτῷ, οὗ ἡ ἀρχή· "Πὰν Πὰν Ἀρκαδίας
μεδέων καὶ σεμνῶν ἀδύτων φύλαξ." ἀλλὰ καὶ ἡ Δημήτηρ ὄναρ
ἐπιστᾶσα αὐτῷ ἐμέμψατο, ὅτι μόνην τῶν θεῶν οὐχ ὕμνησεν. ὁ
δὲ εἰς αὐτὴν ἐποίησε ποίημα οὗ ἡ ἀρχή· "Πότνια θεσμοφόρε
χρυσάννιον." ἀλλὰ καὶ βωμὸν ἀμφοτέρων τῶν θεῶν πρὸ τῆς οἰκίας
τῆς ἰδίας ἱδρύσατο. Παυσανίου δὲ τοῦ Λακεδαιμονίων βασιλέως
ἐμπιπρῶντος τὰς Θήβας ἐπέγραψέ τις τῇ οἰκίᾳ· "Πινδάρου τοῦ
μουσοποιοῦ τὴν στέγην μὴ καίετε·" καὶ οὕτω μόνη ἀπόρθητος
ἔμεινεν· καὶ ἔστι τὸ νῦν ἐν Θήβαις πρυτανεῖον. ἀλλὰ καὶ ἐν
Δελφοῖς ὁ προφήτης μέλλων κλείειν τὸν νεὼν κηρύσσει καθ'
ἡμέραν· "Πίνδαρος ὁ μουσοποιὸς παρίτω πρὸς τὸ δεῖπνον τῷ θεῷ."
καὶ γὰρ ἐν τῇ τῶν Πυθίων ἑορτῇ ἐγεννήθη, ὡς αὐτός φησι· "Πεν-
ταετηρὶς ἑορτὰ βουπομπός, ἐν ᾇ πρῶτον εὐνάσθην ἀγαπατὸς
ὑπὸ σπαργάνοις." λέγεται δὲ θεωροῖς ἀπιοῦσιν εἰς Ἄμμωνος αἰτῆ-
σαι Πίνδαρος τὸ ἐν ἀνθρώποις ἄριστον, καὶ ἀποθανεῖν ἐν ἐκείνῳ
τῷ ἐνιαυτῷ. ἐπέβαλε δὲ τοῖς χρόνοις Σιμωνίδου ἢ νεώτερος
πρεσβυτέρῳ. τῶν γοῦν αὐτῶν μέμνηνται ἀμφότεροι πράξεων.
καὶ γὰρ Σιμωνίδης τὴν ἐν Σαλαμῖνι ναυμαχίαν γέγραφε· καὶ Πίν-
δαρος μέμνηται τῆς Κάδμου βασιλείας. ἀλλὰ καὶ ἀμφότεροι παρὰ
Ἱέρωνι τῷ Συρακουσίων τυράννῳ γεγένηνται. γήμας δὲ Μεγά-
κλειαν τὴν Λυσιθέου καὶ Καλλίνης ἔσχεν υἱὸν Δαΐφαντον, ᾧ καὶ
δαφνηφορικὸν ᾆσμα ἔγραψεν· καὶ θυγατέρας δύο Πρωτομάχην καὶ
Εὔμητιν. γέγραφε δὲ βιβλία ἑπτὰ καὶ δέκα· ὕμνους, παιᾶνας,
διθυράμβων β', προσοδίων β'. φέρεται δὲ καὶ παρθενίων β' καὶ γ',
ὃ ἐπιγράφει κεχωρισμένων παρθενίων· ὑπορχημάτων β', ἐγκώμια,
θρήνους, ἐπικίκων δ'. φέρεται δὲ ἐπίγραμμα ἐπὶ τῇ τελευτῇ αὐ-
τοῦ τόδε·

> ἦ μάλα Πρωτομάχα τε καὶ Εὔμητις λιγύφωνοι
>   Πινδάρου ἔκλαυσαν θυγατέρες πιννταί·
> Ἀργόθεν ἦμος ἵκοντο κομιζούσ' ἐνδόθι κρωσσοῦ
>   λείψαν' ἀπὸ ξείνης ἀθρόα πυρκαϊῆς.

Πινδάρου ἀποφθέγματα.

Ex Vratisl. A.

Πίνδαρος ὁ μελοποιὸς ἐρωτηθεὶς ὑπό τινος, τί πρίονος ὀξύτερον, εἶπε διαβολή.

Παραγενόμενος δὲ εἰς Δελφοὺς καὶ ἐρωτώμενος τί πάρεστι θύσων τῷ Ἀπόλλωνι, εἶπε παιᾶνα.

Ἐρωτηθεὶς πάλιν διὰ τί Σιμωνίδης πρὸς τοὺς τυράννους ἀπεδήμησεν εἰς Σικελίαν, αὐτὸς δὲ οὐ θέλει· ὅτι βούλομαι, εἶπεν, ἐμαυτῷ ζῆν, οὐκ ἄλλῳ.

Ἐρωτηθεὶς διὰ τί τῷ εὖ πράττοντι τὴν θυγατέρα οὐ δίδωσιν· οὐ μόνον δεῖσθαι, φησὶν, εὖ πράττοντος, ἀλλὰ καὶ πράξοντος εὖ.

Ἐρωτηθεὶς πάλιν ὑπό τινος, διὰ τί μέλη γράφων οὐκ ἐπίσταται ᾄδειν, εἶπεν· καὶ γὰρ οἱ ναυπηγοὶ πηδάλια κατασκευάζοντες κυβερνᾶν οὐκ ἐπίστανται.

Τοὺς φυσιολογοῦντας ἔφη ἀτελῆ σοφίας δρέπειν καρπόν.

These biographies are from Böckh. I have not thought worth while to add Eustathios' *Life of Pindar*.

INTRODUCTION.

PINDAR AND HIS POETRY.

THE life of Pindar is full of interest from a historical as
well as from a literary point of view, since it was devoted
to the divers forms of common worship, to the celebration
of the national contests, and the commemoration of the com-
mon traditions which fostered whatever sentiment of Hellenic
unity animated the Hellênes during the heroic period of their
history. Of this Panhellenic spirit the poet was by virtue
of his office, his temperament, and his position as a Theban,
a singularly faithful representative. Unfortunately his bio-
graphies contain few trustworthy facts; but we can gather
from his extant works many valuable traits of character, and
a fair idea of the bent and scope of his genius. While we can
thus from the internal evidence of his works form our estimate
of the man, we must view the few records of his career by the
light thrown upon them by the general history of his times to
discover the circumstances in which he was placed, and the
influences under which the rich fruit of his mind ripened.

He belonged to a family of flute-players of the clan of the
Aegeidae (Pyth. v. 68—77), and was born at Kynoskephalae,
a village of the Theban district, in the year 522 B. C., at the
beginning of the seventeenth Pythiad, according to a fragment,
175 [205], given in the Wratislaw life, πενταετηρὶς ἑορτὰ |
βουπομπὸς ἐν ᾇ πρῶτον εὐνάσθην ἀγαπατὸς ὑπὸ σπαργάνοις. He
was a citizen of Thebes and lived near the fountain of Dirkê,

just outside the *Portae Neitides* (Pausanias, IX. 25), and had
near his house a temple or shrine of the mother of the gods
and Pân, whose cult was natural to flute-players. He is said
to have been the son of Daiphantos, and the pupil of a flute-
player, Skopelinos, who finding him worthy of a higher calling
sent him to Athens to learn the art of lyric composition from
Lasos of Hermione. He is also said to have studied at
Athens under Agathokles or Apollodôros, about 506 B.C. He
probably returned to Thebes before 504 B.C., when the Athe-
nians fought a successful engagement against the Thebans after
the attempt of Kleomenes to overthrow the democracy. He
is further said to have been instructed by the Bœotian poetess
Corinna, who criticised a youthful hymn, of which fragments
are preserved, Frag. 6, 7 [5, 6]. She mentions his contest
with the Bœotian poetess Myrtis thus,

Μέμφομη δὲ κὴ λιγουρὰν Μουρτῖδ' ἰώνγα,
ὅτι βανὰ φοῦσ' ἔβα Πινδάροιο ποτ' ἔριν[1]. Frag. 21.

He composed his earliest extant ode, Pyth. x., for a Thes-
salian dynast, B.C. 502, which fact demonstrates the very early
development of his powers. He travelled about Hellas con-
tinually, visited Sicily B.C. 473, and perhaps went as far as
Kyrêne.

He is said to have died at the age of eighty years, in the
theatre at Argos, in the arms of a youth, Theoxenos of Tene-
dos, on whom he made a skolion, Frag. 101 [88], which con-
tains perfervid expressions of admiration for boyish beauty;
but there is no more ground for accusing the poet of immorality
than there is in the case of Sôkrates, whose purity has been
triumphantly vindicated by Dr Thompson, Mr Henry Jackson,
and others. Tradition concurs with the testimony of his own
words in representing him as an eminently religious man, and
as his poetic pre-eminence must have been largely dependent

---

[1] In Attic the lines would be Μέμφομαι δὲ καὶ λιγυρὰν Μυρτίδ' ἔγωγε |
ὅτι γυνὴ φῦσ' ἔβη Πινδάρου πρὸς ἔριν.

on his deep sympathy with the best and most heartfelt religious feelings of his contemporaries, we cannot apprehend the full significance of his life and work without careful consideration of the extent to which they were influenced by religion. As a lyric poet he held a distinctly sacred office. Out of ten classes of poems which he composed seven are directly devoted to the service of deities. The three remaining varieties are enkômia, skolia, epinikia. Of these the enkômia were probably secular, the skolia might be either sacred or secular, while the epinikia, with which we are chiefly concerned, were of an essentially sacred character. In Pindar's time the great games of Hellas were most solemn religious festivals, held in worship of national deities, according to the institutions of national heroes, hallowed by sacrifices of states and individuals, attended by splendid public embassies, and generally celebrated with every circumstance of sanctity and devotion[1]. The competitors were not vulgar aspirants after notoriety, nor greedy prize-hunters, but devotees who consecrated their wealth or strength to the service of a god. The victors were more than successful men. They were the exponents of the power of their patron deity, and their success was a glorious token of that deity's favor towards their family and state. With us the celebration of an athletic victory, or the winning of a horse-race, could not rise above the level of ephemeral *vers d'occasion*. Pindar justly regarded himself as the inspired dispenser of fame of the highest kind. His care was to associate the common-place individual with the mythical glories of his ancestry, with the festival in which he had distinguished himself, the heroes and deities associated therewith. Hence the impassioned earnestness which constitutes one of Pindar's greatest charms.

It has been suggested that the games lost the exalted character which has been indicated soon after Pindar's death,

---

[1] For several ideas contained in this Essay, I am indebted to the kindness of Prof. Colvin.

but such a view is quite erroneous. The fact that Dorieus, youngest son of Diagoras of Rhodes (Ol. VII.), was given his liberty by the bitterly hostile Athenian assembly (B.C. 407) at the sight of his noble form and on the remembrance of his athletic victories (Pausanias, VI. 7), shows at once that for a full generation after Pindar's death the prestige of the contests had suffered no abatement. It is to be inferred that Pindar's eclectic treatment of myths was due to the influence of the Delphic priesthood, with which he seems to have been very intimate. To this source too may be traced his gnomic style, and perhaps also the traces of Pythagoreanisms which are to be found in his odes. Pindar's lofty conception of his function quite excuses his occasional allusions to his remuneration, which, by the way, seem to me to have been humorous[1]; and as to his acceptance of fees and composing odes to order, we should not compare him in these respects to a laureate, but rather to a first-rate preacher whose sermons are full of enthusiasm, though he takes fee or salary for work which, *theoretically*, he ought to consider it a privilege to perform gratuitously. The personal expenses incident to Pindar's profession must have been considerable, and there is good reason to believe that he expended large sums on sacrifices and offerings. We cannot tell what proportion a payment which he considered adequate bore to the cost of a good chorus; but some passages, which seem to reproach his employers for niggardliness, may refer mainly or entirely to their provision for the recitation of the ode, e.g. Pyth. I. 90. Apart, however, from all thought of gain, he everywhere evinces a pious determination to raise his theme into the empyrean heights of myth, and the ease with which he effects his purpose proves him to have been deeply versed in all varieties of legendary lore, both local and national. In his strong sense of the intimate connection of the present with the heroic past, between

---

[1] Cf. Pyth. XI. 41, Isth. II. 6—11.

the human and the divine[1], the Boeotian minstrel was a faith-
ful representative of the noblest types of Hellênism.

The Delphic philosophy with which he was imbued was in
the main ethical and calls for no comment here. A few traces
of Pythagorean influence are found, especially in the second
Olympian and Nem. III. 70—76. It cannot be shown that he
caught any colour from the speculations of Hêrakleitos, though
it will be seen that he fully recognized the principle of flux
in human affairs, and he certainly agreed with the saying
attributed to Hêrakleitos by Diogenes Laertios, Πολυμαθίη
νόον οὐ διδάσκει. Possibly the strictures of Xenophanes on
the Homeric and Hesiodic accounts of the deities had some-
thing to do with Pindar's tendency to reject unseemly stories,
such as that of the cannibal banquet of Tantalos (Ol. I. 35—
53). More obvious than the influences of Philosophy are
those of art and architecture. He perpetually expresses his
delight in splendour and displays of wealth, which in his age
and land were generally allied with grace and propriety. In
his youth the schools of Chios, Sikyon, Argos and Aegina were
paving the way for the triumph of Athens in the plastic art by
works full of vigour and dignity, temples of perfect design
abounded, and in all productive crafts proportion and beauty
of form were successfully studied. The specimen of goldsmith's
work, from which a metaphor is drawn, Nem. VII. 77—79,
indicates great proficiency—Μοῖσά τοι κολλᾷ χρυσὸν ἔν τε λευκὸν
ἐλέφανθ' ἀμᾷ | καὶ λείριον ἄνθεμον ποντίας ὑφελοῖσ' ἐέρσας. The
poet had the privilege of watching the development of the
arts of representing nature. But his training was received
when they were still struggling with archaic conventionality:
In his prime he doubtless gazed upon the sculptured pediment
of Athene's temple at Aegina. He probably admired many of
Pheidias' works, among them the Athêne Promachos, and the

---

[1] Cf. Nem. VI. 1. Ἐν ἀνδρῶν, ἐν θεῶν γένος· ἐκ μιᾶς δὲ πνέομεν | ματρὸς
ἀμφότεροι.

decorations executed by Polygnôtos for Kimon; but not until
he was about sixty years old.

It is then clear that Pindar, while most susceptible of
elevating impressions, lived and moved in an atmosphere of
ideal art eminently suggestive, but not yet advanced to the
prime of expressive power, and that from this quickening en-
vironment he must have drawn abundant instruction. It
abates not a jot from our high estimate of his genius if we
conclude that he was often indebted to particular specimens of
sculpture or painting for definite ideas and turns of expres-
sion. Nor can it fail to occur to any one at all conversant
with Greek art, that sundry epithets[1] and amplifications,
which seem at first sight needless and without point, may
have been due to the faithful representation of some object of
art, and have therefore impressed the poet's original audience
as happy allusions to familiar and beautiful works of·brush
or chisel. This view applies to the simile of the eagle and
hare (ἄγραν), Nem. III. 80, 81, the subject being exquisitely
treated on many coins, also to the descriptions of Zeus' eagle,
Pyth. I. 6, and of Zêtes and Kalais, Pyth. IV. 182, 183, ἄνδρας
πτεροῖσιν | νῶτα πεφρίκοντας ἄμφω πορφυρέοις, and again to the
account of the birth of Iamos, Ol. VI. 39—42, in which four
lines we have φοινικόκροκον ζώναν, κάλπιδά τ' ἀργυρέαν, λόχμας
ὑπὸ κυανέας and ὁ χρυσοκόμας. It does not come within the
scope of a practical edition to develope such a topic, but it
is too interesting to be passed over entirely. It is more to
the purpose to notice a few obvious allusions to, or distinct
recognitions of, notable specimens of statuary and architec-
ture which display the poet's keen appreciation of these arts.
Perhaps the most interesting is the mention of the Kretan

---

[1] Pindar may have got the wings of the horses given by Poseidon to
Pelops from the chest of Kypselos, Pausan. v. 17. 4, but the chariots are
there *bigae* (owing probably to the difficulty of representing four horses
abreast in an early stage of relief-work); while Pindar seems to imply
quadrigae. The chariots of the nymphs have winged horses, Pausan. v.
19. 2. In my note on φαιδίμας ἵππους, Ol. VI. 14, I have questioned the
rendering 'white mares' derived from Philostratos.

statue τὸν μονόδροπον φυτόν, Pyth. v. 37—39, which was pro-
bably more venerable than graceful. Then there is the simile
derived from the palace of the Iamidae at Stymphalos, Ol. VI.
1—4; the metaphorical passage on the ὕμνων θησαυρός, Pyth.
v. 15—18, and the description of the statue of Thêbê, εὐάρ-
ματε, χρυσοχίτων, ἱερώτατον ἄγαλμα, Θήβα, Frag. 177 [207];
compare χρύσασπι Θήβα, Isth. I. 1. What then was the rela-
tion of Pindar's work to the art of his youth and prime? As
the perfecter of the ideal pure Lyric, he was surely the inter-
preter of the spirit of that art, the appreciative critic who educed
all that it would have delineated, but was compelled for lack of
skill and experience to leave to the imagination; and therefore
his poetry was one of the mightiest of the agencies which de-
veloped the expressive power attained in the heyday of ideal-
istic art by Polygnôtos and Pheidias, and the best of their
contemporaries and scholars. In drama, on the other hand, the
creative power of Aeschylos, with his occasional rigidity, seems
to correspond to the pre-Pheidian idealistic schools of material
representation; that of Sophokles to the Pheidian school—to
which however he stands in the relation of pupil rather than
master—while Euripides' style is in the main realistic.

It is noteworthy that Pindar also witnessed the develop-
ment of the Athenian tragedy, and it is almost certain that he
and his contemporary Aeschylos (B.C. 525—456) must have
derived mutual benefit from each other's work. Pindar was
again contemporary with Epicharmos (B.C. 540 circ.—450 or
443) the father of Megarian (Sicilian) comedy, and his life
extended into the period of the dramatic activity of Krates and
Kratinos. The legends of the Hyperboreans may have been
derived from the epic τὰ Ἀριμίσπεια, and for his mythology
Pindar may have laid the λόγιοι Hekataeos and Charon under
contribution. In every department then of intellectual and
aesthetic culture, mighty waves of progress kept rolling over
Hellas in the first half of the fifth century B.C., communicating
irresistible impulses to a man of Pindar's genius and tem-

perament. This condition of things was intimately connected with the political circumstances of the nation and the various states. It would be sufficient merely to mention the national triumph over the Persian invaders, the strongest stimulus of all to Hellenic life in every aspect, were it not that Pindar has been supposed to have had his sympathy with the national exultation stinted by his humiliation at the sorry part played by Thebes during the crisis. This point demands discussion. Of the poet's love for Thebes there can be no doubt. As to the victory of Marathon, indifference was by no means confined to Thebans. But with respect to the resistance to Xerxes, the destroyer of temples, the religious Pindar clearly felt gratitude to his nation for the liberation of his city from her tyrants and their foreign friends, though he could not feel pride as a participator in the victory. The very fact that he could not glory as a citizen tended to strengthen in him the Panhellénic sentiment with regard to the salvation of Hellas. His profession as a poet, his membership of the widespread clan of the Aegidae, his close connection with Delphi, his well-attested admiration for Athens and Aegina prevented him from entertaining the narrow, selfish, servile views of an ordinary Theban aristocrat. Second only to the Persian wars in impressiveness was the growth of the Athenian democracy.

But turn where one will within the limits of Hellas, the period under review is found to be thickly set with stirring and instructive incidents. The principle which Pindar seems to have thought to be most strikingly illustrated by contemporary history was that of the mutability of human affairs, of the contrasts produced by destiny. That he had ample reason for so thinking is shown by a glance at a chronological table. One sad reverse, the defeat of Thebes at the battle of Oenophyta, B.C. 456, he bewails in touching yet dignified terms in the sixth Isthmian Ode, from the close of which we gather that the establishment of a democracy at Thebes troubled him little, though he was at heart an oligarch (Pyth. xi.

52, 53, II. 86—88). It is very likely that his wide range of observation interfered with any tendency to become strongly attached to a particular form of constitution, and his love for Thebes as a home, for its material beauties and its sanctities and venerable associations, may have been quite independent of keen interest in its polity. There is no ground for regarding his praises of tyrants, always subject to their good behaviour, to have been insincere. His family connection with Sparta and Kyrêne would incline him to look with favour on kingly rule, and if his friendship with the Emmenid Thêro, and Hiero took its origin in their liberal patronage of the arts, yet their share in Gelo's triumph cast a glamour over their unconstitutional sovereignty. It is quite possible that they professed a respect for constitutional forms, and that the poet believed in the actual or future realisation of their professions.

To turn the light afforded by contemporary history on to the scanty materials for Pindar's biography is easier than to point out the characteristics of his genius as exhibited in the extant *Epinikia*, if one may judge from the application thereto of the incompatible epithets 'genial' and 'frigid.' I cannot accept Mr J. A. Symonds' account of Pindar's personality as frigid, austere, not genial, not passionate, hard as adamant. Into criticism of this kind the personal equation must largely enter, so I shall only state my own views briefly and with extreme diffidence. Omitting the obvious and essential features common to all genius, I find lofty serenity and dignity combined with considerable geniality, and as Mr Myers says, 'pre-eminent rapidity' of thought, 'as of an eagle's flight or of very lightning.' His compositions everywhere evince impassioned animation, and marvellous reserve of power. They show traces of humour and of tenderness, of the latter to a surprising extent, considering the nature of his themes. To suggest that he lacked sympathy and tenderness is like finding fault with a march for not being as brisk as

a polka or as solemn as a requiem. Several passages suggest
forcibly that the poet was fond of festivity and good cheer, as
for instance, Frag. 101 [94], Δείπνου δὲ λήγοντος γλυκὺ τρωγά-
λιον καίπερ πεδ᾽ ἄφθονον βοράν, Nem. ix. 48—53; Ol. vii.
1—12; Pyth. iv. 294—297. His vividness of conception and
appreciation of delicate touches of character are, I venture to
say, unrivalled in the whole range of Greek and Latin authors.
Witness the interviews between Pelias and Jason, Pyth. iv.
94—119, 135—167, and between Apollo and Cheiron, Pyth.
ix. 30—65. He seems to have cherished a deeper love of
nature, especially of trees and flowers, than is generally to
be discerned in Greek literature. He is a most effective word-
painter, producing his pictures by a few bold strokes. The
simplicity of his constructions, the grace and freedom of his
forms of expression, the impetuous, elastic movement of his
verse, combine to form almost the ideal of lyric style. Critics
who speak of ‘tumidity,’ ‘overblown exaggeration of phrase,’
‘pomposity,’ and ‘floridity,’ must be thinking of English ver-
sions rather than of the original. The richness of the poet’s
diction, his pregnant phraseology, and his full-sounding com-
pound words, are very apt to make such opprobious epithets
applicable to any literal modern rendering. The attribution
of sententiousness to his style is less unjustifiable. He fre-
quently formulates in fresh, terse terms, a principle, social or
moral, appropriate to the topic in hand. So far he is senten-
tious, even as George Eliot.

To him circumstances and events were not the chaotic
changes of a dream, but the orderly working out of settled
principles; vicissitudes were not the wanton sport of capricious
chance, but the inevitable consequences of the breach or ob-
servance of established rules of conduct. The chief interest
attaching to the achievements and fortunes of legendary heroes
or of his fellow-men lay in the recognition therein of the opera-
tion of these principles, of the validity of these rules. The
utterance of a gnôme then was no empty parade of wisdom, no

indulgence in an appetite for phrase-making, but a natural and reverent comment on some aspect of life, an attempt to solve a problem as well as a didactic admonition. It should be borne in mind that the truisms of to-day have come to be so by a long inductive process, and passed the stages of being newly-discerned truths, unverified propositions, vague surmises. Some of the gnômae which seem common-place to us, may have appeared abstruse to Pindar's original hearers, may have been hailed as the first articulate deliverance of ideas hitherto unborn, the precipitation of a haze of unanalysed, unsummed perceptions in a few clear drops of definite thought. For example, the sentiment τεκμαίρει χρῆμ' ἕκαστον μῶμος, Ol. VI. 73, 74, 'cavil beareth some testimony to every matter,' which I venture to restore, was very likely corrupted owing to not being thoroughly understood. Many of the gnômae have the pith, compactness, and sparkle of epigram, though without the artificial form of that species of composition. Pindar's poems are very rich in metaphors, many being of singular originality. They are frequently drawn from the circumstances of the victory or its celebration, as also are his less numerous similes, e.g. Nem. VII. 70—72, ἀπομνύω μὴ τέρμα προβὰς ἄκονθ' ὥτε χαλκοπάραον ὄρσαι | θοὰν γλῶσσαν, Nem. IV. 93—97.

In elaborate embellishment of an idea and in brief statement he was equally. a master. His extraordinary skill in transition is well exemplified by Ol. III. 9—16, his occasional abruptness by Nem. VI. One of the most conspicuous features of his poetry is its manifold variety both of form and tone. He thoroughly appreciated the effectiveness of contrast, passing from solemn invocation to congratulations almost jovial, from jubilant strains of triumph to impressive warning or tranquil narrative, with diction now exuberant and luscious, now severely plain. We generally find a continuous flow of simply, lightly connected clauses and sentences, but sometimes emphasis is gained by abrupt disconnected utterances. Our appreciation of the ease and spontaneity of Pindar's style must not blind us to the fact, that besides genius he exhibits and glories in consummate art. When most discursive and impetuous, his thoughts are thoroughly under control. Through many of his odes there runs a dominant sentiment, suggested indeed by his immediate theme, but of general application and abiding interest, which knits all the parts of the ode into perfect unity. It is not always clear whether this vein of thought is deliberately followed by the poet or unconsciously, for it is his habit to keep his own personality well in view in his odes, and to give free expression to his own feelings and sentiments with regard to the victor and things in general. Indeed he seems to have thought it a high honour to bring the victor into personal relations with himself. Hence it may be that the connecting idea of some odes was haunting the poet's mind and directing the current of his thoughts without any intention on his part of conveying this idea to his hearers (see Ol. I. Introduction). These suggestions as to a few of the prominent literary characteristics of Pindar's remains will suffice for the present purpose.

His theory of life is extremely interesting. All ἀρεταί and the power of developing them by training are the gifts of deities, bestowed especially on members of ancient families who had preserved the tradition of their descent from heroes and gods; cf. Isth. III. These deities are unwilling that prosperity should abide with a man without intermission or alloy. The jealousy of heaven may however be partially appeased and its action deferred by modesty and upright conduct. He implicitly excuses the φθόνος of the gods by saying that prosperous men seldom escape κόρος and ὕβρις, which prompts them to aspire to the life of immortals, Isth. IV. 13—16. The contemplation of impending reverses ought not to mar the enjoyment of present good, but rather to enhance it by the contrast. The great incentive to discharging rightly the responsibilities entailed by ἀρεταί and external advantages is the

F.

c

desire for posthumous fame ensured by songs, cf. Nem. VII. 9—16; but rewards and punishments in the future state are also taken into account. He inculcates the duty of an active display of heaven-sent powers, the highest field for which is competition in sacred games. He holds that the dead take an interest in the affairs of their kindred on earth. Thus it is the poet's bounden duty to link in song with the present that ideal past to which is owed all that makes life worth living. His interweaving of mythical episodes into his praises of living victors is no mere artistic device, but the spontaneous expression of his innermost convictions. The development of the method suggested by Korinna of adapting Epic subjects to the form and temper of Lyric poetry must have been a congenial study. Though not a bigoted oligarch he was a thorough aristocrat, in so far that he believed in the superiority of the well-born in physical and moral capabilities, but he had a clear view of the rights of the commonalty, and the responsibilities of nobles and rulers. On such points he spoke out boldly though gracefully, even to the most absolute of those whom he addressed.

Pindar's precepts as to conduct are thoroughly chivalrous, with the exception that he thinks it fair after having avowed his enmity to seek to attack his foe at a disadvantage (Pyth. II. 84, 85), a proceeding which modern morality reprobates in private feuds but applauds in warfare. Yet he holds that we ought not to withhold praise, when justly earned, even from foes. His wish was fulfilled that he might die αἰνέων αἰνητά, μομφὰν δ' ἐπισπείρων ἀλιτροῖς (Nem. VIII. 39).

It remains to speak of Pindar's influence. As a popular and eloquent transmitter of ideas that were in his days occupying the minds of the wisest of his countrymen, we may claim that he exercised appreciable influence on Sôkrates and Plato, though without having originated the doctrines to be traced to him, without even having been the sole channel of their transmission. With this proviso it will be advantageous to mention a few points of Sokratic or Platonic theory, which we find expressed or suggested in Pindar's works.

His rejection of unseemly myths has already been noticed, and in this particular he may have influenced Plato. Yet such a tendency had been rendered inevitable by the advance of civilization, and by the speculative theories which had put themselves into competition with the old theology. There was no third alternative for a moral man of high culture besides purifying his conception of Olympos or else rejecting it altogether. Again, apart from the exigences of morality, the Olympic system failed to satisfy the intellectual wants of the age. A unity of design in the universe, the uniform action of great principles in both physics and human affairs had been observed. For this the caprices of the multitudinous theocracy failed to account satisfactorily. There had therefore arisen in the minds even of some of the most loyal adherents of Polytheism vague notions of Monotheism or Pantheism, of a pervading, consistent principle of cosmical government and maintenance. Probably but feeble attempts were made to think out clearly the relations of the gods to this overruling force, and so the old vivid faith and the new misty theological theory could, in spite of their inherent antagonism, coexist in one mind. The personality of Pindar's ὁ μέγας πότμος (Pyth. III. 86), πότμος ἄναξ (Nem. IV. 42), stands in striking contrast to Aeschylos' ἀνάγκη, and rather approximates to the universal νοῦς, symbolized by Zeus in the *Phaedros*, and I believe in sundry passages of Pindar, e.g. Pyth. v. 114. With respect to the 'Orphico-Pythagorean idea' of the future state of the soul, I need only compare Ol. II. 68 with *Phaedros*, p. 249. The most prominent coincidence is that Pindar repeatedly asserts or hints the Sokratic doctrine, that ἀρετή is not διδακτή (cf. Nem. III. 41 ; Ol. II. 86, IX. 100) in the general form, that no excellence can be acquired by training.

One more point in Pindar's life, on which turns the interpretation of two important passages, remains to be noticed.

I still hold the opinion expressed in my paper 'On the First Ages of Written Literature,' published by the Cambridge Philosophical Society, 1868, that Metrical Literature was not committed to writing in Greece for nearly a generation after the Persian wars, i.e. not until Pindar was an old man; so that it is probable that he did not write his odes.

The evidence against his having done so is thus summed up by Professor Paley, in the preface to his translations: 'Not only is there no mention in Pindar of *reading* and *writing*[1] (except the single allusion to a written *name* under the words ἀναγνῶναι and γράφειν[2]), but the oral conveyance by ἄγγελοι is often alluded to, and the words in Ol. VI. 91 seem absolutely to admit of no other interpretation; for the poet there compares the person who is sent to impart the ode to a *scytale* or writing-staff,—a short wooden cylinder round which a paper was wrapped for penning brief messages. If the man carried with him the ode written, the comparison is utterly pointless. He is called a *scytale* because he performs the same part, *vicariously*, of communicating a message. It would be perfectly absurd to call an errand-boy, figuratively 'a note,' simply because he carried a note to a friend's house. I cannot here go into this question at length, though quite prepared to do so, and though it is one of the greatest importance and interest. I will merely state in a few words my present conviction,—that a written literature was entirely unknown to the Greeks even in the times of Pindar.'

In the opening of Olympian XI. where ἀναγιγνώσκω first occurs, the poet's heart is likened to an ἀνάθημα, on which the victory is indelibly recorded, and by which the memory thereof is preserved.

Most of the remarks on the σκυτάλη apply equally to the fragment of Archilochos where it occurs, Ἐρέω σοι αἶνον ἀχνυμένη σκυτάλη, which seems to mean 'a vexed messenger,' not 'no welcome scytale,' as Col. Mure translates it.

---

[1] Ol. XI. 1—3. Compare Ol. III. 30.
[2] Ol. VI. 90; Pyth. IV. 279; Ol. IX. 25, etc.

The best alternative explanation of this difficult phrase σκυτάλη, is to the following effect, that the ἄγγελοι of Pindar are the 'Masters of the Choir,' and that Aeneas is called the scroll-wand of the Muses. 'He is fitted with the power of interpreting poetry by song just as this wand was indispensable to make a letter or document legible, the scroll requiring to be wrapped round it.' Let us analyse the metaphor according to this interpretation. The poem is the scroll, Aeneas with the Music the wand : yet the Muses are supposed to send Aeneas,

' ἐσσὶ γὰρ ἄγγελος ὀρθὸς ἠϋκόμων σκυτάλα Μοισᾶν.'

But surely the sender in using a σκυτάλη would have kept one key-wand himself, while Agêsias would have had the other, and Pindar would have sent the song to the wand : so that the poet is accused of having used a phrase in a confused, not to say erroneous, sense. Professor Paley saves him from such an imputation.

Moreover, it were a strange hyperbole to imply that music was indispensable to make the ᾽Epinikia legible in anything akin to the sense in which the wand was necessary for the reading of the scroll.

Pindar did not, I think, underrate the beauty of his language and his thought; which depended upon music for the enhancement of the delight that they afforded; not for its creation.

Again, the word ὀρθὸς favours Professor Paley's interpretation, for it seems to give the best sense when referred to the correctness of oral transmission. The passage in the fourth Pythian, 279, requires us to translate δι᾽ ἀγγελίας ὀρθᾶς, 'by means of correct reporting,' as a transition to the idea of music would be abrupt and unmeaning.

Lastly, the peculiar use of the word σκυτάλη by Archilochos is in favour of Professor Paley's interpretation.

'If we accept Professor Paley's theory,' said his critic, 'we credit the Greeks of Pindar's age with a power of memory

almost miraculous. Those who have tried in the present day
to commit to memory so much as a portion of one Epinician
ode are fain to confess that the task is extremely arduous.'
I need hardly point out the widely different conditions under
which a modern student and an ancient Greek set themselves
to the task. We must not forget the music, which would aid
the Greek very materially in learning and remembering the bur-
den. Such reference to a modern standard is fatal to a true
and liberal estimate of questions relating to antiquity. After
careful reconsideration of the case and due attention to counte-
arguments, I find nothing that materially modifies the conclu-
sions at which I arrived ten years ago.

The compositions of Pindar comprised :

ὕμνοι, poems in honour of deities sung by a chorus standing
before an altar ;

παιᾶνες, hymns especially consecrated to the worship of
Apollo and Artemis, though composed in honour of other gods,
as of Zeus of Dôdôna, and perhaps even of men ;

διθύραμβοι, choral astrophic songs in honour of Dionysos;

προσόδια, 'processional songs' ;

παρθένια, hymns sung by maidens (cf. Pyth. iii. 77), in-
cluding δαφνηφορικά ;

ὑπορχήματα, songs to very lively dancing performed by
choruses of boys or of boys and young maidens, which were ori-
ginally confined to the worship of Apollo ;

ἐγκώμια, odes in praise of some man, sung by a Kômos ;

σκόλια, songs sung in the course of a banquet or other
festive entertainment ;

θρῆνοι, dirges ;

ἐπινίκια, odes in commemoration of victories in games.

τραγῳδίαι are also attributed to Pindar. These were, pro-
bably, old forms of Satyric Drama, or at least Lyric Dramas
in the Dorian style, quite distinct from the Athenian tragedy
(see note on Ol. xiii. 19).

The Epinikia which we possess are the complete collection known to the grammarians Aristophanes and Aristarchos, with the exception of a few Isthmian odes, but we do not know how or when this collection was first made, and it certainly contained only a portion of the Epinikia actually composed by Pindar. It is, however, almost certain that we have some of the very best specimens of his art in this branch of composition. Out of the forty-four extant odes eleven are in praise of Aeginêtans and fifteen for Sikeliôtes, two for an Epizephyrian Lokrian, and three for Kyrênaeans, and therefore there are only thirteen for the mainland of Hellas, out of which four were in honour of Thebans.

We may conveniently divide his works into three periods, the first beginning B.C. 502 ending B.C. 480, the second ending B.C. 464, in which the dates of the majority of the odes and of most of the best fall, the third ending B.C. 442 (the latest odes date B.C. 452).

The order in which the odes were composed is as follows, so far as can be ascertained :

Pythian IX ....Ol. 69. 3...B.C. 502

    ,, VI. }
    ,, XII. } .... ,, 71. 3... ,, 494

    ,, VII. .... ,, 72. 3... ,, 490

Olympian X. }
    ,, XI. } .... ,, 74. 1... ,, 484

Isthmian V. .... before ,, 75. 1... ,, 480

Nemean V. .... ,, 75. 1... ,, 480

Isthmian III. }
    ,, VII. (?) } ... about ,, 75. 2... ,, 479
Nemean II. }

Pythian IX. }
    ,, XI. } .... ,, 75. 3... ,, 478
Isthmian IV. }

Pythian II. .... ,, 75. 4... ,, 477

Olympian XI. (?) .... OL 75. 4... B.C. 477

" XIV. ⎫
" II. ⎬ .... " 76. 1... " 476
" III. ⎭

Pythian III. ⎫ .... " 76. 3... " 474
" I. ⎭

Nemean I. .... " 76. 4... " 473

Olympian I. .... " 77. 1... " 472
" XII.

Nemean IX. ⎫ ....OL 77. 1 or 3... " 472 or 470
Isthmian II. ⎭

Olympian VI. ⎫ .... OL 78. 1... " 468
" IX. ⎭

Pythian IV. ⎫ .... " 78. 3... " 466
" V. ⎭

Olympian VII. ⎫ .... " 79. 1... " 464
" XIII. ⎭

Nemean X. (?) ... between OL 78. 1 & 80. 3... " 468 and 458

Pythian VIII. .... " 79. 3... " 462

Nemean VII. .... "

Olympian VIII. .... OL 80. 1... " 460

Nemean VI. ....before " 80. 3... " 458

" VIII. ....shortly before " " ... " 458

" IV. ...... " " " " ... " 458

Isthmian I. .... " " ... " 458

" VI. .... " 81. 1... " 456

Olympian IV. ⎫ .... " 82. 1... " 452
" V. ⎭

Nemean XI. gives no clue to its date beyond style, from which it may be inferred that it was not composed later than OL 77. 3, B.C. 470. It is not an Epinikian ode but probably an Enkômion.

PINDAR'S STYLE AND DIALECT.

THE literary characteristics of Pindar's style have been re-marked upon in the foregoing Essay. Here his style will be regarded from a philological point of view.

Most of the difficulties in Pindar's *Odes* arise from his rapidity and fulness of thought, which often seem to have made him sacrifice the formal expression of the connexion of his ideas. Their vividness of presentment and rapidity of sequence interfered with the precise indication of their mutual relations. On the other hand, whenever poetic instinct aims at exhibiting concisely and gracefully the subtle connexions of ideas, a different class of difficulties arises comprising in the main mixtures of construction, and complicated, involved sentences. Pindar shows himself capable of sustained logical effort, but generally his power displays itself first in the design of the whole poem, and then mainly in the moulding of clauses and short phrases, rather than in the welding together of elaborated periods. He deals in divers kinds of abbreviations, fresh combinations of words, inversions, and extensions of the meaning of phrases, and the function of grammatical forms. Yet he set high value on precision and clearness of statement, and made them secondary only to the full outpouring of a fancy which perhaps strained the capa-bilities of current forms of speech, or to an occasional affecta-tion of oracular obscurity. It cannot be doubted that he developed the resources of the artificial Lyric dialect which he used both as to form and substance, and his doing so without often overstepping the natural limits of individual licence, or running counter to the analogies of his language, proves that he possessed a highly sensitive grammatical consciousness, and that owing to intuitive acumen or to reflection, he had a keen appreciation of the nature and qualities of the materials in which he wrought, that is to say, the poetic and colloquial varieties of Hellênic speech. Hence his language as well as his thought is stamped with an individuality so marked that any attempt to account for his idiosyncracies, and to range him with this or that class of authors, or to trace in his works the signs of a period or stage of language, is almost certain to entail misconceptions.

Pindar composed in the αὐστηρὸς χαρακτήρ, αὐστηρὰ ἁρμονία, as to which see Professor Jebb's *Attic Orators*, Vol. I. Chap. II. pp. 21—23. It may be observed that ἁρμονία, style of composition, refers to the putting words together, while λέξις, in a special sense as distinct from ἁρμονία, refers to the choice of words.

As a rule, Pindar's syntax is free and simple, in the λέξις εἰρομένη, 'the jointed style;' see p. XII of Mr Sandys' *Isocratis ad Demonicum et Panegyricus;* but the opening of the first Olympian Ode, and the apologue of the oak in the fourth Pythian, are good examples of exceptionally elaborate structure. He occasionally employs the rhetorical figures of Interrogation and Repetition, but is far less rhetorical than any dramatist. His 'figures of language' are in the main grammatical, generally being such as effect compression directly or indirectly, while perhaps involving incidentally variety or novelty. These, however, appear to be sought to some extent for their own sake. We find then frequent instances of ellipse, especially of the substantive verb (e.g. Pyth. VIII. 95), and of the object of a verb (e.g. Nem. VII. 23). Conspicuous instances of brachyology are Pyth. III. 89—92; Isth. IV. 19.

Pindar's style of diction is variable; sometimes grand and elaborate, like that of Aeschylos, at other times plain, as that of Euripides. Out of the number of compound and derivative words which occur only or first in Pindar, many, we may be sure, were framed by the poet for himself. His later Odes are slightly distinguished by greater obscurity of phraseology, and a larger percentage of non-Epic vocabulary than the earlier compositions, as may be shown by comparing those composed before B. C. 470, with those dated after B.C. 465.

He often uses metaphor where simile might be expected, the substitution denoting vigour and producing compression; e.g. Pyth. III. 75, v. 104, 105; Isth. III. 65, v. 72, 73.

In like fashion Pindar also often suppresses a particle or phrase denoting similitude when introducing a simile; e. g. Ol. XI. 9—12; Pyth. III. 36; Nem. II. 9, IV. 79—84 (where there is also a general apodosis to a particular protasis as in Pyth. XI. 41—44), Nem. XI. 39—42.

Pindar several times confuses a personification with the thing personified; e.g. Ol. VI. 84, VII. 13, 14, VIII. 1, 2; Pyth. IV. 14, IX. 55, Nem. I. 4.

It has already been mentioned that the intensity of his genius makes Pindar venture upon bold inversions; e.g. κεινὰν παρὰ δίαιταν, 'owing to scarcity of sustenance,' Ol. II. 65, καιομένα πυρά, 'the flame of the burning pyre,' Pyth. III. 44, ποθεινὰ Ἑλλας, 'yearning for Hellas,' Pyth. IV. 218; and upon such constructions as ἄνευθε θεοῦ σεσιγαμένου οὐ σκαιότερον χρῆμ' ἔκαστον, Ol. IX. 104, 105, οὔ τοι ἅπασα κερδίων φαίνοισα πρόσωπον, ἀλάθει' ἀτρεκής, Nem. v. 16, 17, and ἵππος δαϊχθείς, 'the wounding of a horse,' Pyth. VI. 32, 33, Ἰφιγένεια σφαχθεῖσα, 'the sacrifice of Iphigeneia,' Pyth. XI. 22, 23.

Hypallage is found several times; e.g. Ol. VIII. 68, XI [X.] 5, 6; Pyth. IV. 255, v. 82, IX. 8.

The causative use of adjectives may be classed with the peculiarities already specified. For instances cf. Ol. VIII. 4; Pyth. IX. 11; perhaps χλωραῖς ἐέρσαις, Nem. VIII. 40.

With regard to the order of words, I venture to suggest that Pindar takes far less licence than is generally supposed, for there is reason to believe that the beginnings of consecutive verses were regarded by the poet as contiguous positions, and so too the endings. Cf. Ol. VII. 13, 15—19, XI [X.] 28—30, XIII. 1—5; Pyth. IX. 23—25, XI. 32. Again, many adjectives placed far from the nouns with which they agree (esp. when there is another adjective in a normal position), are to be taken as extensions of the predicate which are common in Pindar's Odes. Cf. Nem. IV. 4, 41, IX. 48; Isth. III. 77, VII. 70.

When there are two adjectives not coupled by a conjunction, and without a pause between them, in agreement with one substantive, we generally find one adjective definitive, or a constant epithet of distinction, and the other descriptive, cf. Pyth. IX. 8, X. 6. We find a substantive or adjective with the article qualifying a substantive which has also an adjective without the article in agreement with it, Pyth. I. 95, IV. 184, V. 99, 100, IX. 23; Nem. IV. 27. Cumulation of adjectives beyond the limitations here indicated is rare, and in this particular Pindar's verse stands in contrast to the lyric portions of Aeschylos' dramas.

To return to the order of words. Pindar occasionally puts the subject late in the sentence; e.g. Ol. XI. 24—31, XIII. 14—17; Pyth. II. 41, XII. 17; Isth. V. 27—30.

The following are a few peculiarities of idiom :—

A few nouns are feminine, instead of the usual masculine; e. g. Τάρταρος, Pyth. I. 15; Ἰσθμός, Ol. VIII. 48; αἰθήρ is common, see note on Ol. I. 6.

Nouns in the genitive stand in place of adjectives of material; e. g. ἀδάμαντος ἅλοις, Pyth. IV. 71; of place, e. g. ἀγῶνι Κίρρας, Pyth. XI. 12, cf. Nem. VI. 12; of quality, e. g. ἀνάγκας ἔντεσιν, Pyth. IV. 234, ἀνάγκας χερσί, Nem. VIII. 3, δόμους ἁβρότατος, Pyth. XI. 34.

Owing no doubt only to the nature of his themes, we often find substantives, especially those meaning 'victory,' 'glory,' taking datives of place and manner; e. g. Ἰσθμίαν ἵπποισι νίκαν, Isth. II. 13, δόξαν παλαίαν ἅρμασιν, Isth. III. 16; note also τὸν ταύρῳ χαλκέῳ καυτῆρα, Pyth. I. 95, and the possessive dative Ol. IX. 16; Nem. VII. 22; Pyth. IX. 82.

Pindar shows a peculiar partiality for the *dativus termini* with verbs, e. g. Ἀλφεῷ μέσσῳ καταβάς, Ol. VI. 58, νουμηνίᾳ θιγέμεν, Nem. IV. 35; cf. Pyth. IV. 296; καί τιν' ἀελπτίᾳ βαλών, Pyth. XII. 31, ἐφάπτομαι, Pyth. VIII. 60, and with prepositional adverbs, as πέλας, ἄγχι, ὄπιθεν (Ol. III. 33).

His use of prepositions is peculiar both as to their meaning and government. For instance, we find ἀμφί with accusative 'concerning,' e.g. Pyth. II. 15, VIII. 65; Nem. I. 54; Isth. VI. 9; 'according to,' Ol. XI [x.] 77; with dative 'by,' 'in respect of,' Pyth. I. 12, V. 111, VIII. 35; Nem. I. 29, VI. 14; 'within the time of,' Ol. XIII. 37; 'concerning,' Ol. IX. 13; Pyth. II. 62; ἀμφὶς with genitive, ἐσθᾶτος ἀμφίς, 'for' or 'without raiment,' Pyth. IV. 253; ἀνά with accusative, 'within the time of,' Ol. IX. 85; ἐν is sometimes dialectic for εἰς with accusative, cf. Pyth. II. 11; with dative it forms several adverbial expressions, e. g. ἐν χερὸς ἀκμᾷ, Ol. II. 63; ἐν δίκᾳ, Nem. V. 14; it means 'according to,' Pyth. IV. 59, I. 62; 'in the sphere of,' Ol. VI. 7, XIII. 49; Nem. III. 32; 'near,' Ol. VI. 16; Pyth. VIII. 40, IV. 23; 'between,' Pyth. I. 27; ἐπὶ is almost 'in accordance with,' Pyth. II. 49, IX. 89; παρὰ with accusative has no reference to motion, Pyth. IV. 74; Nem. V. 10; Ol. XI (x.) 101; it means 'to,' Pyth. VIII. 59; 'owing to,' 'along of,' Ol. II. 65; περὶ with dative after λέγει, Pyth. II. 69, is noteworthy. For the rest his use of prepositions is far more Epic than it is like Attic.

Pindar is more precise than is generally supposed in his use of καί and τε; for, if τε follows καί, it couples subdivisions of a class which καί couples to a previous idea, as in Ol. III. 8, 9, XII. 17, 18; Pyth. I. 42, IV. 147—149, XI. 60—62; Nem.

III. 60, IV. 8, 78; Frag. 120 [107]; but if τε be the conjunction most used, καί can couple the subdivisions of a class which is coupled by τε, as in Ol. VII. 82, 85, 86. In Pyth. VIII. 99, 100, the two methods are combined. Zeus is coupled to the Aeginêtan heroes by καί, Aeakos' sons and grandson are coupled to him by τε—τε, while Telamon is coupled to his brother Pêleus by καί. With this reservation, however, irregular use of conjunctive particles is conspicuously frequent, especially μὲν—τε, e. g. Nem. II. 9. We find μὲν—οὔτε, Pyth. II. 89; μὲν—ἀλλά, Ol. IX. 5; τε—δέ, Pyth. IV. 81, XI. 30; οὔτ᾽ —τ᾽ οὐκ, Nem. XI. 40; οὔτε—οὐδέ, Pyth. VIII. 85; Isth. II. 44. Pindar differs from Epic poets, in not using ἵνα as a final conjunction. He omits ἄν effectively four or five times; see note on Pyth. IV. 118. The only hypothetical particle he uses is εἰ (not εἰ κε). He places a present indicative in apodosis after εἰ in the optative, Pyth. VIII. 14; Ol. X. 4. For a complicated and varied hypothetical sentence, see Pyth. IV. 263—269, and for a difficult mixed construction, Ol. VIII. 54.

Pindar seems to prefer expressing *purpose* and *result* by a simple infinitive, to using constructions with particles in such cases.

He uses the rare gnômic future, Ol. VIII. 3; Pyth. XII. 30; the prophetic present, Ol. VIII. 42; Pyth. IV. 49; the imperfect where we might expect the aorist, in speaking of Olympic victors, Nem. V. 5, 45; so too the present participle frequently, the pres. inf., Isth. III. 43. He very rarely uses the historic present, but cf. Ol. II. 23; Pyth. IV. 163. We find the present participle for the future, Ol. XIII. 59; Pyth. I. 52, IV. 106.

The *Schema Pindaricum* is oddly enough only found rarely in Pindar's remains, i.e. Ol. X. [XI.] 5, 6, which, however, is not a clear case; Pyth. X. 71, 72; Frag. 53 [45], 15—18, in which two passages, as in Attic, the singular verbs precede the masc. or fem. plural subjects.

Pindar has a plural verb with a neuter plural subject, Ol. II. 84, XI. 85, μολπά...μελέων τὰ φάνεν (here the plural may be used to include μολπά as an antecedent); Pyth. I. 13, IV. 121, where the plural verb may suggest distribution.

We find the active voice where the middle might be expected several times; e.g. ἔπραξε, Ol. II. 40; Isth. IV. 7 ; εὑρεῖν, Pyth. II. 64; ἐστεφάνωσε, Ol. XIV. 22; λύοι, Isth. VII. 45; ἀνέδησαν, Isth. IV. 9; ἀναδήσαντες, Pyth. X. 40.

The above notice of a few idioms either peculiar to, or peculiarly frequent in Pindar's works, is not meant even to approach exhaustiveness; but to furnish hints as to the observation and collection of particulars, or the framing of essays on Pindar's style.

With regard to dialectical peculiarities, it will be better to place particulars before generalizations.

In the inflexion of the Ā- declension ā is preserved where Epic has η; in the genitive sing. masc. we find -ā as well -ao for the termination; in the genitive plur. masc. and fem. the Doric termination -ᾶν is used, even in feminine adjectives, which in Epic are not in this case distinguished from the masculine. Note such Aeolic forms as πάτριᾰ, Ol. VI. 62, Κύκνειᾰ, Ol. XI. 15, Νέμεᾰ, Ol. XIII. 35.

In the Ă- declension the Epic forms are found, except a few instances of the Doric accusative plural in -ος, cf. Ol. I. 53.

In the other declensions the forms used are generally Doric, except that in the dative sing. of I- stems, where Doric has -ῑ, Pindar has -ει, that there is frequent synizesis of -εος genitive termination of stems in -ες, -εϝ, and that the Epic and Aeolic forms from stems in -εϝ, i.e. ῆος, &c., are found. Note the acc. sing. masc. εὐκλεῖα, Nem. VI. 30; perhaps acc. plur. neut. Ol. XIII. 12, and the absence of δ from Θέτιος, Πάριος, &c. Compounds with λαό-ς contract the stem into -λᾱ- and follow the Ā- declension. The Epic stem-endings

-αον, -αων are frequently contracted into -ᾱν-, but we find Ποσείδαον, Ol. I. 75; Ποσειδάωνος, &c., *passim*.

Pindar's pronouns are Epic, especially such Epic forms as coincide with Aeolic; but for the dative of the second personal pronoun he uses σοί τοί and the Doric τίν (the reflexive dative ἵν has no MS. authority). These forms he uses so as to avoid successive syllables beginning with σ and τ (on the same principle he uses πετοῖσαι, πετόντεσσι, ἔμπετες). For the accusative of the third personal pronoun we find the Doric νιν as well as μιν (used especially in the neighbourhood of initial labials), also ἑ and σφε.

In conjugation we find -μᾱν for -μην, the termination of the first person sing. of secondary tenses of the Middle and Passive, and -ᾱν for -ην in Dual terminations. He never uses the Doric -μες in the first plur. Act., but the Aeolo-Epic -μεν. In the third plur. Act. he uses the Doric -οντι and the Aeolic -οισι, -οισιν. His infinitive moods are Epic; but we find two Doric forms, γαρύεν, Ol. I. 3; τράφεν, Pyth. IV. 115.

His participles are Aeolic, i.e. he has -οισα, &c., for -ουσα, &c., and in the first aorist -αις for -ας nom. sing. masc. and -αισα, &c., for -ασα, &c. It is possible that he also used the Epic forms -ας, -ασα, &c., for the first aorist participle, but the variations of MSS. have obscured all evidence on the point.

He quite irregularly doubles the σ of the suffix in θέσσαν (ἔσσαι, Pyth. IV. 273, κάθεσσαν, Pyth. V. 39, show assimilation of the δ of the √ἑδ for √SAD) and possibly in τόσσαις, Pyth. III. 27, perhaps after the analogy of the Epic forms ἔκτισσ', Pyth. I. 62, &c. From verbs in -άζω, -ίζω, -όζω, he uses indifferently the Epic aorist in -σα, &c., and the Doric in -ξα, &c.

In verbs in -μι he has ἔρᾱται, Pyth. IV. 92; third sing. subj. from ἔραμαι, always ᾱ for ῆ as the stem-vowel of verbs which make the second aorist inf. in -ῆναι -άναι, except ἀναστῆῃ, Pyth. IV. 155. The Imp. δίδοι always stands for δίδου.

The substantive verb is Epic except ἐντί, the Doric third plur. present, the frequency of ἔμμεν, the absence of εἶναι, and the fem. part. ἐοῖσα, ἐοῖσαν.

Generally verbs in -άω keep the stem-vowel ᾱ throughout the tenses and derivatives, while verbs in -έω take η; exceptions to this rule are to be explained by the early existence of by-forms in -έω, and are many of them Doric, e.g. καύχημα, Isth. IV. 57, by καυχέομαι, Theokritos.

In adverbs we find -δᾶν for -δην, -ᾳ for -η.

In conjunctions and particles we find ἅς for ἕως, αἴτε, Pyth. IV. 78, for εἴτε which does not occur, ὧτε, θάμα, for which see Lexicon, ὦν Ionic for οὖν.

In prepositions ἐν is occasionally used for ἐς—an Aeolism; and πάρ for παρά, ἄν (ἄμ) for ἀνά before consonants. The ι of περί is elided twice before a vowel. Occasionally πεδά is found for μετά, but not earlier than B.C. 472.

Pindar's instances of crasis seem all to be Doric, even those which are also Ionic as τωὐτοῦ, τωὐτό.

In contraction he follows the Doric dialect, and so too in not contracting terminations in -εος and adjectival forms from stems in -εο-, -εα-. But in these cases the ε (as also ι sometimes before a vowel), seems to have been pronounced nearly as y, without lengthening a preceding short syllable.

With regard to the use of η there are many cases still unmentioned, several of which are Doric as well as Epic. For instance :

Ἥβα, ἥρως are shown by Ahrens to be Doric. Again in several cases, such as Θήβα, μῆλα, where the Boeotian dialect has ει for η, the η is most probably Doric. Without going so far as Ahrens, we may conclude that in this particular the Epic tendencies of Pindar have been exaggerated.

We find the Doric ᾱ for Epic ε in σκιαρός, Ol. III. 14, 19; τράφω, Pyth. II. 44, IV. 115; τράχω, Pyth. VIII. 34; also φρασί for φρεσί, φρένεσσιν, Isth. III. 5.

Pindar preserves the initial digamma in many words, as

F.   d

is shown by the apparent hiatus before them, but he elides
vowels before such words, and they do not affect the quantity
of a short syllable ending with a consonant which precedes;
e.g. δώδεκ' ἀνάκτων, Ol. XI [X.] 49; οὔτ' ἔτος, Pyth. IV. 105;
Πότμὸς ἄναξ, Nem. IV. 42; κείνοισίν εἰπών, Pyth. IV. 105.
The words in question are ἄναξ, ἀνάσσω, ἀνδάνω, ἀχώ, εἴδομαι,
εἶδος, εἰδώς, ἰδεῖν, ἴδρις, ἴσαντι, εἴκοσι, εἰπεῖν, ἔτος, ἐλπίς, ἔλσας (?)
ἔολει (?), ἔργον, ἔρξας, ἑσπέρα, ἔτος, ἦθος, Ἰδαῖος, Ἰλιάδας, ἴσος, οἱ,
ὅς (possessive), οἰκίζω, οἶκος, Ὄανος.

Besides apparent hiatus before words which had an ini-
tial Ϝ we also find hiatus after datives in -ῳ and -ᾳ often, twice
after ῆ, twice after -αί, and six times before Ἰ- in proper
names (twice after -αί and once after ῆ, so these cases are
counted twice); twice after the genitive termination -ου, which
perhaps should be -οι' as in Ol. XIII. 35.

Perhaps the pronunciation of αι before a vowel as a
short syllable is to be explained, as the change of ι to y;
so also Γαίαοχῳ, Ol. XIII. 78. The shortening of ευ may
similarly be a pronunciation of υ as Ϝ. Cf. Pyth. VIII. 35;
Isth. VII. 58; so also as to ἀυάτα. According to Curtius, τὰ
ἐοικότα, Pyth. III. 59, is for τα γεγοικότα.

Before vowels ι is occasionally shortened, as Πιαίνων, Pyth.
IV. 50, μητίονται, Pyth. II. 92. Note ἴκοντ', Pyth. II. 36.

We find Aeolic forms, as κελαδεννός, κλεεννός, φαεννός,
ὄνυμα, αὐάτα, κεχλάδοντας; Doric forms, as ἐσλός.

Some odes show more Aeolic forms than the average,
as Pyth. II.; others more Epic, as Pyth. V.; both being in the
Aeolian rhythm. With this rhythm the diction is more
colloquial than with the Dorian, and exhibits a larger pro-
portion of Aeolic forms, and of rare words which are called
Aeolic, but which may have been deliberately borrowed by
the poet from the dialects of the various localities whither
the odes were respectively destined to go. Thus the form
Ποτειδᾶν in Ol. XIII. is most probably Korinthian, and the
words πεπαρεῖν (Pyth. II. 57), ὑποφαύτιες (ib. 76), may be

Sicilian. The dialect of the odes in Dorian rhythm is, according to Böckh, the common diction of Lyric poetry.

Speaking generally of Pindar's dialect we may quote Hermann's dictum that it is Epic with a tinge of Doric, and sometimes too of Aeolic. The vocabulary is in the main Epic; the inflexions mixed, but with a preponderance of Doric and Aeolic; the pronunciation mainly Doric [1].

PINDAR'S RHYTHMS AND METRES.

IN Greek music there were different modes, τόνοι, which differed in the order of the intervals of the scale and in pitch. The style, ἁρμονία, of Music in the different modes naturally varied, amongst other points apparently in 'time.' The 'rhythm' of an ode is the arrangement of metres and verses which is accommodated to the 'time' of the music. The styles and rhythms chiefly employed by Pindar are the Dorian and the Aeolian. These are to be easily distinguished by the marked contrast of the metres which are used. The Dorian rhythm is comparatively monotonous and severe. The metres are mostly *trochaica dipodia* ($- \cup - \cup$), generally with a *spondaeus* for the last foot, $- \cup - -$, and *dactylica*, especially *trimetri* with a *spondaeus* for the last metre, $- \cup \cup - \cup \cup - -$. *Cretici* are occasionally admitted, but possibly the last long syllable which usually contains a long vowel or diphthong was produced to a double time. *Trochaici semanti* ($\overset{\times}{} -$) are

---

[1] Note the exception that ει and ου are used in compensation for consonantal sound lost immediately after ε and ο.

d 2

found; of which the first syllable was produced to a double time. Resolution of long syllables is comparatively rare. The Aeolic rhythm often resolves long syllables, and has two metric accents or *theses*, which we generally call *arses*, on consecutive syllables, thus ⏑ –́ –́ ⏑ ⏑. Note that in the metrical schemes the accents (*theses*) of the metres are marked, not those of the single feet. The Aeolian rhythm admits *iambi*, *cretici*, *pyrrhici*, *trochaei semanti* (often with the second syllable short, $\overset{x}{-}$ ⏑) and *bacchii*. It is easy to distinguish the admixture of Lydian measures in Dorian rhythms, as we find more *trochaei* than in pure Dorian rhythms, and *pyrrhici* and *cretici*.

The Aeolo-Lydian rhythms are not easily distinguished from the Aeolian. Perhaps short anacruses, frequent *cretici*, and *anapaesti* are the most obvious marks of Lydian rhythm. The odes in this volume may be classed as follows:

Dorian, Ol. III.; Pyth. I. III. IV. XII.;
Dorian and Lydian, Ol. VI. VII. VIII. X [XI.] XII.; Pyth. IX.
Aeolian Ol. I. II. XI [X.]; Pyth. II. V. VI. VII. VIII. XI.
Lokrian (Aeolian), Ol. IX.
Aeolian and Lydian, Ol. IV. V. XIII. XIV.; Pyth. X.

METRICAL SCHEMES.

Ol. I. ⏑⏓⏓⏑⏑—⏑—⏓⏑⏓⏑⏑—⏖   Str.

⏑⏔⏓⏑—⏓⏑⏑—⏑⏑—⏑⏑—⏖

⏓⏑—⏑—⏑⏙

⏓⏑⏓⏑⏑—⏖

⏓⏑—⏑—⏑⏙

⏓⏑—⏑⏔⏑—⏑—⏑—⏑⏓⏑⏑—⏓⏑—⏑⏙

⏓⏑—⏑—⏑—⏑⏓⏑⏑—⏓⏑⏙

⏑⏔⏔⏑—⏑—⏑—⏑⏙

⏑⏔⏓⏑⏑—⏔⏑⏙

⏑⏓⏓⏑—⏑—⏔⏑⏙

⏙⏓⏔⏑—⏑—⏑⏙

⏑⏓⏔⏑—⏑⏑—⏓⏟—⏑—⏓⏑—⏑⏹   Ep.

⏑⏓⏓⏑⏑—⏓⏑⏔⏑—⏑⏙

⏓⏑—⏑—⏑⏓⏑⏑—⏓⏑⏙

⏑⏓⏓⏑—⏓⏑⏑—⏑—⏑⏓⏓⏑⏑—⏖

⏑⏑—⏑⏓⏑⏑—⏓⏑—⏑⏙

—⏓⏑⏑—⏑—⏓⏑—⏑—⏔⏑⏓⏓⏑⏑—⏓⏑⏹

⏑⏓⏓⏑—⏓⏑⏑—⏑—⏓⏑⏑—⏑—⏖

Ol. II. ⏑⏓⏑—⏓⏑—⏖   Str.

⏑⏔⏓⏑—⏓⏑⏝⏓⏑⏝⏓⏑⏙

—⏓⏑—⏓⏑⏝⏓⏑⏝⏝—⏓⏑—⏔⏑⏹

⏓⏑—⏔⏑⏙

—⏓⏑⏝⏓⏑—⏔⏑⏑—⏓⏑⏙

⏑⏓⏓⏑⏝⏓⏑⏝⏝⏓⏑—⏑—⏓⏑—⏖

⏑⏓⏑—⏔⏑⏑—⏑—⏑⏓⏑⏑⏹

Ep.

Ol. III. Str.

Ep.

Ol. IV. Str.

Ep.

⏑ –́ –́ ⏑ – ⏑ – ⏑ –́ ⏑ ⏖ ⏑ –
⏖́ ⏑ ⏖́ ⏑ –́ ⏑ ⏑ –
⏑ –́ ⏑ – ⏑ ⏓

Ol. V. ⏓ – –́ ⏑ ⏑ – –́ ⏑ ⏑ – ⏑ – –́ ⏑ – Str.
⏓ – –́ ⏑ ⏑ – ⏑ ⏑ – ⏖ – –́ ⏑ – ⏑ – ⏒
⏑ ⏑ –́ ⏑ ⏑ – ⏑ – –́ ⏑ – –́ ⏑ – ⏑ – ⏒
⏓ – –́ ⏑ ⏑ – ⏑ ⏑ – ⏑ ⏑ – ⏑ –́ ⏑ – ⏑ – ⏒ Ep.
⏓ – –́ ⏑ ⏑ – ⏑ ⏑ – ⏑ ⏑ – –́ ⏑ – –́ ⏑ – –́ ⏑ – ⏑ – ⏒

Ol. VI. – –́ ⏑ – – –́ ⏑ – – –́ ⏑ ⏑ – ⏑ ⏑ ⏓ Str.
–́ ⏑ ⏑ – ⏑ ⏑ – – –́ ⏑ ⏑ ⏓
–́ ⏑ ⏑ – ⏑ ⏑ – – –́ ⏑ – ⏓
–́ ⏑ – – –́ ⏑ – – –́ ⏑ ⏑ – ⏑ ⏑ – ⏒
– –́ ⏑ – – –́ ⏑ ⏑ – ⏑ ⏑ – ⏑ ⏓
⏑ –́ – –́ ⏑ – – –́ ⏑ – – –́ ⏑ ⏑ – ⏑ ⏑ – ⏒
–́ ⏑ ⏑ – ⏑ ⏑ – – –́ ⏑ – – –́ ⏑ – – –́ ⏑ – ⏒
–́ ⏑ ⏑ – ⏑ ⏑ – – –́ ⏑ – – –́ ⏑ ⏑ – ⏑ ⏑ ⏓ Ep.
–́ ⏑ – – –́ ⏑ – – –́ ⏑ ⏑ – ⏑ ⏑ – ⏑ ⏑ – – –́ ⏑ ⏑ ⏓
–́ ⏑ ⏑ – – –́ ⏑ ⏑ – – –́ ⏑ – – –́ ⏑ ⏓
–́ ⏑ – – –́ ⏑ – ⏒ –́ ⏑ ⏑ – ⏑ ⏑ ⏓
–́ ⏑ ⏑ – ⏑ ⏑ – – –́ ⏑ ⏑ – ⏑ ⏑ ⏓
–́ ⏑ ⏑ – ⏑ ⏑ – – –́ ⏑ ⏑ – ⏑ ⏑ ⏓
–́ ⏑ – –́ ⏑ – – –́ ⏑ – – –́ ⏑ ⏒

Ol. VII. ⏑ ⏑ –́ – –́ ⏑ – – –́ ⏑ ⏑ – ⏑ ⏑ ⏓ Str.
–́ ⏑ – ⏒ –́ ⏑ – – –́ ⏑ ⏓
– –́ ⏑ ⏓
⏒ –́ ⏑ – – –́ ⏑ – – –́ ⏑ ⏑ – ⏑ ⏑ – – –́ ⏑ ⏑ – ⏑ ⏑ ⏓
–́ ⏑ ⏑ – ⏑ ⏑ – – –́ ⏑ – – –́ ⏑ ⏑ – ⏑ ⏑ ⏓
⏑ ⏑ –́ – –́ ⏑ – – –́ ⏑ ⏑ – ⏑ ⏑ – ⏒
–́ ⏑ ⏑ – ⏑ ⏑ – – –́ ⏑ ⏑ – ⏑ ⏑ – – –́ ⏑ ⏓ Ep.
–́ ⏑ – – –́ ⏑ – – –́ ⏑ ⏑ – ⏑ ⏑ – –́ ⏑ ⏓
–́ ⏑ ⏑ – ⏖́ ⏑ –́ ⏑ ⏑ – ⏑ ⏑ – – –́ ⏑ ⏑ – ⏑ ⏑ ⏓
–́ ⏑ – – –́ ⏑ – ⏒

‿‿–‿‿–‿⌒‿––‿‿–‿‿⌣

‿‿––‿‿–‿‿––‿⌣

‿‿––‿‿––‿‿–⌐

Ol. VIII. ‿‿––‿‿‿–‿‿––‿⌣   **Str.**

–‿‿––‿‿‿–‿‿–⌐

‿‿–⌐‿‿‿–‿‿––‿‿‿–‿‿–⌐

‿‿‿–‿‿––‿⌣

‿‿‿–‿‿⌣

‿‿‿–‿‿⌣

‿‿––‿‿⌣

–‿‿‿–‿‿––‿⌣   **Ep.**

‿‿‿–‿‿–⌣‿‿‿–‿‿⌣

‿‿‿–‿‿–⌐‿⌣

‿‿‿–‿‿–⌐

‿‿‿–‿‿––‿‿‿–‿‿–⌐

‿‿‿–‿‿–⌐‿‿‿–‿‿–⌐‿‿‿–

‿‿–‿‿‿–‿‿⌣

⌐‿‿––‿‿⌣

Ol. IX. ‿‿‿–‿‿–‿⌣   **Str.**

⌐‿‿‿–‿–⌶⌐‿‿‿–‿–‿–⌐

⌶⌐‿‿‿–‿⌶⌐‿‿‿–⌐

⌶–‿‿‿–‿⌶–‿‿‿–⌐

⌶⌐‿‿‿–‿⌶⌐‿‿‿–⌐

⌒‿––‿‿‿––‿‿‿–⌐

⌶⌣‿‿‿–‿⌣

–‿‿‿–⌐

‿‿‿‿‿–‿–‿⌣

–‿‿‿–‿‿–⌐‿‿‿–⌐

‿‿‿–‿–‿–   **Ep.**

‿‿‿‿‿–‿–‿–⌐

‿‿‿‿‿‿–⌣

–‿–‿‿‿–‿–‿⌐

‿‿‿–‿–‿–

–‿‿‿–‿‿–‿‿⌣

‒⏑‒⏑‒⏑⏑●‒⏑⏑‒⏑‒

‒⏑‒⏑‒⏑͝ꟿꟿ͓‒⏑⏑‒⏑͝ꟿ͓‒⏑‒⏑⏑‒⏑‒ꟿ

Ol. X.   ‒⏑‒‒‒⏑⏑‒⏑⏑‒‒   Str.

‒⏑‒‒‒⏑⏑‒⏑⏑‒

‒⏑‒‒‒⏑⏑‒

‒⏑‒⏑‒⏑‒‒‒⏑⏑‒⏑⏑‒×

‒⏑‒‒‒⏑‒

‒⏑‒‒‒⏑‒⏑‒⏑⏑‒‒⏑⏑×

‒⏑⏑‒⏑⏑‒‒‒⏑‒‒   Ep.

‒⏑⏑‒⏑⏑‒‒

‒⏑‒͡⏑⏑‒‒‒⏑⏑‒⏑⏑‒

‒⏑‒‒‒⏑‒⏑‒⏑‒

‒⏑‒‒‒⏑‒⏑‒⏑‒

‒⏑‒ꟿ‒⏑‒̇

‒⏑⏑‒⏑⏑‒‒‒⏑‒‒‒⏑×

‒⏑⏑‒‒‒⏑‒‒

‒⏑‒⏑‒⏑‒‒⏑‒‒‒⏑‒ꟿ

Ol. XI.   ⏑⏑‒⏑⏑‒‒⏑‒‒͡⏑⏑×   Str.

ꟿ‒⏑‒‒⏑⏑‒‒⏑×

ꟿ‒⏑‒‒‒͡⏑⏑‒‒‒͡⏑⏑‒‒‒͡⏑⏑‒͓ꟿ‒‒⏑⏑⏑‒⏑⏑×

⏑‒‒⏑⏑ꟿ‒‒⏑×

ꟿ‒⏑‒‒⏑⏑×

ꟿ‒‒⏑⏑‒‒⏑×

⏑‒⏑‒͡⏑‒⏑⏑‒‒‒⏑‒͡⏑×   Ep.

⏑‒‒⏑⏑‒‒⏑⏑×

‒̇‒̇‒̇͡⏑⏑‒‒͡⏑⏑‒‒‒⏑⏑⏑‒ꟿ‒‒⏑×

‒‒⏑⏑⏑‒‒⏑⏑⏑‒‒͡⏑⏑‒‒‒

‒‒⏑⏑⏑‒‒⏑×

‒‒⏑‒‒⏑×

⏑⏑‒⏑⏑×

‒‒⏑⏑⏑‒⏑⏑⏑‒‒⏑×

⏑‒⏑⏑ꟿ‒‒⏑‒͡⏑ꟿ‒⏑‒‒⏑⏑×

Ol. XII.   ‒⏑‒‒‒⏑⏑‒‒⏑⏑×   Str.

‒⏑‒‒‒⏑⏑‒‒⏑⏑‒‒‒⏑⏑‒

INTRODUCTION.

1

⏑ — — ⏑ — — ⏑ —
⏑ — — ⏑ — — ⏑ ⏑ ×
⏑ — — ⏑ ⏑ — ⏑ ⏑ — —
× ⏑ — ⏓ ⏑ — — ⏑ ⏑ — ⏑ ⏑ — — ⏑ — — ⏑ ×
⏑ ⏑ ⏑ — ⏑ ⏑ — — ⏑ — ⏑   **Ep.**
⏑ ⏑ ⏑ — ⏑ ⏑ — — ⏑ — ⏑ ⏑ ×
⏑ — — ⏑ ⏑ ⏑ — ⏑ ⏑ — ⏑ —
— ⏑ ⏑ ⏑ — ⏑ ⏑ — — ⏑ — — ⏑ — —
⏑ — ⏑ ⏑ ⏑ — ⏑ ⏑ —
⏑ — — ⏑ — — ⏑ ⏑ —
⏑ — — ⏑ — — ⏑ — ⏑ ⏑ — — ⏑ — —

Ol. XIII. ⏑ ⏑ — ⏑ ⏑ — ⏓   **Str.**
⏓ — ⏑ — ⏓ — ⏑ — ⏑ ⏑ — ⏓
⏑ — ⏑ ⌒ ⏑ — — ⏑ ×
— — ⏑ ⌒ ⏑ — ⏑ — ⏑ ×
⏑ ⏑ — ⏑ — ⏓ ⏑ — ⏑ ⏑ — ⏓
⏓ — ⏑ — ⏑ ⏑ — — ⏑ — — ⏑ ⏑ — ⏑ ⏑ — ⏑ ×
⏓ — ⏑ ⏑ — ⏑ ⏑ — — ⏑ ⏑ — ⏑ ⏑ — ⏓
⏑ — — ⏑ — — ⏑ ⏑ ×
— ⏑ ⏑ ⏑ — ⏑ ⏑ — ⏑ ⏑ — ⏑ ⏑ — — ⏑ — ⏓   **Ep.**
⏑ — — ⏑ ⏑ ⏑ — ⏑ —
⏑ — ⏓ ⏑ ⏑ — ⏑ — ⏓
⌒ ⏑ — — ⏑ — — ⏑ ×
⏑ — — ⏑ — — ⏑ ⏑ — ⏑ ⏑ ×
⏑ ⏑ — ⏑ — — ⌒ ⏑ ×
⏑ — — × ⏑ — ⏑ — — ⏑ — ⏓

Ol. XIV. — ⏑ ⏑ — ⏑ ⏑ — ⏑ — × — ⏑ — ⏑ ⏑ — ⏑ — ⏑ — —
⏑ ⏑ ⏑ — ⏑ — ⏑ — ⏑ ⏑ — ⏓
⌒ ⏑ — ⏑ ⏑ ⏑ — ⏑ — ⏑ — ⏑ ⏑ ⏑ — ⏑ — ⏑ —
⏑ ⏑ ⏑ — ⏑ — ⏑ ⏑ — ⏑ ⏑ ⏑ — ⏑ —
⏑ ⏑ ⏑ — ⏑ — ⏑ ⏑ ×
⏑ ⏑ ⏑ — ⏑ ⏑ — ⏑ — ⏑ ⏑ — —
⏑ ⏑ — ⏒ — ⏑ ⏑ ⏑ — ⏑ —
⏑ ⏑ ⏑ — ⏒ — ⏑ ⏑ — ⏑ — ⏑ — ⏑ ⏑ ×

‒⏑⏑‒⏑‒⏑⏑‒⏑⏑‒⏑✕

‒⏑⏑⏑‒‒⏑‒

⏑⏑⏑‒⏑‒⏑⏑⏑‒⏑‒⏑‒‒

Pyth. I. ⏑⏑‒‒⏑⏑‒‒⏑⏑⏑‒⏑⏑✕   **Str.**

⏑⏑‒‒⏑⏑⏑‒⏑⏑‒‒⏑⏑⏑‒⏑⏑‒⏑⏑

⏑‒⏑⏑‒‒⏑⏑✕

‒⏑⏑⏑‒⏑⏑‒⏑⏑‒⏑⏑‒‒⏑⏑⏑‒⏑⏑‒

⏑⏑‒‒⏑⏑‒‒⏑⏑✕

⏑⏑⏑‒⏑⏑‒⏑⏑‒‒⏑⏑⏑‒⏑⏑‒‒⏑⏑⏑‒⏑⏑‒

⏑⏑⏑‒⏑⏑‒‒⏑⏑‒‒⏑⏑✕   **Ep.**

⏑⏑⏑‒⏑⏑‒⏑⏑⏑‒‒⏑⏑⏑‒⏑⏑✕

⏑⏑‒‒⏑⏑‒‒⏑⏑‒⏑⏑✕

‒⏑⏑⏑‒⏑⏑‒‒⏑⏑✕

⏑⏑‒‒⏑⏑⏑‒⏑⏑‒⏑⏑‒‒⏑⏑‒

⏑⏑‒‒⏑⏑⏑‒⏑⏑‒‒

⏑⏑‒‒⏑⏑‒‒⏑⏑‒‒⏑⏑‒‒⏑⏑⏑‒⏑⏑✕

⏑⏑⏑‒⏑⏑⏑⏑⏑‒‒⏑⏑‒

Pyth. II. ⏑⏑⏑⏑⏑‒⏑‒⏑‒⏑⏑⏑⏑✕   **Str.**

⏑⏑⏑‒⏑⏑‒⏑⏑⏑⏑⏑‒⏑‒‒⏑⏑⏑‒⏑✕

‒⏑⏑⏑‒⏑⏑‒⏑⏑‒⏑⏑✕

⏑⏑⏑⏑⏑‒⏑⏑‒⏑⏑⏑⏑‒⏑⏑‒⏑✕

‒⏑⏑⏑⏑⏑‒⏑⏑⏑✕

‒⏑⏑⏑⏑⏑‒⏑⏑⏑⏑‒⏑⏑✕

⏑⏑⏑⏑⏑‒⏑⏑⏑‒⏑⏑✕

‒⏑⏑⏑‒⏑‒⏑⏑‒⏑⏑⏑⏑⏑‒⏑‒

⏑⏑⏑⏑⏑‒⏑⏑‒⏑⏑⏑⏑⏑‒⏑⏑⏑‒⏑⏑✕   **Ep.**

⏑⏑⏑⏑⏑‒⏑‒⏑⏑⏑⏑⏑✕

⏑⏑⏑⏑⏑‒⏑‒⏑⏑⏑⏑⏑⏑⏑‒⏑⏑‒

⏑⏑⏑⏑⏑‒⏑‒⏑⏑✕

⏑⏑⏑‒⏑⏑⏑⏑⏑‒⏑‒⏑⏑✕

⏑⏑⏑⏑⏑‒⏑⏑‒

‒‒⏑⏑‒⏑⏑✕

⏑⏑⏑⏑⏑⏑⏑‒⏑‒⏑⏑⏑⏑⏑⏑⏑‒⏑‒

Pyth. III. ⏑⏑‒‒⏑⏑‒⏑⏑×   Str.
    ⏑⏑‒‒⏑⏑‒‒⏑⏑‒‒⏑⏑‒‒⏑×
    ‒⏑⏑⏑‒⏑⏑×
    ⏑⏑⏑‒⏑⏑‒‒⏑⏑‒⏑⏑‒‒⏑⏑‒‒⏑⏑‒‒⏑⏑×
    ⏑⏑⏑‒‒⏑⏑⏑‒⏑⏑‒‒⏑×
    ⏑⏑⏑‒⏑⏑⏑‒⏑⏑‒‒⏑⏑‒‒⏑×
    ⏑⏑⏑‒⏑⏑⏑‒‒⏑⏑‒◡
    ⏑⏑‒‒⏑⏑⏑‒⏑⏑×   Ep.
    ⏑⏑‒‒⏑⏑‒‒⏑×
    ⏑⏑‒‒⏑⏑⏑‒⏑⏑⏑‒‒⏑×
    ⏑⏑‒◡⏑⏑⏑‒⏑⏑⏑‒◡
    ⏑⏑⏑‒⏑⏑⏑‒‒⏑⏑‒‒⏑×
    ⏑⏑⏑‒⏑⏑‒◡⏑‒‒⏑⏑‒‒⏑×
    ⏑⏑⏑‒⏑⏑⏑‒‒⏑⏑⏑‒⏑⏑×
    ⏑⏑‒‒⏑⏑⏑‒⏑⏑⏑‒‒⏑⏑‒◡
    ⏑⏑⏑‒⏑⏑‒‒⏑⏑‒‒⏑×

Pyth. IV. ⏑⏑‒‒⏑⏑⏑‒⏑⏑×   Str.
    ⏑⏑‒‒⏑⏑⏑‒⏑⏑⏑‒‒⏑⏑‒‒⏑⏑⏑‒⏑⏑×
    ⏑⏑‒‒⏑⏑⏑‒⏑⏑⏑‒‒⏑⏑‒‒⏑⏑‒◡
    ⏑⏑⏑‒⏑⏑‒⏑⏑‒‒⏑⏑‒◡
    ⏑⏑⏑‒⏑⏑‒‒⏑⏑‒◡⏑⏑×
    ⏑⏑‒‒⏑⏑‒‒⏑⏑⏑‒⏑⏑‒⏑⏑×
    ⏑⏑‒‒⏑⏑‒‒⏑⏑‒⏑⏑×
    ☊⏑⏑‒‒⏑⏑‒◡
    ⏑⏑‒‒⏑⏑⏑‒⏑⏑⏑‒‒⏑⏑‒‒⏑×   Ep.
    ⏑⏑⏑‒⏑⏑⏑‒‒⏑⏑‒‒⏑⏑⏑‒⏑⏑×
    ⏑⏑‒‒⏑⏑‒‒⏑⏑⏑‒⏑⏑×
    ⏑⏑⏑‒‒⏑⏑‒‒⏑⏑‒‒⏑⏑‒‒⏑⏑⏑‒⏑⏑×
    ‒⏑⏑⏑‒⏑⏑⏑‒⏑⏑‒‒⏑⏑‒◡
    ⏑⏑‒‒⏑⏑‒‒⏑⏑⏑×
    ⏑⏑‒◡⏑⏑⏑‒⏑⏑‒⏑⏑‒◡‒⏑⏑‒◡

Pyth. V. ⏑⏑⏑‒⏑⏑×   Str.
    ⏑⏑⏑◻⏑⏑‒⏑⏑⏑×
    ⏑⏑⏑◻⏑⏑⏑⏑⏑⏑‒⏑‒☊⏑×

⏑⏓⏓⏑⏴
⏑⏓⏑⏑⏴
⏑⏑⏑⏑⏴
⏑⏑⏑⏴
⏑⏑⏑⏑⏑⏑⏑⏴
⏑⏑⏑⏑⏑⏑⏑⏴
⏑⏑⏑⏑⏑⏑⏑⏑⏑⏑⏑⏑⏑⏑⏑⏴
⏑⏑⏑⏑⏑⏑⏑⏑⏑⏴   Ep.
⏑⏑⏑⏑⏑⏑⏑⏑⏑⏑⏑⏑⏑⏑⏑⏑⏑⏑
⏑⏑⏑⏑⏑⏑⏑⏑⏑⏑⏑
⏑⏑⏑⏑⏑⏑⏑⏑⏑⏑
⏑⏑⏑⏑⏑⏑⏑⏑
⏑⏑⏑⏑⏑⏑⏑⏑⏑⏑⏑
⏑⏑⏑⏑⏑⏑⏑⏑⏑
⏑⏑⏑⏑⏑⏴
⏑⏑⏑⏑⏑⏑⏑⏑⏑⏑⏑⏑⏑⏑⏴

Pyth. VI.   ⏑⏑⏑⏑⏑⏑⏑⏑⏑⏑⏑   Str.
⏑⏑⏑⏑⏑⏴
⏑⏑⏑⏑⏑⏑⏑⏑⏑⏴
⏑⏑⏑⏑⏑⏑⏑⏑⏑⏴
⏑⏑⏑⏑⏑⏑⏑⏑⏑⏴
⏑⏑⏑⏑⏑⏑⏑⏑⏑⏴
⏑⏑⏑⏑
⏑⏑⏑⏑⏑⏑
⏑⏑⏑⏑⏑⏑⏑⏑⏴

Pyth. VII. ⏑⏑⏑⏑⏑⏑⏑⏑⏑⏑   Str.
⏑⏑⏑⏑⏑⏑⏑⏑⏑⏑⏑⏑⏑⏑⏑
⏑⏑⏑⏑
⏑⏑⏑⏑⏑
⏑⏑⏑⏑⏑⏑⏑⏑⏑⏑⏑⏑⏑⏴
⏑⏑⏑⏑⏑
⏑⏑⏑⏑⏑
⏑⏑⏑⏑⏑⏑⏑⏑⏑⏑⏑   Ep.

⏑ –́ – –́ ⏑ – – –́ ⏑ ⏑ – ⏑ –
×ϖ ⏑ –́ ⏑ ⏑ – ϖ́ ⏑ – ⏒
–́ ⏑ ⏑ – – –́ ⏑ – ⏑ –́ ⏑ ⏑ –
– –́ ⏑ – –́ ⏑ ⏑ –
⏑ –́ ⏑ ⏑ – –

Pyth. VIII. ×ϖ ⏑ –́ ⏑ ⏑ – ⏑ ⏓ Str.
×–́ ⏑ –́ ⏑ ⏑ ϖ ⏑ ⏓
– –́ ⏑ –́ ⏑ ⏑ ⏓
⏑ –́ ⏑ – –́ ⏑ ⏑ – ⏑ ⏓
–́ ⏑ ⏑ – ×– ⏒ ×–́ ⏑ –́ ⏑ ⏑ – ⏑ ⏓
⏒ –́ ⏑ –́ ⏑ ⏑ – ×– ⏒ –́ ⏑ – ⏑ ⏓
⏒ –́ ⏑ – ⏒ –́ ⏑ – ⏑ ⏓
⏑ –́ ⏑ –́ ⏑ ⏑ – ⏑ – –́ ⏑ – ⏑ ⏓ Ep.
⏒ –́ ⏑ –́ ⏑ ⏑ – ×– ⏒ –́ ⏑ ⏑ – ⏒
×– ⏒ –́ ⏑ ⏑ – ⏑ – ×– – –́ ⏑ ⏑ – ⏒
– –́ ⏑ ⏑ – –́ ⏑ ⏑ – ⏑ – ⏑ –
⏑ –́ –́ ⏑ ⏑ – ⏑ – ×–́ ⏑ –́ ⏑ ⏑ – ⏑ ⏓
⏑ –́ ⏒ ×– ⏒ –́ ⏑ ⏑ – ⏑ – ⏑ – ⏒

Pyth. IX. ⏑ ⏑ –́ ⏑ –́ ⏑ ⏑ – ⏑ ⏑ – – Str.
–́ ⏑ – – –́ ⏑ – –́ ⏒
⏑ ⏑ –́ ⏑ –́ ⏑ ⏑ – ⏑ ⏑ – ⏒
–́ ⏑ ⏑ – ⏑ ⏑ – – –́ ⏑ ⏑ – ⏑ ⏑ – ⏒
–́ ⏑ – – –́ ⏑ ⏑ – ⏑ ⏑ – – –́ ⏑ – – –́ ⏑ ⏑ – ⏑ ⏑ ⏓
–́ ⏑ ⏑ – ⏑ ⏑ – – –́ ⏑ ⏑ – ⏑ ⏑ – – –́ ⏑ ⏑ – ⏑ ⏑ – ⏒
–́ ⏑ ⏑ – ⏑ ⏑ – –́ ⏑ – – –́ ⏑ ⏓
–́ ⏑ – – –́ ⏑ – – –́ ⏑ – – –́ ⏑ – ⏒
– –́ ⏑ ⏑ – ⏑ ⏑ – – –́ ⏑ – Ep.
–́ ⏑ ⏑ – ⏑ ⏑ – – –́ ⏑ – – –́ ⏑ – – –́ ⏑ ⏑ – ⏑ ⏑ ⏓
–́ ⏑ – – –́ ⏑ ⏑ – ⏑ ⏑ – – –́ ⏑ ⏓
–́ ⏑ – – –́ ⏑ – –
–́ ⏑ – ⏒ –́ ⏑ ⏑ – ⏑ ⏑ – ⏒ –́ ⏑ ⏓
–́ ⏑ – – –́ ⏑ ⏑ – ⏑ ⏑ ⏓
–́ ⏑ – – –́ ⏑ ⏑ – ⏑ ⏑ – – –́ ⏑ – – –́ ⏑ ⏓

Pyth. X.   Str.

                                          Ep.

Pyth. XI.   Str.

                                          Ep.

Pyth. XII.   Str.

OLYMPIA I.

ON THE VICTORY OF HIERO'S RIDING HORSE PHERENIKOS, B.C. 472.

INTRODUCTION.

CHRONOLOGY.

	B.C.
HIERO wins the prize with the single horse, Gelo with the four-horse chariot at Olympia	488
Pindar goes to Sicily. Death of Thêro. Hiero rises to the height of his power, the tyranny at Agrigentum being upset. Nem. I. composed	473
Hiero's second victory with the single horse at Olympia. Pindar composes Ol. I. and XII., Nem. IX., Isthm. II. .	472
Hiero wins with the four-horse chariot (according to the poet's hope, vv. 109, 111) at Olympia. The poet was at Thebes this year[1]	468

[1] Pausanias, VIII. 42, tells us that Hiero did not pay his vows for his victories to Olympian Zeus; but that Deinomenes his son did so after his father's death. The following epigrams are quoted:

σὸν τοτε νικήσας, Ζεῦ Ὀλύμπιε, σεμνὸν ἀγῶνα
τεθρίππῳ μὲν ἅπαξ μουνοκέλητι δὲ δίς,
δῶρ' Ἱέρων τάδε σοι ἐχαρίσσατο, παῖς δ' ἀνέθηκεν
Δεινομένης πατρὸς μνῆμα Συρακοσίου.

and   υἱὸς μέν γε Μίκωνος Ὀνατᾶς ἐξετέλεσσεν
νάσῳ ἐν Αἰγίνῃ δώματα ναιετάων.

The gifts (Paus. VI, 12) were a bronze chariot and driver, by Onâtâs of Aegina, and on each side a horse, with a young rider by Kalamis. From

F.   1

The ode is composed in Aeolian rhythm (*v.* 102), with accompaniment of the Dorian cithern (*v.* 17), for a banquet at Syrakuse (*v.* 17), at which the poet was probably present. It was sung by a chorus of men (*v.* 17, ἄνδρες).

ANALYSIS.

vv.

1—7. A highly elaborated comparison illustrating the superlative renown of the Olympian games.

7—17. They inspire minstrels to sing the praises of Hiero, whose royalty, virtues, and musical taste are touched upon.

17—24. Praise of Pherenikos' easy victory at Pisa, the new home of Pelops.

25—27. Love of Poseidon for Pelops of the white shoulder from his birth.

28—34. The power of Song to give currency to falsehoods.

35. It is fitting to speak well of Deities. [These two considerations appropriately introduce what follows.]

the omission of Kalamis' name in the épigrams we may infer either that Kalamis' riding horses and their riders were offered later than the date of the epigrams, and Onâtâs' work (which cannot be safely dated earlier than, Ol. 79, B. C. 464, the first Olympian festival after Hiero's death), or that Kalamis was Onâtâs' assistant, and had not acquired independent fame. Hence Kalamis' 'floruit' ought not, as Professor Jebb suggests, to be placed so early as Ol. 78.

De Jongh places Hiero's first Olympian victory B. C. 476, and to it refers this ode, as he would have been Αἰτναῖος not Συρακόσιος, B.C. 472, he having founded Aetna, B. C. 476. The Schol. refer both first victory and this ode to B.C. 488, the latter wrongly beyond doubt. De Jongh thinks the error is owing to a confusion between Hiero's single-horse victory, and Gelo's chariot victory gained in that year. The Schol. on v. 23 (35) cites Didymos as saying on Apollodôros' authority that Hiero was Συρακούσιος, not Αἰτναῖος, at the date of the ode, but as the fancy for exalting Aetna at the expense of Syrakuse did not in likelihood last for more than one Olympiad, De Jongh is not justified in rejecting the date B.C. 472. According to Didymos, Hiero was Αἰτναῖος at the time of his last two Olympian victories, and yet the first epigram quoted from Pausanias makes him Συρακόσιος. Thêro was at war with Hiero, B.C. 476, and it is not likely that Thêro's friend, as Pindar was before he was Hiero's, should get a commission from Hiero before the reconciliation with Thêro.

36—45. Pindar's version of Pelops' disappearance, viz. his abduction by Poseidon.

46—51. The false myth invented through envy.

52—53. Deprecation of evil-speaking.

54—66. Bliss, insolence, and punishment of Tantalos, and consequent return of Pelops to earth.

67—89. Episode of Pelops' race with Oenomaos, including his invocation of Poseidon (*vv.* 75—85).

90—96. Pelops' posthumous glory at Olympia.

97—100. Happiness of victors.

100—111. Mention of Hiero's equestrian victory and of his excellence; expression of a hope that he will win the Chariot race.

111—end. Parallel of Pindar's paramount position as poet with Hiero's as king, and a prayer for the continuance of their exalted position during Hiero's life-time.

Throughout the whole Ode, which insists on the blessings of fame, there runs a subtly-veiled depreciation of long life. Tantalos' heaven-favored prosperity ends in woe. The crime for which he suffered was attempting to make men immortal. Pelops despises life in comparison with glory (*vv.* 82, 83). He had much trouble in life and great glory after death. Again, *vv.* 97—100 and 113, 114 inculcate contentment with present satisfaction of high ambition. Of course the more transparent bearing of the myth of Tantalos is on the danger of satiety and the sure punishment of insolence, while Pelops' connection with Poseidon, one of the Triopean Deities, links him to Hiero (Pyth. II. 11, 12), in whose family that cult was hereditary. Again, his being the first winner at Olympia makes his story generally appropriate to the Ode. Still I cannot help feeling that the Poet was influenced by his knowledge that Hiero's years were numbered. See Introduction to Pyth. III.

Στρ. α΄.

Ἄριστον μὲν ὕδωρ, ὁ δὲ χρυσὸς αἰθόμενον πῦρ
ἅτε διαπρέπει νυκτὶ μεγάνορος ἔξοχα πλούτου·
εἰ δ᾿ ἄεθλα γαρύεν   5
ἔλδεαι, φίλον ἦτορ,
5 μηκέτ᾿ ἀελίου σκόπει

1—9. 'Of sovereign worth is
water, while gold, as blazing fire
at night shines out, is beyond com-
pare the brightest treasure of lordly
wealth. But if thou art fain to
celebrate games, heart of mine,
look thou no more for other star
by day more genial than the sun
in the waste of heaven; so surely
shall we not name a contest trans-
cending Olympia's; inspired where-
by the hymn of high renown steals
o'er minstrels' faculties so that they
laud the son of Kronos.' Com-
pare the opening of Ol. x.
1. Ἄριστον μὲν ὕδωρ.] That this
was a proverbial expression in Pin-
dar's time is to be inferred from the
form in which it is given in the
third Olympian Ode, which is earlier
than this, i.e. v. 42, εἰ δ᾿ ἀριστεύει
μὲν ὕδωρ, κτεάνων δὲ χρυσὸς αἰδοιέ-
στατον. In all likelihood this simple
expression is nearly as old as the
sentiment, which Thales found,
say, B.C. 600, and formulated into
his Kosmical theory. Plato refers to
this place, Euthydem. p. 304 B, τὸ
γὰρ σπάνιον τίμιον· τὸ δὲ ὕδωρ εὐωνό-
τατον, ἄριστον ὄν, ὡς ἔφη Πίνδαρος.
Arist. Rhet. I. 7 § 14 quotes καὶ τὸ
σπανιώτατον (μεῖζον) τοῦ ἀφθόνου·
οἷον χρυσὸς σιδήρου, ἀχρηστότερος
ὢν· μεῖζον γὰρ ἡ κτῆσις διὰ τὸ χαλε-
πωτέραν εἶναι. ἄλλον δὲ τρόπον τὸ
ἄφθονον τοῦ σπανίου, ὅτι ἡ χρῆσις
ὑπερέχει· τὸ γὰρ πολλάκις τοῦ ὀλι-
γάκις ὑπερέχει· ὅθεν λέγεται ἄ. μ. ὑ.
It has not been generally noticed
that this praise of water is con-
siderably qualified by being the
anticlimax in the scale of super-

latives. We must mentally supply
'of things abundant and useful.'
Herod. VII. 16 makes Artabanos
call the sea τὴν πάντων χρησιμωτά-
την ἀνθρώποισι. Though one of the
uses of water was to mix with
wine, a banquet was not the oc-
casion for a lover of good cheer
to insist upon its transcendant
excellence. The omission of a
comparison, by which Pindar illus-
trates the supremacy of gold over
things rare and ornamental, and of
the Olympic contest among games
(things honourable), is scarcely to
be regarded as a distinction.
αἰθόμενον.] It is true that the
verb αἴθω is usually intrans.; but
the intrans. part., as αἰθοίσας, Ol.
VII. 48, is rare. The pass. αἰθό-
μενος is found thrice as an epithet
of πῦρ in the Hesiodic poems, once
of δᾷς, once of ἱερά, and more than
twenty times with πῦρ, δᾷς, λαμπ-
τήρ, δαλὸν in the Homeric. Don.'s
note seems likely to mislead. The
simile of fire blazing at night may
have reference to the eruption of
Aetna, which began B.C. 479.
2. ἔξοχα.] Cf. Ol. VIII. 23, ἔνθα
...ἀσκεῖται Θέμις ἔξοχ᾿ ἀνθρώπων,
Pyth. v. 24, φίλει δὲ Κάρρωτον ἔξοχ᾿
ἑταίρων.
πλούτου.] Equivalent to κτεάνων,
cf. Φιδίλαν, πάγχρυσον κορυφὰν κτεά-
νων, Ol. VII. 4, and Ol. III. 42.
5. ἀελίου.] So the best MSS.
There is a slight balance of evi-
dence that Pindar always used this
form, with synizesis when needful.
That he always used ἀεθλο- is
tolerably certain.

ἄλλο θαλπνότερον ἐν ἀμέρᾳ φαεννὸν ἄστρον ἐρήμας
    δι' αἰθέρος,   10
μηδ' Ὀλυμπίας ἀγῶνα φέρτερον αὐδάσομεν·
   ὅθεν ὁ πολύφατος ὕμνος ἀμφιβάλλεται

6. ἄστρον.] Frag. 84 [74] (on an eclipse), the sun is ἄστρον ὑπέρτατον.

ἐρήμας.] The adjective refers to the apparent absence of stars, and is different from Homer's ἀτρύγετος, Il. XVII. 425, of the empty αἰθήρ in which nothing offers resistance to the passage of σιδήρειος ὀρυμαγδός. Cf. Ol. XIII. 88.

αἰθέρος.] Fem. in Hom., masc. in Att. Prose and Tragic Iambics (except once in Eurip.). Pindar has it fem. here and in Ol. XIII. 88, both Aeolian odes, but twice masculine in Dorian rhythms, Ol. VII. 67, Nem. VIII. 42, ὑγρὸν αἰθέρα.

7. μηδ' αὐδάσομεν.] In Soph. Aj. 572, καὶ τἀμὰ τεύχη μήτ' ἀγωνάρχαι τινὲς | θήσουσ' Ἀχαιοῖς μήθ' ὁ λυμεὼν ἐμός, which Schn. quotes, μήτε is explained by the previous ὅπως according to Prof. Jebb. Here it is simplest to regard the previous imperative clause as equivalent to an expletive and cite Ar. Eccl. 999, μὰ τὴν Ἀφροδίτην μὴ 'γὼ σ' ἀφήσω, id. Av. 194, μὰ γῆν μὰ παγίδας μὰ νεφέλας μὰ δίκτυα μὴ 'γὼ νόημα κομψότερον ἤκουσά πω. We find, Il. ϙ 330, XV. 42, μὴ with ind. after ἴστω νῦν. Mr Jackson suggests that cases of μὴ with ind. in such solemn forms of asseveration are survivals of an old idiom. Now the Sanskrit mā shows us that μὴ is probably older than οὐ, and again the use of μὴ in prohibitions, wishes, &c., suggests that it is of stronger force, and might therefore be retained occasionally in emphatic negation. Is οὐ μὴ to be explained as the old strong negative retained with the newer, weaker sign of negation added to

distinguish the function of the μή, which might be liable to misconception after its general disuse as a particle of direct negation? We find μή irregularly used in rhetorical interrogations, e.g. Dem. F. L. 444, πῶς οὖν μήτε ψεύσομαι φανερῶς, μήτ' ἐπιορκεῖν δόξας πάνθ' ὅσα βούλομαι διαπράξομαι; Plat. Gorg. 510 D, Phileb. 18 E, Krat. 429 D (all due to Mr Jackson).

Ὀλυμπίας.] For comparatio compendiaria cf. Madv. § 90, Rem. 1, Il. XXI. 191, κρείσσων δ' αὖτε Διὸς γενεὴ Ποτάμοιο τέτυκται where Ποτάμοιο = γενεῆς Ποτάμοιο or ἢ γενεὴ Ποτάμοιο. Here then we must say Ὀλυμπίας = ἀγῶνος Ὀλυμπίας, or ἢ ἀγῶνα Ὀλυμπίας, a less usual construction than ἀγῶνος Ὀλυμπίου or ἢ ἀγῶνα Ὀλύμπιον, so that it almost seems as if this genitive takes the place of an adjective. Cf. however Nem. VI. 12 Νεμέας ἐξ δέθλων, Pyth. XI. 12 ἀγῶνι Κίρρας.

8. ὅθεν.] Cf. τὰς ἀπὸ θεύμοροι νίσσοντ' ἐπ' ἀνθρώπους ἀοιδαί, Ol. III. 9, Ὀρτυγία...σέθεν | ἁδνεπὴς ὕμνος ὁρμᾶται θέμεν | αἶνον ἀελλοπόδων μέγαν ἵππων, Nem. I. 4.

ἀμφιβάλλεται.] Cf. Eur. Bacch. 384, ἀνδράσι κρατήρ | ὕπνον ἀμφιβάλλῃ. Il. X. 535, ἀμφὶ κτύπος οὔατα βάλλει. Dissen explains 'is comprehended' comparing the metaphorical use of περιβάλλεσθαι (mid.), amplecti, 'to comprehend.' If we understand a word meaning motion with ὅθεν, as in Ol. I. 19, Pyth. IX. 29, we might render 'hath its foundations laid all about by minstrel skill.' Cf. Frag. 176, quoted on v. 16. For Od. XXIII. 192, τῷ...ἀμφιβαλὼν θάλαμον δέμον means 'having laid foundations'

σοφῶν μητίεσσι, κελαδεῖν　　　　　　　15
10 Κρόνου παῖδ' ἐς ἀφνεὰν ἱκομένους
μάκαιραν Ἱέρωνος ἐστίαν,

'Αντ. α'.

θεμιστεῖον ὃς ἀμφέπει σκᾶπτον ἐν πολυμάλῳ
Σικελίᾳ, δρέπων μὲν κορυφὰς ἀρετᾶν ἄπο πασᾶν,　　　20
ἀγλαΐζεται δὲ καὶ
15 μουσικᾶς ἐν ἀώτῳ,
οἷα παίζομεν φίλαν
ἄνδρες ἀμφὶ θαμὰ τράπεζαν.　ἀλλὰ Δωρίαν ἀπὸ φόρ-
μιγγα πασσάλου

or 'first courses about it, I built a chamber.' Two interpretations of Schol., προβάλλεται, περιγράφεται (cf. *Il.* XXIII. 255), support this view, which is at least as legitimate as Tafel's 'is discharged all about by poets' minds (as arrows are by bows).' Surely we should expect ὕμνοι ἀμφιβάλλονται, as Pindar's darts and arrows of song have definite marks, which they hit. I only defend my suggestion as next best to the rendering given above after Heyne, Böckh and Don. Herm. explains 'i. q. ἀναβάλλεται, ἐμβάλλεται.' Welcker thought there was a metaphor from a robe, cf. Schol. κοσμεῖται. Wakefield compares Ar. *Lysistr.* 28. In short, if once the simplest meaning be set aside there is no limit to conjecture.

9. σοφῶν.] Cf. Pyth. I. 42. Here the Chorus is included.

κελαδεῖν.] For inf. cf. Goodwin, § 97, note 2, Nem. III. 81, 82, Pyth. X. 48, Ol. III. 34, IX. 80.

12. θεμιστεῖον.] This derivative does not mean 'lawful,' 'righteous,' but 'of judicial authority.' Cf. *Il.* II. 206, βασιλεύς, ᾧ ἔδωκε Κρόνου παῖς... | σκῆπτρόν τ' ἠδὲ θέμιστας ἵνα σφίσιν ἐμβασιλεύῃ, and IX. 99.

13. δρέπων.] Act. instead of usual mid. four times, e.g. Pyth. I.

49, IV. 130; mid. twice, e. g. Nem. II. 9.

κορυφάς.] Cf. Nem. I. 34, ἐν κορυφαῖς ἀρετᾶν μεγάλαις, Ol. V. 1.

14. ἀγλαΐζεται.] 'He rejoiceth in music's rarest bloom, to wit, in such festive strains as we men ofttimes raise around the friendly board.' Gloss, λαμπρύνεται. *Il.* X. 331, Simon. Amorg. Frag. 7 line 70, Suidas' ἠγλαϊσμένη· χαίρουσα, λαμπρυνομένη, also Hesiod's and Pindar's use of ἀγλαΐα are conclusive against Böckh's 'is adorned.'

15. ἐν.] Cf. Nem. III. 82, παλαιαῖσι δ' ἐν ἀρεταῖς γέγαθε Πηλεὺς ἄναξ, where Don. alters needlessly. There it='in the possession of,' here 'in the encompassing sound of.'

16. οἷα.] For the indefinite relative introducing epexegesis or expansion of a definite antecedent cf. Pyth. II. 75, οὐδ' ἀπάταισι θυμὸν τέρπεται ἔνδοθεν οἷα ψιθύρων παλάμαις ἕπετ' αἰεὶ βροτῷ. III. 18, VI. 21, Frag. 176 [206], κεκρότηται χρυσέα κρηπὶς ἱεραῖσιν ἀοιδαῖς | οἷα τειχίζομεν ἤδη ποικίλον κόσμον αὐδάεντα λόγων, Nem. IX. 9, Ol. X. 8.

17. θαμά.] Sometimes in Pindar equivalent in *sense* to ἅμα, though *not* etymologically connected. θαμά 'in crowds, together' is to θαμά 'often' as *farcio*, φράσσω to *fre-*

λάμβαν', εἴ τί τοι Πίσας τε καὶ Φερενίκου χάρις
νόον ὑπὸ γλυκυτάταις ἔθηκε φροντίσιν
20 ὅτε παρ' Ἀλφεῷ σύτο δέμας
ἀκέντητον ἐν δρόμοισι παρέχων,
κράτει δὲ προσέμιξε δεσπόταν,

Ἐπ. α'.

Συρακόσιον, ἱπποχάρμαν βασιλῆα· λάμπει δέ οἱ κλέος
ἐν εὐάνορι Λυδοῦ Πέλοπος ἀποικίᾳ·
25 τοῦ μεγασθενὴς ἐράσσατο Γαιάοχος
Ποσειδᾶν, ἐπεί νιν καθαροῦ λέβητος ἔξελε Κλωθώ,   40
ἐλέφαντι φαίδιμον ὦμον κεκαδμένον.
ἢ θαυματὰ πολλά, καί πού τι καὶ βροτῶν φάτιν ὑπὲρ
τὸν ἀλαθῆ λόγον

quens, and as saepio to saepe;
while ἅμα is akin to Skt. sam- 'to-
gether,' Lat. sim-ul. For separation
of prep. from case cf. Pyth. II. 66.
18. Φερενίκου.] The Schol. on
the heading of the Ode has a frag.
of Bakchylides on this horse, ξανθό-
τριχα μὲν Φερένικον Ἀλφεὸν παρ' εὐ-
ρυδίναν πῶλον ἀελλοδρόμον νικήσαντα.
Now if this refers to this victory
B.C. 472, Don. must be wrong as to
this Pherenikos being mentioned
in Pyth. III. for victories dated B.C.
486, 482. A fifteen-year-old is
scarcely πῶλος. Even if Bakchy-
lides were referring to Hiero's first
Olympian victory B.C. 488, compo-
sing long after the event as Pindar
does in Pyth. III., we have a seven-
teen-year-old winner in B.C. 472.
Surely the Pherenikos of Pyth. III.
was grandsire to the Pherenikos of
Ol. I. See Introduction to Pyth.
III. Had the horse won before the
occasion celebrated in Ol. I., Pindar
would probably have alluded to the
fact.
21. ἀκέντητον.] Cf. Plat. Phaedr.
253 D (of the good horse), ἄπληκτος,
κελεύματι μόνῳ καὶ λόγῳ ἡνιοχεῖται.
22. For the idiom cf. v. 78, Ol.
XI. 104, Nem. I. 18, ὀλυμπιάδων φύλ-

λοις ἐλαιᾶν χρυσέοις μιχθέντα, ib. II.
22, ὀκτὼ στεφάνοις ἐμίχθεν ἤδη, Isth.
III. 3, ἄξιος εὐλογίαις ἀστῶν μεμίχθαι,
Soph. Antig. 1311, δειλαίᾳ δὲ συγκέ-
κραμαι δύᾳ, Isth. II. 19, κλειναῖς
Ἐρεχθειδᾶν χαρίτεσσιν ἀραρώς.
δεσπόταν.] 'His master.' De
Jongh joins δεσ. Συρ., comparing
wrongly Ol. VI. 18, ἀνδρὶ κώμου
δεσπότᾳ πάρεστι Συρακοσίῳ. Be-
ware of joining Συρ. βασιλῆα. Pin-
dar would use gen. plur., which
many MSS. give against the scan-
sion. Cf. Pyth. I. 73, Συρακοσίων ἀρχῷ.
23. ἱπποχάρμαν.] Pindaric for
ἱππιοχάρμης, which clearly does not
mean 'rejoicing in horses,' but
'fighting as a horseman,' lit.
'horse-fight-some.' Cf. Pyth. II. 2.
οἱ.] For the king.
24. ἀποικίᾳ.] Pisa. Pelops was
ἄποικος from Lydia; so that his
new home is appropriately called
ἀποικίᾳ in connection with Λυδοῦ.
26. καθαροῦ.] 'Purifying.' Cf. κ.
θεείῳ sulfure puro, Theok. XXIV. 95.
Κλωθώ.] The fates assisted at
births, cf. Nem. VII. 1, Ἐλείθυια
πάρεδρε Μοιρᾶν βαθυφρόνων, Ol. VI.
42, XI. 52.
28. ἢ θαυματὰ πολλά.] 'Verily
tales of marvel are rife, and per-

δεδαιδαλμένοι ψεύδεσι ποικίλοις ἐξαπατῶντι μῦθοι. 45

Στρ. β'.

30 χάρις δ', ἅπερ ἅπαντα τεύχει τὰ μείλιχα θνατοῖς,
ἐπιφέροισα τιμὰν καὶ ἄπιστον ἐμήσατο πιστὸν 50
ἔμμεναι τὸ πολλάκις·
ἀμέραι δ' ἐπίλοιποι
μάρτυρες σοφώτατοι.

35 ἔστι δ' ἀνδρὶ φάμεν ἐοικὸς ἀμφὶ δαιμόνων καλά· μείων
γὰρ αἰτία. 55
υἱὲ Ταντάλου, σὲ δ' ἀντία προτέρων φθέγξομαι,
ὁπότ' ἐκάλεσε πατὴρ τὸν εὐνομώτατον 60
ἐς ἔρανον φίλαν τε Σίπυλον,
ἀμοιβαῖα θεοῖσι δεῖπνα παρέχων,
40 τότ' Ἀγλαοτρίαιναν ἁρπάσαι

Ἀντ. β'.

δαμέντα φρένας ἱμέρῳ χρυσέαισιν ἀν' ἵπποις
ὕπατον εὐρυτίμου ποτὶ δῶμα Διὸς μεταβᾶσαι·

chance to some extent too the bruit of mortals is led all astray by fables tricked out beyond the truth with varied garniture of lies.' Most mss. read θαῦμα τὰ πολλά. Several editors read θαύματα πολλά, which Don. says is not Greek, because ἔστι the predicate is never omitted. But why not explain θαύματά ἐστι πολλά 'wonders are rife?' However θαυμστὰ is supported by the Schol. Vet. Don. cites Soph. Ant. 332, πολλὰ τὰ (Don. τε) δεινὰ κοὐδὲν ἀνθρώπου δεινότερον πέλει. For sentiment, cf. Pyth. x. 48.

φάτιν.] mss. φάτις; and φρένας, which is clearly a correction, but supports an acc. For sentiment, cf. Nem. vii. 23. σοφία δὲ κλέπτει παράγοισα μύθοις, also Thuk. i. 21. 1, but see note on v. 47.

30. χάρις.] A personification of the charm of beauty, social harmony, or minstrelsy (Ol. vii. 11,

xiii. 18, Nem. iv. 7).

31. 'By adding her authority contriveth that even the incredible be ofttimes credible.'

33. For sentiment cf. Ol. xi. 53.

35. μείων γὰρ αἰτία.] Cf. Pyth. i. 82. For sentiment, cf. Ol. ix. 87.

38. ἔρανον.] Cf. Pyth. v. 72. This particular feast is called ἔρανος by Euripides Hel. 388, and Epicharmos uses ἔρανος for a feast generally.

41. χρυσέαισιν ἀν' ἵπποις.] For ἵπποι 'chariot' see L. and S.

42. μεταβᾶσαι.] Inf. extra structuram after ἁρπάσαι, cf. Pyth. iv. 146, or else after δαμέντα φρένας ἱμέρῳ, cf κελαδεῖν, v. 9 supra. If the latter construction be preferred, render 'snatched thee, his heart constrained by yearning to bear thee off,' if the former, place a comma after 'yearning.'

ἔνθα δευτέρῳ χρόνῳ
ἦλθε καὶ Γανυμήδης
45 Ζηνὶ τωὖτ' ἐπὶ χρέος.
    ὡς δ' ἄφαντος ἔπελες, οὐδὲ ματρὶ πολλὰ μαιόμενοι
        φῶτες ἄγαγον,
    ἔννεπε κρυφᾷ τις αὐτίκα φθονερῶν γειτόνων   75
    ὕδατος ὅτι σε πυρὶ ζέοισαν ἀμφ' ἀκμὰν
    μαχαίρᾳ τάμον κατὰ μέλη,
50 τραπέζαισί τ' ἀμφὶ δεύματα κρεῶν   80
    σέθεν διεδάσαντο καὶ φάγον.

                                                   Ἐπ. β'.

    ἐμοὶ δ' ἄπορα γαστρίμαργον μακάρων τιν' εἰπεῖν· ἀφί-
        σταμαι·
    ἀκέρδεια λέλογχεν θαμινὰ κακαγόρος.   85
    εἰ δὲ δή τιν' ἄνδρα θνατὸν Ὀλύμπου σκοποὶ
55 ἐτίμασαν, ἦν Τάνταλος οὗτος· ἀλλὰ γὰρ καταπέψαι
    μέγαν ὄλβον οὐκ ἐδυνάσθη, κόρῳ δ' ἕλεν

---

43. Pindar and Euripides, *Troad.*
821, follow the legend that Ga-
nymede was the son of Pelops'
contemporary Laomedon, others
make him Laomedon's brother,
Homer his uncle, namely son of
Trôs.

47. As Envy is said to have
given rise to the rejected story, *vv.*
28—31 scarcely refer to exaggera-
tion or embellishment as Thuk. I.
21, but mean that poetic art will
give currency to the most impro-
bable slanders.

48. ὑδ. ζε. ἀκ.] Schol. ὕδωρ
ἀκμαίως ζέον. Our phrase '.boiling
point' accidentally corresponds to
Pindar's ornate turn.

τραπ. ἀμφι.] For each man
having a table, cf. Hom. *Od.* XVII.
333, 447.

50. δεύματα] Almost all MSS.
δεύτατα, which is as old as Athên-
aeos (A.D. 230), but one of the
oldest MSS. gives the text. δεύτατα
would be 'second course,' as Athên.,
or ' the end of the banquet.'

52. ἄπορα.] For plur. cf. Pyth.
I. 34, II. 81, IV. 247.

τινα.] Dêmêter was supposed to
have eaten the shoulder.

53. ἀκέρδεια λέλογχεν.] 'Sore loss
hath oft befallen evil-speakers.'
The use of the perfect indicates
the abiding effect of their sin on
them. So τὰν Διὸς εὐναὶ λάχον, Pyth.
II. 27. τῷ σκληρῷ δαίμονος ὅς με λέ-
λογχε, Theok. IV. 40. For the Doric
(and Boeotian) acc. plur. -ος for -ονς*
instead of -ους, Dor. -ως, cf. Hes.
Scut. Herc. 302, λαγός. Cf. νᾶσος,
Ol. II. 71, ὑπέροχος, ἐσλός, Nem.
III. 24, 29.

55. καταπέψαι.] For metaph.
cf. *Il.* I. 81, χόλον καταπέψῃ. Here
the use is slightly different, but
circumstances may be said to form
the food of character.

ἄταν ὑπέροπλον, ἅν οἱ πατὴρ ὑπὲρ κρέμασε καρτερὸν
    αὐτῷ λίθον,   90
τὸν αἰεὶ μενοινῶν κεφαλᾶς βαλεῖν εὐφροσύνας ἀλᾶται.
                                      Στρ. γ´.

ἔχει δ᾽ ἀπάλαμον βίον τοῦτον ἐμπεδόμοχθον,   95
60 μετὰ τριῶν τέταρτον πόνον, ἀθανάτων ὅτι κλέψαις
    ἁλίκεσσι συμπόταις
νέκταρ ἀμβροσίαν τε   100
δῶκεν, οἷς μιν ἄφθιτον
θέσσαν. εἰ δὲ θεὸν ἀνήρ τις ἔλπεταί τι λαθέμεν ἔρδων,
    ἁμαρτάνει.
65 τοὔνεκα προῆκαν υἱὸν ἀθάνατοί οἱ πάλιν   105
μετὰ τὸ ταχύποτμον αὖτις ἀνέρων ἔθνος.
πρὸς εὐάνθεμον δ᾽ ὅτε φυὰν
λάχναι νιν μέλαν γένειον ἔρεφον,   110
ἑτοῖμον ἀνεφρόντισεν γάμον
                                  Ἀντ. γ´.

70 Πισάτα παρὰ πατρὸς εὔδοξον Ἱπποδάμειαν

57. Euripides (Orest. 6) again
follows the same legend as Pindar,
and differs from Homer (Od. xi.
582).

οἱ...αὐτῷ.] The two pronouns
are suspicious. mss. give τῷ οἱ;
I think for ἐν τοι.

58. 'Ever eager to cast which
from his head he suffers banish-
ment from joy.'

κεφαλᾶς βαλεῖν.] The construc-
tion is not paralleled. The alter-
native rendering 'ever expecting
which to hit him on the head' is
scarcely better supported. Il. xiv.
264, μενοινᾷς certainly seems to
mean 'are you apprehensive about,'
but κεφ. βαλεῖν 'to hit his head'
is not well defended. Perhaps
μολεῖν should be read, comparing
for gen. ἀκροβόλων δ᾽ ἐπαλξέων λιθάς
ἔρχεται, Aesch. Sept. c. Th. 146
(P.). For confusion of μ and β cf.

Il. xxiv. 81. ἐμβεβανῖα, cited Plato
Ion, p. 538 c, ἐμμεμνῖα (Paley), Ol.
ix. 8.

ἀλᾶται.] Cf. ψυχὴν ἀλᾶται τῆς
πάροιθ᾽ εὐπραξίας, Eur. Troad. 642.

59. ἀπάλαμον.] For meaning
and quantity cf. Hes. W. and D.
20.

βίον.] Of existence after death,
cf. Ol. ii. 63, βίοτον, 67, αἰῶνα.

60. τριῶν.] Ixion, Sisyphus, Ti-
tyos.

63. οἷς μιν.] Bergk suggests οἷς
νιν for the MS. reading οἷσιν.

67. πρός.] 'Towards,' 'about
the time of.' Pyth. ix. 25, πρὸς
αὠ, see L. and S.

68. μέλαν.] Proleptic. See Essay
on Style.

69. ἑτοῖμον.] Though the con-
ditions were hard and success very
difficult, still the match was open
to all.

σχεθέμεν. ἐγγὺς ἐλθὼν πολιᾶς ἁλὸς οἶος ἐν ὄρφνᾳ 115
ἄπυεν βαρύκτυπον
Εὐτρίαιναν· ὁ δ᾽ αὐτῷ
πὰρ ποδὶ σχεδὸν φάνη.
75 τῷ μὲν εἶπε· Φίλια δῶρα Κυπρίας ἄγ᾽ εἴ τι, Ποσεί-
δαον, ἐς χάριν 120
τέλλεται, πέδασον ἔγχος Οἰνομάου χάλκεον,
ἐμὲ δ᾽ ἐπὶ ταχυτάτων πόρευσον ἁρμάτων 125
ἐς Ἇλιν, κράτει δὲ πέλασον.
ἐπεὶ τρεῖς τε καὶ δέκ᾽ ἄνδρας ὀλέσαις
80 μναστῆρας ἀναβάλλεται γάμον

Ἐπ. γ΄.

θυγατρός. ὁ μέγας δὲ κίνδυνος ἄναλκιν οὐ φῶτα λαμ-
βάνει.
θανεῖν δ᾽ οἷσιν ἀνάγκα, τί κέ τις ἀνώνυμον 131
γῆρας ἐν σκότῳ καθήμενος ἕψοι μάταν,
ἁπάντων καλῶν ἄμμορος; ἀλλ᾽ ἐμοὶ μὲν οὗτος ἄ-
εθλος 135
85 ὑποκείσεται· τὺ δὲ πρᾶξιν φίλαν δίδοι.
ὣς ἔννεπεν· οὐδ᾽ ἀκράντοις ἐφάψατο ἔπεσι. τὸν μὲν
ἀγάλλων θεὸς
ἔδωκεν δίφρον τε χρύσεον πτεροῖσιν τ᾽ ἀκάμαντας ἵπ-
πους.

Στρ. δ΄.

ἕλεν δ᾽ Οἰνομάου βίαν παρθένον τε σύνευνον·
τέκε τε λαγέτας ἐξ ἀρεταῖσι μεμαλότας υἱούς. 145

71. ἐν ὄρφνᾳ.] Iamos invokes Poseidon and Apollo, νυκτὸς ὑπαί-θριος, Ol. vi. 61.
75. Cf. Soph. Aj. 520, ἀνδρί τοι χρεὼν | μνήμην προσεῖναι, τερπνὸν εἴ τί του πάθοι, Verg. Aen. iv. 307, fuit aut tibi quidquam | dulce meum.
77. ταχ. ἁρμ.] A Lydian Chariot was proverbial for swiftness, cf. Frag. 190 [222].
78. Cf. v. 22.

81. λαμβάνει.] Cf. Pyth. iv. 70.
83. ἕψοι.] Lit. 'coddle.' Cf. Pyth. iv. 186.
88. ἕλεν.] Generally in zeugma one verb is suppressed: here the verb refers to two objects, but in different senses. Cf. Soph. Trach. 353, ταύτης ἕκατι κεῖνος Εὔρυτόν θ᾽ ἕλα | τὴν θ᾽ ὑψίπυργον Οἰχαλίαν.
89. ἀρεταῖσι.] Pindar probably follows the Pythagorean division

90 νῦν δ' ἐν αἱμακουρίαις
ἀγλααῖσι μέμικται,
'Αλφεοῦ πόρῳ κλιθείς,
τύμβον ἀμφίπολον ἔχων πολυξενωτάτῳ παρὰ βωμῷ.
τὸ δὲ κλέος   150
τηλόθεν δέδορκε τᾶν 'Ολυμπιάδων ἐν δρόμοις
95 Πέλοπος, ἵνα ταχυτὰς ποδῶν ἐρίζεται   155
ἀκμαί τ' ἰσχύος θρασύπονοι·
ὁ νικῶν δὲ λοιπὸν ἀμφὶ βίοτον
ἔχει μελιτόεσσαν εὐδίαν

'Αντ. δ'.

ἀέθλων γ' ἕνεκεν. τὸ δ' αἰεὶ παράμερον ἐσλὸν   160
100 ὕπατον ἔρχεται παντὶ βροτῷ. ἐμὲ δὲ στεφανῶσαι
κεῖνον ἱππίῳ νόμῳ

of virtues into four, temperance,
courage, justice, prudence. Cf. Nem.
III. vv. 70—75. For phrase, cf. εὐ-
θυμίᾳ τε μέλων εἴην, Frag. 132 [127].
90. αἱμακουρίαις.] Pausanias
tells us that a black ram was sacri-
ficed yearly to Pelops as the *blood*
offering to *satisfy* his shade. ἐν...
μέμικται=ἐμμέμικται per tmesin.
93. Cf. Ol. XI. 24.
94. τηλόθεν.] ' Now long after,'
lit. ' from far off time.' Cf. Pyth.
II. 54, ἑκὰς ἐών.
δέδορκε.] Cf. Nem. III. 84, δέ-
δορκεν φάος, Nem. IX. 41.
ἐν δρόμοις.] Depends on τὸ κλέος
(Cf. Ol. VIII. 56, 83, Pyth. VI. 18,
ἅρματι νίκαν Κρισαίαισιν ἐν πτυχαῖς,
Pyth. VII. 13), and takes a double
genitive, cf. Pyth. IX. 39. For τᾶν
'Ολ. ἐν δρομ. cf. Πυθιάδος δ' ἐν δρόμῳ,
Pyth. I. 32.
95, 96. '.Where is rivalry in
swiftness of foot and toil-braving
feats of strength.'
ἐρίζεται.] If this be an inversion
for ταχύτατα ἐρίζοντι it is very pe-
culiar, not to say unique. We find
Hes. *Sc.* 5, νόον οὔτις ἔριζε without
a dat., but νόον seems to the ana-

lyst to be an accusative of respect,
though not necessarily so to a
Greek, and it may ·be on this
very phrase that Pindar's artificial
turn is framed. The alternative is
to take the verb as middle, in the
same sense as the active, and then
the next verse means ' and toil-
braving strength developed to the
highest point.' In our athletic
dialect ἀκμὴ ἰσχύος is 'prime con-
dition,' and the plural is distribu-
tive, indicating the various kinds
of physical excellence needed for
the several exercises.
97—99. For sentiment, cf. Pyth.
I. 46 note, Plato *Rep.* v. 465 D,
ζήσουσι τοῦ μακαριστοῦ βίου ὃν οἱ
'Ολυμπιονῖκαι ζῶσι μακαριώτερον. As
the poet immediately speaks of
further contests, and we know that
one Olympian victory did not con-
tent victors, εὐδίαν must mean the
calm satisfaction caused by having
once attained the highest object of
ambition.
99. τὸ δ' αἰεὶ παρ.] 'Ever fresh,' as
the renown of an Olympian victory.
101. ἱππίῳ.] 'An equestrian
strain' is called a Καστόρειον,Pyth. II.

Αἰοληΐδι μολπᾷ
χρή· πέποιθα δὲ ξένον 165
μή τιν' ἀμφότερα καλῶν τε ἴδριν ἀλλὰ καὶ δύναμιν
κυριώτερον
105 τῶν γε νῦν κλυταῖσι δαιδαλωσέμεν ὕμνων πτυχαῖς. 170
θεὸς ἐπίτροπος ἐὼν τεαῖσι μήδεται
ἔχων τοῦτο κῦρος, Ἱέρων,
μερίμναισιν· εἰ δὲ μὴ ταχὺ λίποι,
ἔτι γλυκυτέραν κεν ἔλπομαι 175
Ἐπ. δ'.

110 σὺν ἅρματι θοῷ κλείξειν ἐπίκουρον εὑρὼν ὁδὸν λό-
γων,
παρ' εὐδείελον ἐλθὼν Κρόνιον. ἐμοὶ μὲν ὦν
Μοῖσα καρτερώτατον βέλος ἀλκᾷ τρέφει· 180
ἐπ' ἄλλοισι δ' ἄλλοι μεγάλοι· τὸ δ' ἔσχατον κορυφοῦται

69. Αἰολ. μολπᾷ is in apposition to νόμῳ. It does not follow from the mention of the Dorian lyre, v. 17, that this ode was not thoroughly Aeolian in rhythm and accompaniment. Aristot. *Polit.* vi. (iv.) ch. iii. tells us that some say there are only two ἁρμονίαι, the Dorian and Phrygian, τά τ' ἄλλα συντάγματα τὰ μὲν Δώρια τὰ δὲ Φρύγια καλοῦσιν. Thus the Aeolian would be included in the Dorian class. There was not a distinct Aeolian lyre, so that the epithet Δωρίαν (φόρμιγγα) seems to have been merely ornamental.

104. ἀλλὰ καί.] Most mss. give ἅμα καί, others ἄλλον ἤ, or ἄλλον καί. Hermann's emendation is almost certainly right, as M and ΛΛ are often confused. For ἀμφότερα, cf. Ol. vi. 17, Pyth. iv. 79, Isth. i. 42.

105. πτυχαῖς.] Don. 'with artificial turns of song.'

106. θεός.] Not Poseidon, but ὁ μέγας πότμος, cf. Pyth. iii. 85, λαγέταν γάρ τοι τύραννον δέρκεται

εἴ τιν' ἀνθρώπων ὁ μ. π.

109. κεν.] For ἄν (κε κεν) with Fut. Inf. see Goodwin § 41. 4, who is somewhat too sceptical, and ignores this passage (note 2).

110. σὺν ἅρματι.] For σὺν cf. Nem. x. 48 σὺν ποδῶν σθένει νικᾶσαι, Pyth. i. 38. For dependence on γλυκ. (μέριμναν) cf. νίκα ἅρματι, quoted on v. 94, and passim; so too νίκα ἵπποις, Isth. ii. 13.

ὁδόν.] Cf. Nem. vii. 51, ὁδὸν κυρίαν λόγων.

111. Κρόνιον.] Κρόνιος or Κρόνιος λόφος, Ol. v. 17, was a hill at the N.W. corner of the Olympian Valley.

112. βέλος.] Pindar is fond of likening his thoughts and words to missiles, Ol. ii. 83, 89, βέλη, ὀϊστοί, Ol. ix. 5, βέλη, Ol. xiii. 93, Nem. vii. 71, Pyth. i. 44, ἄκων, Isth. iv. 47 τοξεύματ'; so the tones of the lyre are κῆλα, Pyth. i. 12; ἐτόξευον ὕμνους, Isth. ii. 3.

ἀλκᾷ.] Hermann attaches this word to τρέφει 'for my defence.' But for dat. of manner, cf. Ol.

βασιλεῦσι.   μηκέτι πάπταινε πόρσιον.
115 εἴη σέ τε τοῦτον ὑψοῦ χρόνον πατεῖν, ἐμέ τε τοσσάδε
    νικαφόροις
ὁμιλεῖν πρόφαντον σοφίᾳ καθ᾽ Ἕλλανας ἐόντα παντᾷ.

II. 6, IV. 24, XIII. 52.
  114. πάπταινε.] Cf. Pyth. III.
22.   For sentiment, cf. Ol. III. 44.
  115. χρόνον.] For sense of 'life-
time,' cf. Pyth. V. 118.

πατεῖν.]   Cf. ἐν εὐθείαις ὁδοῖς στεί-
χοντα, Nem. I. 25, also Ol. II. 21, 22.
  τοσσάδε.] For neut. plur. instead
of masc. or fem. sing. of pronoun,
cf. v. 16 οἷα, Ol. X. 8.

OLYMPIA II.

INTRODUCTION.

CHRONOLOGY.

Thêro's pedigree was Aenêsidâmos, Pataekos (who, or his father
Emmenides or Emmenes, went to Agrigentum from Gela, and the
last named, or his father Chalkiopeus, emigrated from Rhodes to
Gela)......Têlemachos (who migrated from Thêra to Rhodes), Samos,
Thêras (who colonized Thêra from Lakônia), Autesion, Tisamenos,
Thersandros, Polyneikes (m. Argia daughter of Adrastos), Oedipus,
Laios, Labdakos, Polydôros, Kadmos.

ANALYSIS.

vv.

1—6.   Threefold theme of the ode, Zeus, Hêrakles, Thêro, set forth.

6, 7.   Praise of Thêro and mention of his glorious ancestors.

7—11.   Their settlement in Sicily and prosperity there.

12—15.   Prayer to Olympian Zeus for its continuance.

15—22.   Not even Time can undo deeds once done, but good fortune brings forgetfulness of troubles.

22—45.   This truth is illustrated by the fortunes of Kadmos' family, which lead up to

45, 46.   Thêro's descent from Thersandros and Adrastos.

46—51.   So that it is natural that Thêro and his brother should be victorious in games.

51, 52.   Victory releases competitors from troubles.

53—56.   Opportunities for distinction are afforded by wealth combined with virtues, and if a wealthy man knows what is to be—

57—77.   That the unjust are punished but the just lead a life of delight in the Isles of the Blest,

78—83.   Where are Thêro's ancestor Kadmos and his prototype Achilles—

83—86.   If one is intelligent by nature he will understand my sayings;

86—88.   But detractors, such as mine for instance, are mere learners.

89—95.   Complimentary mention of Akragas and high praise of Thêro for kindness and bounty.

95—98.   Yet unjust envy attacks his fame.

98—100.   His bounties are innumerable.

For the bearing of the last 17 lines see note on *v.* 56.

Στρ. α´.

Ἀναξιφόρμιγγες ὕμνοι,
τίνα θεόν, τίν᾽ ἥρωα, τίνα δ᾽ ἄνδρα κελαδήσομεν;
ἤτοι Πίσα μὲν Διός· Ὀλυμπιάδα δ᾽ ἔστασεν Ἡρακλέης 5
ἀκρόθινα πολέμου·
5 Θήρωνα δὲ τετραορίας ἕνεκα νικαφόρου
γεγωνητέον, ὄπι δίκαιον ξένον, ἔρεισμ᾽ Ἀκράγαντος, 10
εὐωνύμων τε πατέρων ἄωτον ὀρθόπολιν·

Ἀντ. α´.

καμόντες οἳ πολλὰ θυμῷ
ἱερὸν ἔσχον οἴκημα ποταμοῦ, Σικελίας τ᾽ ἔσαν
10 ὀφθαλμός, αἰών τ᾽ ἔφεπε μόρσιμος, πλοῦτόν τε καὶ
χάριν ἄγων   20

1. The vocal melody of course determines the instrumental accompaniment.

2. Observe the emphatic δέ. The Games and founder settled the two first questions. Those who bring against Pindar the thoughtless accusation of irrelevance should learn from this passage, copied by Horace, *Od.* i. 12, that the victor was by no means all his theme.

3. For the legend of the founding of the Olympian games by Hêrakles, cf. Ol. xi. 21 sqq. Zeus is to be celebrated as patron deity of the Olympian games, Hêrakles as their founder, and in this instance owing to his connection with Thebes, whence Thêro derived his ancestry.

4. ἀκρόθινα.] In this passage, Pindar pronounced the ι of the neut. plur. subst. ἀκρόθινια as a y, so also the ε of θεὸς, Pyth. i. 56. In τετραορίας (v. 5) αο is pronounced as one long syllable (synizesis). To illustrate the apposition Dissen cites an epigram in Paus. v. 27 fin. Ζηνὶ θεῶν βασιλεῖ μ᾽ ἀκροθίνιον ἐνθάδ᾽ ἔθηκαν Μενδαῖοι: but ἀκροθ. is here an adj. Don.'s paraphrase 'from the chief spoils,' is misleading as to

the grammar of the phrase, as also is L. and S. The neut. plur. subs. means 'an offering,' or 'offerings, of prime spoils.' Here then it means 'as his offering of prime spoils,' epexegetic of ἔστασεν Ὀλυμπιάδα, not merely in apposition with Ὀλυμπιάδα; cf. Soph. *El.* 130 (Jebb).

6. ὄπι.] Hermann reads this instead of mss. ὄπι, and ξένων, but for ὄπις without gen. cf. Hom. *Od.* xiv. 82, ἀτὰρ σιάλους γε σύας μνηστῆρες ἔδουσιν, | οὐκ ὄπιδα φρονέοντες ἐνὶ φρεσὶν οὐδ᾽ ἐλεητύν. Herm. formerly read ὄπιν, and left ξένον. For the quantity ὄπι cf. Epic μῆτι.

7. ἄωτον.] This word may here mean 'choicest honour to,' as in Ol. iii. 4, but as this would *imply* his was the best of the line why not render 'choicest flower' with gen., as in Thuk. i. 1, ἀξιολογώτατον τῶν προγεγενημένων? The compound ὀρθόπολιν is strictly 'upright-city-ed.'

9. ἔσχον.] 'Gat.' Cf. Pyth. i. 65. ποταμοῦ.] Cf. Eur. *Med.* 846, ἱερῶν ποταμῶν πόλις, Ol. vi. 84, Ἀλφεὸν οἰκεῖν. The neighbourhood of the river made the dwelling-place ἱερόν.

10. ὀφθαλμός.] Cf. Pyth. v. 17.

F.   2

γνησίαις ἐπ' ἀρεταῖς.

ἀλλ' ὦ Κρόνιε παῖ 'Ρέας, ἕδος 'Ολύμπου νέμων
ἀέθλων τε κορυφὰν πόρον τ' Ἀλφεοῦ, ἰανθεὶς ἀοιδαῖς 25
εὔφρων ἄρουραν ἔτι πατρίαν σφίσιν κόμισον

'Επ. α'.

15 λοιπῷ γένει. τῶν δὲ πεπραγμένων
ἐν δίκᾳ τε καὶ παρὰ δίκαν ἀποίητον οὐδ' [ἂν]   30
χρόνος ὁ πάντων πατὴρ δύναιτο θέμεν ἔργων τέλος·
λάθα δὲ πότμῳ σὺν εὐδαίμονι γένοιτ' ἄν.
ἐσλῶν γὰρ ὑπὸ χαρμάτων πῆμα θνάσκει   35
20 παλίγκοτον δαμασθέν,

Στρ. β'.

ὅταν θεοῦ Μοῖρα πέμπῃ
ἀνεκὰς ὄλβον ὑψηλόν. ἔπεται δ' ὁ λόγος εὐθρόνοις
Κάδμοιο κούραις, ἔπαθον αἱ μεγάλα, πένθος δὲ πιτνεῖ
βαρὺ   40
κρεσσόνων πρὸς ἀγαθῶν.
25 ζώει μὲν ἐν 'Ολυμπίοις, ἀποθανοῖσα βρόμῳ   45

ἔφετε.] An inversion of the common Epic use. For suppression of object, cf. Ol. I. 40, Pyth. II. 17.

12. Κρόνιε.] Cf. Pyth. II. 18.

13. πόρον τ'.] For the simple connective where we might expect a preposition, cf. v. 47.

14. σφίσιν...γένει.] Don. says σφίσιν for αὐτῶν. But rather the second dative explains and extends the first. Cf. Ol. VIII. 83, ὃν σφιν Ζεὺς γένει ὤπασεν, Pyth. I. 7, ἐπί οἱ νεφέλαν ἀγκύλῳ κρατί...κατέχευας. Eur. Bacch. 336, ἡμῖν τε τιμὴ παντὶ τῷ γένει προσῇ.

16. ἐν.] Cf. v. 63, Ol. VI. 12, VII. 69. For sentiment cf. Simonides, Frag. 69 (111), τὸ γὰρ γεγενημένον οὐκέτ' ἄρεκτον ἔσται.

19. 'For by noble delights a cruel trouble is subdued and dies away, whensoever the Fate of God

sends uppermost high bliss.' Cf. Eur. Herc. Fur. 101, κάμνουσι γάρ τοι καὶ βροτῶν αἱ συμφοραί.

21. The metaphor is probably from the turning of a wheel, which alternately raises and lowers any point on the periphery. Cf. Tib. I. 5. 70, Versatur celeri Fors levis orbe rotae.

22. ὑψηλόν.] Proleptic. εὐθρόνοις.] From Pyth. III. 94 this would seem to be more than a mere epithet of royalty.

23. δὲ πιτνεῖ.] The corrections δ' ἐπίτνει and δ' ἐπίτνεν are unwarranted. The overthrow of the calamity would not be regarded as a continuous act in any case, nor was bliss attained gradually in these particular instances, therefore the Historic Pres. is far better than the Imp.

κεραυνοῦ ταννέθειρα Σεμέλα, φιλεῖ δέ μιν Παλλὰς αἰεί,
καὶ Ζεὺς πατὴρ μάλα, φιλεῖ. δὲ παῖς ὁ κισσοφόρος. 50

'Αντ. β'.

λέγοντι δ' ἐν καὶ θαλάσσα
μετὰ κόραισι Νηρῆος ἁλίαις βίοτον ἄφθιτον
30 'Ινοῖ τετάχθαι τὸν ὅλον ἀμφὶ χρόνον. ἤτοι βροτῶν
γε κέκριται   55
πεῖρας οὔ τι θανάτου,
οὐδ' ἀσύχιμον ἀμέραν ὁπότε παῖδ' ἀελίου
ἀτειρεῖ σὺν ἀγαθῷ τελευτάσομεν· ῥοαὶ δ' ἄλλοτ'
ἄλλαι   60
εὐθυμιᾶν τε μετὰ καὶ πόνων ἐς ἄνδρας ἔβαν.

'Επ. β'.

35 οὕτω δὲ Μοῖρ', ἅ τε πατρώϊον   65
τῶνδ' ἔχει τὸν εὔφρονα πότμον, θεόρτῳ σὺν ὄλβῳ
ἐπί τι καὶ πῆμ' ἄγει παλιντράπελον ἄλλῳ χρόνῳ·
ἐξ οὗπερ ἔκτεινε Λᾷον μόριμος υἱὸς   70

26. Παλλάs.] Mentioned because
of the worship of Pallas Onka at
Thebes, cf. Aesch. Sept. c. Theb.
164, and of Pallas Lindia at Agri-
gentum, the building of whose
temple offered Thêro the oppor-
tunity of seizing the tyranny.
30. κέκριται.] 'Verily for mor-
tals no set time of death is deter-
mined, nor (is it determined) if
ever we shall bring to its close a
peaceful day, child of the Sun,
with unimpaired good; for at dif-
ferent times divers currents come
to men bearing both joys and
trials.' Cf. Theognis 381 (373), οὐδέ
τι κεκριμένον πρὸς δαίμονός ἐστι βρο-
τοῖσιν, | οὐδ' ὁδός, ἥν τις ἰὼν ἀθανά-
τοισιν ἅδοι.
32. ὁπότε.] Cf. Thuk. I. 2,
ἄδηλον ὅν ὁπότε τις ἐπελθὼν......ἄλλος
ἀφαιρήσεται.
παῖδ' ἀελίου.] For confusion of
objects and Personifications, cf. Ol.

x. 2, Pyth. IV. 14.
33. ῥοαί.] Cf. Nem. XI. 46, προ-
μαθείας δ' ἀπόκεινται ῥοαί, 'currents
(of future events) lie out of reach
of foresight.' For form of expres-
sion, cf. Ol. VII. 95, Pyth. III. 104,
Isth. III. 23. Heyne and Böckh
join μετέβαν, but the compound
with ἐς would require the indica-
tion or implication of the place
whence. For position of καὶ cf. v.
28, of prep. Pyth. II. 11. The me-
taphor in ῥοαί is not from tides,
which are insignificant in the Me-
diterranean. Cf. Isth. III. 18, Eur.
Andr. 349, Herc. Fur. 739, παλίρ-
ρους πότμος.
35. πατρώϊον.] Extension of pre-
dicate. For sentiment cf. Nem. v.
40, πότμος συγγενής.
37. πῆμα παλιντρ.] 'Sad re-
verse.'
38. μόριμος.] Cf. Ol. III. 10, VI.
8, Pyth. II. 2.

2—2

συναντόμενος, ἐν δὲ Πυθῶνι χρησθὲν
40 παλαίφατον τέλεσσεν.

Στρ. γ΄.

ἰδοῖσα δ᾽ ὀξεῖ᾽ Ἐρινὺς
ἔπεφνέ οἱ σὺν ἀλλαλοφονίᾳ γένος ἀρήϊον·   75
λείφθη δὲ Θέρσανδρος ἐριπέντι Πολυνείκει, νέοις ἐν
    ἀέθλοις
ἐν μάχαις τε πολέμου
45 τιμώμενος, Ἀδραστιδᾶν θάλος ἀρωγὸν δόμοις·   80
ὅθεν σπέρματος ἔχοντα ῥίζαν πρέπει τὸν Αἰνησιδάμου
ἐγκωμίων τε μελέων λυρᾶν τε τυγχανέμεν.   85

Ἀντ. γ΄.

Ὀλυμπίᾳ μὲν γὰρ αὐτὸς
γέρας ἔδεκτο, Πυθῶνι δ᾽ ὁμόκλαρον ἐς ἀδελφεὸν

40. παλαίφατον.] As noun; 'an-
tient oracle,' lit. 'antiently spoken.'
41. ὀξεῖα.] Paley best, 'keen-eyed.'
The adj. is in fact adverbial. Cf.
Nem. x. 62, ὀξύτατον ὄμμα.
43. Θέρσανδρος.] An Adrastid
by his mother Argia, daughter of
Adrastos.
ἐριπέντι.] The reading of the
best MSS. and Aldine Ed., found
also by Apollônios Dyskolos the
grammarian (A.D. 117—161), and
needlessly altered by him to ἐρι-
πόντι, from analogy of Homeric
intrans. ἤριπον.
νέοις.] The only instance I know
of νέος = 'of the young,' as epithet
of externals, is Soph. Aj. 510, νέας
τροφῆς στερηθείς. νέα φροντίς, ν.
διάνοια, νεαρὰν ἀρετάν, are not to
the point. I have thought that the
games instituted by Adrastos (cf.
Nem. IX. 9—12) at Sikyôn are
meant.
44. μάχαις.] In the war of the
Epigoni and the fight in Mysia, in
which he showed himself the fore-
most of the Hellênes in prowess
and was slain by Têlephos.
46. σπέρματος.] I take the geni-

tive to be in a sort of apposition
with ὅθεν, cf. Ol. VII. 24; as the
poet would hardly make ῥίζαν ante-
cedent to σπέρμα. Don. is mislead-
ing, for here the ῥίζαν is derived from
the θάλος, through, as I take it, the
σπέρμα which the θάλος bears, while
in Aesch. Suppl. 105, which he
compares, νεάζει πυθμὴν δι᾽ ἁμὸν
γάμον τεθαλώς (far better than τὸ
θάλλος, see Paley), the old stock
sprouts.
ἔχοντα.] Most MSS. give ἔχοντι
ῥίζαν. πρ. .... Besides the awk-
wardness of the asyndeton, and
the necessity of supplying a subject
for ἔχοντι from v. 36, the Pindaric
doctrine of γνήσιαι ἀρεταί is not
so well enforced as by the text.
Four MSS. (three 13th cent.) give
the v. l. ἔχοντα. We can infer from
the Schol. that Aristarchos (B.C.
156) read ἔχοντα, but that Didymos
got his punctuation with the read-
ing ἔχοντι, probably a careless al-
teration due to the neighbourhood
of πρέπει.
47. λυρᾶν τε.] Cf. v. 18.
49. For victories of Xenokra-
tes, Thêro's brother, see Introd.

50 Ἰσθμοῖ· τε κοιναὶ Χάριτες ἄνθεα τεθρίππων δυωδεκα-
    δρόμων   ·90
ἄγαγον· τὸ δὲ τυχεῖν
πειρώμενον ἀγωνίας, παραλύει δυσφρονᾶν.   95
ὁ μὰν πλοῦτος ἀρεταῖς δεδαιδαλμένος φέρει τῶν τε καὶ
    τῶν
καιρόν, βαθεῖαν ὑπέχων μέριμναν ἀγροτέραν,   100
                                    Ἐπ. γ´.

55 ἀστὴρ ἀρίζηλος, ἐτυμώτατον
    ἀνδρὶ φέγγος· εἰ δέ μιν ἔχων τις οἶδεν τὸ μέλλον,

ὁμόκλαρον.] Cf. Nem. IX. 5.

50. Χάριτες.] They are givers of victory here as in Ol. VI. 76, Nem. V. end, X. 38.

ἄνθεα.] 'Crowns of four-horse teams which twelve times run the course.' For the crowning of the horses or mules cf. Ol. XIII. 10.

51. τὸ δὲ τυχεῖν.] 'Now to win when essaying a contest sets one free from its hardships.' τυχεῖν equiv. to εὐτυχεῖν. Cf. Pyth. III. 104.

52. δυσφρονᾶν.] So Dindorf. Most editors, after inferior mss., read δυσφρόνων. Most mss. give the obvious gloss δυσφροσύναν or -ας, perhaps suggested by Hes. Theog. 528, ἐλύσατο δυσφροσυνάων.

53. For sentiment, cf. Pyth. V. 1—4.

φέρει.] 'Bringeth opportunity for divers aims, suggesting a deep yearning for noble quests.'

τῶν τε καὶ τῶν.] Cf. Pyth. VII. 22. Generally used of varieties; but of opposites Isth. III. 51, Theogn. 398.

54. μέριμναν.] Cf. Ol. I. 108.

ἀγροτέραν.] On the form, cf. Pyth. III. 4. Here 'eager in pursuit.' Pyth. IX. 6, 'huntress.'

55. ἀρίζηλος.] From ἀρι-διηλος, ἀρι-διϝηλος, from √ DIV. For termination, cf. ἔκ-ηλος. In δῆλος the iota is absorbed.

ἐτυμώτατον.] Both ἐτήτυμος and ἔτυμος are, I believe, superlative forms connected with ἐτεό-ς. Cf. Skt. satyatama-s. In ἔτυμος either -τη- is dropped by dissimilation, as in τράπεζα from τετραπεζα, or it is formed with -ma instead of -tama, and y is dropped. The reading of the best mss. is rejected here for ἐτήτυμον, the loss of the syllable being set straight by taking ὀρθαῖς, ἔβα, for the better supported ὀρθαῖσι, ἐπέβα, vv. 75, 95. In vv. 15, 35, τετραγμένων, πατρώϊον have the first syllable scanned long. The fault lies with the metrical Schol. who may have gone by the first two epodes, reckoning the doubtful syllables short, and the grammarians who interpolated ἀλαθινόν. I venture to think the metre of the text is more consonant with the rest of the rhythm than that of the critics.

56. εἰ δέ μιν ἔχων τις.] This is the reading of best mss. authority. I hold that the apodosis of the sentence is lost by reason of the long digression vv. 57—83, and that the poet intended, 'But if one possessing wealth combined with virtues knows what is to be, that if he be just he will attain bliss after death, he will understand my sayings (v. 83), and strong in my praises will not heed the censures of the envious'

ὅτι θανόντων μὲν ἐνθάδ᾽ αὐτίκ᾽ ἀπάλαμνοι φρένες   105
ποινὰς ἔτισαν, τὰ δ᾽ ἐν τᾷδε Διὸς ἀρχᾷ
ἀλιτρὰ κατὰ γᾶς δικάζει τις ἐχθρᾷ
60 λόγον φράσαις ἀνάγκᾳ·

Στρ. δ΄.

ἴσαις δὲ νύκτεσσιν αἰεί,
ἴσαις δ᾽ ἀμέραις ἀέλιον ἔχοντες, ἀπονέστερον   110
ἐσλοὶ δέκονται βίοτον, οὐ χθόνα ταράσσοντες ἐν χερὸς
ἀκμᾷ
οὐδὲ πόντιον ὕδωρ   115
65 κεινὰν παρὰ δίαιταν· ἀλλὰ παρὰ μὲν τιμίοις
θεῶν, οἵτινες ἔχαιρον εὐορκίαις, ἄδακρυν νέμονται   120

(v. 95). Böckh suggests εἰ γέ μιν ἔχων, the sense of which is grammatically clear, but not in accordance with Pindar's views; for he would not think the glory to be attained through wealth combined with virtues dependent on knowledge of the after-life. Rauchenstein, Tafel, Don. read εὖ δέ μιν ἔχων 'if a person possesses this (i.e. wealth adorned by virtue), he well knows, &c.' But again this knowledge is not dependent on wealth.

57. θανόντων μέν.] Opposed by ἴσαις δέ (v. 61). The δ᾽ of vv. 58, 62, is in both cases quite subordinate. Rauchenstein's explanation is condemned by his separation of ἐνθάδε from θανόντων.

ἀπάλαμνοι.] Solon, Frag. 27 (3) 12, οὐδ᾽ ἔρδειν ἔθ᾽ ὅμως ἔργ᾽ ἀπάλαμνα θέλει. Theogn. v. 281, δειλῷ γάρ τ᾽ ἀπάλαμα βροτῷ πάρα πόλλ᾽ ἀνελέσθαι | πὰρ ποδός, ἡγεῖσθαί θ᾽ ὡς καλὰ πάντα τιθεῖ. With this passage compare Frag. 106 [95].

59. δικάζει τις.] The Schol. says Pluto is meant, but it might be Minos. The indefinite pronoun is used in solemn reticence, as in Aesch. Eum. 860, σπευδόμεναι δ᾽ ἀφελεῖν τινὰ τάσδε μερίμνας.

61, 62. Interpolated mss. read ἴσων...ἴσα δ᾽ ἐν for metrical reasons, which however are not conclusive. The text reminds one of the curious description of Laistrygonia, Od. x. 82—86.

62. ἀπονέστερον.] Far easier than life on earth.

63. δέκονται.] So Wüstemann after one ms. Most read δέρκονται, a mistake suggested by the two preceding lines. Cf. Isth. v. 15.

οὐ χθόνα, κ.τ.λ.] Cf. Isth. i. 48, 49, which suggest that ταράσσοντες πόντιον ὕδωρ means fishing, while Hes. W. and D. 236 makes for navigation generally.

ἀκμᾷ.] 'With utmost stress of handiwork.' For ἐν with dat. used adverbially cf. v. 16. For phrase cf. d. ποδῶν, Isth. vii. (viii.) 38, d. φρενῶν, Nem. iii. 39.

65. κεινάν.] 'Owing to lack of sustenance.' Cf. Thuk. i. 141, § 9.

τιμίοις θεῶν.] Dissen and Don. understand 'those who are honoured by the gods;' but the gen. cannot be defended except as a partitive. I take the Chthonian deities to be meant, and οἵτινες to refer back to ἐσλοί.

αἰῶνα· τοὶ δ' ἀπροσόρατον ὀκχέοντι πόνον.

'Αντ. δ'.

ὅσοι δ' ἐτόλμασαν ἐστρὶς
ἑκατέρωθι μείναντες ἀπὸ πάμπαν ἀδίκων ἔχειν   125
70 ψυχάν, ἔτειλαν Διὸς ὁδὸν παρὰ Κρόνου τύρσιν· ἔνθα
    μακάρων
νᾶσος ὠκεανίδες
αὖραι περιπνέοισιν· ἄνθεμα δὲ χρυσοῦ φλέγει,   130
τὰ μὲν χερσόθεν ἀπ' ἀγλαῶν δενδρέων, ὕδωρ δ' ἄλλα
    φέρβει,
ὅρμοισι τῶν χέρας ἀναπλέκοντι καὶ στεφάνοις,   135

'Επ. δ'.

75 βουλαῖς ἐν ὀρθαῖσι 'Ραδαμάνθυος,
ὃν πατὴρ ἔχει Κρόνος ἑτοῖμον αὐτῷ πάρεδρον,
πόσις ὁ πάντων 'Ρέας ὑπέρτατον ἐχοίσας θρόνον. 140
Πηλεύς τε καὶ Κάδμος ἐν τοῖσιν ἀλέγονται·
'Αχιλλέα τ' ἔνεικ', ἐπεὶ Ζηνὸς ἦτορ
80 λιταῖς ἔπεισε, μάτηρ·

Στρ. έ.

ὃς "Εκτορ' ἔσφαλε, Τροίας   145

---

67. τοὶ δ'.] Opposed to ἐσλοί; 'but the wicked.'

68. ἐστρίς.] The number three, and the metempsychosis here implied, are probably Pythagorean. Cf. Plat. *Phaedr.* p. 249 A.

70. Διὸς ὁδόν.] There seems to have been a legend of Zeus paying solemn visits to the Isles of the Blest, which Plato used *Phaedr.* 246 E.
Κρόνου.] Cf. Hes. *W. and D.* 169.

71. νᾶσος.] Cf. Ol. I. 53.

72. χρυσοῦ.] For gen. instead of adj., cf. Ol. I. 7.

74. καὶ στεφάνοις.] 'And (their heads) with crowns.' The suppression of κεφαλάς, which Böckh read for στεφάνοις, made alteration almost inevitable. Most good MSS.

read στεφάνους. For the ὅρμοι twined about, i. e. carried in, their hands, cf. Isth. I. 66.

75. Rhadamanthys here seems to play the part given to Minos Plat. *Gorg.* 526 c.
ἐν.] Cf. Pyth. IV. 59.

76. Κρόνος.] The reading of the interpolated MSS. for the obviously corrupt γᾶς. I suspect that πατρὸς was the original reading, as Κρόνος was Rhadamanthys' grandfather. After πατήρ, πατρὸς might easily drop out.

78. Πηλεύς.] Pêleus is suggested by Kadmos, cf. Pyth. III. 87. Achilles the great adversary of Troy is apposite to Thêro, foe of the Elymi of Trojan descent. Kyknos and Memnon suggest Thêro's Phoenician enemies.

ἄμαχον ἀστραβῆ κίονα, Κύκνον τε θανάτῳ πόρεν,
'Αοῦς τε παῖδ' Αἰθίοπα. πολλά μοι ὑπ' ἀγκῶνος ὠκέα
βέλη   150
ἔνδον ἐντὶ φαρέτρας
85 φωνάεντα συνετοῖσιν· ἐς δὲ τὸ πᾶν ἑρμηνέων
χατίζει. σοφὸς ὁ πολλὰ εἰδὼς φυᾷ· μαθόντες δὲ λά-
βροι   155
παγγλωσσίᾳ, κόρακες ὥς, ἄκραντα γαρύετον

                                                    'Αντ. ε'.

Διὸς πρὸς. ὄρνιχα θεῖον.
ἔπεχε νῦν σκοπῷ τόξον. ἄγε θυμέ, τίνα βάλλομεν 160
90 ἐκ μαλθακᾶς αὖτε φρενὸς εὐκλέας. ὀιστοὺς ἱέντες; ἐπί
τοι
'Ακράγαντι τανύσαις   165
αὐδάσομαι ἐνόρκιον λόγον ἀλαθεῖ νόῳ,
τεκεῖν μή τιν' ἑκατόν γε ἐτέων πόλιν φίλοις ἄνδρα
μᾶλλον   170
εὐεργέταν πραπίσιν ἀφθονέστερόν τε χέρα

                                                    'Επ. ε'.

95 Θήρωνος. ἀλλ' αἶνον ἐπέβα κόρος

85. ἐς δέ.] 'But for the majority they need interpreters.'
86. φυᾷ.] Cf. τὸ δὲ φυᾷ κράτιστον ἅπαν, Ol. ix. 100, Plat. Phaedr. p. 245 ε.
87. παγγλωσσίᾳ.] Reckless unstinted speech. A wealth of words poured forth without thought or scruple. License of tongue. See Isokrates' use of παρρησία.
ἄκραντα.] Cf. Aesch. Choeph. 884, ἄκραντα βάζω, Eur. Suppl. 770.
γαρύετον.] Simonides and Bakchylides. Their envy of Pindar is probably introduced to associate the poet with the victor and emphasize his sympathy.
90. Cf. Pyth. iv. 4.
91. τανύσαις.] Böckh takes this as optative, cf. Ol. ix. 14, and puts

a colon after it, against a slight preponderance of ms. authority and the Schol. Moreover τοι is more likely to be used in affirmation than with the precative.
93. ἐτέων.] For gen. cf. Madv. § 66 a. However the number of years is said by the Schol. to refer to the age of Akragas, which was 106 years old at the date of this ode. Accordingly the gen. might as far as grammar goes qualify πόλιν (Madv. § 54 b), but this construction would limit the compliment strangely. I think the limit of time hints at a tradition of superlative hospitality indulged in by one of Tháro's ancestors. ἔτος, akin to vetus, had an initial ϝ.
95. 'But praise is attacked by disgust, not paying heed to justice,

οὐ δίκᾳ συναντόμενος, ἀλλὰ μάργων ὑπ' ἀνδρῶν, 175
τὸ λαλαγῆσαι θέλων κρύφον τε θέμεν ἐσλῶν καλοῖς
ἔργοις. ἐπεὶ ψάμμος ἀριθμὸν περιπέφευγεν·
ἐκεῖνος ὅσα χάρματ' ἄλλοις ἔθηκεν, 180
100 τίς ἂν φράσαι δύναιτο;

but felt by covetous men, eager that prating should bring obscurity (*lit.* for prating and bringing obscurity) on fair deeds of noble men.' For this κόρος cf. Ol. XIII. 10.

· 96. συναντόμενος.] Cf. Isth. II. 2, κλυτᾷ φόρμιγγι σ.

μάργων.] Cf. Theognis 581, ἐχθαίρω δὲ γυναῖκα περίδρομον ἄνδρα τε μάργον, | ὃς τὴν ἀλλοτρίην βούλετ' ἄρουραν ἀροῦν.

97. The construction is θέλων τὸ λαλαγῆσαι θέμεν ꞏε κρύφον. Cf. Soph. Œd. Kol. 442, τὸ δρᾶν οὐκ ἠθέλησαν. Hermann makes θέμεν govern τὸ λαλαγῆσαι, as well as the rare subst. κρύφον. He also proposes τιθέμεν for τε θέμεν, 'eager

that babbling bring obscurity over.' The mss. give θέλων, but elsewhere Pindar always uses the form ἐθέλων. I would suggest κακολογῆσαι for τὸ λαλαγῆσαι. True, κακολογέω is not found in poets, but cf. the Pindaric παλαιμονέω, also εὐμενέω, ναυστολέω, μοναρχέω, which are not found in earlier extant works. Pindar uses the equally unpoetical κακολόγος. I imagine that κολαλογῆσαι was the corruption, and the text its correction.

98. ψάμμος.] Cf. Ol. XIII. 45, Hor. Od. I. 28. 1.

99. ἔθηκεν.] The Aor. is frequentative.

OLYMPIA III.

ON THERO OF AKRAGAS, COMPOSED FOR THE
THEOXENIA.

INTRODUCTION.

THIS Ode was composed for the same victory as that celebrated in Ol. II.

From the greater prominence given to the victory and to the Olympian games in this Ode, and from the αὖτε of Ol. II. 90, we may infer with tolerable certainty that this Ode was composed before Ol. II.

It was probably for recitation at the Theoxenia[1], a festival supposed to have been instituted by the Dioskuroi, who with their sister Helenê were said to have entertained the Gods, and it was probably sung in a temple at Agrigentum, while Thêro stood crowned with victor's chaplet (vv. 6, 13).

The Schol. tells us that Aristarchos explained the theme of the Ode by stating that the Dioskuroi were held in high honour at Agrigentum.

From the intimate connection of the Emmenidae with the cult of the Divine Twins, to which Pindar alludes vv. 38—41, we may infer that this Doric worship was transmitted to Sicily from Lakônia through Thêra with Thêro's ancestors, or was even brought with them to Lakônia from Argos where the cult flourished. Cf. Ol. II. 43—46.

The propriety of celebrating the Tyndaridae in connection with an Olympian victory appears from vv. 36, 37.

The rhythm is Dorian, the accompaniment being a new combination of cithern and flute (vv. 4, 5, 8).

---

[1] According to the heading given in the best MSS., the Schol., and also the allusion in v. 40. The Schol. Ol. IX. 146 (98) makes the Theoxenia of Pellêne a festival of Apollo and Hermes.

ANALYSIS.

vv.

1—4. The theme of Thêro's victory is commended to the Dioskuroi and Helenê,

4—6. For which the Muse had helped the poet to invent a new variety of Dorian song,

6—9. Since Thêro's victory made it incumbent on the poet to invent a combination of lyre and flute in the accompaniment, and he was required to sing by Pisa,

9—13. Whence odes come for all whom the Hellânodikas crowns with a wreath of olive,

13—34. Which Hêrakles brought from the Hyperboreans. Myth of his journey to their land and back to the then treeless Olympia.

34, 35. He now attends the Theoxenia with the Twins.

36—38. Them he had enjoined to superintend the Olympian games.

38—41. The poet expresses conviction that to the Twins is Thêro's glory due in requital of pious worship.

42—44. So surely as water and gold are supreme of their kind, so Thêro's achievements reach as far as the Pillars of Hêrakles.

44, 45. Further none can pass. The poet declines to suggest such a thing.

$$Στρ. \ α'.$$

Τυνδαρίδαις τε φιλοξείνοις ἀδεῖν καλλιπλοκάμῳ θ' Ἑλένᾳ

1. φιλοξείνοις.] The epithet is appropriate to the Theoxenia and perhaps glances at Thêro's hospitality, cf. Ol. II. 93—95.

ἀδεῖν.] 'I am confident that I shall please.' For the Aorist referring to future, cf. Pyth. I. 35. The primitive meaning of εὔχομαι may have been 'to speak out,' but it very early got the special signification of 'to utter a wish,'

for εὔχομαι 'I pray' for εὔσκομαι is connected with Old High German *wunsc*, Eng. *wish*. The passage to the meaning 'boast' seems to be through 'to utter a realized wish,' hence 'to utter that which gives mental satisfaction.' Curtius connects αὐχέω, which I prefer to group with καυχάομαι. The Skt. root νᾶς, ἠχή, Lat. *vāgīre*, all originally, as it would seem, ap-

κλεινὰν 'Ακράγαντα γεραίρων εὔχομαι,
Θήρωνος 'Ολυμπιονίκαν ὕμνον ὀρθώσαις, ἀκαμαντο-
πόδων   5
ἵππων ἄωτον. Μοῖσα δ' οὕτω τοι παρέστα μοι νεο-
σίγαλον εὑρόντι τρόπον
5 Δωρίῳ φωνὰν ἐναρμόξαι πεδίλῳ

                                                     'Αντ. α'.

ἀγλαόκωμον· ἐπεὶ χαίταισι μὲν ζευχθέντες ἔπι στέφ-
ανοι   10
πράσσοντί με τοῦτο θεόδματον χρέος,
φόρμιγγά τε ποικιλόγαρυν καὶ βοὰν αὐλῶν ἐπέων τε
θέσιν

---

plying to inarticulate sound, should
be kept distinct from Skt. *vāch*,
Greek Ϝεπ., Lat. *voc-*, as well as
from εὔχομαι.

3. ὀρθώσαις.] The Aor. is used
because ὀρθώσαις gives the cause of
which γεραίρων expresses the effect.;
cf. Ol. IX. 13. The metaphor is
according to Dissen from setting
up a στήλη to commemorate a
victory, cf. Ol. VII. 86, 87, Nem. IV.
81.

4. ἄωτον.] Cf. Ol. II. 7, v. 1.

οὕτω.] With the above-men-
tioned result in view.

παρέστα.] Cf. κώμῳ μὲν ἀδυμελεῖ
Δίκα παρέστακεν, Pyth. VIII. 70, just
before which, as here, we have
εὔχομαι.

νεοσίγαλον.] In σίαλος 'fat' (subs.)
the γ is probably dropt after ι as in
Φιαλία by Φιγαλία, Boeōt. ἰών (ἰγών)
=ἐγώ. The full form was probably
swigala, cf. A. S: *svegle* 'bright.'
The metaphor is from the glossiness
of new cloth, which seems to have
been partly at least due to the use
of oil in the weaving; cf. Il. XVIII.
596, *Od.* VII. 107.

5. πεδίλῳ.] 'Measure.' Owing
to the intimate connection between
song and dance in Greece, musical

time was named from the move-
ment of the *feet*. The rhythmic
stress originally coincided with the
putting down (θέσις) of the foot,
the lighter part of the metre with
the raising (ἄρσις) of the foot. The
Latin metricians inverted these
Greek terms.

6. ἀγλαόκωμον.] 'Of festive
revellers.' Cf. the Hesiodic use of
ἀγλαΐα. For κῶμος cf. Ol. IV. 9.

7. θεόδματον.] 'God-built' is a
strange epithet for a debt, but it
should be understood to refer to
the hymn, which the poet several
times likens to a building, esp. Ol.
VI. 1—4, Frag. 176 [206].

8. 'That in honour of Aenēsi-
dāmos' son I should fittingly com-
bine the varied melody of the
cithern with the air played on
flutes and the verses set thereto.'

τε—καί—τε.] The last τε by unit-
ing βοὰν αὐλῶν to ἐπέων θέσιν distin-
guishes the sound of the flutes from
that of the cithern and clearly sug-
gests that the whole air was played
on the former; cf. Ol. VII. 12, and,
for similar conjunction, Pyth. I.
42, IV. 149. Former commentators
seem to have acquiesced in the co-
ordinate use of τε after καί by

Αἰνησιδάμου παιδὶ συμμίξαι πρεπόντως, ἅ τε Πίσα
   με γεγωνεῖν· τᾶς ἄπο   15
10 θεύμοροι νίσοντ' ἐπ' ἀνθρώπους ἀοιδαί,

'Επ. α'.

ᾧ τινι, κραίνων ἐφετμὰς Ἡρακλέος προτέρας   20
ἀτρεκὴς Ἑλλανοδίκας γλεφάρων Αἰτωλὸς ἀνὴρ ὑψόθεν
ἀμφὶ κόμαισι βάλῃ γλαυκόχροα κόσμον ἐλαίας, τάν
   ποτε
Ἴστρου ἀπὸ σκιαρᾶν παγᾶν ἔνεικεν Ἀμφιτρυωνιάδας, 25
15 μνᾶμα τῶν Οὐλυμπίᾳ κάλλιστον ἀέθλων,

Στρ. β'.

δᾶμον Ὑπερβορέων πείσαις Ἀπόλλωνος θεράποντα
   λόγῳ.
πιστὰ φρονέων Διὸς αἴτει πανδόκῳ   30

Pindar, which I dispute. Both by
Pindar and Plato ποικίλος, &c., are
often applied to music.
   9. γεγωνεῖν.] Sc. πράσσει from
v. 7, 'And Pisa claims that I lift
up my voice.'
   10. θεύμοροι.] Cf. Ol. vi. 8.
   νίσοντ'.] So the best mss. for
the usual νίσσοντ'.   ▸
   11. ᾧ τινι.] For ὅστις (ὃς ἂν,
εἴ τις, ἤν τις) with plur. antecedent,
cf. Madv. § 99 d.
   12. Ἑλλανοδίκας.] The Hellâno-
dikae were the judges at the
Olympic games. In Pindar's time
there were two, afterwards the
number increased to nine, ten,
twelve and lastly to fifty. The
Elean judge is called Αἰτωλὸς from
the colony of the Aetôlian Oxylos.
   ὑψόθεν.] Cf. Apoll. Rhod. Arg.
II. 806, ὑ. ἄκρης. Adverbs of place
in -θεν often signify position simply,
instead of motion from.
   13. ἐλαίας.] Pindar seems to
have confused the cultivated olive
with the wild (κότινος).
   14. Ἴστρου.] As the Hyper-
boreans are generally, as in Isth.

v. (vi.) 23, placed in the North,
Pindar may have heard of the
northward direction of the Danube
above the confluence of the Drave
and no more. Hêrodotos' Hyper-
boreans are beyond his Scythians,
i. e. N. or N.E. of the Lower
Danube, the source of which river
he places in the west of Europe,
Her. iv. 33, 49.
   Ἀμφιτρυωνιάδας.] Hêrakles, son
of Zeus, but called the son of his
mother's husband, as Polydeukes
alone is ὁ Τυνδαρίδας Nem. x. 73.
So Eurytos and Kteatos sons of
Poseidon are Ἀκτορίωνε, cf. on Ol.
xi. 34.
   16. Ὑπερβορέων.] Cf. Pyth. x.
30—44.
   λόγῳ.] Critics, stumbling at the
asyndeton of the next line, have
read ὅγε found in inferior mss.
   17. πιστὰ φρονέων.] 'With loyal
intent was he entreating.' The
poet lays stress on the bona fides of
the transaction on Hêrakles' part.
His persuasion was effected by
telling the truth or making pro-
mises which he intended loyally

ἄλσει σκιαρόν τε φύτευμα ξυνὸν ἀνθρώποις στέφανόν
     τ᾽ ἀρετᾶν.
ἤδη γὰρ αὐτῷ, πατρὶ μὲν βωμῶν ἁγισθέντων, διχό-
     μηνις ὅλον χρυσάρματος   35
20 ἑσπέρας ὀφθαλμὸν ἀντέφλεξε Μήνα,
                                              ᾿Αντ. β'.

καὶ μεγάλων ἀέθλων ἁγνὰν κρίσιν καὶ πενταετηρίδ᾽
     ἀμᾷ
θῆκε ζαθέοις ἐπὶ κρημνοῖς ᾿Αλφεοῦ·
ἀλλ᾽ οὐ καλὰ δένδρε᾽ ἔθαλλεν χῶρος ἐν βάσσαις Κρον-
     ίου Πέλοπος.   40
τούτων ἔδοξεν γυμνὸς αὐτῷ κᾶπος ὀξείαις ὑπακουέμεν
     αὐγαῖς ἀελίου.
25 δὴ τότ᾽ ἐς γαῖαν πορεύειν θυμὸς ὥρμαιν᾽   45
                                              ᾿Επ. β'.

᾿Ιστρίαν νιν· ἔνθα Λατοῦς ἱπποσόα θυγάτηρ

to fulfil. The needless conjecture
῎Αλτει for αἴτει is at once disposed
of by the planting of ·the trees
outside the Altis (vv. 33, 34).

19, 20. 'For already, when the
altars were consecrated to his sire,
the midmonth moon with car of
gold had lit up to the full, right
opposite to him, the eye of even-
ing.'

19. αὐτῷ.] Hêrakles faced the
East as he sacrificed and so the
full moon faced him. The Olympic
games fell from the 11th to the
15th of Hekatombaeon. Cf. Ol. xi.
73—75.

20. ἑσπέρας.] Authorities say
'in the evening,' though the moon
is called νυκτὸς ὀφθαλμός, Sept.
contr. Theb. 385. Aeschylos might
have borrowed the expression from
Pindar. Now ὅλον ὀφθαλμὸν can
scarcely mean 'all her light' (cf.
ὄμμα='light' Eur. Iph. in Taur.
194, ἱερὸν ὄμμ᾽ αὐγᾶς, cf. Soph. Ant.

879) and certainly not 'all her eye.'
The logical connection between
διχόμηνις and ὅλον is shown by their
contiguity.

21. καί.] For καὶ (τε) after μὲν
cf. Ol. vii. 12, 69, 88, Ol. vi. 4, 88,
Ol. xiii. 52, Pyth. ii. 58, vi. 39, xi.
46, Nem. ii. 9, &c.

22. θῆκε.] Observe the change
of subject.

23. ἔθαλλεν.] For the half cog-
nate accusative, cf. θαλέθω.

24. τούτων.] Cf. κολεοῦ γυμνὸν
φάσγανον, Nem. i. 52. 'Bare of
these the demesne seemed to be
exposed to the keen rays of the
sun.'

κᾶπος.] This use supports the
connection with campus, which
seems primarily to have meant
an enclosed or marked-out level
place.

26. ἱπποσόα.] For Artemis' con-
nection with horses cf. Pyth. ii. 7,
Ol. xiii. 65.

δέξατ᾽ ἐλθόντ᾽ Ἀρκαδίας ἀπὸ δειρᾶν καὶ πολυγνάμπτων.
μυχῶν,
εὗτέ μιν ἀγγελίαις Εὐρυσθέος ἔντυ᾽ ἀνάγκα πατρόθεν 50
χρυσόκερων ἔλαφον θήλειαν ἄξονθ᾽, ἄν ποτε Ταϋγέτα
30 ἀντιθεῖσ᾽ Ὀρθωσίᾳ ἔγραψεν ἱράν.

Στρ. γ'.

τὰν μεθέπων ἴδε καὶ κείναν χθόνα πνοιαῖς ὄπιθεν
Βορέα   55
ψυχροῦ· τόθι δένδρεα θάμβαινε σταθείς.
τῶν νιν γλυκὺς ἵμερος ἔσχεν δωδεκάγναμπτον περὶ
τέρμα δρόμου
ἵππων φυτεῦσαι. καὶ νῦν ἐς ταύταν ἑορτὰν ἵλαος ἀντι-
θέοισιν νίσεται   60
35 σὺν βαθυζώνου διδύμνοις παισὶ Λήδας.

Ἀντ. γ'.

τοῖς γὰρ ἐπέτραπεν Οὐλυμπόνδ᾽ ἰὼν θαητὸν ἀγῶνα
νέμειν   65

---

28. εὗτε.] For ἐστε for γοτε (orig. yakâ) which usually becomes ὅτε.

ἀγγελίαις.] Cf. Il. xv. 639 (Περιφήτην) ὃς Εὐρυσθῆος ἄνακτος | ἀγγελίης (?) οἴχνεσκε βίῃ Ἡρακληείῃ, where ἀγγελίης if correctly read may mean 'to convey commands,' a rare genitive of motive or reason, cf. Madv. § 170 c, Rem. Perhaps ἀγγελίῃ should be restored, a dative of the motive or end; cf. Isth. vi. 7.

30. ἀντιθεῖσ᾽.] The Schol. Vat. says that Taygeta was turned into a stag by Artemis to enable her to escape Zeus' importunities.

ἔγραψεν.] Render 'in her own stead branded as sacred,' As Pausanias (viii. 10) gives an Arkadian legend of a hind with a collar (ψέλλιον) inscribed Νεβρὸς ἐὼν ἑάλων ὅτ᾽ ἐς Ἴλιον ἦκ᾽ Ἀγαπήνωρ, inscribed collars may be older than

Pindar, else the inscription might be on the golden horn. In a hind ordinary horns are peculiar outside the region of myth.

31. πνοιαῖς.] So most MSS. (Böckh and Don. πνοαῖς.) Mommsen points out that Pindar is partial to the dativus termini, as with ἐγγὺς and πέλας. Pindar however twice uses the genitive after ὄπισθε, ὄπιθε, but in neither case as here with only the simple notion of location behind.

34. φυτεῦσαι.] For Inf. cf. Ol. i. 9.

ἑορτάν.] The Theoxenia.

35. βαθυζώνου.] Cf. βαθυκόλπου, Pyth. i. 12.

36. The Dioskuroi were ἐναγώνιοι θεοί, Nem. x. 53, and were worshipped at the starting-place in the Hippodrome as ἀφετήριοι, Paus. v. 15.

ἀνδρῶν τ' ἀρετᾶς πέρι καὶ ῥιμφαρμάτου
διφρηλασίας. ἐμὲ δ' ὧν πᾳ θυμὸς ὀτρύνει φάμεν,
    Ἐμμενίδαις
Θήρωνί τ' ἐλθεῖν κῦδος εὐίππων διδόντων Τυνδαριδᾶν,
    ὅτι πλείσταισι βροτῶν   70
40 ξεινίαις αὐτοὺς ἐποίχονται τραπέζαις,

                                                    Ἐπ. γ'.

εὐσεβεῖ γνώμᾳ φυλάσσοντες μακάρων τελετάς.
εἰ δ' ἀριστεύει μὲν ὕδωρ, κτεάνων δὲ χρυσὸς αἰδοι-
    έστατον,   75
νῦν γε πρὸς ἐσχατιὰν Θήρων ἀρεταῖσιν ἱκάνων ἅπτεται
οἴκοθεν Ἡρακλέος σταλᾶν. τὸ πόρσω δ' ἔστι σοφοῖς
    ἄβατον
45 κἀσόφοις. οὔ μιν διώξω· κεινὸς εἴην.

37. ῥιμφαρμάτου.] Lit, 'swift-wheeled driving of cars.' Cf. Pyth. II. 10, 11.

38. πᾳ.] Böckh and Don. read πάρ.

39. 'Because more than all mortals besides they do them grateful service with tables set for guests, in pious spirit scrupulously observing the rites of the Blessed.'

40. ἐποίχονται.] For the notion of reciprocity in the preposition, cf. Pyth. II. 24. Cf. also Pyth. v. 80, θυσίαισιν ἄνδρες οἰχνέοντές σφε, VI. 4, ὀμφαλὸν ἐριβρόμου | χθονὸς ἀένναον προσοιχόμενοι.

41. φυλάσσοντες.] Cf. Ol. VII. 40.

42. Cf. Ol. I. 1.

43, 44. 'Now at least hath Théro by his merit reached (glory's) utmost bound, and journeyed all the way from home to Hêrakles' pillars.'

43. ἐσχατιάν.] Note that this word is in form collective as the accent shows. It meant primarily a *linear* limit, the *locus* of ἔσχατα 'extreme *points*,'

44. οἴκοθεν.] Don. 'By his own innate virtues,' cf. Nem. III. 31, VII. 52, but cf. Isth. III. 30. To go *from home* to the Pillars of Hêrakles means to go through a difficult business without exceptional advantages or assistance. In Pindar's time the Pillars of Hêrakles were the farthest bounds of western voyage. However Samian mariners had ventured to the mouth of the R. Baetis.

τὸ πόρσω.] For sentiment cf. Ol. I. 114.

σοφοῖς.] Here as generally in Pindar 'minstrels;' so that ἀσόφοις only means 'laymen' such as Théro who were men of action rather than of song. At first sight ἄβατον ἀσόφοις recalls Pope's 'fools rush in.'

45. εἴην.] For omission of ἄν (κε) cf. Pyth. IV. 118, Ol. X. 21. Dissen's 'opinio sine conditione' is wrong, as a condition is certainly suppressed here. The sense is, 'I *should* be foolish (if I were to do so, but I certainly shall not).'

OLYMPIA IV.

ON THE VICTORY OF PSAUMIS OF KAMARINA WITH THE MULE-CHARIOT.

INTRODUCTION.

KAMARINA was restored, to a great extent by the exertions of Psaumis, B.C. 461. The victory commemorated in this and the following ode was gained B.C. 452.

Pausanias (v. 9) tells us that the mule-chariot race was introduced Ol. 70 (B.C. 500), and put down by proclamation Ol. 84 (B.C. 444). Polemo (early in the 2nd century B.C.), quoted by Schol., agrees in the latter date, but says there were only 13 victories, so the first victory was probably Ol. 71, the last Ol. 83.

The rhythm of this and the next ode is a mixture of Lydian and Aeolian. They are both supplications on an occasion when two disappointments toned down one success, which may account for the employment of the somewhat plaintive and tender rhythm appropriate, as Böckh shows, to the praises of the young, of suppliants, or of mourners. Psaumis seems to have been elderly.

Pindar was present at Olympia (v. 3) and composed this ode to be sung at the altar of Zeus in the Altis on the evening of the victory.

ANALYSIS.

vv.

1—3. Invocation to Zeus the Thunderer, whose daughters the Seasons sent the poet to witness the Olympian games.

4, 5. [Reason for the invocation given.] The success of friends makes worthy men show joy.

F. 3

6—12. [Invocation resumed.] Prayer to Zeus of Aetna to receive graciously the Kômos of Psaumis.

12, 13. Prayer that the god may grant his other prayers;

13—16. Since he is enthusiastic with respect to horses, hospitable and devoted in singleness of heart to his city's well-being.

17, 18. Trial is the test of men.

19—23. The which saved the grey-haired Erginos from being disparaged by the Lêmnian women, when he won as ὁπλιτοδρόμος and said:

24—28. 'Such am I in speed; my strength and courage correspond. Grey hair often comes to young men.'

Στρ.

Ἐλατὴρ ὑπέρτατε βροντᾶς ἀκαμαντόποδος Ζεῦ· τεαὶ γὰρ ὧραι
ὑπὸ ποικιλοφόρμιγγος ἀοιδᾶς ἑλισσόμεναί μ᾽ ἔπεμ-
ψαν   5
ὑψηλοτάτων μάρτυρ᾽ ἀέθλων.

1. According to Dissen βροντᾶς means 'thundering steeds,' cf. Hor. Od. I. 34. 7, 8, and he suggests that thunder had been heard during Psaumis' race or sacrifice. This is too fanciful. Aetnaean Zeus is naturally the lord and hurler of thunderbolts, cf. Pyth. I. ad init. The Epic use of ἐλαύνειν, 'to drive a weapon through,' with reference to Zeus' lightning is illustrated by Pyth. III. 57, 58. The substantive of the compound ἀκαμαντόποδος is redundant.

τεαὶ γὰρ ὧραι.] The Horae were daughters of Zeus, Hes. Theog. 901, and the season of the Olympian games was sacred to him, so that here we have a confusion of personification and time, see Essay on Style. For γὰρ after voc. cf. Plato Laws I. p. 626 D, 629 B, Herod. I. 30, Eur. Bacch. 521, 1329, Iph. in Aul. 909, Tro. 235, El. 82, Hek. 1114. So Verg. Aen. I. 65, Hor. Od. III. 11. 1.

2. ὑπό.] With genitive of musical accompaniment, cf. Ol. VII. 13, Soph. El. 630, Hes. Scut. Herc. 280, οἱ δ᾽ ὑπὸ φορμίγγων ἄναγον χόρον ἱμερόεντα, also 278, 281; see ὑπαί. So 'by the light of,' Il. XVIII. 492, and Eur. Ion, 1474, οὐχ ὑπὸ λαμπάδων οὐδὲ χορευμάτων | ὑμέναιος ἐμός, | τέκνον, ἔτικτε σὸν κάρα. Eur. Iph. in Aul. v. 1036 is interesting for its alternative preps. τίς ἄρ᾽ ὑμέναιος διὰ λωτοῦ Λίβυος μετά τε φιλοχόρου κιθάρας συρίγγων θ᾽ ὕπο καλαμοεσσᾶν ἔστασεν ἰαχάν; on the more general use cf. Pretor's Trachiniae v. 419, though I do not dare to be positive as to the 'priority' of the meaning 'to the sound of,' over 'by the light of.'

ἑλισσόμεναι.] This is more likely to allude to the whirling in dance of the Seasons than merely to their cyclic revolution.

3. μάρτυρ.] Isth. III. 28, ὅσσα δ᾽ ἐπ᾽ ἀνθρώπους ἄηται | μαρτύρια φθιμένων ζωῶν τε φωτῶν | ἀπλέτου

ξείνων δ' εὖ πρασσόντων ἔσαναν αὐτίκ' ἀγγελίαν
5 ποτὶ γλυκεῖαν ἐσλοί.
   ἀλλ', ὦ Κρόνου παῖ, ὃς Αἴτναν ἔχεις   10
   ἶπον ἀνεμόεσσαν ἑκατογκεφάλα Τυφῶνος ὀβρίμου,
   Οὐλυμπιονίκαν δέκευ
   Χαρίτων θ' ἔκατι τόνδε κῶμον,   15

'Αντ.

10 χρονιώτατον φάος εὐρυσθενέων ἀρετᾶν. Ψαύμιος γὰρ
   ἵκει
   ὀχέων, ὃς ἐλαίᾳ στεφανωθεὶς Πισάτιδι, κῦδος ὄρσαι 20

δόξας, makes it doubtful whether,
though Pindar was at Olympia, this
word was intended to indicate the
fact.
   4. ἔσαναν.] Of the metaphori-
cal uses of this verb that of Aesch.
Ag. 798 perhaps comes nearest to
this passage, οὐκ ἔστι λαθεῖν ὄμματα
φωτὸς | τὰ δοκοῦντ' εὔφρονος ἐκ δια-
νοίας | ὑδαρεῖ σαίνειν φιλότητι, where
it means 'feign joy;' here 'show
joy.' The poet here gives in gene-
ral terms the reason for his joyful
invocation.
   ἀγγελίαν.] The herald's procla-
mation of the victory. Cf. Pyth. I.
32.
   6. ἀλλ'.] Resumptive; cf. Ol.
II. 12, and VIII. 9, 10, whence pro-
bably came δέξαι, first as a gloss,
and then substituted for δέκευ in
the old mss.
   ὃς Αἴτναν ἔχεις.] Cf. Pyth. I. 29,
30, Ζεύ...ὃς τοῦτ' ἐφέπεις ὄρος, Ol. VI.
96, Nem. I. 6, Ζηνὸς Αἰτναίου.
   7. ἶπον.] Cf. ἰπούμενος ῥίζαισιν
Αἰτναίαις ὕπο, Aesch. *Prom.* 365,
cf. Pyth. I. 17—20.
   9. 'Welcome the Olympian vic-
tor, and welcome in the Graces'
behoof this minstrel-band.'
   θ'.] The translation shows that
it is not necessary to reject this
particle which the best mss. give.
It is not likely to have been inter-

polated as it stands, but it might
be a correction for τ, due to a scribe
beginning τόνδε, and after seeing
his mistake forgetting to erase the
redundant letter. Rauch. retains
δ'. No doubt ἔκατι began originally
with υ (F); but it is not proved
that Pindar retained it, though
Bergk reads σέο Fέκατι, Isth. IV.
(v.) 2 (mss. γ' ἐκ.). Still Hesiod,
W. and D. 4, exhibits F, so its
retention by Pindar is probable.
But, though he retained F before
ἔπος (cf. Ol. VI. 16, Nem. VII. 48),
yet we find οὔτ' ἔπος, Pyth. IV. 105.
So πείθεσθ' (F)ἀναξίαις ἑκόντες, Nem.
VIII. 10. Hence Bergk's argument
against θ', founded on the presence
of F, is not conclusive.
   κῶμον.] Here the Κῶμος is the
procession of the victor, his friends,
and a chorus, to the altar of the
Olympian Zeus in the Altis on the
evening of the victory.
   10. χρονιώτατον.] For senti-
ment, cf. Nem. IV. 6, 7, ῥῆμα δ'
ἐργμάτων χρονιώτερον βιοτεύει.
   Ψαύμ. γὰρ ἵκ. ὀχ.] Equals ἵκει
γὰρ ὁ κῶμος, Ψαύμιος ὀχέων ὤν (Don.).
ὄχος and ἀπήνη, Ol. V. 3, are 'mule-
chariots.' The Sicilian mules were
famous; cf. Frag. 83 [73] ἅρμα
Θηβαίων (Θηβαῖον· ἀλλ', Bergk) ἀπὸ
γᾶς ἀγλαοκάρπου. Σικελίας δ' ὄχημα
δαιδάλεον ματεύειν.

3—2

σπεύδει Καμαρίνα. θεὸς εὔφρων
εἴη λοιπαῖς εὐχαῖς· ἐπεί μιν αἰνέω, μάλα μὲν
τροφαῖς ἑτοῖμον ἵππων,
15 χαίροντά τε ξενίαις πανδόκοις,   25
καὶ πρὸς Ἁσυχίαν φιλόπολιν καθαρᾷ γνώμᾳ τετραμ-
μένον.
οὐ ψεύδεϊ τέγξω λόγον·
διάπειρά τοι βροτῶν ἔλεγχος·   30
                                                          Ἐπ.

ἅπερ [καὶ] Κλυμένοιο παῖδα·
20 Λαμνιάδων γυναικῶν
ἔλυσεν ἐξ ἀτιμίας.
χαλκέοισι δ' ἐν ἔντεσι νικῶν δρόμον   35
ἔειπεν Ὑψιπυλείᾳ, μετὰ στέφανον ἰών·

13. λοιπ. εὐχ.] To win a horse-
race; Psaumis having failed with
the four-horse chariot and the
riding horse. See Introduction to
the Ode.
15. τε.] After μέν, cf. Pyth.
XI. 1, II. 31, Ol. v. 11, VI. 4, 88,
VII. 13, 88, III. 21.
16. Cf. Pyth. I. 70, δᾶμον γε-
ραίρων τράποι σύμφωνον ἐφ' ἀσυχίαν.
It looks as if Psaumis' efforts at
Olympia were ascribed to political
ambition.
17. Cf. Pyth. IV. 99, ἐχθίστοισι
μὴ ψεύδεσιν καταμιάναις εἰπὲ γένναν.
19. καί.] Omitted in Cod. Ambr.
but found in most old MSS. ΚΑΙ
would easily be inserted or lost
before ΚΑΤ. The metre is deci-
sive against its genuineness.
Κλυμ. παῖδα.] The Minyan Er-
ginos of Orchomenos, an Argonaut,
who won as ὁπλιτοδρόμος in the
Funeral Games for Thoas, held by
his daughter Hypsipyle, cf. Pyth.
IV. 253. The point of this allusion
cannot be merely that Psaumis
was derided for being grey-haired,
as any decrepit or invalid could
win a chariot race as owner; and

if Psaumis had been his own
charioteer the poet would surely
have observed upon it. I take it
that the Schol. is right as to the
derision; but that it was elicited
by his making his *first* appearance
among owners of race-horses as a
grey-beard. His country might
well suspect a sinister motive in
an elderly man taking up a sport,
the votaries of which are generally
initiated in youth. Pindar repels
insinuations that his friend had
secret, sordid views of personal
aggrandizement by comparing the
youthful vigour and generosity of
his temperament with the strength
and agility of the hoary Erginos,
who *may*, of course, have been
reckoned amongst Psaumis' an-
cestry.
22. νικῶν.] From the pres.,
though it often means 'as victor,'
'being a victor,' we may infer that
he ran straight up to Hypsipyle for
his wreath, speaking as he ap-
proached, thus showing great fresh-
ness. For running up to the prize,
cf. Pyth. IX. 118—120. For the
ὁπλιτοδρόμοι cf. Pyth. IX. Introd.

οὗτος ἐγὼ ταχυτᾶτι·
25 χεῖρες δὲ καὶ ἦτορ ἴσον.
φύονται δὲ καὶ νέοις ἐν ἀνδράσι πολιαὶ   40
θαμάκι παρὰ τὸν ἁλικίας
ἐοικότα χρόνον.

24. οὗτος.] 'Such an one am I in speed.' Cf. ἔσομαι τοῖος, Pyth. IV. 157, Dem. de Corona, p. 320, σὺ τοίνυν οὗτος εὑρέθης. So ταύταν χάριν, Ol. VIII. 57, κεῖνος ἀνήρ, Ol. VI. 7.

ταχυτᾶτι.] For dat. of manner cf. Ol. I. 112.

26. That Psaumis was really old appears from Ol. v. · 22, while this concluding sentence is far more appropriate and humorous on the supposition that Erginos was really old, and said in effect, 'Do not judge by external appearances. I, though I look and am old, have still the constitution of a youth beyond my time, and again youths (note the καί) often get grey before their time.'

OLYMPIA V.

ON THE VICTORY OF PSAUMIS OF KAMARINA WITH THE MULE-CHARIOT.

INTRODUCTION.

SUNG at Kamarina on the return of Psaumis, probably at the shrine of Kamarina near the temple of Athêne Polias. Böckh thinks it was sung at Athêne's temple, near to which were Kamarina's shrine and Zeus' temple or statue. See Ol. IV. Introd.

ANALYSIS.

vv.

1—8. Prayer to Kamarina asking her to accept the worship of Psaumis, who has brought her honour.

9—14. Address to Pallas and mention of natural features of the neighbourhood.

15, 16. While the result is doubtful, competition involves only expense, trouble, struggle, but success makes even fellow-townsmen give one credit for wisdom.

17—23. Invocation to Zeus Sôter of Olympia that he bring divers glories on the citizens of Kamarina, and prayer that Psaumis may reach a hale old age.

23, 24. If a man have health, wealth and renown, let him not seek to become a god.

Στρ. α΄.

Ὑψηλᾶν ἀρετᾶν καὶ στεφάνων ἄωτον γλυκὺν
τῶν Οὐλυμπίᾳ, Ὠκεανοῦ θύγατερ, καρδίᾳ γελανεῖ 5
ἀκαμαντόποδός τ᾽ ἀπήνας δέκευ Ψαύμιός τε δῶρα·

Ἀντ. α΄.

ὃς τὰν σὰν πόλιν αὔξων, Καμάρινα, λαοτρόφον,
5 βωμοὺς ἓξ διδύμους ἐγέραρεν ἑορταῖς θεῶν μεγίσταις 10
ὑπὸ βουθυσίαις ἀέθλων τε πεμπταμέροις ἀμίλλαις,

Ἐπ. α΄.

ἵπποις ἡμιόνοις τε μοναμπυκίᾳ τε.   τὶν δὲ κῦδος
ἁβρὸν 15
νικάσαις ἀνέθηκε, καὶ ὃν πατέρ᾽ Ἄκρων᾽ ἐκάρυξε καὶ
τὰν νέοικον ἕδραν.

Στρ. β΄.

ἵκων δ᾽ Οἰνομάου καὶ Πέλοπος παρ᾽ εὐηράτων 20
10 σταθμῶν, ὦ πολιάοχε Παλλάς, ἀείδει μὲν ἄλσος ἁγνὸν
τὸ τεόν, ποταμόν τε Ὤανιν, ἐγχωρίαν τε λίμναν, 25

1. ἄωτον.] Cf. Ol. II. 7.
2. Ὠκεανοῦ θύγ.] Kamarina,
nymph of the lake on the river
Hipparis, whence the city got its
name.
3. ἀπήνας.] Cf. Ol. IV. 11.
4. αὔξων.] A Hêsiodic form,
used in this sense Pyth. VIII. 38,
ἀ. πάτραν, and often elsewhere.
5. ἓξ διδύμους.] The six double
altars to the Olympian Deities
were—1, to Zeus and Poseidon, 2,
to Hêra and Athêna, 3, to Hermes
and Apollo, 4, to the Charites and
Dionysos, 5, to Artemis and Al-
pheos, 6, to Kronos and Rhea.
6. πεμπταμέροις.] This has been
corrected to πεμπ-, πεντ-, πενθ-;
but the ordinal form is supported
by ἑβδομήκοντα, ὀγδώκοντα, by the
other compounds with the cardi-
nal. Dissen explains the number
five, referring only to three con-
tests, by the supposition that these

were on the first, third, and fifth
days respectively. A comma after
ἀμίλλαις removes all difficulty, se-
parating the general statement
from the particular. Moreover, I
think the epithet refers back to
βουθυσίαις.
7. μοναμπυκίᾳ.] 'Single-horse-
riding.' Probably coined by Pin-
dar. Don. should not have said
that μονάμπυξ is common in the
poets.
8. νέοικον.] It had been de-
stroyed by Gelo, and resettled
B.C. 461.
10. πολιάοχε.] It is difficult to
account for the α unless by false
analogy with cases where the first
element of the compound was a
stem in α.
μέν.] Not answered by δέ, v. 15,
but by τε. Cf. Ol. IV. 15.
11. Ὤανιν] Also Ἄνις. Curt.
thinks that the Ω represents F. I

Ἀντ. β'.

καὶ σεμνοὺς ὀχετούς, Ἵππαρις οἷσιν ἄρδει στρατόν,
κολλᾷ δὲ σταδίων θαλάμων ταχέως ὑψίγυιον ἄλσος, 30
ἀπ' ἀμαχανίας ἄγων ἐς φάος τίνδε δᾶμον ἀστῶν·

Ἐπ. β'.

15 αἰεὶ δ' ἀμφ' ἀρεταῖσι πόνος δαπάνα τε μάρναται πρὸς
ἔργον 35
κινδύνῳ κεκαλυμμένον· ηὖ δ' ἔχοντες σοφοὶ καὶ πολί-
ταις ἔδοξαν ἔμμεν.

Στρ. γ'.

Σωτὴρ ὑψινεφὲς Ζεῦ, Κρονίίν τε ναίων λόφον 40
τιμῶν τ' Ἀλφεὸν εὐρὺ ῥέοντ' Ἰδαῖόν τε σεμνὸν ἄντρον,
ἱκέτας σέθεν ἔρχομαι Λυδίοις ἀπύων ἐν αὐλοῖς, 45

Ἀντ. γ'.

20 αἰτήσων πόλιν εὐανορίαισι τάνδε κλυταῖς

think perhaps Ὤανις may be for
ϜαϜᾶνις.

λίμναν.] The lake Kamarina.

13. κολλᾷ.] Generally taken to
mean 'builds.' I take it to mean
'makes into rafts,' and σταδίων
θαλάμων 'for stoutly-built dwell-
ings.' I do not think ὑψίγυιον
ἄλσος can mean 'a high-storied
group,' or 'a lofty forest' of dwell-
ings. The epithet is only appli-
cable to separate trees, 'a grove
of lofty trunks.'

14. δᾶμον.] Perhaps in the
early sense 'township,' 'enclosure.'
There is a great preponderance of
ms. authority for ὑπ' 'from under'
instead of ἀπ'.

15, 16. The poet seems to
glance at adverse criticisms on Psau-
mis' trouble and expenditure (cf.
Ol. IV. 19) which ought to be
silenced by success.

15. μάρναται.] Observe the sing.
number according to what the
grammarians call the schema Alc-
manicum. πόνος δαπάνα τε = 'costly
trouble.'

16. κινδύνῳ.] The perils of the
course which might destroy the
chance of a chariot in spite of un-
deniable superiority over the rest.

καί.] Even to his fellow-citizens
who would naturally be critical.
Don. wrongly makes σοφοὶ καί an
hyperbaton for καὶ σοφοί; appa-
rently because the Schol. on Nem.
I. 13 quotes a fragment of Euri-
pides, τὸν εὐτυχοῦντα καὶ φρονεῖν νο-
μίζομεν. For sentiment cf. Nem. I.
10, 11.

17. Σωτήρ.] A special title of
the deities invoked by mariners.

18. Ἰδαῖον ἄντρον.] Dêmêtrios
of Skêpsis (abt. B.C. 160) states
according to the Schol. that there
was an Idaean cave at Olympia.
Anyhow there was an altar of the
Idaean goddess Rhea, and the in-
vocation is appropriate in a city in
which, upon its restoration by
Psaumis, many Cretans of Gela
settled.

19. ἐν αὐλοῖς.] Cf. Ol. VII. 12,
παμφώνοισι ἐν ἔντεσιν αὐλῶν.

20. 'To beseech thee to bedeck

δαιδάλλειν, σέ τ', 'Ολυμπιόνικε, Ποσειδανίαισιν ἵπ-
          ποις   50
ἐπιτερπόμενον φέρειν γῆρας εὔθυμον ἐς τελευτάν,
                                              'Επ. γ'.
υἱῶν, Ψαῦμι, παρισταμένων. ὑγίεντα δ' εἴ τις ὄλβον
     ἄρδει,   55
ἐξαρκέων κτεάτεσσι καὶ εὐλογίαν προστιθείς, μὴ μα-
     τεύσῃ θεὸς. γενέσθαι.

this city with *various* renown of
goodly sons, and (to grant) that
thou &c.'
   23. *ὑγίεντα.*] Perhaps an exten-
sion of the predicate. Cf. Nem. I.

32, ἀλλ' [ἔραμαι] ἐόντων εὖ τε παθεῖν
καὶ ἀκοῦσαι φίλοις ἐξαρκέων.
   24. *μὴ ματεύσῃ θεὸς γενέσθαι.*]
For sentiment, cf. Pyth. III. 61, μή,
φίλα ψυχά, βίον ἀθάνατον σπεῦδε.

OLYMPIA VI.

ON THE VICTORY OF AGESIAS OF SYRAKUSE WITH
THE MULE-CHARIOT, B.C. 468.

INTRODUCTION.

AGESIAS the Iamid was a citizen of Syrakuse, being a descendant
of an Iamid who was associated with Archias in founding Syrakuse
(*v.* 6). He was a friend of Hiero, but seems to have been unpopular
among the citizens (*vv.* 19, 74, 100); indeed the Schol. says that he
was killed by them three years after this victory. He was also a
citizen of Stymphalos in Arkadia, and treasurer to or diviner at the
great altar of Zeus at Olympia (*v.* 5). The ἄφθονοι ἀστοὶ of *v.* 7
are citizens of Stymphalos where this ode was sung, probably at a
banquet in a grand palace belonging to the Iamid family. It was
sent from Thebes (*vv.* 85, 86), by the mouth of Aeneas, who was pro-
bably an Iamid of Stymphalos (*v.* 88), as Xenophon mentioned a
Stymphalian general of that name (*Hell.* VII. 3. 1), and Pausanias
mentioned Aeneas as father of a seer of Mantinea at the time of the
Achaean league. From *v.* 98, perhaps supported by *v.* 86, it may be
inferred that Pindar composed another ode on this victory to be
sung at Syrakuse.

If the first syllable of an epitrite were present at the beginning
of the 6th strophic verse and the third syllable of the last verse of
the epodes scanned as two long (the vowels being all long by nature
or nasalized, and therefore capable of production), the rhythm would
be Doric. (For πάρεστι, *v.* 18, inferior MSS. suggest νῦν ἐστί.)

ANALYSIS.

vv.

1—4. The proëm of an ode ought to be striking as the façade of a noble building.

4—9. Agêsias' various claims to be the theme of song.

9—11. Achievements are famous in proportion to their difficulty.

12—18. Agêsias, as seer and warrior, is compared to Amphiarâos.

19—21. The poet vows he is of peaceable disposition.

22—27. The charioteer Phintis is asked to yoke his mules to the car of poetry and drive the poet to the origin of the family.

28—34. Myth of the birth of Euadne daughter of Pitane, and her adoption by Aepytos of Phaesane.

35—56. Beautiful myth of the birth and naming of Euadne's son Iamos.

56—61. His invocation of Poseidon and Apollo.

61—63. Apollo in answer summons him to Olympia.

64—70. The two-fold gift of divination granted to Iamos and his seed.

71—73. Their wealth and fame.

73—76. Conspicuous merit as of Olympian victors is sure to incur envious cavil.

77—81. Agêsias' victory attributed to his ancestral god Hermes Enagônios of Arkadia, and to Zeus.

82—87. The poet is inspired by the thought of the mythical connection between Thebes and Arkadia.

87—91. Address to Aeneas teacher of the chorus.

92—97. Mention of Syrakuse and praise of Hiero.

98—100. A hope that Hiero will receive kindly the Kômos of Agêsias when he arrives at Syrakuse from Stymphalos.

100, 101. The two homes likened to two anchors in stormy weather.

101, 102. A blessing on the citizens of both places.

103—105. Poseidon is invoked to give Agêsias a safe voyage to Syrakuse, and to make the poet's song acceptable.

Στρ. ά.

Χρυσέας ὑποστάσαντες εὐτειχεῖ προθύρῳ θαλάμου
κίονας, ὡς ὅτε θαητὸν μέγαρον,
πάξομεν· ἀρχομένου δ᾽ ἔργου πρόσωπον
χρὴ θέμεν τηλαυγές. εἰ δ᾽ εἴη μὲν Ὀλυμπιονίκας,　5
5 βωμῷ τε μαντείῳ ταμίας Διὸς ἐν Πίσᾳ,
συνοικιστήρ τε τᾶν κλεινᾶν Συρακοσσᾶν· τίνα κεν
φύγοι ὕμνον
κεῖνος ἀνήρ, ἐπικύρσαις ἀφθόνων ἀστῶν, ἐν ἱμερταῖς
ἀοιδαῖς;　　　　　　　　　　　　　　　　　　10

1. Χρυσέας.] For the gilding of buildings in poetry compare the description of the palace of Alkinoos, Hom. *Od.* vii. 88—90, where, however, the pillars are not gilt. Pindar has χρυσέα κρηπίς, Frag. 176 [206]. It must not be inferred that gilding of walls and pillars was common in real life even in the most magnificent houses. Indeed Pindar several times uses χρύσεος merely in the sense 'fair,' 'brilliant.' The vestibule was formed by the prolongation of two side walls of the building with two or more pillars to support the roof between the columnar front ends of these walls (παραστάδες).

εὐτειχεῖ.] The πρόθυρον had wall at the sides and back, the decorations whereof would contribute to the splendour of the façade.

θαλάμου.] Used of buildings generally, Ol. v. 13.

2. ὡς ὅτε.] For the supplying of the verb from πάξομεν, cf. Pyth. xi. 39, ἤ μέ τις ἄνεμος ἔξω πλόου ἔβαλεν ὡς ὅτ᾽ ἄκατον εἰναλίαν, Nem. ix. 16, ἀνδροδάμαντ᾽ Ἐριφύλαν, ὅρκιον ὡς ὅτε πιστόν, | δόντες Οἰκλείδᾳ γυναῖκα.

3. ἀρχομένου δ᾽.] 'For at the outset of a work we must make the front to shine afar.' The simile does not go quite on all fours, as the

completion of the front is not the first stage in the process of building. The προοίμιον is aptly likened to the front of a completed building and the words ἀρχ. ἔργ. refer only, or at any rate specially, to the beginning of an ode. The δ᾽ is epexegetic. The πρόσωπον is clearly *not* 'the entablature' but the whole façade.

4. εἴη μέν.] For omission of τις, cf. Nem. ix. 46, Isth. i. 41. For μέν followed by τε, cf. Ol. iv. 15.

5. 'And dispenser of oracles at the altar of Zeus in Pisa.'

6. συνοικιστήρ.] From this passage it would seem that the descendants of an οἰκιστής retained the title. See Introduction.

7. κεῖνος.] Equiv. to τοιοῦτος, if referring to a definite person. Cf. Ol. iv. 24. 'What song of (in the sphere of) bewitching minstrelsy would such an one escape if he happened on fellow-townsmen void of envy?' Two good mss. for κεν read καὶ which is much more forcible, cf. Pyth. iv. 118. Also φύγη is well supported, which suggests καὶ φύγῃ, the Epic subj. in indefinite future sense. For the use of φεύγειν in this context cf. ἀρετὰς ὕμνῳ διώκειν, Isth. iii. 21. In Pindar's earliest extant Ode, ἐπικύρσαι takes the dat. but in Aesch. *Pers.* 853 the gen.

'Αντ. α'.

ἴστω γὰρ ἐν τούτῳ πεδίλῳ δαιμόνιον πόδ' ἔχων
Σωστράτου υἱός. ἀκίνδυνοι δ' ἀρεταὶ
10 οὔτε παρ' ἀνδράσιν οὔτ' ἐν ναυσὶ κοίλαις   15
τίμιαι· πολλοὶ δὲ μέμνανται, καλὸν εἴ τι ποναθῇ.
'Αγησία, τὶν δ' αἶνος ἑτοῖμος, ὃν ἐν δίκᾳ
ἀπὸ γλώσσας·· "Αδραστος μάντιν Οἰκλείδαν ποτ' ἐς
'Αμφιάρηον   20

ἐν.] Cf. Ol. xiii. 51.
8. ἴστω γάρ.] 'This I say, for
let Sostratos' son know that by
divine grace he hath his foot in
this sandal.' For the adverbial
use of δαιμόνιον, cf. Ol. ii. 38, iii.
10, xiii. 17. Pindar also has ἴστω
λαχών, Nem. ix. 45, ἴστω αὔξων,
Isth. vi. 27. There was a proverbial
expression no doubt, like our 'dead
men's shoes,' 'wouldn't be in
your (his, &c.) shoes;' but Don.'s
reference, after Böckh, to Lucian's
ὡς ἔστι μοι τὸ χρῆμα τοῦτο περὶ πό-
δα, 'suits me exactly,' is not quite
to the point; and περὶ πόδα, περὶ
κάρα, Aesch. Eum. 159 (P.), wrongly
cited by Don., is simply 'about the
foot, about the top (of the altar).'
9. ἀκίνδυνοι.] For different ex-
pression of the sentiment, cf. Ol.
i. 81, v. 15, Pyth. iv. 186. Similar
are τῆς δ' ἀρετῆς ἱδρῶτα θεοὶ προπά-
ροιθεν ἔθηκαν | ἀθάνατοι, Hes. W. and
D. 287, cited by Plato, Rep. p.364c,
and Theognis v. 464, χαλεπῷ δ'
ἔργματι κῦδος ἔπι. Cf. Ar. Eth. Nik.
ii. iii. 10. The peaceful achieve-
ment of winning the mule-race in-
volved κίνδυνος, cf. Ol. v. 15; but
here the poet, wishing to add
Agesias' prowess as a warrior to
his previously mentioned merits,
uses κίνδυνος in the higher sense
and involves himself in a half-
contradiction.
10. παρ' ἀνδράσιν.] 'Warriors
on land.' The occasional limita-
tion in meaning of ἀνήρ is justified

by the higher antiquity of land
battles, which would make the
term denoting a well-born warrior
naturally apply to them unless the
sea was specially indicated. Per-
haps we have the same distinction
Nem. v. 9, (Αἴγιναν) τάν ποτ' εὐαν-
δρόν τε καὶ ναυσικλυτὰν θέσσαντο.
11. τίμιαι.] Of course an Ὀλυμπι-
ονίκας without incurring κίνδυνος in
the sense of peril was τίμιος, but
in a lower sense than a brave
warrior.
ποναθῇ.] Pindar seems to have
kept α in forms from πονάω=
'toil at,' 'perform by toil,' but
used η in forms from πονέω='I
toil, am distressed' (πονεῖ, Pyth.
iv. 151, is causal); cf. Pyth. iv.
236, ἐξεπόνασ' ἐπιτακτὸν ἀνήρ | μέ-
τρον, Pyth. ix. 93. For sentiment
cf. Ol. x. (xi.) 4.
12. τίν.] This is a true dat.=
Lat. tibi from tva-bhyam, σοί, τοὶ
being locatives.
ἑτοῖμος.] A metaphor from money
ready to be drawn, cf. Pyth. vi. 7,
ἑτοῖμος ὕμνων θησαυρός. More than
once too Pindar speaks of the debt
of song due to excellence, cf. Ol.
xi. 7.
ἐν δίκᾳ.] Cf. Ol. ii. 16, vii. 69,
Nem. v. 14.
13. ἀπὸ γλώσσας.] Cf. Pyth.
iii. 2. Don. 'openly'; but Tyr-
taeos, Frag. 12, vv. 6, 7, οὐδ' εἰ......
γλῶσσαν δ' Ἀδρήστου μειλιχόγηρυν
ἔχοι, suggests 'glibly' or 'im-
promptu.'

φθέγξατ', ἐπεὶ κατὰ γαῖ' αὐτόν τέ νιν καὶ φαιδίμας
ἵππους ἔμαρψεν,

Ἐπ. α'.

15 ἑπτὰ δ' ἔπειτα πυρᾶν νεκρῶν τελεσθέντων Ταλαϊονίδας
εἶπεν ἐν Θήβαισι τοιοῦτόν τι ἔπος· Ποθέω στρατιᾶς
ὀφθαλμὸν ἐμᾶς   25
ἀμφότερον μάντιν τ' ἀγαθὸν καὶ δουρὶ μάρνασθαι. τὸ
καὶ
ἀνδρὶ κώμου δεσπότᾳ πάρεστι Συρακοσίῳ.   30
οὔτε δύσηρις ἐὼν οὔτ' ὢν φιλόνεικος ἄγαν,
20 καὶ μέγαν ὅρκον ὀμόσσαις τοῦτό γέ οἱ σαφέως   35
μαρτυρήσω· μελίφθογγοι δ' ἐπιτρέψοντι Μοῖσαι.

Στρ. β'.

Ὦ Φίντις, ἀλλὰ ζεῦξον ἤδη μοι σθένος ἡμιόνων,
ᾇ τάχος ὄφρα κελεύθῳ τ' ἐν καθαρᾷ

14. φαιδίμας.] Adrastos was represented in art as driving a pair of white mares, but, as Euripides (Suppl. 925 (P.)) tells us καὶ μὴν τὸν Οἰκλέους γε γενναῖον τόκον | θεαὶ ζῶντ' ἀναρπάσαντες ἐς μυχοὺς χθονὸς | αὐτοῖς τεθρίπποις εὐλογοῦσιν ἐμφανῶς, the picture is no evidence for Pindar's usage of φαιδίμας, which I render 'glossy.' The seer was engulphed at Potniae near Thebes.

15. ἐπτά.] 'After the bodies of seven pyres had been consumed.' There were only four chiefs to bury; so we must suppose that a large pyre for each of the seven contingents is intended, cf. Nem. IX. 21—27. According to Euripides (Supplices 757 (P.)) the funeral rites were held in Attica. Bergk reads νεκρῶν τ' ἐδεσθέντων, which is ingenious and would be safe were πυρὶ or φλογὶ present.

16. ἐν.] 'Near.' Cf. Ol. IX. 17. Pyth. IV. 16, VIII. 39, 40. Herod. VII. 166, ἐν Σαλαμῖνι.

ὀφθαλμόν.] Cf. Ol. II. 10 for metaphorical use of this word and

ὄμμα. So Milton Par. Reg. Bk. IV. 'Athens, the eye of Greece.'

17. ἀμφότερον.] Cf. Ol. I. 104, Hom. Il. III. 179, ἀμφότερον βασιλεύς τ' ἀγαθὸς κρατερός τ' αἰχμητής. For the variety of construction Schneid. cites Xenophanes Frag. 2, v. 15, οὔτε γὰρ εἰ πύκτης ἀγαθὸς λαοῖσι μετείη, | οὔτ' εἰ πενταθλεῖν οὔτε παλαισμοσύνην | οὐδὲ μὲν εἰ ταχυτῆτι ποδῶν.

τὸ καί.] 'This praise doth even so apply to the worthy Syrakusan, master of this triumphal chorus. Though neither quarrelsome nor contentious overmuch, even with confirmation of a mighty oath will I to this at least bear him witness.'

22. Φίντις.] For Φίλτις, probably a Sicilian name. He is Agesias' charioteer.

σθένος ἡμ.] Cf. Pyth. II. 12, v. 32, and infr. v. 95.

23. ᾇ τάχος.] Equivalent to ὡς τάχος, cf. Pyth. IV. 164, nearly, but lit. 'by the quickest way,' cf. Theokr. XIV. 68, ἐπιόντα ᾇ τ.

βάσομεν ὄκχον, ἵκωμαί τε πρὸς ἀνδρῶν   40
25 καὶ γένος· κεῖναι γὰρ ἐξ ἀλλᾶν ὁδὸν ἁγεμονεῦσαι
ταύταν ἐπίστανται, στεφάνους ἐν Ὀλυμπίᾳ
ἐπεὶ δέξαντο· χρὴ τοίνυν πύλας ὕμνων ἀναπιτνάμεν
αὐταῖς·   45
πρὸς Πιτάναν δὲ παρ' Εὐρώτα πόρον δεῖ σάμερόν μ'
ἐλθεῖν ἐν ὥρᾳ·

                                         Ἀντ. β'.

ἅ τοι Ποσειδάωνι μιχθεῖσα Κρονίῳ λέγεται
30 παῖδ' ἰοβόστρυχον Εὐάδναν τεκέμεν.   50
κρύψε δὲ παρθενίαν ὠδῖνα κόλποις·
κυρίῳ δ' ἐν μηνὶ πέμποισ' ἀμφιπόλους ἐκέλευσεν
ἥρωι πορσαίνειν δόμεν Εἰλατίδᾳ βρέφος,   55
ὃς ἀνδρῶν Ἀρκάδων ἄνασσε Φαισάνᾳ, λάχε τ' Ἀλ-
φεὸν οἰκεῖν·
35 ἔνθα τραφεῖσ' ὑπ' Ἀπόλλωνι γλυκείας πρῶτον ἔψαυσ'
Ἀφροδίτας.

                                         Ἐπ. β'.

οὐδ' ἔλαθ' Αἴπυτον ἐν παντὶ χρόνῳ κλέπτοισα θεοῖο
γόνον·   60

εἰς Αἴγυπτον. I therefore join it with βάσομεν; 'drive the car with all speed and on an open road.' For the latter phrase cf. θεοδότων ἔργων κέλευθον ἂν καθαράν, Isth. IV. 23 and infr. v. 73. Note the (indefinite future) subj. expressing the object of the future βάσομεν. The Poet identifies the ἀπήνη of Agesias with the Μοισᾶν δίφρος, Ol. IX. 81, Isth. II. 2, ἅρμα Πιερίδων τετράορον, Pyth. X. 65, Μοισαῖον ἅρμα, Isth. VII. 62.

25. καί.] For the position cf. Ol. VII. 26.

ἐξ ἀλλᾶν.] i.e. ὁδῶν. For the sense 'beyond others' we should expect a superlative phrase.

30. ἰοβόστρυχον.] Cf. Pyth. I. 1. The best mss. give ἰοπλόκαμον

against rhythm. The same occurs Isth. VI. 23. Bergk reads in both places Ϝιοπλοκο-; but the scansion of Pyth. I. 1 is against the Ϝ.

31. 'She hid her pregnancy unhallowed by wedlock with the folds of her robe.'
παρθενίαν.] Cf. Pyth. III. 34.
κόλποις.] Cf. Pyth. I. 12.
33. πορσαίνειν.] Cf. Pyth. III. 45, IV. 115.
Εἰλατίδᾳ.] Aepytos.
34. Ἀλφεόν.] Cf. Ol. II. 9 for the identification of the riparian district with the river.
36. κλέπτοισα.] 'Hide' was the earliest meaning of √κλεπ, a secondary form of a √ΚΑΛ, whence Lat. celare clam occulere. But the Lat. clepo, Goth. hliftus 'thief,'

ἀλλ' ὁ μὲν Πυθῶνάδ', ἐν θυμῷ πιέσαις χόλον οὐ
   φατὸν ὀξείᾳ μελέτᾳ,
ᾤχετ' ἰὼν μαντευσόμενος ταύτας περ' ἀτλάτου πάθας. 65
ἁ δὲ φοινικόκροκον ζώναν καταθηκαμένα
40 κάλπιδά τ' ἀργυρέαν λόχμας ὑπὸ κυανέας
   τίκτε θεόφρονα κοῦρον. τᾷ μὲν ὁ Χρυσοκόμας   70
   πραΰμητίν τ' Ἐλείθυιαν παρέστασέν τε Μοίρας·

                                           Στρ. γ'.

ἦλθεν δ' ὑπὸ σπλάγχνων ὑπ' ὠδῖνός τ' ἐρατᾶς Ἴαμος
   ἐς φάος αὐτίκα. τὸν μὲν κνιζομένα   75
45 λεῖπε χαμαί· δύο δὲ γλαυκῶπες αὐτὸν
   δαιμόνων βουλαῖσιν ἐθρέψαντο δράκοντες ἀμεμφεῖ
   ἰῷ μελισσᾶν, καδόμενοι. βασιλεὺς δ' ἐπεὶ   80
   πετραέσσας ἐλαύνων ἵκετ' ἐκ Πυθῶνος, ἅπαντας ἐν
      οἴκῳ
   εἴρετο παῖδα, τὸν Εὐάδνα τέκοι· Φοίβου γὰρ αὐτὸν φᾶ
      γεγάκειν
                                           Ἀντ. γ'.

50 πατρός, περὶ θνατῶν δ' ἔσεσθαι μάντιν ἐπιχθονίοις 85

our *shoplifter*, show the antiquity
of the special sense of √KALP,
KLAP 'hide the property of an-
other.'
   39. Here follows one of Pindar's
exquisite word-pictures. Note the
contrasts of colour.
   42. Μοίρας.] Cf. Ol. I. 26.
   43. ὑπὸ σπλάγχνων.] 'From
under.' Cf. Pyth. XI. 18, τὸν δὴ...
χειρῶν ὕπο κρατερᾶν τροφὸς ἄνελε,
Nem. I. 35, σπλάγχνων ὕπο ματέρος
αὐτίκα θαητὰν ἐς αἴγλαν παῖς Διὸς
ὠδῖνα φεύγων......μόλεν, Pyth. IX.
61, Ol. v. 14.
   ὑπ' ὠδῖνος.] 'By travail dearly
longed for.'
   44. κνιζομένα.] 'Though sore
distressed.' Translators are hard
on the mother in not showing that
the desertion of the child was the
cause of this poignant grief.

   46. δράκοντες.] So of Erichtho-
nios, Eur. *Ion*, 21 sqq. Serpents
were symbols of prophecy, cf. Pyth.
VIII. 46.
   47. ἰῷ μελισσᾶν.] Honey is only
called 'venom' with a qualifying
epithet as administered by the
serpents, which animals, by the
way, were thought to be fond of
dainties. For the connection be-
tween honey and prophecy, cf.
Pyth. IV. 60. Note that Pindar
gives a choice of derivations for
the name Ἴαμος, viz. ἴο-ς, ἴο-ν.
   50. περί.] Usually explained
per tmesin for περιέσεσθαι, but cf.
Il. IV. 257, περί μέν σε τίω Δαναῶν,
ib. v. 325. The position of δὲ sug-
gests its construction with θνατῶν
ἔξοχον, as also does the addition of
the latter word.

ἔξοχον, οὐδέ ποτ' ἐκλείψειν γενεάν.
ὡς ἄρα μᾶνε. τοὶ δ' οὔτ' ὦν ἀκοῦσαι
οὔτ' ἰδεῖν εὔχοντο πεμπταῖον γεγεναμένον. ἀλλὰ
κέκρυπτο γὰρ σχοίνῳ βατίᾳ τ' ἐν ἀπειράτῳ,   90
55 ἴων ξανθαῖσι καὶ παμπορφύροις ἀκτῖσι βεβρεγμένος ἁβρὸν
σῶμα· τὸ καὶ κατεφάμιξεν καλεῖσθαί νιν χρόνῳ σύμ-
παντι μάτηρ

'Επ. γ'.

τοῦτ' ὄνυμ' ἀθάνατον. τερπνᾶς δ' ἐπεὶ χρυσοστεφ-
άνοιο λάβεν   95
καρπὸν "Ηβας, 'Αλφεῷ μέσσῳ καταβὰς ἐκάλεσσε
Ποσειδᾶν' εὐρυβίαν,
ὃν πρόγονον, καὶ τοξοφόρον Δάλου θεοδμάτας σκοπ-
όν,   100
60 αἰτέων λαοτρόφον τιμάν τιν' ἐᾷ κεφαλᾷ,
νυκτὸς ὑπαίθριος. ἀντεφθέγξατο δ' ἀρτιεπὴς   105
πατρία ὄσσα, μετάλλασέν τέ νιν· "Ορσο, τέκος,

---

53. ἀλλά...γάρ.] 'But as he had been hidden......therefore indeed' (τὸ καί, v. 56).
54. ἀπειράτῳ.] Pindaric for ἀπείραστος like θαυματός.
55. ἴων.] Prof. Paley rightly, I believe, calls these λευκόϊα 'pansies.'
56. κατεφάμιξεν.] 'She declared in accordance with the omen that he should be called.' The ceremony of name-giving, performed by the mother in the absence of the father, is no doubt meant; but Don.'s citation ὄνομα φημίζεται, Demosth. p. 417, does not show that φημίζειν without ὄνομα expressed means 'to give a name.' However ἐπιφημίζειν seems almost equivalent to φήμης ἔνεκα ἐπονομάζειν in Plato Krat. p. 417 c, and to ἐπονομάζειν, Tim. p. 73 D; but in both passages the context clearly

suggests the special meaning. In deference to authority I render τὸ 'wherefore' (cf. τὸ καὶ κλαίουσα τέτηκα, Il. III. 176), but I incline to govern τὸ by the verb, 'the which omen she accepted by declaring that, &c.,' explaining the inf. according to Goodwin § 15. 2, note 3, § 92. 2; though it is generally explained ut vocaretur, ib. § 92. 1. The pansy remains in bloom a long time and was therefore an omen of the perpetuation of the Iamidae: so that there is peculiar force in ὄνυμ' ἀθάνατον.
57. χρυσοστεφάνοιο.] A Hesiodic epithet of Hêbê, Theog. 17.
58. Cf. Ol. I. 71 for the descent to the water to invoke Poseidon at night.
59. σκοπόν.] Cf. Ol. I. 54.
62. μετάλλασεν.] So the best MSS., others giving μετάλλασσεν.

δεῦρο πάγκοινον ἐς χώραν ἴμεν φάμας ὄπισθεν.

Στρ. δ΄.

ἵκοντο δ᾽ ὑψηλοῖο πέτραν ἀλίβατον Κρονίου   110
65 ἔνθα οἱ ὤπασε θησαυρὸν δίδυμον
μαντοσύνας, τόκα μὲν φωνὰν ἀκούειν
ψευδέων ἄγνωστον, εὖτ᾽ ἂν δὲ θρασυμάχανος ἐλθὼν
Ἡρακλέης, σεμνὸν θάλος Ἀλκαϊδᾶν, πατρὶ   115
ἑορτάν τε κτίσῃ πλειστόμβροτον τεθμόν τε μέγιστον
   ἀέθλων,
70 Ζηνὸς ἐπ᾽ ἀκροτάτῳ βωμῷ τότ᾽ αὖ χρηστήριον θέσθαι
   κέλευσεν.

Ἀντ. δ΄.

ἐξ οὗ πολύκλειτον καθ᾽ Ἕλλανας γένος Ἰαμιδᾶν·   120

I cannot agree with Don. that μετάλλατον implies an *answer*, Pyth. iv. 164, q. v. I construe after the Schol. Vet. ' and sought him out.' The god Apollo is at Olympia (δεῦρο πάγκοινον ἐς χώραν), and the voice of his answer is represented by a half personification as going in search of Iamos. ' ὅρσο &c.' give the substance of ὄσσα in a sort of apposition. Dissen agrees except as to the god being so far off as Olympia. Heyne, Buttmann and Don. render 'addressed him.' Böckh interprets ἐφιλοφρονήσατο. Hermann, approved by Rauchenstein, reads μεταλλάσαντί ἰν or μιν. The reading μετάλλασσεν gives a graphic imperfect and = μετῴκιζεν.

63. πάγκοινον.] Proleptic, cf. Ol. i. 68, iii. 17.

φάμας.] The sound of the ὄσσα which would on its return direct Iamos to his new home.

64. ἵκοντο.] i.e. Iamos and his followers.

ἀλίβατον.] The etymology is doubtful. But Buttmann's shortened form of ἠλιτόβατος, analogous to ἠλιτόεργος, and Döderlein's connection with λέπας (*lapis*) λόφος

klippe are clearly wrong, except perhaps in the case of *lapis*, which Corssen (p. 545) connects with *rumpo rupes* Eng. 'reef.' To the two root phases RAP (LAP) RUP, we may add RIP, whence ἐρείπω, ἤριπον, and perhaps ἠ-λίβ-ατος (steep, broken), αἰγί-λιψ (causing goats to fall). For the termination -ατο- cf. ἠλακ-άτη. For the prosthetic ἠ cf. ἠ-ρέμα.

66. τόκα μέν.] ' There and then.' If, as most editors &c. seem to imply, the privilege of hearing Apollo's voice ceased when that of divining ἐμπύροις began, the word δίδυμον is meaningless. Whether correctly or not Pindar's expression suggests the permanence of the earlier gift.

70. The altar of Zeus, between the temple of Hêra (N. of the great temple of Zeus) and the precinct of Pelops, consisted of two tiers, the lower (πρόθυσις) 125 feet round, where victims were offered, the upper 32 feet round, where the thighs were used for divination. To the establishment of this oracle the words χρηστήριον θέσθαι κέλευσεν refer.

ὄλβος ἅμ' ἕσπετο· τιμῶντες δ' ἀρετὰς
ἐς φανερὰν ὁδὸν ἔρχονται. τεκμαίρει
χρῆμ' ἕκαστον μῶμος· ἐκ δ' ἄλλων κρέμαται φθονεόν-
    των   125
75 τοῖς οἷς ποτὲ πρώτοις περὶ δωδέκατον δρόμον
ἐλαυνόντεσσιν αἰδοία ποτιστάζει Χάρις εὐκλέα μορφάν.
εἰ δ' ἐτύμως ὑπὸ Κυλλάνας ὅραις, 'Αγησία, μάτρωες
    ἄνδρες   130
                                'Επ. δ'.

ναιετάοντες ἐδώρησαν θεῶν κάρυκα λιταῖς θυσίαις
πολλὰ δὴ πολλαῖσιν 'Ερμᾶν εὐσεβέως, ὃς ἀγῶνας ἔχει
    μοῖράν τ' ἀέθλων,   135
80 'Αρκαδίαν τ' εὐάνορα τιμᾷ· κεῖνος, ὦ παῖ Σωστράτου,
σὺν βαρυγδούπῳ πατρὶ κραίνει σέθεν εὐτυχίαν.
δόξαν ἔχω τιν' ἐπὶ γλώσσᾳ ἀκόνας λιγυρᾶς,   140

72. τιμῶντες.] 'But through setting great store by brilliant achievements.'

73. τεκμαίρει.] mss. have μῶμος δ' ἐξ against scansion. I hold the error to be due to the separation of μῶμος from the previous sentence, to which I restore it, rendering, 'Cavil affords ground for true inference as to every transaction. For owing to the envy of others it hangeth o'er &c.' Dissen interprets *probat res quemque*. Cf. Ol. iv. 18; Don. 'it is indeed money which distinguishes a man, cf. Isth. ii. 11.' I cannot catch a satisfactory line of thought on either view. My slight emendation falls in thus; 'your family have been prosperous and famous. True you are troubled by the envy of the Syrakusans, but their cavil is the best evidence of your success and worth.' Thus the poet consoles the victor for his trouble by a flattering turn. That hostile criticism bears even stronger testimony to real merit than eulogy is now a truism; but it was scarcely so in Pindar's time, and if my suggestion be accepted I may claim to have rescued from oblivion an important and pithy gnômê; cf. Pyth. xi. 29, for the sentiment.

76. αἰδοία.] The epithet implies that Χάρις produces αἰδώς, cf. Pyth. iv. 29, Mr Fanshawe has pointed out to me that the attendance of Charis on victors expresses the physical fact that they generally keep their style and grace to the end of a race, while the beaten present a comparatively wretched spectacle.

77. μάτρωες.] The Arkadians, especially Aepytos' family. Euadne was not Arkadian but Lakônian by birth, see vv. 32—34.

78. ἐδώρησαν.] Note the non-Attic active voice. Cf. Hesiod, *W. and D.* 82.

λιταῖς.] Adj. as in Pyth. iv. 217.

80. εὐάνορα.] Gives the best sense as an extension of predicate.

82. 'I have a kind of feeling as of a shrill whetstone on my

ἅ μ' ἐθέλοντα προσέρπει καλλιρόοισι πνοαῖς·
ματρομάτωρ ἐμὰ Στυμφαλίς, εὐανθὴς Μετώπα,

tongue.' Pindar uses the metaphor of forging the tongue on an anvil for forming a habit of speech, Pyth. I. 86, q. v.; and here a happy thought is said to whet the forged point or edge (στόμα), cf. Soph. *Oed. Col.* 794. According to Prof. Jebb στόμα, *Aj.* 651, does not mean 'edge of my words,' as Don. explains it. For mixture of metaphor see *Essay on Style*, and cf. Nem. III. 79, τόμ' ἀοίδιμον Αἰολῇσιν ἐν πνοαῖσιν αὐλῶν.

83. προσέρπει.] So all good MSS. Dissen, Don. and others prefer the poorly supported προσέλκει, 'which draws me on nothing loth.' Dissen takes πνοαῖς to mean *ad cantus;* it is better to explain it as a Dat. of manner, with either reading. I render 'which steals over me nothing loth with fair streams of inspiration,' cf. Aesch. *Sept. c. Theb.* 110, Eur. *Bacch.* 1094. There is no authority for πνοαί in the sense of 'breaths of song,' or 'sound,' without the words signifying the utterer, Μοῖσ' ἀδύπνοος, Ol. XIII. 22, or the instrument, see last note, Eur. *Orest.* 144, ἅ, ἅ σύριγγος ὅπως πνοὰ | λεπτοῦ δόνακος, ὦ φίλα, φώνει μοι. Prof. Paley gives 'as with gentle breezy airs.' The reading προσέρπει is open to the objection that Sophokles uses the dat. after this verb, but προσελθεῖν takes both dat. and acc. Don.'s second objection, 'when a verb of motion is combined with a part. signifying will or choice, the part.

is in the dat., not the acc. case,' needs qualification. The dat. is wanted when the reference of the motion to a person's feelings is prominent, and the direction of the motion is sufficiently indicated without the dative. To take his instance, Aristoph. *Pax* 582, ὡς ἦλθες ἡμῖν ἀσμένοις, the notion of *your coming* is combined with the notion of *our gladness,* not the notion of *your coming to us* with *our gladness* as in Eur. *Ion* 1438, ἀσμενός σ' ἰδὼν πρὸς ἀσμένας πέπτωκα σὰς παρηΐδας. Here to make Don.'s 2nd objection valid we must render 'steals near with my ready consent,' or something of the kind, not 'steals over *me* with my ready consent.' However, ἐθέλοντα is a little awkward, and the signification of προσ- is strained by rendering it 'over,' 'upon,' as is required, for which we should expect ἐφέρπει, so that there are grounds for suspicion that ἅ μ' ἐ. προπέμπει may have been the original reading, the meaning being 'escorts me,' or 'leads me forward, though I need no extra inducements to proceed on my path of song.' Prof. Paley rightly regards δόξαν as the antecedent to ἅ.

84. ματρομάτωρ.] 'A nymph of Stymphalos was mother of my mother,' i.e. of the tutelary goddess of my country. Cf. Μᾶτερ ἐμὰ χρύσασπι Θήβα, Isth. I. 1*. For the confusion of place and person see *Essay on Style.*

---

* The pedigree given by the Schol. Vet. is as follows:

Okeanos = Têthys   Lâdon (a river of Arkadia)

Asôpos   =   Metôpê (a lake fed thereby)

| Kerkyra | Aegina | Salamis | Thêbê | Harpinna | Nemea. |

Στρ. ε'.

85 πλάξιππον ἃ Θήβαν ἔτικτεν, τᾶς ἐρατεινὸν ὕδωρ 145
πίομαι ἀνδράσιν αἰχματαῖσι πλέκων
ποικίλον ὕμνον. ὄτρυνον νῦν ἑταίρους,
Αἰνέα, πρῶτον μὲν Ἥραν Παρθενίαν κελαδῆσαι, 150
γνῶναί τ' ἔπειτ', ἀρχαῖον ὄνειδος ἀλαθέσιν
90 λόγοις εἰ φεύγομεν, Βοιωτίαν ὗν· ἐσσὶ γὰρ ἄγγελος
ὀρθός,
ἠϋκόμων σκυτάλα Μοισᾶν, γλυκὺς κρατὴρ ἀγαφθέγκ-
των ἀοιδᾶν· 155

Ἀντ. ε'.

εἰπὸν δὲ μεμνᾶσθαι Συρακοσσᾶν τε καὶ Ὀρτυγίας·
τὰν Ἱέρων καθαρῷ σκάπτῳ διέπων,
ἄρτια μηδόμενος, φοινικόπεζαν
95 ἀμφέπει Δάματρα, λευκίππου τε θυγατρὸς ἑορτάν, 160

85. πλάξιππον.] Cf. Βοιωτοὶ πλ.
Hes. Scut. 24.
86. πίομαι.] This seems to refer
to the immediate future. He will
get special inspiration from Dirke's
fount for the rest of the ode. Cf.
Isth. v. 74.
πλέκων.] The metaphor of weav-
ing a crown of song is peculiarly
appropriate to a crowned victor.
It is kept up in ὕμνων ἄνθος, v. 105.
Cf. Nem. vii. 77, εἴρειν στεφάνους
ἐλαφρόν· ἀναβάλεο· Μοῖσά τοι | κολλᾷ
χρυσόν, ἔν τε λευκὸν ἐλέφανθ' ἁμᾷ | καὶ
λείριον ἄνθεμον ποντίας ὑφελοῖσ' ἐ-
έρσας.
88. Αἰνέα.] Two Arkadians, one
an Iamid, of this name are known,
so he was probably a Stympha-
lian, and ἑταίρους are especially,
but not necessarily exclusively, the
chorus.
Παρθενίαν.] At Stymphalos Hêra
was worshipped as παῖς, τελεία,
χήρα.
89. γνῶναί τ'.] The Schol.
Rec., Heyne, and Don. take this as

transitive ('make known') com-
paring γνώσομαι, Ol. xiii. 3. Prof.
Paley, Dissen and others take it
intransitively 'to make up their
minds.' For τε after μέν, cf. Ol.
iv. 15, supra v. 4.
ἀλαθέσιν λόγοις.] 'If the truth
be told.'
90. Βοιωτίαν ὗν.] The Schol.
Vet. quotes from a Dithyramb of
Pindar's, ἦν ὅτε σύας τὸ Βοιώτιον
ἔθνος ἔλεγον (better ἔνεπον) Frag. 51
(60), and from Kratinos, οὗτοι δ'
εἰσὶν Συοβοιωτοί. The name is fur-
ther said to have come from cer-
tain Hyantes who dwelt in Boeotia.
It was at any rate used to reproach
the Boeotians for their reputed
ἀμουσία.
ὀρθός.] 'Correct,' 'accurate.' Cf.
Pyth. iv. 279. For a full discus-
sion of this passage cf. Essay on
Pindar and his Poetry.
95. These deities were Triopean,
cf. Ol. i. Introd. end.
λευκίππου.] White horses de-
noted royalty, and hence divinity.

καὶ Ζηνὸς Αἰτναίου κράτος. ἀδύλογοι δέ μιν
λύραι μολπαί τε γινώσκοντι. μὴ θραῦσαι χρόνος ὄλβον
     ἐφέρπων.
σὺν δὲ φιλοφροσύναις εὐηράτοις 'Αγησία δέξαιτο κῶ-
     μον   165
                                             'Επ. ε΄.

οἴκοθεν οἴκαδ' ἀπὸ Στυμφαλίων τειχέων ποτινισόμενον,
100 ματέρ' εὐμήλοιο λείποντ' 'Αρκαδίας. ἀγαθαὶ δὲ πέλοντ'
     ἐν χειμερίᾳ   170
νυκτὶ θοᾶς ἐκ ναὸς ἀπεσκίμφθαι δῦ' ἄγκυραι. θεὸς
τῶνδε κείνων τε κλυτὰν αἶσαν παρέχοι φιλέων.   175
δέσποτα ποντόμεδον, εὐθὺν δὲ πλόον καμάτων
ἐκτὸς ἐόντα δίδοι, χρυσαλακάτοιο πόσις
105 'Αμφιτρίτας, ἐμῶν δ' ὕμνων ἀέξ' εὐτερπὲς ἄνθος.

---

97. θραῦσαι.] MSS. θραῦσοι; but
the fut. opt. is not found in
Classical Greek when a wish is
expressed. Cookesley supposes a
metaphor from a chariot upset on
the course, citing Eur. *Herc. Fur.*
780, ἔθραυσε δ' ὄλβου κελαινὸν ἅρμα.
     99. As a citizen of both Stym-
phalos and Syrakuse Agésias had
two homes.
     100. ματέρ'.] Stymphalos, which
Pindar chooses to call the mother
city of Arkadia; cf. Ol. ix. 20.
     101. δῦ' ἄγχυραι.] Prof. Paley

is right as to the two anchors being
on either side of the prow. When
the stem was made fast it was to
the shore with cables (πρυμνήσια),
as Hobart Pasha's fleet was se-
cured in the port of Batoum.
     102. τῶνδε κείνων τε.] ' Of Stym-
phalians and Syrakusans.'
     103. εὐθὺν πλόον.] Literally—
a direct, i.e. a good voyage to
Syrakuse.
     104. δίδοι.] Doric Imperative.
     105. εὐτερπές.] Extension of
the predicate.

OLYMPIA VII.

ON DIAGORAS OF RHODES, THE BOXER.

INTRODUCTION.

THIS ode commemorates, apparently, the first Olympian victory of the Rhodian boxer Diagoras, B.C. 464, though he had previously gained four Isthmian victories. He was the son of Dâmâgêtos who was probably a Prytanis (v. 17), the descendant of Kallianax (v. 93), of the clan of the Eratidae, Dorian oligarchs of Iâlysos. It has been thought probable that Diagoras had clouded his victory by some inadvertent transgression, cf. vv. 24, 25, most likely the slaughter of his opponent (vv. 27—30), which would in likelihood debar him from the usual sacrifice after a victory. He probably gained his first Pythian victory B.C. 466 (vv. 10, 17). It is not until we get to vv. 87, 88, that we find the ode is formally Olympian and not equally a commemoration of the Pythian victory. I am therefore inclined to suppose that the transgression occurred in connection with the Pythian victory, which in consequence could not be formally celebrated, but might be mentioned as in vv. 10, 17, in connection with a subsequent achievement.

The Hellenic feeling on the subject of bloodshed was so strong that it is next door to certain that no Kômos would raise an ode of triumph for a victory which had proved fatal to one of the vanquished, and so cast a gloom over the festal gathering. Dâmâgêtos, great-grandfather of Diagoras, is said to have married a daughter of the great Messenian leader Aristomenes. Diagoras' sons were celebrated athletes, especially Dôrieus, cf. Cic. *Tusc.* I. 46. 111; Paus. VI. 7. They were banished in a revolution promoted by the Athenians, but probably not for twenty years at least after the date of this victory, so that it is very doubtful whether, as Böckh surmises, these political troubles are foreboded vv. 92—95. According to the

Schol. Gorgo the historian of the Rhodians says that this ode was preserved in the temple of Athêne at Lindos, inscribed on a gold tablet. It was probably sung at Iâlysos, at a banquet. The rhythm is a mixture of Dorian with a few Lydian measures, and the accompaniment, like that of OL. III., was on the cithern and flute (*vv.* 12, 13).

ANALYSIS.

vv.	
1—10.	Comparison of the ode to a betrothal goblet.
10.	He is happy whom good report attends.
11, 12.	Charis, Epinikian song, regards different men at different times.
13—19.	To the sound of flute and cithern the poet has come to Rhodes to praise the Olympian and Pythian victor and his father.
20—24.	He commends to the Hêrakleid descendants of Tlêpolemos his legend.
24, 25.	Occasions for error beset men, but none can tell how any event will turn out in the end.
26—31.	For instance, Tlêpolemos, the Dorian colonist of Rhodes, killed his mother Alkmênê's half-brother in wrath.
31—34.	Whereupon he consults the Delphic oracle, whose answer introduces—
35—49.	The myth of Lindian Athêne's birth, and the omission of the Hêliadae to offer burnt sacrifices to her,
49—53.	Yet they are greatly blessed—
54—69.	The absence of Hêlios from the allotment of the earth among the gods,
69—71.	Which resulted in his acquiring the new island Rhodes,
71—76.	Where Rhodos bare him seven sons, one of whom was father of the eponyms Iâlysos, Lindos, Kameiros.
77—80.	In Rhodes Tlêpolemos is honoured with games;
80—87.	In which Diagoras has been twice victorious, as in many other places.
87—93.	Invocation to Zeus, praying him to honour the ode and to give the victor favour with all men, since he is modest and wise.
93, 94.	The state rejoices in the triumphs of the Eratidae.
94, 95.	But fortune quickly varies.

Στρ. α΄.

Φιάλαν ὡς εἴ τις ἀφνειᾶς ἀπὸ χειρὸς ἑλὼν
ἔνδον ἀμπέλου καχλάζοισαν δρόσῳ
δωρήσεται
νεανίᾳ γαμβρῷ προπίνων οἴκοθεν οἴκαδε, πάγχρυσον,
κορυφὰν κτεάνων,   5
5 συμποσίου τε χάριν κᾶδός τε τιμάσαις ἑόν, ἐν δὲ φίλων
παρεόντων θῆκέ νιν ζαλωτὸν ὁμόφρονος εὐνᾶς·   10

Ἀντ. α΄.

καὶ ἐγὼ νέκταρ χυτόν, Μοισᾶν δόσιν, ἀεθλοφόροις
ἀνδράσιν πέμπων, γλυκὺν καρπὸν φρενός,   15
ἱλάσκομαι,

1. 'As when one takes and gives out of a wealthy hand a goblet all of gold, prime of his treasures, bubbling within with dew of the vine, to a youth, welcoming him as son-in-law with a friendly draught from home to home both for good-fellowship's sake and to do honour to his own connection, and the while should friends be present maketh him envied for a love match; So I sending to winners of prizes liquid nectar, the Muses' gift, sweet fruit of my mind, make libation in their honour as victors at Olympia and Pytho.'

ἑλών.] So often used in Homer. However, ἀφν. ἀπὸ χειρὸς may be taken with the part. almost as if in the Dat., but indicating that wealth is the antecedent of which a rich present is the consequence. Without the epithet ἀπὸ χειρὸς would not do.

2. καχλάζοισαν.] Primarily means the noise of water flowing over loose pebbles, and so well applicable to the sound accompanying the 'creaming' of sparkling wine. Cf. Vergil's spumantem pateram, Aen. I. 739.

δρόσῳ.] Cf. Nem. III. 77, πέμπω

μεμιγμένον μέλι λευκῷ | σὺν γάλακτι, κιρναμένα δ᾽ ἔερσ᾽ ἀμφέπει.

3. δωρήσεται.] The not very common gnomic Future taken up v. 6 by the Aor. θῆκε.

4. προπίνων.] The word is here somewhat pregnant owing to the context. Shilleto on Dem. De Fals. Leg. 384 questioned the notion that it ever meant dono donare as the Scholl. say. In all passages where this notion seems to be supported 'betray,' 'abandon recklessly' suits better, as in Eur. Rhes. 405: Ἕλλησιν ἡμᾶς προὔπιες τὸ σὸν μέρος. Xenophon An. VII. iii. 26—30, has four chances of using προπίνω='I give,' but does not take them. It seems to have been a method of betrothal for the daughter or her father to drink to the suitor and present him with the cup.

5. φίλων παρ.] A gen. abs.; not dependent on ζαλωτόν.

6. ὁμόφρονος.] Cf. Hom. Od. VI. 181, ἄνδρα τε καὶ οἶκον καὶ ὁμοφροσύνην ὀπάσειαν (θεοὶ Ναυσικάᾳ). | Ἐσθλὴν οὐ μὲν γὰρ τοῦ γε κρεῖσσον καὶ ἄρειον, | ἢ ὅθ᾽ ὁμοφρονέοντε νοήμασιν οἶκον ἔχητον | ἀνὴρ ἠδὲ γυνή, Eur. Med. 13.

9. ἱλάσκομαι.] For the meaning

10 Οὐλυμπίᾳ Πυθοῖ τε νικώντεσσιν· ὁ δ' ὄλβιος, ὃν φᾶμαι
　κατέχοντ' ἀγαθαί.
　ἄλλοτε δ' ἄλλον ἐποπτεύει Χάρις ζωθάλμιος ἁδυμε-
　λεῖ　　　　　　　　　　　　　　　　　　　　　　20
　θαμὰ μὲν φόρμιγγι παμφώνοισί τ' ἐν ἔντεσιν αὐλῶν.
　　　　　　　　　　　　　　　　　　　　　　'Επ. α'.
　καί νυν ὑπ' ἀμφοτέρων σὺν Διαγόρᾳ κατέβαν, τὰν
　ποντίαν
　ὑμνέων παῖδ' Ἀφροδίτας, Ἀελίοιό τε νύμφαν, Ῥόδον, 25
15 εὐθυμάχαν ὄφρα πελώριον ἄνδρα παρ' Ἀλφειῷ στεφα-
　νωσάμενον

and construction without acc. cf.
Hes. *W. and D.* 334, κὰδ' δύναμιν δ'
ἔρδειν ἱέρ' ἀθανάτοισι θεοῖσιν | ἁγνῶς
καὶ καθαρῶς, ἐπὶ δ' ἀγλαὰ μηρία
καίειν. ἄλλοτε δὲ σπονδῇσι θύεσσί
τε ἱλάσκεσθαι.

10. κατέχοντι.] 'Encompass,'
cf. Pyth. I. 96, ἐχθρὰ Φάλαριν κατέ-
χει παντᾷ φάτις.

11. ἐποπτεύει.] Cf. Pyth. III.
85.

12. μέν.] Cf. IV. 15, infr. v. 88.
The combination of lyre and
flute seems to have been devised
by Pindar about B.C. 476. Cf. Ol.
III. 8, whence it is to be infer-
red that παμφώνοισι here means
'playing all the melody,' while the
cithern only played some passages
or did not follow the voice so
closely. It would be out of place
to discuss the point here, but it
seems that Böckh is right in sup-
posing that the old Greeks used
harmonies, those in this ode and
the third Olympian being major
thirds and minor fourths, not to
mention octaves and even a major
fifth, if the ὑπάτη (lowest note) of
the flute octave was sounded with
the νήτη of the lyre. The notes of
the flute, being capable of prolonga-
tion, would go more closely with
the voice and thus give more of

the melody than the cithern if
they sounded note for note all
through the piece. Cf. Pyth. XII.
19. The Greek art of counter-
point consisted simply in combin-
ing instruments or modes (τόνοι),
the corresponding notes of which,
owing to the order of the intervals
as well as the general pitch, would
produce harmonious chords. If
the spaces between a short line
and a long denote half a tone
ascending from left to right, the

intervals between the correspond-
ing notes of the Dorian lyre (top
numbers) and the Lydian flute
(lower numbers) can be observed at
a glance by the diagram.

ἐν.] Governs φόρμιγγι. For posi-
tion, cf. Ol. VIII. 47, Pyth. II. 10,
11; for force, Ol. I. 15. We may
render ἔντεσιν 'stops' (Myers).

13. ὑπ'.] Cf. Ol. IV. 2.

κατέβαν.] The poet identifies
himself with his ode here as else-
where. Note the confusion of place
and person.

15. εὐθυμάχαν.] 'For his fair
fighting,' taken with αἰνέσω as well

αἰνέσω πυγμᾶς ἄποινα　　　　　　　　　　　30
καὶ παρὰ Κασταλίᾳ, πατέρα τε Δαμάγητον ἀδόντα
　　Δίκᾳ,
'Ασίας εὐρυχόρου τρίπολιν νᾶσον πέλας
ἐμβόλῳ ναίοντας 'Αργείᾳ σὺν αἰχμᾷ.　　　　　35
　　　　　　　　　　　　　　　　　　　　Στρ. β'.

20 ἐθελήσω τοῖσιν ἐξ ἀρχᾶς ἀπὸ Τλαπολέμου
ξυνὸν ἀγγέλλων διορθῶσαι λόγον,
'Ηρακλέος
εὐρυσθενεῖ γέννᾳ. τὸ μὲν γὰρ πατρόθεν ἐκ Διὸς εὔχον-
　　ται· τὸ δ' 'Αμυντορίδαι　　　　　　　　　　40
ματρόθεν 'Αστυδαμείας. ἀμφὶ δ' ἀνθρώπων φρασὶν
　　ἀμπλακίαι
25 ἀναρίθμητοι κρέμανται· τοῦτο δ' ἀμάχανον εὑρεῖν, 45

as πυγμᾶς ἄποινα. Cf. Ol. XIII. 1. For the two accusatives cf. Isth. III. 7, εὐκλέων δ' ἔργων ἄποινα χρὴ μὲν ὑμνῆσαι τὸν ἐσλόν, Madv. § 26 b, Aristoph. Acharn. 1231, ἀλλ' ἐψόμεσθα σὴν χάριν | τήνελλα καλλίνικον ᾆ- | δοντες σὲ καὶ τὸν ἀσκόν, Ol. XI. 78. Note that στεφ. is lit. ' caused himself to be crowned.'

17. ἀδόντα.] 'For that he is well-pleasing.' Perhaps he was a Prytanis.

18. εὐρυχόρου.] Cf. Hes. Theog. 63, ἔνθα σφιν λιπαροί τε χοροὶ καὶ δώματα καλά, where χοροί are ' open spaces.'

19. ἐμβόλῳ.] 'A headland.' The promontory of Kynosêma in the Kârian Peraea. 'Αργ. σὺν αἰχ., i. e. with warrior colonists from Epidauros. Cf. μυρίαν ἄγων λόγχην, Eur. Phoen. 445, 'a vast host of spearmen,' cf. the use of ἀσπὶς for ἀσπισταί, ὅπλα for ὁπλῖται.

20. 'I shall readily proclaim with thorough accuracy a tale that is of common interest to those originally descended from Tlêpolemos, a widely-potent offspring of Hêrakles.' The distant, flourishing colonies of Rhodes make the epithet εὐρυσθενὴς quite appropriate to the Rhodian branch of the Hêraklidae.

23. τὸ δ', &c.] 'While they claim to be Amyntoridae on the mother's side, Astydameia.' For the apposition of 'Αστυδαμείας and ματρόθεν, cf. Ol. II. 46.

24. ἀμφὶ δ', &c.] 'Now occasions of wrong-doing beset men's minds in countless number.' The moral of the tale is that men are so liable to do wrong that it is idle to repine if one has got into a scrape, and whatever may be the immediate consequences all may come right eventually. I suspect that, as Dissen suggests, Diagoras had killed or injured an opponent in the boxing match, a circumstance likely to trouble him, as he was of large stature and therefore probably kind-hearted.

25. τοῦτο.] It is better to render ' This is impossible to find,' than 'It is impossible to find this.' Cf. Ol. VIII. 25, XIII. 13, 47; Nem. IV. 94, v. 18, x. 20, 72; Isth. II. 87; Madv. § 150 a.

'Αντ. β'.

ὅ τι νῦν ἐν καὶ τελευτᾷ φέρτατον ἀνδρὶ τυχεῖν.
καὶ γὰρ Ἀλκμήνας κασίγνητον νόθον   50
σκάπτῳ θενὼν
σκληρᾶς ἐλαίας ἔκτανεν Τίρυνθι Λικύμνιον ἐλθόντ' ἐκ
    θαλάμων Μιδέας
30 τᾶσδέ ποτε χθονὸς οἰκιστὴρ χολωθείς. αἱ δὲ φρενῶν
    ταραχαὶ   55
παρέπλαγξαν καὶ σοφόν. μαντεύσατο δ' ἐς θεὸν ἐλθών·

'Επ. β'.

τῷ μὲν ὁ Χρυσοκόμας εὐώδεος ἐξ ἀδύτου ναῶν πλόον
εἶπε Λερναίας ἀπ' ἀκτᾶς εὐθὺν ἐς ἀμφιθάλασσον
    νομόν,   60
ἔνθα ποτὲ βρέχε θεῶν βασιλεὺς ὁ μέγας χρυσέαις
    νιφάδεσσι πόλιν,
35 ἁνίχ' Ἀφαίστου τέχναισιν   65
χαλκελάτῳ πελέκει πατέρος Ἀθαναία κορυφὰν κατ'
    ἄκραν
ἀνορούσαισ' ἀλάλαξεν ὑπερμάκει βοᾷ.
Οὐρανὸς δ' ἔφριξέ νιν καὶ Γαῖα μάτηρ.   70

Στρ. γ'.

τότε καὶ φαυσίμβροτος δαίμων Ὑπεριονίδας

26. Cf. οὗτος μὲν πανάριστος ὃς
αὐτὸς πάντα νοήσῃ | φρασσάμενος τά
κ'. ἔπειτα καὶ ἐς τέλος ᾖσιν ἀμείνω,
Hes. W. and D. 293. For inf.
τυχεῖν see last note. But it is rare
to find the noun in agreement with
the adj. the subject of the inf., cf.
Madv. l. c. Rem. 1.

31. ἐς θεόν.] To the oracle at
Delphi which directed Greek colo-
nization generally. For the ex-
pression, cf. Ar. Av. 619, εἰς Ἄμμων
ἐλθών.

32. εὐώδεος.] Fragrant with
bay leaves, the odour of which
increased the frenzy of the Py-
thoness. Cf. Lucr. l. 739, Pythia

quae tripodi a Phoebi lauroque
profatur.

33. εὐθύν.] Mommsen reads
ὅρσαι, as a verb is to be expected
after εἶπε, while Bergk would
change ναῶν to νωμᾶν. However,
as Dissen remarks, Pindar is imi-
tating oracular diction, therefore
we need not stick at a phrase re-
presenting faithfully πλόος εὐθὺς of
oratio recta. The best mss. give
εὐθυν' against scansion. For εὐθύν,
cf. Ol. vi. 103.

39. Ὑπεριονίδας.] i. e. Hyperion.
For the extended form, cf. Ταλαϊο-
νίδας, Ol. vi. 15, though Ταλαΐων
would = son of Talaos.

40 μέλλον ἔντειλεν φυλάξασθαι χρέος
παισὶν φίλοις,
ὡς ἂν θεᾷ πρῶτοι κτίσαιεν βωμὸν ἐναργέα, καὶ σεμνὰν
θυσίαν θέμενοι 75
πατρί τε θυμὸν ἰάναιεν κόρᾳ τ' ἐγχειβρόμῳ. ἐν δ'
ἀρετὰν
ἔβαλεν καὶ χάρματ' ἀνθρώποισι Προμαθέος αἰδώς· 80
Ἀντ. γ'.

45· ἐπὶ μὰν βαίνει τι καὶ λάθας ἀτέκμαρτα νέφος,
καὶ παρέλκει πραγμάτων ὀρθὰν ὁδὸν 85
ἔξω φρενῶν.
καὶ τοὶ γὰρ αἰθοίσας ἔχοντες σπέρμ' ἀνέβαν φλογὸς
οὔ· τεῦξαν δ' ἀπύροις ἱεροῖς
ἄλσος ἐν ἀκροπόλει. κείνοις ὁ μὲν ξανθὰν ἀγαγὼν
νεφέλαν 90

40. 'Had enjoined his dear children to pay diligent heed to a service soon to become due.' The παῖδες are the Hêliadae of Rhodes, see v. 77. The service was the worship with burnt offerings of the new goddess Athêne, who would abide for ever with the people who first duly performed her rites. This privilege, lost by the Hêliadae, fell to the Athenians.

43. ἐν δ', κ.τ.λ.] 'Now it is scrupulous regard to duty born of forethought that brings on men high merit and (consequent) blessings. Howbeit a cloud of forgetfulness comes over them unaccountably and causes the correct course of conduct to pass from the mind.' Don. renders αἰδώς 'sense of honour,' ἀρετὴν 'bravery,' χάρματα 'usefulness in battle,' thus quite detaching the passage from its context. Dissen renders αἰδὼς prudentiae reverentia; Paley 'respectful obedience.' In reference to battle αἰδὼς may be rendered ' sense

of honour,' as it means prospectively 'fear of shortcomings,' cf. Pyth. iv. 173, 'shame' being retrospective. For Προμ. αἰδ., cf. Ἐπιμαθέος—θυγατέρα πρόφασιν, Pyth. v. 25; (τύχα) Εὐνομίας τε καὶ Πειθοῦς ἀδελφὰ καὶ Προμαθείας θυγατήρ, Alkman Frag. 62 (Bergk). We find νεφέλα used metaphorically of sleep, Pyth. i. 7.

48. οὔ.] Note the emphatic position. For σπέρμα cf. Pyth. iii. 37.

49. Note that Pindar's point in this ode is to show that men may be blessed in spite of transgression, so that it is quite natural for him to go at once from their omission of fire to the marks of divine favour which they received. The story of Zeus raining gold on Rhodes probably arose from the literal interpretation of a metaphorical description of a sudden influx of great wealth. Cf. Il. ii. 670, καί σφιν θεσπέσιον πλοῦτον κατέχευε Κρονίων, the seventeen lines before which give the story of Tlêpolemos.

50 πολὺν ὗσε χρυσόν· αὐτὰ δέ σφισιν ὤπασε τέχναν

　　　　　　　　　　　　　　　　　　　　'Επ. γ'.

πᾶσαν ἐπιχθονίων Γλαυκῶπις ἀριστοπόνοις χερσὶ κρα-
　　τεῖν.

ἔργα δὲ ζωοῖσιν ἑρπόντεσσί θ' ὁμοῖα κέλευθοι φέρον·　95
ἦν δὲ κλέος βαθύ. δαέντι δὲ καὶ σοφία μείζων ἄδολος
τελέθει.

φαντὶ δ' ἀνθρώπων παλαιαὶ　　　　　　　　　100
55 ῥήσιες, οὔπω ὅτε χθόνα δατέοντο Ζεύς τε καὶ ἀθάνατοι,
φανερὰν ἐν πελάγει 'Ρόδον ἔμμεν ποντίῳ,
ἁλμυροῖς δ' ἐν βένθεσιν νᾶσον κεκρύφθαι.　　　105

　　　　　　　　　　　　　　　　　　　　Στρ. δ'.

ἀπεόντος δ' οὖτις ἔνδειξεν λάχος 'Αελίου·
καί ῥά μιν χώρας ἀκλάρωτον λίπον,
60 ἁγνὸν θεόν.

μνασθέντι δὲ Ζεὺς ἄμπαλον μέλλεν θέμεν. ἀλλά νιν
οὐκ εἴασεν· ἐπεὶ πολιᾶς　　　　　　　　　110

52. 'Works of art like unto living and moving creatures used to move about their streets,' Dissen; 'were placed in the high roads,' Don. and Cookesley.

53. βαθύ.] Cf. Pyth. i. 66.

δαέντι δέ.] 'For to a good judge ('in a skilled artist,' Paley) even skill free from trickery is superior,' i.e. the illusions of legitimate art are preferable to those produced by magic or jugglery. Heyne detected a covert reference to the Telchines, magical workmen whose legend somewhat clashes with Pindar's account of the Hēliadae. The force of καὶ is seen if we consider that primarily objection to trickery is ethical, but is here transferred to aesthetics. The fair fighting of Diagoras is glanced at under the more obvious allusion to artistic skill. For the use of μείζων, cf. Soph. Ant. 637, ἐμοὶ γὰρ οὐδεὶς ἀξίως ἔσται γάμος | μείζων φέρεσθαι.

58. Pindar implies that Hēlios made a mistake which at first sight seemed to involve loss; but all came right notwithstanding.

61. 'But on his mentioning it, Zeus was on the point of holding a second lottery.' Böckh reads ἄμπαλον μ. θ. for μέλλεν ἀναθέμεν πάλον, supporting the sense given to ἀναθέμεν by ἀναθέσθαι, 'to correct a (bad or false) move at backgammon,' and then generally 'to correct' for one's own benefit, so that to 'make over again' for another's benefit (μνασθέντι being dat. commodi), would make the active appropriate. He regards a substantive ἀνάπαλος as against analogy, but Mommsen cites ἄνοδος (cf. Pindaric ἄμπνευμα, ἄναπνοά), and moreover says the word may be an adjective. Mommsen also quotes κατ' ἄνπαλον μισθούντω(ν) from a recently discovered Maltese inscr. edited by Ussing. Besides

εἶπέ τιν' αὐτὸς ὁρᾶν ἔνδον θαλάσσας αὐξομέναν πε-
δόθεν
πολύβοσκον γαῖαν ἀνθρώποισι καὶ εὔφρονα μήλοις. 115
'Αντ. δ'.

ἐκέλευσεν δ' αὐτίκα χρυσάμπυκα μὲν Λάχεσιν
65 χεῖρας ἀντεῖναι, θεῶν δ' ὅρκον μέγαν 120
μὴ παρφάμεν,
ἀλλὰ Κρόνου σὺν παιδὶ νεῦσαι, φαεννὸν ἐς αἰθέρα μιν
πεμφθεῖσαν ἑᾷ κεφαλᾷ
ἐξοπίσω γέρας ἔσσεσθαι. τελεύταθεν δὲ λόγων κορ-
υφαὶ 125
ἐν ἀλαθείᾳ πετοῖσαι· βλάστε μὲν ἐξ ἁλὸς ὑγρᾶς
'Επ. δ'.

70 νᾶσος, ἔχει τέ μιν ὀξειᾶν ὁ γενέθλιος ἀκτίνων πατήρ,
πῦρ πνεόντων ἀρχὸς ἵππων· ἔνθα 'Ρόδῳ ποτὲ μιχθεὶς
τέκεν 130
ἑπτὰ σοφώτατα νοήματ' ἐπὶ προτέρων ἀνδρῶν παρα-
δεξαμένους
παῖδας, ὧν εἷς μὲν Κάμειρον 135
πρεσβύτατόν τε 'Ιάλυσον ἔτεκεν Λίνδον τ'· ἀπάτερθε
δ' ἔχον,
75 διὰ γαῖαν τρίχα δασσάμενοι πατρωΐαν,

defending ἄμπαλον, he impugns ἀμ
in tmesi.
64. Λάχεσιν.] Lachesis, 'the
Allot-er,' appropriately confirms the
allotments of the λάχος.
65. θεῶν ὅρκ. μέγ.] By the Styx.
Cf. Hes. Theog. 397—400 (P.).
66. παρφάμεν.] 'To utter guile-
fully.'
68. 'And the main purport of
their words in the issue fell out
truly.' For λόγ. κορ. cf. Pyth. III.
80, λόγων κορυφὰν συνέμεν. The
plur. κορυφαί is here used because
the words of two persons at least
were fulfilled. For ἐν, cf. ἐν δίκᾳ,
Ol. II. 16.

72. 'Seven sons inheriting from
him (lit. 'having received') minds
wiser than any in the days of by-
gone heroes.' Of the four names
on which accounts agree three are
epithets of the sun personified, viz.
Aktis, Triopês, Phaëthon, and the
fourth Makar, or Makareus, is said
to be a form of Melkart the Tyrian
sun-god.
75. As triple division was a note
of Dorian occupation, this legend
of the founding of the Rhodian
Tripolis is probably a Dorian adap-
tation of an older Hêliad myth.
The name of the father of the
three eponymi, Kerkaphos (Schol.

ἀστέων μοῖραν, κέκληνται δέ σφιν ἔδραι.   140

Στρ. ε΄.

τόθι λύτρον συμφορᾶς οἰκτρᾶς γλυκὺ Τλαπολέμῳ
ἵσταται Τιρυνθίων ἀρχαγέτᾳ,
ὥσπερ θεῷ,
80 μήλων τε κνισάεσσα πομπὰ καὶ κρίσις ἀμφ' ἀέθλοις.
τῶν ἄνθεσι Διαγόρας   145
ἐστεφανώσατο δίς, κλεινᾷ τ' ἐν Ἰσθμῷ τετράκις εὐ-
τυχέων,
Νεμέᾳ τ' ἄλλαν ἐπ' ἄλλᾳ, καὶ κρανααῖς ἐν Ἀθά-
ναις.   150

Ἀντ. ε΄.

ὅ τ' ἐν Ἄργει χαλκὸς ἔγνω νιν, τά τ' ἐν Ἀρκαδίᾳ
ἔργα καὶ Θήβαις, ἀγῶνές τ' ἔννομοι   155
85 Βοιωτίων,
Πελλανά τ', Αἴγινά τε νικῶνθ' ἑξάκις· ἐν Μεγάροισίν
τ' οὐχ ἕτερον λιθίνα
ψᾶφος ἔχει λόγον. ἀλλ' ὦ Ζεῦ πάτερ, νώτοισιν Ἀτα-
βυρίου   160
μεδέων, τίμα μὲν ὕμνου τεθμὸν Ὀλυμπιονίκαν,

Ἐπ. ε΄.

ἄνδρα τε πὺξ ἀρετὰν εὑρόντα, δίδοι τέ οἱ αἰδοίαν χάριν

Vet.) reminds one of Kekrops.
Join διὰ-δασσάμενοι.
76. σφιν.] 'By their names.'
Dat. commodi.
79. The deification of founders
of colonies lasted until after Milti-
ades' death, cf. Herod. vi. 38.
82. ἄλλαν ἐπ' ἄλλᾳ.] Sc. νίκαν
cognate accus. after εὐτυχέων. 'And
two successive victories at Nemea
and at rocky Athens.' If ἄλλ. ἐπ'
ἄλλ. did not apply to Athens καὶ
would not be used.
83. χαλκός.] A bronze shield
given as the prize.
ἔγνω.] Cf. Ol. vi. 97.
84. ἔργα.] Works of art given
as prizes, such as cups, tripods, cf.

Ol. xiii. 36.
85. So Codex Ambrosianus A.
Most old mss. Βοιωτῶν. Cf. Μήδειοι
for Μῆδοι, Pyth. i. 78. Among
these games were the Erôtidia at
Thespiae, the Eleutheria at Pla-
taea, the Amphiaraia at Orôpos,
the Dêlia at Dêlium.
86. ἐν Μεγάροισίν τ'.] 'And at
Megara the memorial column of
stone bears the same tale;' i.e. of
six victories. For use of ψᾶφος,
cf. Pyth. iv. 265.
88. ὕμνου τεθμόν.] 'The pre-
scribed song in thanksgiving for
an Olympian victory.' For μὲν—τε,
cf. v. 12.
89. ἀρετάν.] 'A character for

90 καὶ ποτ' ἀστῶν καὶ ποτὶ ξείνων. ἐπεὶ ὕβριος ἐχθρὰν
   ὁδὸν   165
εὐθυπορεῖ, σάφα δαεὶς ἅ τε οἱ πατέρων ὀρθαὶ φρένες
   ἐξ ἀγαθῶν
ἔχρεον. μὴ κρύπτε κοινὸν   170
σπέρμ' ἀπὸ Καλλιάνακτος· Ἐρατιδᾶν τοι σὺν χαρίτ-
   εσσιν ἔχει
θαλίας καὶ πόλις· ἐν δὲ μιᾷ μοίρᾳ χρόνου
95 ἄλλοτ' ἀλλοῖαι διαιθύσσοισιν αὖραι.   175

bravery.' Cf. Nem. VII. 59, τόλμαν
τε καλῶν ἀραμένῳ, Thuk. I. 33,
φέρουσα ἀρετήν.
   εὑρόντα.] Cf. Pyth. II. 64.
   90. ὕβριος ἐχθράν.] 'That shuns
insolence.'
   92. ἔχρεον.] So Cod. Ambr. A
'Were wont to suggest.' Cf. Herod.
VII. 38, χρήσαις ἄν τι τεῦ βουλοίμην
τυχεῖν.
   μὴ κρύπτε.] 'Cast not into ob-
scurity the seed of Kallianax, in
whom all take interest.' The next
sentence amplifies the κοινόν.
   93. Kallianax was the founder
of Diagoras' family. The Eratidae
were the Dorian aristocracy of
Iálysos.
   95. For sentiment, cf. Ol. II.
33—37, Pyth. III. 104. From the
context of the latter passage, the
meaning seems to be 'rejoice now
you have occasion.' I cannot agree
with Böckh that Pindar is referring
to impending troubles for the

Eratidae. He has been inculcating
so strongly that good follows bad,
that for truth's sake he gives the
reverse in vague terms.
   So far from anticipating a revol-
ution, the poet seems to tell the
citizens to rejoice now over the
success of their favourite Diagoras,
for that they the citizens may not
again for some time have such an
occasion for rejoicing. This pas-
sage rightly considered is evi-
dence that Athenian influence had
scarcely showed itself at Rhodes at
this date.
   διαιθύσσοισιν.] For intransitive
use of αἰθύσσω, cf. Pyth. I. 87, IV.
83. 'But in one allotted space of
time shifting breezes blow from
divers points at different times.'
Probably the poet attached no defi-
nite limits such as those of 'year,'
'generation,' 'lifetime,' to μοῖρα
χρόνου. It cannot mean 'point of
time,' as ἄλλοτε subdivides it.

OLYMPIA VIII.

ON ALKIMEDON OF AEGINA, VICTOR IN THE WRESTLING MATCH OF BOYS.

INTRODUCTION.

THIS victory was won B.C. 460. The victor belonged to a family, the Blepsiadae, which could boast of six athletic successes; but it may be inferred that before the Nemean victory of Alkimedon's brother Timosthenes two generations had failed to win, see note on *v. 46.* It appears that the diviners at the great altar of Zeus had foretold Alkimedon's victory. For the mention of Timosthenes see note on *v.* 15; and for that of the Athenian trainer Melêsias on *vv.* 53, 66. A lack of unity in the construction of this ode makes itself felt, and *vv.* 68, 69 almost appear to be borrowed from Pyth. VIII.; but there is reason for these shortcomings, compensated as they are by several beauties, seeing that it was sung in the στεφανα- φορία directly after the victory, when the Kômos attended the victor to the altar of Zeus in the Altis. Hence, unless the poet trusted the diviners sufficiently to prepare the ode beforehand the compo- sition must have been very rapid. The rhythm is a mixture of Dorian and Lydian.

ANALYSIS.

vv.

1—11. Invocation to Olympia, where Zeus' diviners are consulted as to the issue of the contests, and to Pisa's precinct.

12—14. There is diversity of blessings.

15—18. Thou Timosthenes, for instance, art a Nemean victor, thy brother an Olympian.

19, 20. Praise of Alkimedon who proclaimed as his country Aegina;

21—30. Which is renowned for fair-dealing, having been ruled by Dorians from the time of Aeakos.

31—40. Myth of the building of Troy's walls by Apollo, Poseidon, and Aeakos, and of the surmounting thereof by one serpent out of three that tried.

41—45. Apollo's prophecy of the fall of Troy.

45—52. Return of the three builders.

53—66. After an apologetic preface the praise of Melêsias the trainer of Alkimedon is sung.

.67—73. Alkimedon's victory and triumphant return are celebrated, and the delight of his grandfather.

74—76. Commemoration of six victories won by Blepsiads.

77—84. As success of relations is dear to the dead, Angelia, daughter of Hermes, will tell of Alkimedon's crown to Iphion and Kallimachos.

84—88. Wish that Zeus will give health, harmony, and a life free from trouble to the Blepsiads and Aegina.

$$\Sigma\tau\rho.\ a'.$$

Μᾶτερ ὦ χρυσοστεφάνων ἀέθλων, Οὐλυμπία,
δέσποιν' ἀλαθείας, ἵνα μάντιες ἄνδρες
ἐμπύροις τεκμαιρόμενοι παραπειρῶνται Διὸς ἀργι-
κεραύνου,   5
εἴ τιν' ἔχει λόγον ἀνθρώπων πέρι
5 μαιομένων μεγάλαν
ἀρετὰν θυμῷ λαβεῖν,
τῶν δὲ μόχθων ἀμπνοάν

1. χρυσοστεφάνων.] The χρυσο-
must not be taken literally. Cf. Ol.
x. 13, στεφάνῳ χρυσέας ἐλαίας, Pyth.
x. 40, δάφνᾳ χρυσέᾳ. The personi-
fication is illustrated by a coin of
Elis, on which is a noble female
head with the legend Olympia.

2. μάντιες.] The Iamidae, about
whom see Ol. vi., Clytiadae and Tel-
liadae.

3. ἀργικεραύνου.] The epithet is
illustrated by the frequency of the
thunderbolt on the coins of Elis.

6. ἀρετάν.] 'Glory,' cf. Pyth. iv.
187. For construction, cf. Aesch.
Choëph. 773 (P.).

θυμῷ.] To be taken with μαιομέ-
νων as therefore also is μεγ. ἀρ.

7. ἀμπνοάν.] Cf. Ol. i. 98.

'Αντ. ά'.

ἄνεται δὲ πρὸς χάριν εὐσεβίας ἀνδρῶν λιταῖς.   10
ἀλλ' ὦ Πίσας εὔδενδρον ἐπ' Ἀλφεῷ ἄλσος,
10 τόνδε κῶμον καὶ στεφαναφορίαν δέξαι. μέγα τοι κλέος
    αἰεί,
ᾧτινι σὸν γέρας ἔσπητ' ἀγλαόν.   15
ἄλλα δ' ἐπ' ἄλλον ἔβαν
ἀγαθῶν, πολλαὶ δ' ὁδοὶ
σὺν θεοῖς εὐπραγίας.

'Επ. ά'.

15 Τιμόσθενες, ὔμμε δ' ἐκλάρωσεν πότμος
Ζηνὶ γενεθλίῳ· ὃς σὲ μὲν Νεμέᾳ πρόφατον,   20
Ἀλκιμέδοντα δὲ πὰρ Κρόνου λόφῳ
θῆκεν Ὀλυμπιονίκαν.
ἦν δ' ἐσορᾶν καλός, ἔργῳ τ' οὐ κατὰ εἶδος ἐλέγχων   25
20 ἐξένεπε κρατέων πάλᾳ δολιχήρετμον Αἴγιναν πάτραν·
ἔνθα Σώτειρα Διὸς ξενίου
πάρεδρος ἀσκεῖται Θέμις

8. 'For there is fulfilment for men's prayers in return for pious worship.' Ἄνεται is here impersonal. Mommsen considers that ἄνω like ἀνύω='perform,' 'accomplish;' ἄνω, ἄνυμι 'to consume,' 'hasten over.' So here he explains 'ἄνεται scil. ὁδὸς...corripitur via ad gratiam (i.e. praemium) pietatis.'
9. ἀλλ'.] Resumptive, cf. Ol. IV. 6.
11. ἔσπητ'.] I regard this form and ἔσπωνται, Od. XII. 349, as reduplicated Aorists.
12. ἄλλα.] For neut. plur. with plur. vb. cf. Pyth. I. 13.
13. ἀγαθῶν.] The partitive genitive here is curious. For sentiment cf. Ol. IX. 104.
15. The mention of Timosthenes immediately after the above truism, combined with the prayer of v. 86, almost proves that he was at least

inclined to be jealous of Alkimedon's Olympian victory, which of course threw his own Nemean success into the shade.
ὔμμε.] Though not usually dual in meaning, here clearly addressed to the two brothers. For the notion of their being allotted to Zeus, God of the Family, cf. Ol. IX. 15.
16. σὲ μέν.] The σὲ seems against the scansion, and MSS. read σὲ μὲν ἐν; but μὲν seems out of place, and I would suggest σ' ἔμμεν; cf., for inf. after θῆκε, Nem. X. 48.
19. Cf. Simon. Epigr. 149. 3 (Bergk), κάλλιστον μὲν ἰδεῖν, ἀθλεῖν οὐ χείρονα μορφῆς of an Aeginetan boy who won the wrestling prize at Olympia, Tyrtaeos 10. 9 (Bergk), αἰσχύνει τε γένος κατὰ δ' ἀγλαὸν εἶδος ἐλέγκει.
21. Σώτειρα.] Don. has a long note to show that the epithet

Στρ. β΄.

ἔξοχ᾿ ἀνθρώπων. ὅ τι γὰρ πολὺ καὶ πολλᾷ ῥέπῃ, 30
ὀρθᾷ διακρῖναι φρενὶ μὴ παρὰ καιρόν,
25 δυσπαλές, τεθμὸς δέ τις ἀθανάτων καὶ τάνδ᾿ ἁλιερκέα
χώραν
παντοδαποῖσιν ὑπέστασε ξένοις 35
κίονα δαιμονίαν,
ὁ δ᾿ ἐπαντέλλων χρόνος
τοῦτο πράσσων μὴ κάμοι,

Ἀντ. β΄.

30 Δωριεῖ λαῷ ταμιευομέναν ἐξ Αἰακοῦ 40
τὸν παῖς ὁ Λατοῦς εὐρυμέδων τε Ποσειδᾶν,
Ἰλίῳ μέλλοντες ἐπὶ στέφανον τεῦξαι, καλέσαντο συν-
εργὸν
τείχεος, ἦν ὅτι νιν πεπρωμένον
ὀρνυμένων πολέμων 45

originally attached to the gods of mariners. Here Θέμις and, Ol. IX. 15, Εὐνομία receive the title as the preservers of civilised society. Themis is the goddess of universal right, while Δίκη ξύνεδρος Ζηνὸς (Soph. Oed. Kol. 1382) is justice. according to particular institutions. Cf. Bacchylides, Frag. 29 (Bergk).

21 sqq.] 'Where Saviour Themis, who sitteth in judgment by Zeus, god of strangers, is honoured more than among all men beside. For whatsoever maketh the scale sway much and in many ways is hard to wrestle with so as to decide with upright mind not unsuitably to (sundry) occasions; but as it were an ordinance of the immortals set up even this sea-girt land as a pillar by grace divine for strangers from every land.'

The Aeginetans were renowned for their probity in commercial transactions, which of course presented many perplexing, delicate points for judicial decision.

24. For the Inf., cf. Ol. VII. 25.
25. δυσπαλές.] The metaphor is appropriate to the theme of the ode.

On the authority of Cod. Ambr. A. and two inferior MSS. Don. and others place a comma after ἀθανά-των, supplying ἐστὶ and taking καὶ = 'and.' But the force of 'even' is brought out by reference to Thuk. I. 37. As being ἁλιερκής, Aegina was, though not so much as Kerkyra, αὐτάρκη θέσιν κειμένη.

28, 29. A parenthesis, as ταμι-ευομέναν agrees with χώραν, v. 25.

30. As the Myrmidones of old Aegina and Phthia were not Dorian, we have here again an adapted myth. Cf. Ol. VII. 75.

32. στέφανον.] 'A wall.' Cf. Pyth. II. 58, Eur. Tro. 779. Join ἐπὶ—τεῦξαι.

33. νιν.] Refers to τείχεος or στέφανον.

·35 πτολιπόρθοις ἐν μάχαις
λάβρον ἀμπνεῦσαι καπνόν.

'Επ. β'.

γλαυκοὶ δὲ δράκοντες, ἐπεὶ κτίσθη νέον,
πύργον ἐσαλλόμενοι τρεῖς, οἱ δύο μὲν κάπετον,   50
αὖθι δ' ἀτυζομένω ψυχὰς βάλον,
40 εἷς δ' ἐσόρουσε βοάσαις.
ἔννεπε δ' ἀντίον ὁρμαίνων τέρας εὐθὺς 'Απόλλων·
Πέργαμος ἀμφὶ τεαῖς, ἥρως, χερὸς ἐργασίαις ἁλίσκ-
    εται·   55
ὡς ἐμοὶ φάσμα λέγει Κρονίδα
πεμφθὲν βαρυγδούπου Διός·

Στρ. γ'.

45 οὐκ ἄτερ παίδων σέθεν, ἀλλ' ἅμα πρώτοις ἄρξεται 60
καὶ τετράτοις. ὡς ἄρα θεὸς σάφα εἴπαις
Ξάνθον ἤπειγεν καὶ 'Αμαζόνας εὐίππους καὶ ἐς 'Ίστρον
ἐλαύνων.
'Ορσοτρίαινα δ' ἐπ' 'Ισθμῷ ποντίᾳ
ἄρμα θοὸν τάννυεν,   65

37. For nom. cf. Madv. § 50,
Rem. 4.
38. κάπετον.] So καβαίνων, Alk-
man, Frag. 38 (Bergk), κασπολέω,
Sappho, Frag. 80. The assimila-
tion without the loss of the as-
similated letter is more common,
e.g. κάββαλλε, Alkaeos, Frag. 34,
κακχέεται, Sappho 2. 12. The two
serpents that died typify Achilles
and Aias, perhaps also remotely
Iphion and Kallimachos, vv. 81,
82, who may have contended un-
successfully at Olympia. The one
successful serpent is Neoptolemos,
and again perhaps Alkimedon.
42. 'Pergamos is taken, hero,
where thy hands have wrought.'
For the hypallage cf. v. 68, Ol. xi. 6.
For the prophecy of a vulnerable
point in the defences, cf. Il. vi.
433—439. Observe the prophetic

present for future.
44. Διός.] Gen. after φάσμα, not
after πεμφθέν, which governs ἐμοὶ
even more than does λέγει, cf. v. 75.
45. ἄρξεται.] Used passively, as
is more often the case with denom-
inative than primary futures. We
find ἄρξονται, Aesch. Pers. 591, in
a passive sense.
46. τετράτοις.] As Neoptolemos
was only two generations from
Telamon, who assisted Herakles in
taking Troy (Nem. iv. 25), this
should be τρίτοις, but perhaps the
poet made the mistake advisedly
because Alkimedon's great-grand-
father had been a victor.
47. ἐς.] For the position, cf.
Ol. vii. 12. Apollo goes to his
favourite Hyperboreans.
49.] Observe the imperfect here
and above, v. 47, for which cf.

50 ἀποπέμπων Αἰακὸν
δεῦρ' ἀν' ἵπποις χρυσέαις,

'Αντ. γ'.

καὶ Κορίνθου δειράδ' ἐποψόμενος δαιτακλυτάν.
τερπνὸν δ' ἐν ἀνθρώποις ἴσον ἔσσεται οὐδέν. 70
εἰ δ' ἐγὼ Μελησίᾳ ἐξ ἀγενείων κῦδος ἀνέδραμον ὕμνῳ,

Poppo on Thuk. i. 26. In this chapter Mr Shilleto finds three *panoramic imperfects;* but I venture to suggest that Poppo is right as to ἔπεμπον (cf. κάπεμπόμην, Soph. *El.* 680), and that ἐκέλευον, ἐδέοντο are frequentative.

51. δεῦρ'.] 'To Aegina.' The word is used of the place spoken of, though the speaker is not there. Cf. Plato, *Phaedo,* 58 B. For Poseidon's chariot, ef. Ol. i. 41.

52. So Mommsen. The common reading is καὶ Κ. δειρὰδ' ἐ. δαῖτα κλυτάν, making δειρὰδ' an *acc. termini* which is harsh after ἀποπέμπων δεῦρο, after which we should expect καὶ to introduce another participle instead of going back to ἅρμα τάννεν or the general idea of motion conveyed by that phrase. Mommsen's conjectural compound, formed with the rare δαίτη, is closer to mss. than Bergk's δαιτικλυτάν. There is no support for taking δειρὰδ' as dat. with elision of ι.

53. 'Nothing pleasant is equally so among all men.' This deprecatory saw introduces the praise of an Athenian, the trainer (ἀλείπτης) Melêsias, which might might well give offence in Aegina.

54. 'For if I had, in honour of Melêsias, gone back to his glory won off boys—let no grudging prejudice smite me with a jagged stone. For indeed I shall speak of such a victory at Nemea, and at the same time of the subsequent struggle with men in the quinquertium.'

Μελησίᾳ.] So *Cod. Ambr. A* in text and one Schol. and *Vat. B.* Other mss. give genitive Μελησία.

ἀνέδραμον.] This verse cannot refer to the previous celebration of Melêsias' pupils, unless we render ἀνέδραμον 'increased' in the transitive sense, with Don., which is unwarrantable, or alter the text, which is needless. Yet I cannot agree with Dissen, that it and ἀνέκραγον, Nem. vii. 75, are *futura exacta.* The εἰ with the latter aorist is rather concessive than hypothetical, and the aorist refers to the former part of the ode as in Ol. xi. 98, 100. The other instances of Pindar using an aorist in speaking of himself given by Don., viz. θέμιτες ὦρσαν, Ol. xi. 25, ἔβαν, Ol. xiii. 93, Nem. iv. 74, vi. 59, ἦλθον, Ol. ix. 89, ἔμολον, Ol. xiv. 18, refer the first to the time before the ode was composed, the rest to the time before it was sung by the poet's representatives, and consequently do not illustrate the passage as I take it. Here, according to my view, we have an artistic anakoluthon. The poet, giving an instance of the general sentiment set forth in the previous verse, begins in the hypothetical form, but instead of *stating* the consequence he *deprecates* it, as though suddenly, upon uttering *v.* 54, he had changed his mind and resolved to brave the consequences. For the imaginary presentment of a condition as past, cf. Eur. *Orestes,* 1132, where Pylades says, with reference to the *contemplated* slaughter of Klytaemnêstrạ, εἰ μὲν γὰρ ἐς

55 μὴ βαλέτω με λίθῳ τραχεῖ φθόνος·
　καὶ Νεμέᾳ γὰρ ὁμῶς
　　ἐρέω ταύταν χάριν,　　　　　　　　　75
　τὰν δ' ἔπειτ' ἀνδρῶν μάχαν,

　　　　　　　　　　　　　　　　'Επ. γ'.

　ἐκ παγκρατίου.　τὸ διδάξασθαι δέ τοι
60 εἰδότι ῥᾴτερον· ἄγνωμον δὲ τὸ μὴ προμαθεῖν·
　κουφότεραι γὰρ ἀπειράτων φρένες.　　　80
　　κεῖνα δὲ κεῖνος ἂν εἴποι
　ἔργα περαίτερον ἄλλων, τίς τρόπος ἄνδρα προβάσει
　ἐξ ἱερῶν ἀέθλων μέλλοντα ποθεινοτάταν δόξαν φέ-
　ρειν.　　　　　　　　　　　　　　　85

γυναῖκα σωφρονεστέραν | ξίφος με-
θεῖμεν δυσκλεὴς ἂν ἦν φόνος. Prof.
Goodwin, § 54. 3, seems to take
μεθεῖμεν for the optative; it is how-
ever the ind. as well, and therefore
we need not regard the sentence
as grammatically irregular. I take
the praise of the Nemean victor
Melêsias as a salve for the envious
Timosthenes, cf. vv. 15, 16. For
the sense given to ἀνέδραμον, cf.
Simonid. Amorg. Frag. 10, Bergk, τί
ταῦτα μακρῶν διὰ λόγων ἀνέδραμον;
from the Schol. on Eur. Phoen.
207, who says ἀντὶ τοῦ ἀναδραμεῖν
μέλλω; and one Schol. explains
our lemma as ἀντὶ τοῦ ἀναδραμοῦμαι,
forcing grammar to suit his view
of the passage.

56. Νεμέᾳ.] For dat. of place
after a subs. cf. infra, v. 88, Pyth.
VII. 14, VIII. 37.

57. ταύταν.] Cf. Ol. IV. 24,
Nem. VI. 36. 'Such' (as Alkime-
don's).

58. μάχαν.] Nowhere else is
μάχα used by Pindar in reference
to games (but εὐθύμαχον, Ol. VII.
15); while it seems better that ἐκ
παγκρ. should follow χάριν or an
equivalent. Rauch. suggests ἔχειν,
Schn. λαχεῖν; still I do not think

that alteration is absolutely neces-
sary. If I altered at all I would
read ταύταν μάραις | τὰν δ' ἔπειτ'
ἀνδρῶν χάριν | ἐκ παγκρατίου, 'such a
victory as Alkimedon's with hands
(i.e. in wrestling) and the following
victory in the quinquertium of
grown men.' If χάριν and μάραις
got transposed, the latter would of
course be soon altered. As in v. 75
χειρῶν ἄωτον ἐνίνικον is used ap-
parently with special or at least
principal reference to wrestling,
I think it highly probable that this
is the passage whence the Schol.
on the Il. (Frag. 276, Pind.) got
μάρη ἡ χεὶρ κατὰ Πίνδαρον.

59. διδάξασθαι.] 'To teach.'
Does the middle voice apply to
Melêsias' professional teaching for
his own benefit? Cf. Simonides
(on himself), Frag. 145, διδαξάμενος
χορόν, Aristoph. Nubes, 781. The
sentiment is found Ar. Metaph. I.
1, ὅλως τε σημεῖον τοῦ εἰδότος καὶ
τὸ δύνασθαι διδάσκειν ἐστί.

60. ἄγνωμον.] 'Not to have
had previous learning prevents
good judgment.' This passage re-
calls Alkman, cited by Schol. Isth.
I. 56 (40), πεῖρά τοι μαθήσιος ἀρχά.

65 νῦν μὲν αὐτῷ γέρας Ἀλκιμέδων
νίκαν τριακοστὰν ἑλών·

Στρ. δ΄.

ὃς τύχᾳ μὲν δαίμονος, ἀνορέας δ᾽ οὐκ ἀμπλακών
ἐν τέτρασιν παίδων ἀπεθήκατο γυίοις   90
νόστον ἔχθιστόν καὶ ἀτιμοτέραν γλῶσσαν καὶ ἐπί-
κρυφον οἶμον,
70 πατρὶ δὲ πατρὸς ἐνέπνευσεν μένος
γήραος ἀντίπαλον.
Ἀΐδα τοι λάθεται   95
ἄρμενα πράξαις ἀνήρ.

Ἀντ. δ΄.

ἀλλ᾽ ἐμὲ χρὴ μναμοσύναν ἀνεγείροντα φράσαι
75 χειρῶν ἄωτον Βλεψιάδαις ἐπίνικον,
ἕκτος οἷς ἤδη στέφανος περίκειται φυλλοφόρων ἀπ᾽
ἀγώνων.   100
ἔστι δὲ καί τι θανόντεσσιν μέρος
κὰν νόμον ἐρδόμενον·
κατακρύπτει δ᾽ οὐ κόνις
80 συγγόνων κεδνὰν χάριν.   105

66. The thirtieth victory won by Melêsias' pupils. Another besides the two sung of here is commemorated in Nem. IV.

67. 'Who by heaven-sent good luck, but in prowess verily not remiss, did on the bodies of four boys put off from himself a most hateful return, and talk of honour sullied, and a skulking route.' Cf. Pyth. VIII. 81—87.

68. τέτρασιν.] According to any reasonable plan of matching the competitors there must have been an entry of at least eleven, which number would give for first ties five pairs and an ἔφεδρος, second ties three pairs, third ties one pair and an ἔφεδρος, so that a victor, to throw four boys, could not be

ἔφεδρος either time. On the other hand, there may have been as many as sixteen. For the dat. of the adj. where we should expect a gen. in agreement with παίδων, cf. Ol. XI. 6.

73. ἄρμενα.] i.e. ἐῦ. The sentiment seems to refer to the grandfather having attained the wish of his heart.

77. 'That the dead too should have some share paid to them is meet and right. For the dust concealeth not the kinsmen's glory dear to them.' For the connection of the first words of consecutive verses, cf. Ol. VII. 15. For the constr., cf. Ol. IX. 103. For the sentiment, cf. Ar. Nik. Eth. I. x. §§ 3—5.

'Eπ. δ'.

'Ερμᾷ δὲ θυγατρὸς ἀκούσαις Ἰφίων
'Αγγελίας, ἐνέποι κεν Καλλιμάχῳ λιπαρὸν
κόσμον 'Ολυμπίᾳ, ὃν σφι Ζεὺς γένει
ὤπασεν. ἐσλὰ δ' ἐπ' ἐσλοῖς   110
85 ἔργα θέλοι δόμεν, ὀξείας δὲ νόσους ἀπαλάλκοι.
εὔχομαι ἀμφὶ καλῶν μοίρᾳ νέμεσιν διχόβουλον μὴ
    θέμεν·
ἀλλ' ἀπήμαντον ἄγων βίοτον   115
αὐτούς τ' ἀέξοι καὶ πόλιν.

81. The introduction of Hermes is appropriate, he being ἐναγώνιος, god of Heralds and conductor to Hades. The herald would proclaim (ἀγγέλλειν) probably Iphion as the victor's father; so that 'Αγγελία is doubly significant. In the similar passage, Ol. xIV. 20—24, 'Αχὼ is represented as πατρὶ κλυτὰν φέροισ' ἀγγελίαν.
83. 'Ολυμπίᾳ.] For dat. of place with subs. cf. supra, v. 56.

σφι—γένει.] Cf. Ol. II. 14, 15.
85. Probably there is a reference to the diseases which had proved fatal to Iphion and Kallimachos.
86. διχόβουλον.] 'Of divided counsels.' Cf. supra, v. 15.
88. Pindar evidently did not anticipate that before the next Olympic festival Aegina would be reduced by Athens.

OLYMPIA IX.

ON THE VICTORY OF EPHARMOSTOS OF OPUS IN THE
WRESTLING MATCH.

INTRODUCTION.

EPHARMOSTOS was a renowned wrestler who seems to have
excelled more by great skill than extraordinary strength. He was
an Opuntian of a noble family, perhaps a magistrate, *v.* 56. The
date of this victory is uncertain. The Scholl. give B.C. 488 as the
date of his Olympian and Pythian victories; but also the thirtieth
Pythiad, B.C. 470, for the Pythian, and one MS. gives Pythiad 33, B.C.
458, whence Böckh adopts B.C. 456 as the date of this Olympian
victory. But I cannot believe that this ode was composed the year
after the battle of Oenophyta and the reduction of Aegina, when the
Athenian power threatened the overthrow of the Lokrian Oligarchs;
if indeed it had not overthrown them. I place it Pyth. 30, B.C. 468,
when Simonides may have been alive (see *v.* 48, note). The ode
was sung after crowning the altar of the Opuntian Hero Aias Oïleus,
perhaps at a banquet. The rhythm is Lokrian, a variety of Aeolian.

ANALYSIS.

vv.
1—10. Archilochos' short triumphal song sufficed at Olympia;
    but now address the following ode to the height of Elis,
    Pelops' wedding gift to Hippodameia,

11, 12. And address Pytho.

12—14. Not in vain will you praise Opus and her son;

15—20. Opus renowned for good government and Pythian and Olympian victories.

21—27. I will spread this city's fame far and wide, if any poetic skill has been given me by fate.

28, 29. For poesy gives delight, but both poetic skill and prowess depend on the deity.

29—35. Else how could Hêrakles have withstood gods at Pylos?

35—39. Peace. It is hateful to speak ill of gods, and unseasonable vaunting is akin to madness.

40, 41. Do not connect gods with war and strife.

41—47. Speak of Opus where Deukalion and Pyrrha made men from stones.

48, 49. Praise old wine, newer lays.

49—53. They say there had been a flood.

53—66. Genealogical myth of Opus' hero eponymos.

67—70. His friendships, especially with Menoetios.

71—79. Of Menoetios' son Patroklos and Achilles.

80—83. May I have poetic skill, courage, and versatility.

83—85. For I come to aid Lampromachos, proxenos of Thebes, who won an Isthmian victory on the same day as his friend Epharmostos.

86—99. Mention of other victories of Epharmostos.

100—108. Excellence which comes by nature and is the gift of God is the best. Some pursuits are more glorious than others and all need training, but we are not all *naturally* constituted so as to benefit by the same training.

109—112. Praise of Epharmostos for heaven-directed skill and bravery, and mention of his crowning the altar of Aias Oïleus.

Throughout the ode runs the idea that natural gifts are superior to acquired skill, these gifts being of course developed by the favour of the gods. Now about Epharmostos' skill there is no doubt, so it is probable that the victor had been disparaged as deficient in natural advantages and as winning rather by artifice than straightforward play. The ill-natured criticisms and controversies of athletes are now endless, and probably have always been so. Scholarship however, cannot in this particular vaunt itself over gymnastic. It is not easy to see the connection of *vv.* 49—53.

Στρ. α'.

Τὸ μὲν Ἀρχιλόχου μέλος
φωνᾶεν Ὀλυμπίᾳ, καλλίνικος ὁ τριπλόος κεχλαδώς,
ἄρκεσε Κρόνιον παρ' ὄχθον ἀγεμονεῦσαι   5
κωμάζοντι φίλοις Ἐφαρμόστῳ σὺν ἑταίροις·
5 ἀλλὰ νῦν ἑκαταβόλων Μοισᾶν ἀπὸ τόξων
Δία τε φοινικοστερόπαν σεμνόν τ' ἐπίνειμαι   10
ἀκρωτήριον Ἄλιδος
τοιοῖσδε βέλεσσιν,
τὸ δή ποτε Λυδὸς ἥρως Πέλοψ   15
10 ἐξάρατο κάλλιστον ἕδνον Ἱπποδαμείας·

1. The song of triumph here mentioned was usually sung by a victor's kômos at Olympia, if a special ode was not composed for him. One Schol. cites it as τήνελλα καλλίνικε χαῖρ' ἄναξ Ἡράκλεις (leg. -εες) αὐτός τε καὶ Ἰόλαος αἰχμητὰ δύο τήνελλα καλλίνικε χαῖρ' ἄναξ Ἡράκλεις (leg. -εες). Another says it was called τριπλός from τήνελλα being thrice repeated. Another because the whole was thrice repeated. Yet another gives Eratosthenes' authority for καλλίνικος being thrice repeated, which Pindar's phrase supports. So it is likely that τήνελλα καλλίνικε was repeated at the end again. Cf. Archil. Frag. 119 (Bergk).

2. φωνᾶεν.] The position of the adjective clause is justified by its beginning the verse next to that which the article begins. Cf. Ol. VIII. 78, VII. 15, 18. But cf. Pyth. VI. 32.

κεχλαδώς.] 'Joyous.' Cf. Pyth. IV. 179.

5. ἀλλά.] Often follows μὲν in Homer.

6. φοινικοστερόπαν.] The thunderbolt is especially common on the reverse of Zeus-bearing coins of Elis, so we need not fancy any allusion to a Lokrian worship in this ode. True, the Lokri Epizephyrii

worshipped the Thunderer; but this variety of cult was chiefly determined by the prevalence of storms in a particular district.

ἐπίνειμαι.] This word, which Don., New Crat. (2nd. Ed.) § 174, shows to mean 'trespass' on sacred ground, is, with βέλεσσι, singularly appropriate to the consecrated district of Olympia. To discharge darts thereon literally would have been a 'violation' of the sacred territory and truce. That Δία and ἀκρωτήριον make up a hendiadys is suggested by their positions, though there is the alternative of taking ἐπίνειμαι with Δία by zeugma. Render 'the inviolable crest of Elis consecrate to Zeus, lord of ruddy lightning, do thou ply with missiles such as these.' The expression involves an oxymoron like γλυκὺν ὄιστὸν below.

7. ἀκρωτήριον.] The Κρόνιος λόφος which here stands for the district of Olympia.

8. βέλεσσιν.] The oldest MSS. give μέλεσι or μέλεσσιν, but Pal. C, Par. A and others furnish good authority for the text.

10. Note that he did not win Olympia with Hippodameia, but for her.

'Αντ. α'.

πτερόεντα δ' ἴει γλυκὺν
Πυθώναδ' ὀϊστόν· οὔτοι χαμαιπετέων λόγων ἐφάψεαι,
ἀνδρὸς ἀμφὶ παλαίσμασιν φόρμιγγ' ἐλελίζων   20
κλεινᾶς ἐξ 'Οπόεντος, αἰνήσαις ἓ καὶ υἱόν,
15 ἃν Θέμις θυγάτηρ τέ οἱ σώτειρα λέλογχε   25
μεγαλόδοξος Εὐνομία. θάλλει δ' ἀρεταῖσι
σόν τε, Κασταλία, παρὰ
'Αλφεοῦ τε ῥέεθρον·
ὅθεν στεφάνων ἄωτοι κλυτὰν   30
20 Λοκρῶν ἐπαείροντι ματέρ' ἀγλαόδενδρον.

'Επ. α'.

ἐγὼ δέ τοι φίλαν πόλιν
μαλεραῖς ἐπιφλέγων ἀοιδαῖς,
καὶ ἀγάνορος ἵππου   35
θᾶσσον καὶ ναὸς ὑποπτέρου παντᾷ

12. χαμαιπετέων.] The Schol.
explains this as a metaphor from
arrows that miss the mark, as the
context suggests. For ἐφάψεαι with
dat. referring to a special speech,
not as here and Pyth. VIII. 60 to a
pursuit generally, cf. Ol. I. 86.
13. ἀμφί.] Cf. ἀμφ' ἀρετᾷ κελα-
δέων, Pyth. II. 62. For ἐλελίζων, cf.
Pyth. I. 4.
14. αἰνήσαις.] The balance of
ms. authority is against placing a
full stop before this word, as do
several editors making it optative.
The present participle gives the
effect of which αἰνήσαις 'having
composed a song of praise' gives
the cause; cf. Ol. III. 3 where how-
ever the performance of the ode is
the cause of τὸ γεραίρειν.
15. οἱ.] For this rare dat. cf.
ψεύδεσί οἱ, Nem. VII. 22. It is to be
distinguished from σφίσιν—λοιπῷ
γένει, Ol. II. 14, 15 q.v.
16. ἀρεταῖσι.] mss. read ἀρε-
ταῖς ἴσον τε κασταλία. Cod. Ambr. A
with Schol. favours both the text

and ἀρεταῖσιν ἔν τε Κασταλίᾳ
(Böckh, Don., Mommsen) which
I believe to be a correction after
the dropping of one of the two
collocations ισ. The fact that ἐν
= 'near' with names of towns and
islands (cf. Ol. VI. 16) does not
justify such a use with the name of
a spring, in the vicinity too of a
mountain and temple of at least
equal celebrity. In vv. 17, 18,
mss. give παρ' 'Αλφεοῦ, παρ' 'Αλ-
φεοῦ.
19. κλυτάν.] 'To fame.' Ex-
tension of Predicate.
20. ματέρ'.] Cf. Ol. VI. 100.
22. The metaphor is from the
lighting up a height with a beacon-
fire. The comparison with a ship
is meant to suggest that the fame
conferred by the poet's praise will
spread over sea as well as land.
24. ὑποπτέρου.] Cf. λινόπτερ' ηὗρε
ναυτίλων ὀχήματα, Aesch. P. V. 476
(P.), Hes. W. and D. 628, εὐκόσμως
στολίσας νηὸς πτερὰ ποντοπόροιο.

.25 ἀγγελίαν πέμψω ταύταν,
εἰ σύν τινι μοιριδίῳ παλάμᾳ
ἐξαίρετον Χαρίτων. νέμομαι κᾶπον 40
κεῖναι γὰρ ὤπασαν τὰ τέρπν᾽· ἀγαθοὶ δὲ καὶ σοφοὶ
κατὰ δαίμον᾽ ἄνδρες

                                    Στρ. β΄.

ἐγένοντ᾽. ἐπεὶ ἀντίον
30 πῶς ἂν τριόδοντος Ἡρακλέης σκύταλον τίναξε χερ-
σίν, 45
ἀνίκ᾽ ἀμφὶ Πύλον σταθεὶς ἤρειδε Ποσειδᾶν,
ἤρειδεν δέ μιν ἀργυρέῳ τόξῳ πολεμίζων
Φοῖβος, οὐδ᾽ Ἀΐδας ἀκινήταν ἔχε ῥάβδον, 50
βρότεα σώμαθ᾽ ᾇ κατάγει κοίλαν πρὸς ἀγυιὰν
35 θνασκόντων; ἀπό μοι λόγον
τοῦτον, στόμα, ῥῖψον· 55
ἐπεὶ τό γε λοιδορῆσαι θεοὺς
ἐχθρὰ σοφία, καὶ τὸ καυχᾶσθαι παρὰ καιρὸν

28. Cf. Ol. xiv. 5—7. By ἀγα-
θοὶ καὶ σοφοὶ the Poet means 'brave
victors like Epharmostos and poets
like me,' cf. Pyth. i. 42.
κατὰ δαίμον᾽.] Not by 'favour of
the deity,' Don.; but 'in divine
measure,' the opposite to κατ᾽ ἄν-
θρωπον. By the favour of the
Graces is implied of course. That
he means to imply an extravagant
compliment to Epharmostos with
a word for himself is clear from
v. 38, καὶ τὸ καυχᾶσθαι παρὰ καιρὸν
μανίαισιν ὑποκρέκει.
29. ἐπεί.] 'For else.'
30. Homer Il. v. 395—398,
represents Hêrakles as an archer
in this contest. From Il. xi. 687—
695, Hêrakles would appear to
have been an ally of the Epeians,
and cf. v. 58 for the mythological
connection between Epeians and
Opus. According to the Schol. on
the latter passage Hêra was Hêra-
kles' third divine opponent, not as
here Phoebos.
31. ἀμφὶ Π. στ.] 'In defence
of Pylos.' Cf. ἀμφιβαίνω.
32. πολεμίζων.] Prof. Paley and
Bergk suggest πελεμίζων; but as
Hêrakles triumphed, the notion of
'driving back' is out of place.
Moreover πόλεμον, v. 40, favours
the text.
35. θνασκόντων.] 'As men die.'
Gen. abs. a noun being understood
out of βρότεα. Note that σώματα
here means 'shapes,' 'forms' with-
out any idea of solidity. For gen.
abs. without noun expressed cf.
Pyth. iv. 25, viii. 43, Aesch. Suppl.
437 (P.).
37. γε.] The force of the par-
ticle is shown by Ol. i. 35, where it
is suggested that it is a serious
responsibility to speak at all of the
gods.
38. ἐχθρά.] 'Is a baneful ex-
ercise of skill.'
καυχᾶσθαι.] Lit. 'to speak loud;'

'Αντ. β'.

μανίαισιν ὑποκρέκει.

40 μὴ νῦν λαλάγει τὰ τοιαῦτ'· ἔα πόλεμον μάχαν τε
      πᾶσαν   60
χωρὶς ἀθανάτων· φέροις δὲ Πρωτογενείας
ἄστει γλῶσσαν, ἵν' αἰολοβρόντα Διὸς αἴσᾳ   65
Πύρρα Δευκαλίων τε Παρνασοῦ καταβάντε
δόμον ἔθεντο πρῶτον, ἄτερ δ' εὐνᾶς ὁμόδαμον
45 κτησάσθαν λίθινον γόνον·   70
λαοὶ δ' ὀνόμασθεν.
ἔγειρ' ἐπέων σφιν οἶμον λιγύν,

but here, and generally, metaphorically 'to speak extravagantly,' 'to vaunt,' 'boast.'

παρὰ καιρόν.] Cf. πὰρ μέλος, Nem. VII. 69.

39. 'Has the true ring of madness.' Lit. 'strikes a note in unison with madness,' a metaphor from the lyre in accompaniment.

40. ἔα.] 'Let war and struggle of any kind be left apart from the immortals.' Gymnastic contests would seem to be comprised in μάχαν πᾶσαν. The fundamental meaning of μάχη is 'strength' hence 'trial of strength.'

41. Πρωτογενείας.] Clearly the daughter of Opus (cf. v. 58) the hero epónymos of Opus in Elis who was the son of Prôtogeneia daughter of Deukalion and Pyrrha. The younger Prôtogeneia was the mother of the hero epónymos of the Lokrian Opus. For φέροις γλ. cf. Pyth. v. 55.

44. ὁμόδαμον.] Extension of Predicate.

46. λαοί.] This myth is probably etymological in origin. The words λαὸς and λᾶας are probably not connected, though formed from roots so similar in sound that we cannot distinguish between them except by the meaning. The

Teutonic liud-, our lewd, Germ. Leute, is connected with the Goth. liudan, 'to grow' from the old root RUDH 'grow,' 'mount.' The Greek λαὸς for λαϝος seems to be from a primary root RU (to which RUDH is secondary), whence also ῥώννυμι, &c. and Lat. Roma; while λᾶας for λαϝας is most likely from the root RU 'break,' 'tear' the primary of RUP, whence Lat. rupes. Hermann quotes from Strabo VII. p. 321, 322 these Hesiodic verses. ἤτοι γὰρ Λοκρὸς Λελέγων ἡγήσατο λαῶν, | τοὺς ῥά ποτε Κρονίδης Ζεὺς ἄφθιτα μήδεα εἰδὼς | λεκτοὺς ἐκ γαίης λᾶας πόρε Δευκαλίωνι.

47. οἶμον.] MSS. give οἶμον which has been considered incompatible with ἔγειρε. For the emendation of Gedike, οὖρον, cf. Pyth. IV. 8, Nem. VI. 29. I do not think it is necessary; as οἶμον is not placed emphatically and moreover has not the meaning of a material roadway closely attached to it, being, Pyth. IV. 248, contrasted with ἁμαξιτόν. Surely ἐπέων οἶμος and οἶμος ἀοιδῆς, Hom. Hymn. in Merc. 451, are synonyms for οἶμη and might replace it in any context. It is supposed however, that οἶμον is a mistake due to οἶνον in the next verse.

αἴνει δὲ παλαιὸν μὲν οἶνον, ἄνθεα δ' ὕμνων

'Επ. β'.

νεωτέρων. λέγοντι μὰν 75
50 χθόνα μὲν κατακλύσαι μέλαιναν
ὕδατος σθένος, ἀλλὰ
Ζηνὸς τέχναις ἀνάπωτιν ἐξαίφνας
ἄντλον ἑλεῖν. κείνων δ' ἔσσαν
χαλκάσπιδες ὑμέτεροι πρόγονοι, 80
55 ἀρχᾶθεν Ἰαπετιονίδος φύτλας
κοῦροι κορᾶν καὶ φερτάτων Κρονιδᾶν, ἐγχώριοι βασι-
λῆες αἰεί.

Στρ. γ'.

πρὶν Ὀλύμπιος ἀγεμὼν 85
θύγατρ' ἀπὸ γᾶς Ἐπειῶν Ὀπόεντος ἀναρπάσαις, ἕκαλος
μίχθη Μαιναλίαισιν ἐν δειραῖς, καὶ ἔνεικεν
60 Λοκρῷ, μὴ καθέλοι νιν αἰὼν πότμον ἐφάψαις 90

But a Schol. Vet. gives traces of a reading ὅρμον, which corruption of οἶμον slightly increases the presumption of its antiquity.

σφίν.] i.e. ἀστοῖς suggested by ἄστει, v. 42.

48. The Scholl. Vett. say that this expression is aimed at Simonides, who had expressed his envy of Pindar in the phrase ἐξελέγχει ὁ νέος οἶνος οὔπω πέρυσι δῶρον ἀμπέλου, Frag. 75 (Bergk). However that may be, the Poet seems to mean 'choose old themes but fresh modes of expression.'

49. It is very probable that the floods of which traditions have been preserved were occasioned by some catastrophe which raised the waters of the Black Sea. A very slight rise in the Aegaean consequent on the escape of pent-up waters from the Euxine would submerge the lowlands of Thessaly.

53. κείνων.] i.e. λαῶν, v. 56. It is governed by ἐγχώριοι βασιλῆες.

54. ὑμέτεροι.] 'Of your family.'

56. κορᾶν.] Plural for singular, meaning the younger Prôtogeneia, as also Κρονιδᾶν meaning Zeus.

57. πρίν.] 'Before that,' i. e. before they got the kingdom of Lokris. The Poet proceeds to explain v. 56. It is probably the fact that the Lokri had not kings in Pindar's time that makes Bergk and others take πρίν = 'until,' thereby reducing the time indicated by αἰεί to nought, since the races of Iapetos and Kronos were not mixed before the event introduced by πρίν. Epharmostos may have held an office something like that of the ἄρχων βασιλεὺς at Athens only hereditary, or again αἰεί need not be carried down to the present time. Hermann denies that πρίν can = olim without comparison with a later time.

60. Λοκρῷ.] He might be a son, but was probably grandson of Deukalion whose great-grand-

ὀρφανὸν γενεᾶς. ἔχεν δὲ σπέρμα μέγιστον
ἄλοχος, εὐφράνθη τε ἰδὼν ἥρως θετὸν υἱόν,   95
μάτρωος δ᾽ ἐκάλεσσέ νιν
ἰσώνυμον ἔμμεν,
65 ὑπέρφατον ἄνδρα μορφᾷ τε καὶ
ἔργοισι. πόλιν δ᾽ ὤπασεν λαόν τε διαιτᾶν.   100

                                                      Ἀντ. γ´.

ἀφίκοντο δέ οἱ ξένοι
ἔκ τ᾽ Ἄργεος ἔκ τε Θηβᾶν, οἱ δ᾽ Ἀρκάδες, οἱ δὲ καὶ
    Πισᾶται·
υἱὸν δ᾽ Ἄκτορος ἐξόχως τίμασεν ἐποίκων   105
70 Αἰγίνας τε Μενοίτιον. τοῦ παῖς ἅμ᾽ Ἀτρείδαις
    Τεύθραντος πεδίον μολὼν ἔστα σὺν Ἀχιλλεῖ
μόνος, ὅτ᾽ ἀλκάεντας Δαναοὺς τρέψαις ἁλίαισιν   110
πρύμναις Τήλεφος ἔμβαλεν·
ὥστ᾽ ἔμφρονι δεῖξαι
75 μαθεῖν Πατρόκλου βιατὰν νόον·   115
ἐξ οὗ Θέτιος * γόνος * οὐλίῳ νιν ἐν Ἄρει

daughter he married presumably in his old age. This Legend suggests the early presence of Lokrians in Elis and an early Lelegian league.

62. θετόν.] 'Adopted'= ποιητόν.
63. μάτρωος.] His mother's father Opus. For the gen. cf. Pyth. ι. 30, Madv. § 63 d. Rem.
64. ἔμμεν.] Cf. Ol. vi. 56.
65. Note how Pindar jumps from birth to manhood in putting ὑπέρφατον ἄνδρα simply in agreement with μιν.
68. Note that Epharmostos had won prizes at the games connected with these four names which seem to be selected out of the localities and tribes connected with the Leleges, to which people the Aegidae may have belonged.
71. The plain of Teuthras is Mysia. Prof. Paley points out that

this episode is not found in the Homeric poems.
74. 'So that it' (the circumstance related in the foregoing clause) 'showed for the appreciation of a shrewd understanding the warrior spirit of Patroklos.' For the redundant μαθεῖν cf. Nem. vi.. 8, τεκμαίρει καὶ νῦν Ἀλκιμίδας τὸ συγγενὲς ἰδεῖν | ἄγχι καρποφόροις ἀρούραισιν, Soph. Oed. Kol. 791, γένος δ᾽ | ἄτλητον ἀνθρώποισι δηλώσοιμ᾽ ὁρᾶν.
76. γόνος.] So all mss.; but the first syllable should belong, so Böckh and Don. accept Hermann's γ᾽ οὐλίῳ γόνος. Others without displacing οὐλίῳ read γ᾽ ἶνις, γ᾽ υἱὸς, θετιόγνητος γ᾽ ὄξυς, βλαστός. I propose κοῦρος as very likely to be lost or mutilated before οὐλίῳ, when γόνος would be inserted to fill the gap. The phrase οὔλιος Ἄρης is Hesiodic.

Ἐπ. γ´.

παραγορεῖτο μή ποτε
σφετέρας ἄτερθε ταξιοῦσθαι
δαμασιμβρότου αἰχμᾶς.
80 εἴην εὑρησιεπὴς ἀναγεῖσθαι   120
πρόσφορος ἐν Μοισᾶν δίφρῳ·
τόλμα δὲ καὶ ἀμφιλαφὴς δύναμις
ἕσποιτο. προξενίᾳ δ᾽ ἀρετᾷ τ᾽ ἦλθον
τιμάορος Ἰσθμίαισι Λαμπρομάχου μίτραις, ὅτ᾽ ἀμφό-
τεροι κράτησαν   125

Στρ. δ´.

85 μίαν ἔργον ἀν᾽ ἀμέραν.
ἄλλαι δὲ δύ᾽ ἐν Κορίνθου πύλαις ἐγένοντ᾽ ἔπειτα
χάρμαι,
ταὶ δὲ καὶ Νεμέας Ἐφαρμόστῳ κατὰ κόλπον·   130

80. It may be inferred that the poet implies that friendship exists between Epharmostos and Lampromachos like to that between Achilles and Patroklos; cf. Ol. xi. 16—19. Having embarked on an epic theme he checks himself, saying in effect 'I should certainly be able to pursue such a theme had I not other work in hand.' The δ᾽ of v. 83 is like the Homeric ἀλλά = εἰ μή. But here after τόλμα... ἕσποιτο the εἰ μή, which would make the simplest construction immediately after εἴην...δίφρῳ, would be awkward. For this optative without ἄν, cf. Pyth. iv. 118. Render 'I should surely be able to fashion heroic verse so as to drive straight on, a fit servant of the muses, in their car, and daring and widely ranging power would attend me. But I am come for state-friendship's and prowess' sake to do honour to the Isthmian fillets of Lampromachos (gained) when they both won a victory on one

day.' For sentiment cf. Ol. xiii. 11, 96.

80. ἀναγεῖσθαι.] For Inf. cf. Ol. i. 41. The verb means 'to narrate continuously,' cf. Nem. x. 19, Isthm. v. 56, and 'to lead on continuously.' Here it is used in a double sense suitable to the regular progress of epic narrative.

83. προξενίᾳ.] For dat. of cause cf. Madv. § 41. Lampromachos was it seems πρόξενος of Thebes at Opus. He was probably related to Epharmostos.

84. For the μίτραι of the Isthmian games cf. Isth. iv. 62.

85. ἔργον.] 'In a contest.' For this sense cf. Isth. iii. 869, ἰσχύος ἔργον. For acc. cf. Madv. § 26, Rem. 1, 2, and Pyth. viii. 80.

86. Κορ. πύλ.] 'At the Isthmos.' Any kind of pass was πύλαι to the Greeks. Tafel thinks games at Korinth other than Isthmian may be meant, e.g. the Hellôtia, cf. Ol. xiii. 40. In this verse ἀμφοτέροις is to be understood.

Ἄργει τ' ἔσχεθε κῦδος ἀνδρῶν, παῖς δ' ἐν Ἀθάναις.
οἷον δ' ἐν Μαραθῶνι συλαθεὶς ἀγενείων   135
90 μένεν ἀγῶνα πρεσβυτέρων ἀμφ' ἀργυρίδεσσιν·
φῶτας δ' ὀξυρεπεῖ δόλῳ
ἄπτωτι δαμάσσαις
διήρχετο κύκλον ὅσσα βοᾷ,   140
ὡραῖος ἐὼν καὶ καλὸς κάλλιστά τε ῥέξαις.

'Αντ. δ'.

95 τὰ δὲ Παρρασίῳ στρατῷ
θαυμαστὸς ἐὼν φάνη Ζηνὸς ἀμφὶ πανάγυριν Λυκ-
αίου,   145
καὶ ψυχρᾶν ὁπότ' εὐδιανὸν φάρμακον αὐρᾶν
Πελλάνᾳ φέρε· σύνδικος δ' αὐτῷ Ἰολάου   150
τύμβος εἰναλία τ' Ἐλευσὶς ἀγλαΐαισιν.
100 τὸ δὲ φυᾷ κράτιστον ἅπαν· πολλοὶ δὲ διδακταῖς
ἀνθρώπων ἀρεταῖς κλέος
ὤρουσαν ἀρέσθαι.
ἄνευ δὲ θεοῦ σεσιγαμένον   155

88. ἀνδρῶν.] 'Men's glory,' i.e. glory won in the contest of men.

89. 'What a contest with the elders for silver cups did he maintain at Marathon, soon as removed from the youths! and after worsting the men by a quickly-throwing trick that saved him from a fall, with what cheers did he pass round the ring, being in the bloom of youth and of noble form and having most nobly wrought!' ὀξυρεπὴς is 'sharply turning off one's balance.'

95. τὰ δέ.] 'And again' or 'and further,' cf. Ol. xiii. 55, Pyth. viii. 28, Isthm. iii. 11.

97. φάρμακον.] 'A warm antidote to chilling blasts.' Pindar seems to have adopted this phrase from Hipponax who several times uses φάρμακον metaphorically, cf. Frag. 19 Bergk. Ἐμοὶ γὰρ οὐκ ἔδωκας

οὔτε κω χλαῖναν | δασεῖαν, ἐν χειμῶνι φάρμακον ῥίγευς, οὔτ' ἀσκέρῃσι τοὺς πόδας δασείῃσιν | ἔκρυψας, ὡς μή μοι χίμετλα ῥήγνυται. Here the use is 'prophylactic' elsewhere 'corrective,' as in Soph. Aj. 1255.

98. σύνδικος.] Cf. Pyth. i. 2.

100. For sentiment, cf. Ol. ii. 86, Eur. Hippol. 79, 80.

103. 'When a god hath no part, far better is it that every matter be veiled in silence.' For the personal construction with a participle instead of an impersonal expression with acc. and inf. cf. Soph. Aj. 635, Madv. § 177, Rem. 4, where however, in the translation at least, it is limited to ἀρκῶ, ἱκανός, κρείττων, βελτίων εἰμί. Cf. Pyth. iv. 151, οὐ πονεῖ με...ταῦτα πορσύνοντα, Ol. viii. 77, 78, Nem. v. 16, οὔτοι ἅπασα κερδίων φαίνοισα πρόσωπον ἀλάθει' ἀτρεκὴς (with this

οὐ σκαιότερον χρῆμ' ἕκαστον· ἐντὶ γὰρ ἄλλαι

'Επ. δ'.

105 ὁδῶν ὁδοὶ περαίτεραι,
μία δ' οὐχ ἅπαντας ἄμμε θρέψει   160
μελέτα· σοφίαι μὲν
αἰπειναί· τοῦτο δὲ προσφέρων ἄεθλον,
ὄρθιον ὤρυσαι θαρσέων,
110 τόνδ' ἀνέρα δαιμονίᾳ γεγάμεν
εὔχειρα, δεξιόγυιον, ὁρῶντ' ἀλκάν·   165
* Αἰάντεόν τ' ἐν δαίθ' ὅς* Ἰλιάδα νικῶν ἐπεστεφάνωσε
βωμόν.

ἅπασα 'in every case' cf. ἅπαν supra v. 100), Ar. Vesp. 27, δεινόν γε τοῦστ' ἄνθρωπος ἀποβαλὼν ὅπλα, 47, οὔκουν ἐκεῖν' ἀλλοκότον ὁ Θέωρος κόραξ γενόμενος. Not very unlike is Horace's syllaba longa brevi subjecta vocatur iambus. I cannot think it correct to take ἄνευθε θεοῦ closely with χρῆμ' ἕκαστον, 'Everything that is done with the god.' Rather ἄν. θε. go with the whole sentence and mean 'If you cannot speak of a god.'

104. ἐντί.] It is not easy to see the exact drift of these reflections unless we suppose Epharmostos to have failed in some more ambitious project than the winning of a wrestling prize.

108. ἄεθλον.] The Ode is meant by 'this prize.'

110. It would appear that Epharmostos was famed for the originality of his style of wrestling.

111. ὁρῶντ'.] Cf. Pyth II. 20.

112. The text is Böckh's suggested by inferior mss. The best read δαιτὶ without ὅς. I propose Αἰάντεον ὅς τ' ἐν δαιτὶ Ἰλιάδα, κ.τ.λ., scanning -τεον as a short syllable, cf. θεός, Pyth. I. 55. If ὅς did not drop out by accident it would stand a great chance of being expunged by a metrist. Ἰλεύς, Ἰλεάδης had the digamma which in Homer became 'O. Curtius suggests a connection with ῑλη-. Ileus was greatgrandson of Opus.

νικ. ἐπεστ.] i.e. 'being a victor crowned in commemoration.' Commentators neglect the preposition. For Αἰάντεον instead of Αἴαντος with the gen. Ἰλιάδα, cf. Ol. II. 12, Il. II. 54, Νεστορέῃ παρὰ νηὶ Πυλοιγενέος βασιλῆος.

OLYMPIA X. [XI.]

ON THE VICTORY OF AGESIDAMOS, AN EPIZEPHYRIAN LOKRIAN, IN THE BOYS' BOXING-MATCH.

INTRODUCTION.

THIS ode was sung after the victory, at Olympia, B.C. 484. It alludes to a promise to compose an ode to be sung after the victor's return home, which was tardily fulfilled by the next ode. The rhythm is a mixture of Lydian and Dorian.

ANALYSIS.

vv.

1—6. Winds are needed at one time, showers at another, but for a victor songs are (ever) needed to remind posterity of his merits.

7—8. The praise they initiate is ever ready for Olympian victors.

8—10. This my tongue desires to promote; but upon God depends immortality of song.

11—15. Promise of an ode on Agêsidâmos' victory in honour of the Lokri Epizephyrii.

16—19. The muses are assured that they will find them hospitable, poetic and warlike.

19—21. For foxes and lions would never under any circumstances change their nature.

Στρ.

Ἔστιν ἀνθρώποις ἀνέμων ὅτε πλεῖστα
χρῆσις, ἔστιν δ᾽ οὐρανίων ὑδάτων
ὀμβρίων, παίδων νεφέλας.
εἰ δὲ σὺν πόνῳ τις εὖ πράσσοι, μελιγάρυες ὕμνοι
5 ὑστέρων ἀρχαὶ λόγων   5
τέλλεται καὶ πιστὸν ὅρκιον μεγάλαις ἀρεταῖς.

'Αντ.

ἀφθόνητος δ᾽ αἶνος 'Ολυμπιονίκαις
οὗτος ἄγκειται. τὰ μὲν ἀμετέρα

1. For the form of the exordium
cf. Ol. I. 1 sqq. For the sentiment
cf. Nem. III. 6, διψῇ δὲ πρᾶγος ἄλλο
μὲν ἄλλου. | ἀεθλονικία δὲ μάλιστ᾽
ἀοιδὰν φιλεῖ, | στεφάνων ἀρετῶν τε
δεξιωτάταν ὀπαδόν. Dissen thinks
the choice of winds to illustrate
the general statement was due to
Agêsidâmos having to return home
by sea. Here however, Pindar
seems to me to suggest more than
in the passage just quoted, namely
the unintermittent value of poetic
praise as opposed to the intermit-
tent demand for the most useful
thing. Beware of supposing that
ἐνίο-τε from anya-kâ, 'some-when,'
is a corruption of ἔστιν ὅτε. There
is a half personification in νεφέλας.
4. Cf. Ol. VI. 11.
5. Prof. Paley renders 'are an
introduction to an after address;'
but the interpretation of the Schol.
is preferable, 'honey-voiced odes
are found to be the ground of the
talk of posterity, yea, a trusty wit-
ness on oath to mighty exploits.'
6. τέλλεται.] This is not a very
good instance of the Schema Pin-
daricum, for which cf. Pyth. x. 71,
as, if ἀρχὰ (Cod. Ambr. A) be not
read, there may be an attraction
of the number to ὅρκιον. Observe
that strictly τέλλεσθαι, τελέθειν
mean more than 'to be,' viz. 'to
be in the issue.'

ὅρκιον.] Cf. ἔξορκος, Ol. XIII. 100.
It is a mistake to render this 'a
pledge' here, though it has that
signification Nem. IX. 16. Here it
is lit. 'evidence delivered on oath.'
7. ἀφθόνητος.] Extension of
Predicate. 'Without stint.' Prof.
Paley understands 'without jea-
lousy' comparing Ol. XIII. 25.
8. ἄγκειται.] Cf. Ol. XIII. 36.
τὰ μέν.] Cf. Ol. I. 16. The
reference is not to ὕμνοι, but to
αἶνος, i. e. ὕστεροι λόγοι. Prof.
Paley renders 'some part of it my
tongue desires to keep in store,'
explaining thus—'The metaphor
in ποιμαίνειν is from a flock tended
and fed until required for use.'
But I do not think that τὰ μὲν can
mean 'some part' unless 'the
whole' or 'another part' is indi-
cated in the clause introduced by
δέ, as is not here the case. Com-
mentators either ignore the diffi-
culty of this whole passage or else
misinterpret it. The connection is
best shown by a paraphrase. 'This
song-caused praise of posterity is
laid up without stint for Olympian
victors, the which my tongue is
ready and willing to promote. But
it is God's gift for a man to bloom
for ever by means of the produc-
tions of poetic talent.' The general
sense is the same if ἀνήρ means
'the poet,' in which case σοφαῖς

γλῶσσα ποιμαίνειν ἐθέλει·
10 ἐκ θεοῦ δ᾽ ἀνὴρ σοφαῖς ἀνθεῖ ἐσαεὶ πραπίδεσσιν.   10
ἴσθι νῦν, Ἀρχεστράτου
παῖ, τεᾶς, Ἀγησίδαμε, πυγμαχίας ἕνεκεν

'Επ.

κόσμον ἐπὶ στεφάνῳ χρυσέας ἐλαίας
ἀδυμελῆ κελαδήσω,
15 τῶν Ἐπιζεφυρίων Λοκρῶν γενεὰν ἀλέγων.   15
ἔνθα συγκωμάξατ᾽· ἐγγυάσομαι
μή μιν, ὦ Μοῖσαι, φυγόξενον στρατὸν
μήδ᾽ ἀπείρατον καλῶν,
ἀκρόσοφον δὲ καὶ αἰχματὰν ἀφίξεσθαι. τὸ γὰρ

πραπίδεσσιν is a dative of manner; viz. I am *willing* to immortalize victors, but can only do so if God is willing to confer immortality by means of (or on) my verse. He goes on to express his conviction that in Agêsidâmos' case God is willing to do so.

9. ποιμαίνειν.] The metaphor is most closely illustrated by ποιμένες Κυπρίας δώρων, Nem. viii. 6. The sheep are, in these two passages, gifts which the shepherd brings to perfection and provides. There is no support for the renderings 'enfold,' 'keep in store.'

10. πραπίδεσσιν.] A highly probable derivation for πραπίδες is to take it as a corruption of σπραπίδες from an extension with π of the √SPAR whence σπαίρω, ἀσπαίρω, πάλλω. With this I would connect σπλή-ν and σπλάγχ-νο-ν, the latter from a nasalized extension with χ for early *gh*. The entrails might well be designated as 'quiverers' by folk who were used to sacrificing animals.

13. κόσμον.] 'My voice shall set the adornment of a sweet strain upon thy crown of glistening olive.' For κόσμον of song cf. Frag. 176 [206] quoted Ol. i. 16.

χρυσέας.] Cf. Ol. viii. 1.

15. ἀλέγων.] 'Doing honour to.' The Schol. explains ὑμῶν, citing Alkaeos, οὐκ ἐγὼ λύκον ἐν Μούσαις ἀλέγω, Frag. 58. [43.]

16. συγκωμάξατε.] 'There do ye join in the triumphal song;' i.e. when I send it as I promise. I suspect that συγκωμάξετε. was the original reading. There is no stop after it in the best MSS. Most editors place a comma.

17. μιν.] Refers to γενεάν. 'I shall stand surety that ye will not, Muses, find it on arrival a host that puts (unprotected) strangers to flight nor unskilled in noble pursuits, but unsurpassed in minstrelsy and warlike withal.' The epithet φυγόξενος doubtless may refer to the Doric ξενηλασία which the Panhellenic Pindar would abhor; but, whether the Lokri Epizephyrii owned an Ozolian founder as Strabo says or an Opuntian as Ephoros, they were not Dorians. The epithet here serves as a correlative to αἰχματάν. These Lokri could boast of at least two poets, Xenokritos and Erasippos, and a poetess Theano, cf. Ol. xi. 13—15.

19. αἰχματάν.] Cf. Thuc. i. 5. They had gained a famous victory

20 ἐμφυὲς οὔτ' αἴθων ἀλώπηξ   20
   οὔτ' ἐρίβρομοι λέοντες διαλλάξαιντο ἦθος.

over the Sybarites on the river
Sagra.
20. αἴθων.] 'Tawny.'
21. διαλλάξαιντο.] For the omis-
sion of ἀν cf. Pyth. IV. 118. There
is no real hiatus, as ἦθος had an
initial F, being akin to Lat. sue-
sco. For ἐμφυὲς ἦθος cf. συγγενὲς
ἦθος, Ol. XIII. 13. The particular
shade of emphasis expressed by the

omission of ἀν is to be brought out
by reflecting that the Lokri had
been for a long time far removed
from their metropolis, yet had not
changed, and were not at all likely
to do so under any circumstances.
The fox is probably proverbial and
has no reference to Lokrian charac-
teristics, while the lions are a com-
plimentary addition by the poet.

OLYMPIA XI. [X.]

ON THE VICTORY OF AGESIDAMOS, AN EPIZEPHYRIAN
LOKRIAN, IN THE BOYS' BOXING-MATCH.

INTRODUCTION.

THIS ode is on the same victory as the last, in which there is
allusion to a promised ode in praise of the Lokrians. It was pro-
bably composed for the return of an Olympian festival, and I
venture to suggest that it was the second return, i.e. B.C. 476. This
conjecture is mainly founded on the mention of Hêrakles' repulse
by Kyknos and the recital of the fate of Augeas[1], and especially the
dictum of *vv.* 39, 40. This applies exactly to the relations between
Anaxilâos and Hiero and between the Lokrians and both tyrants,
which subsisted about the date of the second Pythian Ode, and are
discussed in the introduction thereto. The death of Anaxilâos fell
in B.C. 476. About this period Pindar must have had his attention
called to any promise he had made to a member of the Lokrian
state. Again, the length of time which I ascribe to Pindar's delay
seems to suit the tone of the apology and the last six verses, from
which it appears that Agêsidâmos was quite grown up at the date
of composition. Had Pindar been to Sicily previously he would
scarcely have avoided being reminded of his debt, and in such case

---

[1] The Scholl. take the allusion to Hêrakles and Kyknos as referring
to Agêsidâmos, who, they say, almost gave in, but was encouraged by
Ilas and went on to victory. But they tell us also that Kyknos when
aided by Ares repulsed Hêrakles, but when alone was killed by him;
while Hêrakles is not said to have been backed up on either occasion.
The parallel suggested then is very incomplete, and moreover is scarcely
complimentary to the victor Agêsidâmos. Now the Lokri must have
been humiliated by Anaxilâos before they applied for aid to Hiero; but
he in his turn suffered humiliation even as Augeas. It should be observed
that praise of Hêrakles, the traditional enemy of the Pylians, would be
grateful to foes of the Messênian Anaxilâos.

the opening of the ode would be inappropriate; so that B.C. 472 is almost out of the question. It is, on the other hand, very likely that Pindar would take care to discharge his obligation before going into his creditor's neighbourhood.

ANALYSIS.

vv.

1—8. Acknowledgment of the long-standing debt.

9, 10. But payment with interest will acquit the poet from blame. Simile of a wave washing down an accumulation of shingle.

11, 12. For his friend's sake the poet will make payment of a rede of common interest.

13—16. Praise of the Lokri Epizephyrii for strict justice, poetic accomplishments and bravery.

16—19. Mention of Ilas, Agêsidâmos' trainer.

20, 21. By God's help a trainer can develope natural excellence,

22, 23. But few attain success at Olympia without toil.

24—42. The ordinances of Zeus bade sing of the best of games, which Hêrakles founded when he had overcome the perfidious Augeas and his kin. The gnômê—'A quarrel with superiors is most hard to be rid of'—is introduced *vv.* 39, 40.

43—51. Description of the institution of the Olympian games.

51—55. Mention of the presence thereat of the Fates and Time, the ultimate establisher of truth.

55—59. Time has given testimony as to Hêrakles' institution of the games.

60—77. Commemoration of the first contests and subsequent festivities.

78—83. Zeus' thunderbolt must be sung of.

84, 85. At last a song to the flute has come from Thebes.

86—90. Simile of the child of a wealthy man's old age.

91—93. Prowess is useless if one dies unsung.

93—96. Agêsidâmos, however, is sure of the renown promoted by song.

97—99. Complimentary mention of the Lokri.

99—105. Praise of Agêsidâmos.

Στρ. α'.

Τὸν 'Ολυμπιονίκαν ἀνάγνωτέ μοι
'Αρχεστράτου παῖδα, πόθι φρενὸς
ἐμᾶς γέγραπται· γλυκὺ γὰρ αὐτῷ μέλος ὀφείλων ἐπι-
λέλαθ'. ὦ Μοῖσ', ἀλλὰ σὺ καὶ θυγάτηρ   5
'Αλάθεια Διός, ὀρθᾷ χερὶ
5 ἐρύκετον ψευδέων
ἐνιπὰν ἀλιτόξενον.

'Αντ. α'.

ἔκαθεν γὰρ ἐπελθὼν ὁ μέλλων χρόνος
ἐμὸν καταίσχυνε βαθὺ χρέος.   10
ὅμως δὲ λῦσαι δυνατὸς ὀξεῖαν ἐπιμομφὰν τόκος. ὁράτω
νῦν ψᾶφον ἑλισσομέναν

1. ἀνάγνωτέ μοι.] The sense is pregnant, 'read and tell me.' For the subject of the dependent clause as the object of the principal clause cf. Madv. § 191. The construction is used to give the noun prominence. Aeschylos several times uses this metaphor from inscriptions or memoranda, *Prom. V.* 807 (P.), *Choëph.* 441, *Eum.* 265, *Suppl.* 175.

2. φρενός.] For this partitive genitive cf. Madv. § 50 *b*.

3. ὀφείλων.] Cf. Eur. *Bacch.*, ἐπιλελήσμεθ' ἡδέως | γέροντες ὄντες. Compare μέμνημαι with part., Madv. § 178.

4. ὀρθᾷ.] Schol. δικαίᾳ, Dissen, *erecta.* I prefer the latter interpretation. It might be used causatively 'correcting.' Cf. χερὶ κούφᾳ, Pyth ix. 11.

6. ἀλιτόξενον.] For the agreement with ἐνιπὰν instead of ψευδέων (hypallage) cf. Pyth. vi. 5, Πυθιόνικος ὕμνων θησαυρος, Pyth. iv. 255, ὑμετέρας ἀκτῖνος ὄλβου, Ol. viii. 42, 68, cf. also Soph. *Aj.* 8, and Jebb's note. For the magnitude of the offence, cf. Aesch. *Eum.* 260, 261.

7. 'For the coming time (i.e. the season of the Olympian games) having approached again from a distant date made me feel the disgrace of my deep debt.' The usual interpretation of ὁ μέλλων χρόνος is 'the time then future,' i.e. when the promise was made. To speak of the immediate future as having come round is less awkward than this. It seems, however, questionable whether ὁ μέλλων χρόνος can 'refer to the time fixed for the performance of the promised task' (Don.), or any other *fixed time.* Have we here a bold expression for '*the time of my delay* having advanced from a distant date'?

8. For the Aorist here and in v. 24, cf. Ol. viii. 54.

9. ὁράτω.] Adapted from Schneidewin's ὁρᾶτ' ὤν. mss. give, best τόκος θνατῶν, inferior ὁ τόκος ἀνδρῶν. Hermann proposed τόκος ὀνάτωρ, 'beneficial interest,' which is read by Don. and Bergk. Rauchenstein and Kayser agree with Schn. that ὄπα requires a verb before it. I doubt Pindar using ὤν with the imperative. He generally has another particle (δ', μὲν, γὰρ, οὖτ',

10 ὀπᾷ κῦμα κατακλύσσει ῥέον,   15
    ὀπᾷ τε κοινὸν λόγον
    φίλαν τίσομεν ἐς χάριν.

'Επ. α'.

νέμει γὰρ 'Ατρέκεια πόλιν Λοκρῶν Ζεφυρίων,
    μέλει τέ σφισι Καλλιόπα
15 καὶ χάλκεος "Αρης. τράπε δὲ Κύκνεια μάχα καὶ ὑπέρ-
    βιον   20
    'Ηρακλέα· πύκτας δ' ἐν 'Ολυμπιάδι νικῶν
    "Ιλᾳ φερέτω χάριν
    'Αγησίδαμος ὡς
    'Αχιλεῖ Πάτροκλος.
20 θήξαις δέ κε φύντ' ἀρετᾷ ποτὶ
    πελώριον ὁρμάσαι κλέος ἀνὴρ θεοῦ σὺν παλάμαις. 25
                                       Στρ. β'.

ἄπονον δ' ἔλαβον χάρμα παῦροί τινες,
    ἔργων πρὸ πάντων βιότῳ φάος.

αἴτ') before it. By ψᾶφον is meant
the accumulation of censure, and
the κῦμα is the ode.
10. κατακλύσσει.] The -σσ- is
due to the assimilation of the y of
the future suffix sya- which be-
comes σι°ₐ, σε°ₑ in Doric, σ°ₑ in Attic.
11. κοινόν.] Schneidewin ren-
ders 'the account that stands be-
tween us:' but the settlement of an
account is hardly ἐς χάριν; and for
'a rede of common interest,' cf.
Ol. vii. 21, Isth. v. 69.
12. φίλαν.] This supports my
reading ὀρᾶτω above. Were not
Archestratos' son already alluded
to in the sentence we should ex-
pect φίλῳ or φίλον. Render ' as a
friendly favour.'
13. γάρ.] The particle simply
marks the beginning of the pay-
ment just announced. The com-
pliment involved in 'Ατρέκεια is not
high; there is a mere allusion to

Zaleukos' Code. It may be in-
ferred from Pyth. ii. that Pindar
had not a high opinion of the
Lokrian state.
14. Cf. Ol. x. 18.
17. Ilas was aleípta to Agêsi-
dâmos or at any rate acted as
such.
20. θήξαις.] Lampo who had
trained his two sons is said, Isth.
v. 72, 73, ἀνδράσιν ἀθληταῖσιν
ἔμμεν | Ναξίαν πέτραις ἐν ἄλλαις
χαλκοδάμαντ' ἀκόναν.
In this and the next verse Pindar
reconciles the facts of education
with his theory of the natural and
divine character of all excellence
and his depreciation of διδακταὶ
ἀρεταί, Ol. ix. 100, ii. 86. The
same problem is treated of Ol. ix.
104—107.
23. ἔργων.] Here ἔργα may
mean victories, cf. Ol. ix. 85. For
βιότῳ φάος cf. Ol. ii. 55.

ἀγῶνα δ' ἐξαίρετον ἀεῖσαι θέμιτες ὦρσαν Διός, ὃν
    ἀρχαίῳ σάματι πὰρ Πέλοπος   30
25 βωμῶν ἐξάριθμον ['Ηρακλέης] ἐκτίσσατο,
ἐπεὶ Ποσειδάνιον
πέφνε Κτέατον ἀμύμονα,

                                                   'Αντ. β'.

πέφνε δ' Εὔρυτον, ὡς Αὐγέαν λάτριον
    ἀέκονθ' ἑκὼν μισθὸν ὑπέρβιον   35
30 πράσσοιτο, λόχμαισι δὲ δοκεύσαις ὑπὸ Κλεωνᾶν
    δάμασε καὶ κείνους 'Ηρακλέης ἐφ' ὁδῷ,
ὅτι πρόσθε ποτὲ Τιρύνθιον   40
ἔπερσαν αὐτῷ στρατὸν
μυχοῖς ἥμενον Ἄλιδος

                                                   'Επ. β'.

Μολίονες ὑπερφίαλοι. καὶ μὰν ξεναπάτας
35 'Επειῶν βασιλεὺς ὄπιθεν

---

25. The text is adopted by Mommsen from the *Cod. Ambr.* A; other good MSS. give βωμῶν ἐξάριθμον 'Ηρακλέης. Inferior MSS. give βίη 'Ηρακλέος, a confessed interpolation. The only objection to the text is that all the corresponding verses begin with a short syllable. This is not absolutely fatal, and if it were βωμῶν might be an early gloss, substituted for πυρῶν or some other word suggesting 'altar.' It is highly probable that a genitive followed by ἐξάριθμον is the original reading, 'Ηρακλέης having been interpolated to supply a subject which was wanting owing to a vicious full stop after πράσσοιτο, v. 30. Hermann would read βίᾳ 'Ηρ., supposing the text to have arisen from a gloss on ἐξήριτον which he regards as the original of ἐξαίρετον. For a late position of the subject cf. *Essay on style*, Ol. XIII. 14—17. For the number cf.

Ol. v. 5, βωμοὺς ἐξ διδύμους. The genitive depends on the substantive element in the compound adjective (for which compare τοσουτάριθμον), cf. Madv. § 63 d. Rem.

28. ὡς] 'That he might exact by overwhelming force in despite of the unwillingness of Augeas the wage for his service.' The ἑκὼν is added to give force to ἀέκοντα. It is clear that ὑπέρβιον is used adverbially as in Homer.

33. ἥμενον.] So MSS. and Bergk. Heyne and other editors ἥμενοι, most unnecessarily. If one alters at all ᾧ μένον suits the legend quite as well as ἥμενοι.

34. Μολίονες.] The above-mentioned Kteatos and Eurytos. The name is probably a *patronymic* from the maternal grandfather. *Il.* XI. 750 they are called Ἀκτορίωνε Μολίονε παῖδε. Homer makes them survive the contest with Hêrakles.

οὐ πολλὸν ἴδε πατρίδα πολυκτέανον ὑπὸ στερεῷ πυρὶ 45
πλαγαῖς τε σιδάρου βαθὺν εἰς ὀχετὸν ἄτας
ἴζοισαν ἑὰν πόλιν.
νεῖκος δὲ κρεσσόνων
40 ἀποθέσθ' ἄπορον.
καὶ κεῖνος ἀβουλίᾳ ὕστατος
ἁλώσιος ἀντάσαις θάνατον αἰπὺν οὐκ ἐξέφυγεν.   50

Στρ. γ'.

ὁ δ' ἄρ' ἐν Πίσᾳ ἔλσαις ὅλον τε στρατὸν
λαΐαν τε πᾶσαν Διὸς ἄλκιμος
45 υἱὸς σταθμᾶτο ζάθεον ἄλσος πατρὶ μεγίστῳ· περὶ δὲ
πάξαις Ἄλτιν μὲν ὅγ' ἐν καθαρῷ   55
διέκρινε, τὸ δὲ κύκλῳ πέδον
ἔθηκε δόρπου λύσιν,
τιμάσαις πόρον Ἀλφεοῦ

Ἀντ. γ'.

μετὰ δώδεκ' ἀνάκτων θεῶν· καὶ πάγον
50 Κρόνου προσεφθέγξατο· πρόσθε γὰρ   60
νώνυμνος, ἃς Οἰνόμαος ἄρχε, βρέχετο πολλᾷ νιφάδι.
ταύτᾳ δ' ἐν πρωτογόνῳ τελετᾷ

37. βαθύν.] 'Settling down in-
to the deep watercourse of ca-
lamity.' To be taken with πατρίδα
ὑπὸ πυρί as well as with (ὑπὸ) πλα-
γαῖς ἑὰν πόλιν which are what the
τε couples. Here we have a metă-
phor from banks and buildings
thereon being undermined by a
torrent.

39, 40.] 'Right hard is it to rid
oneself of a quarrel with higher
powers.' Cf. ἔρις κρεσσόνων, Nem.
x. 72. 'So even he through his
evil counsels at the last confronted
cupture and escaped not death's
steep.'

42. αἰπύν.] Like the Homeric
αἰπὺν ὄλεθρον. Don. compares En-
nius, aut intra muros aut extra
praecipe casu.

43. ἔλσαις.] This should be
Ϝέλσαις, cf. Pyth. IV. 233.

45. περὶ δέ.] 'And by fencing
round the Altis he marked it off'
(from the rest of the ἄλσος or
'sacred precinct')'in a clear space,
and the plain around he made a
resting-place for the evening meal
in honour of Alpheos' ford together
with the twelve sovereign deities.
And to the hill of Kronos he gave
its name.' For ἐν καθαρῷ, cf. Il.
x. 199, and for the lack of trees in
early times at Olympia, cf. Ol. III.
18—23.

47. δόρπου λύσιν.] The gen.
was originally definitive 'the even-
ing-meal halt.'

51. ἄς.] Aeolo-Doric for ἧος,
ἕως, Skt. yâvat. It is not at all

παρέσταν μὲν ἄρα Μοῖραι σχεδὸν　　　　　　65
ὅ τ᾽ ἐξελέγχων μόνος
ἀλάθειαν ἐτήτυμον
　　　　　　　　　　　　　　　　'Επ. γ´.

55 χρόνος τόδε σαφανὲς ἰὼν πόρσω κατέφρασεν,
ὅπᾳ τὰν πολέμοιο δόσιν
ἀκρόθινα διελὼν ἔθυε καὶ πενταετηρίδ᾽ ὅπως ἄρα　70
ἔστασεν ˙ἑορτὰν σὺν 'Ολυμπιάδι πρώτᾳ
νικαφορίαισί τε.
60 τίς δὴ ποταίνιον
ἔλαχε στέφανον
χείρεσσι ποσίν τε καὶ ἄρματι,
ἀγώνιον ἐν δόξᾳ θέμενος εὖχος, ἔργῳ καθελών ;　.75
　　　　　　　　　　　　　　　　Στρ. δ´.

στάδιον μὲν ἀρίστευσεν, εὐθὺν τόνον
65 ποσσὶ τρέχων, παῖς ὁ Λικυμνίου
Οἰωνός˙ ἵκεν δὲ Μιδέαθεν στρατὸν ἐλαύνων˙ ὁ δὲ
πάλᾳ κυδαίνων 'Έχεμος Τεγέαν˙　　　　80

clear what this mention of snow means. At any rate the poet seems to make two propositions in one sentence, 'it was nameless' and 'it used to be besprinkled with much snow,' or to invert 'the snowclad hill was nameless.' Now to speak of the winter aspect of the hill, which is not so high as to be under ordinary circumstances covered with snow except in winter, in connection with a summer festival, is curious: so that we may conclude that the poet has inserted a tradition of greater cold in early times. Hêrakles was supposed to be contemporary with Oenomaos' grandson Atreus.

52. The Fates assisted as at a birth, cf. Ol. vi. 42.

53. This sentence may contain a side allusion to Time having at last proved the poet true to his promise. For the sentiment, cf.

Ol. i. 31, Simonides, Frag. 175 (Bergk), οὐκ ἔστιν μείζων βάσανος χρόνου οὐδενὸς ἔργου.

55—59. The logic is not very strict; though doubtless the relics, annals, observances and associations of Olympia tended to foster belief in the story of the foundation of the games.

*57. ἀκρόθινα.] Cf. Ol. ii. 4.

63. 'Having set before him in anticipation glory in the games, having won it in deed.' Don. points out that θέσθαι with a competitor as subject is the proper correlative to τίθημι in Soph. Ajax, 572, τεύχη ἀγωνάρχαι θήσουσι 'will propose as prizes,' and to the verbal element in ἀγωνοθέτης, &c., cf. κεῖτο τέλος, Isth. i. 27. For καθελών, cf. Herod. vii. 50, μεγάλα γὰρ πρήγματα μεγάλοισι κινδύνοις ἐθέλει καταιρέεσθαι, Pyth. v. 20, εὖχος ἑλών.

66. ὁ δὲ πάλᾳ.] 'He that gat

Δόρυκλος δ᾽ ἔφερε πυγμᾶς τέλος,
Τίρυνθα ναίων πόλιν·
ἀν᾽ ἵπποισι δὲ τέτρασιν

'Αντ. δ'.

70 ἀπὸ Μαντινέας Σᾶμος ἀλιρροθίου·
ἄκοντι Φράστωρ ἔλασε σκοπόν·　　85
μᾶκος δὲ Νικεὺς ἔδικε πέτρῳ χέρα κυκλώσαις ὑπὲρ
ἁπάντων, καὶ συμμαχία θόρυβον
παραίθυξε μέγαν· ἐν δ᾽ ἕσπερον　　90
ἔφλεξεν εὐώπιδος
75 σελάνας ἐρατὸν φάος.

'Επ. δ'.

ἀείδετο δὲ πᾶν τέμενος τερπναῖσι θαλίαις
τὸν ἐγκώμιον ἀμφὶ τρόπον.
ἀρχαῖς δὲ προτέραις ἑπόμενοι καί νυν ἐπωνυμίαν χά-
ριν　　95
νίκας ἀγερώχου, κελαδησόμεθα βροντὰν
80 καὶ πυρπάλαμον βέλος

renown (for his native place) in wrestling was Echemos for Tegea.'
67. ἔφερε.] Graphic imperf. For τέλος=prize, cf. Pyth. IX. 118, Isth. I. 27.
70. Best MSS. give σᾶμ' 'Αλιρροθίου; inferior MSS. σᾶμος ἠείδετο (the latter imported from v. 76). Σᾶμος is supported by Diphilos, τρέψας δὲ πώλους ὡς ὁ Μαντινεὸς Σῆμος | ὃς πρῶτος ἅρματ' ἤλασεν παρ' 'Αλφειῷ. ἀλιρροθίου is for ὁ 'Αλιρροθίου the ι being pronounced as y, cf. Ol. II. 4, XIII. 6.
71. Phrastor and Enikeus or Nikeus (Cod. Ambr. A) are distinguished by the asyndeton and the omission of their native place. It is to be inferred that they were Lokrian heroes perhaps regarded as ancestors of Agêsidâmos. The other heroes mentioned are of Arkadia or Argolis, cf. Ol. IX. 68.

For the dat. πέτρῳ, cf. Isthm. I. 24, χερσὶν ἀκοντίζοντες αἰχμαῖς.
73. παραίθυξε.] Cf. Pyth. I. 87. ἐν δ'.] 'And meanwhile.' Apart from the suggestion of a beautiful scene, the poet calls attention to the institution of the time of year at which the games were held.
76. ἀείδετο.] This construction almost answers to our colloquial ' is besung,' cf. αὐλεῖται πᾶν μέλαθρον ' is be-fluted,' Eur. Iph. Taur. 367. θυηπολεῖται ἄστυ ' is be-sacrificed,' id. Heracl. 401. The grammatical irregularity is not unlike that of Ol. I. 95, ταχυτὰς ποδῶν ἐρίζεται. Note that in all these instances the verb is denominative.
78. ἐπωνυμίαν.] For this adj. with gen. cf. Pyth. I. 30, Ol. IX. 63.
χάριν.] ' A song,' cognate acc. with κελαδησόμεθα. For the double acc. cf. Pyth. I. 97, Ol. VII. 16.

F.　　　　　　　　　　　7

ὀρσικτύπου Διός,
ἐν ἅπαντι κράτει
αἴθωνα κεραυνὸν ἀραρότα.
χλιδῶσα δὲ μολπὰ πρὸς κάλαμον ἀντιάξει μελέων, 100

Στρ. ε΄.

85 τὰ παρ᾽ εὐκλέϊ Δίρκᾳ χρόνῳ μὲν φάνεν·
ἀλλ᾽ ὥτε παῖς ἐξ ἀλόχου πατρὶ
ποθεινὸς ἵκοντι νεότατος τὸ πάλιν ἤδη, μάλα δέ οἱ
θερμαίνει φιλότατι νόον· 105
ἐπεὶ πλοῦτος ὁ λαχὼν ποιμένα
ἐπακτὸν ἀλλότριον,
90 θνάσκοντι στυγερώτατος·

Ἀντ. ε΄.

καὶ ὅταν καλὰ ἔρξαις ἀοιδᾶς ἄτερ,
Ἀγησίδαμ᾽, εἰς Ἀΐδα σταθμὸν 110
ἀνὴρ ἵκηται, κενεὰ πνεύσαις ἔπορε μόχθῳ βραχύ τι
τερπνόν. τὶν δ᾽ ἁδυεπής τε λύρα
γλυκύς τ᾽ αὐλὸς ἀναπάσσει χάριν· 115
95 τρέφοντι δ᾽ εὐρὺ κλέος
κόραι Πιερίδες Διός.

---

83. ἀραρότα.] 'Associated with all success.' For ἀραρότα, cf. Isthm. II. 19, κλειναῖς Ἐρεχθειδᾶν χαρίτεσσιν ἀραρώς. This is the usual interpretation. Is it not rather, 'In all success appropriate'? For the sentiment cf. Pyth. IV. 197, 198. For ἐν cf. Ol. XIII. 51. The worship of Zeus the Thunderer was especially cultivated by the Epizephyrian Lokrians whose coins display the device of a thunderbolt; but the passage seems appropriate to Zeus of Olympia with whom the thunderbolt is associated.

84. 'And there shall answer to the pipe a swelling melody of song.'

85. φάνεν.] For plur. with neut.

subj. cf. Ol. II. 84, Pyth. I. 13.

87. 'When come already to youth's opposite.'

91. καί.] 'So.' Cf. Ol. VII. 7. This comparison is suggested by the poet's delay in sending this ode. Dissen infers that Agēsidāmos had become elderly. Why not just as plausibly that he was the son of his father's old age? ἔρξαις should be Ϝέρξαις, cf. our 'work.'

93, 94. We must not infer that cithern and flute were combined in the accompaniment of this ode, for if so v. 84 would be quite misleading. There is no special reference to this ode; else συν- v. 97, is without force.

'Επ. ε'.

ἐγὼ δὲ συνεφαπτόμενος σπουδᾷ, κλυτὸν ἔθνος
Λοκρῶν ἀμφέπεσον μέλιτι
εὐάνορα πόλιν καταβρέχων· παῖδ᾽ ἐρατὸν δ᾽ Ἀρχεσ-
τράτου   120
100 αἴνησα, τὸν εἶδον κρατέοντα χερὸς ἀλκᾷ
βωμὸν παρ᾽ Ὀλύμπιον·
κεῖνον κατὰ χρόνον
ἰδέᾳ τε καλὸν
ὥρᾳ τε κεκραμένον, ἅ ποτε
105 ἀναιδέα Γανυμήδει πότμον ἄλαλκε σὺν Κυπρογενεῖ. 125

97. 'And I with them zeal-
ously applying myself did honour
to the Lokrians' famous tribe by
besprinkling with honey a city
happy in her sons.'

104. κεκραμένον.] Cf. Ol. i. 22,
Pyth. x. 41.
105. ἀναιδής.] Equivalent to
improbus, 'with no sense of pro-
priety,' and so 'ruthless.'

OLYMPIA XII.

ON THE VICTORY OF ERGOTELES OF HIMERA IN THE LONG FOOT-RACE.

INTRODUCTION.

ERGOTELES, son of Philânor, had been driven from Knôsos in Krête by civil disturbances and settled in Himera, of which colony he had become a citizen, and had already won two Pythian victories, the last B.C. 474, and two Isthmian victories when he won this Olympian victory, the first of two, B.C. 472. He also won twice at Nemea. The year before this ode was written Hiero had assisted the Himeraeans in expelling the tyrant Thrasydaeos, son of Thêro. Either on this occasion or before, on freeing themselves from the tyranny of Terillos, a temple was dedicated to Zeus the Liberator. The ode was probably sung in the temple of Tychê. Pindar composed it when in Sicily soon after the victory. The rhythm is a mixture of Dorian and Lydian.

ANALYSIS.

vv.
1, 2.   Prayer that Tychê will cherish Himera,
3—5.   For she guides ships, wars, public councils.
5—9.   Men's hopes, however, are tossed like ships at sea, and indications of the future are obscure.
10—12.   Good and bad befall men in unexpected alternation.
13—16.   Had not Ergoteles suffered banishment he would not have won fame,
17—19.   But as it is, he has been successful at great games and exalted his adopted city.

Στρ.

Λίσσομαι, παῖ Ζηνὸς Ἐλευθερίου,
Ἱμέραν εὐρυσθενέ ἀμφιπόλει, Σώτειρα Τύχα·
τὶν γὰρ ἐν πόντῳ κυβερνῶνται θοαὶ
νᾶες, ἐν χέρσῳ τε λαιψηροὶ πόλεμοι   5
5 κἀγοραὶ βουλαφόροι. αἵ γε μὲν ἀνδρῶν
πόλλ᾽ ἄνω, τὰ δ᾽ αὖ κάτω ψεύδη μεταμώνια τάμνοισαι
κυλίνδοντ᾽ ἐλπίδες·

Ἀντ.

σύμβολον δ᾽ οὔ πώ τις ἐπιχθονίων   10
πιστὸν ἀμφὶ πράξιος ἐσσομένας εὗρεν θεόθεν·

2. εὐρυσθενέα.] This should be
taken proleptically; otherwise it
is outrageously flattering.

Σώτειρα.] Cf. Ol. VIII. 21, Aesch.
Agam. 647 (P.) τύχη δὲ σωτὴρ ναῦν
θέλουσ᾽ ἐφέζετο.

Τύχα.] According to Pausanias
(VII. 26), Pindar in a hymn to
Tychê made her one of the Fates,
who are called daughters of Zeus
and Themis by Hêsiod, while Tychê
is daughter of Okeanos. She is a
personification of the Course of
Events or of Vicissitude, not of un-
intelligent, undetermined Chance.
The Hellênic conception of ' For-
tune' is well illustrated by the fol-
lowing verses, Frag. Adesp. 139
Bergk.

...... Τύχα, μερόπων ἀρχὰ
καὶ τέρμα· τὺ καὶ σοφίας θακεῖς ἕδρας,
καὶ τιμὰν βροτέοις ἐπέθηκας ἔργοις·
καὶ τὸ καλὸν πλέον ἢ κακὸν ἐκ σέθεν,
ἅ τε χάρις λάμπει περὶ σὰν πτέρυγα
χρυσέαν.
καὶ τὸ τεᾷ πλάστιγγι δοθὲν μακαρι-
στότατον τελέθει.
τὸ δ᾽ ἀμαχανίας πόρον εἶδες ἐν ἀλγε-
σιν,
καὶ λαμπρὸν φάος ἄγαγες ἐν σκότῳ,
προφερεστάτα θεῶν.

4. λαιψηροί.] 'Speedily deci-
sive,' opposed to βουλαφόροι. The
Himeraeans had had two conspicu-
ous examples of speedily decisive
wars, in that terminated by the
great battle of Himera and in their
contest with Thrasydaeos. It is
probable that λαιψ-ηρὸς is from RIP
a phase of the root RAP whence
ἀρπαλέος, rapidus, &c. For the ex-
tension of the root by a sibilant,
cf. ἔψω.

πόλεμοι.] Prof. Paley compares
Thuk. I. 140, and on ἀγοραὶ βουλα-
φόροι says, 'in public councils it
was a formula to commence ἀγαθῇ
τύχῃ, "May this prove lucky to the
state," etc. See Aristoph. Thesm.
350.' The deliberative assemblies
of the Himeraeans would probably
be oligarchic.

5. αἵ γε.] 'At least'—i.e. even
if I have exaggerated the influence
of Τύχα, it is certain that—'men's
hopes are tossed ofttimes up but at
other times again down as they
plough a sea of vain illusions.' For
πόλλ᾽—τὰ δ᾽, cf. Nem. IX. 43, πολλὰ
μὲν ἐν κονίᾳ χέρσῳ, τὰ δὲ γείτονι
πόντῳ φάσομαι. For τάμνοισαι, cf.
Pyth. III. 68, Ἰονίαν τέμνων θάλασ-
σαν, Hor. Od. I. 1. 14, Myrtoum
pavidus nauta secet mare. Don. cites
a similar passage from Spenser's
Faerie Queen Bk. IV, canto 3, st. 1.

8. πιστόν.] Here the word does
not mean ' credible' so much as

τῶν δὲ μελλόντων τετύφλωνται φραδαί.

10 πολλὰ δ' ἀνθρώποις παρὰ γνώμαν ἔπεσεν,
   ἔμπαλιν μὲν τέρψιος, οἱ δ' ἀνιαραῖς   15
   ἀντικύρσαντες ζάλαις ἐσλὸν βαθὺ πήματος ἐν μικρῷ
   πεδάμειψαν χρόνῳ.

                                              'Επ.

   υἱὲ Φιλάνορος, ἤτοι καὶ τεά κεν
   ἐνδομάχας ἅτ' ἀλέκτωρ συγγόνῳ παρ' ἑστίᾳ   20

'clear,' 'unmistakable.' Cf. τὸ δ'
ἐκ Διὸς ἀνθρώποις σαφὲς οὐχ ἕπεται
τέκμαρ, Nem. xi. 43, a frag. of Hes.,
Μάντις δ' οὐδάς ἐστιν ἐπιχθονίων
ἀνθρώπων, ὅστις ἂν εἰδείη Ζηνὸς νόον
αἰγιόχοιο. Pindar did not doubt
that oracles and omens were truly
fulfilled, cf. ἀληθείας 'oracular
truth,' Ol. viii. 2; but he doubt-
less felt that their practical utility
was considerably impaired by their
obscurity and vagueness.

9. 'For signs of events to come
have been darkened;' i.e. oracles
and omens and even ordinary
means of forecasting the future
have been enveloped in obscurity
and uncertainty. Cf. Hor. Od. iii.
29. 29, *Prudens futuri temporis
exitum | caliginosa nocte premit
deus.*

10. ἔπεσεν.] The mss. give σ
except in two instances, namely
πετοῖσαι, Ol. vii. 69, πετόντεσσιν,
Pyth. v. 48, there being a sibilant
in the termination in both cases,
so that the variety is probably due
to the principle of dissimilation.
The metaphor is from dice-throw-
ing.

11. ἔμπαλιν μέν.] i.e. τοῖς μὲν
ἔμπ. κ.τ.λ. For the phrase, cf.
ἔμπ. γνώμας, Pyth. xii. 32.

12. ζάλαις.] Fick with proba-
ble correctness takes ζάλη to be
for ζασλη for yaslā from √YAS
whence ζέω, ζωμός. Here it means
the waves that break over a storm-
tossed ship.

ἐσλόν.] 'Have got rich blessings

in exchange for misery.' Cf. Pyth.
iii. 96, ἐκ καμάτων μεταμειψάμενοι
χάριν Διός. For βαθύ, cf. Ol. xiii.
62. It is a mistake to suppose that
πεδά and μετά are etymologically
connected. All analogies of pho-
netic change are against it.

14. ἐνδομάχας.] 'As a cock whose
battles are confined to the poultry
yard,' if we compare Aesch. *Agam.*
1671, κόμπασον θαρσῶν, ἀλέκτωρ
ὥστε θηλείας πέλας. Cf. *Eum.* 861—
866. But I prefer 'who fights only
in private matches' as being a more
appropriate simile for one who
would have taken part in regular
contests but in the comparatively
private arenas of Krête. Cf. Xen.
Anab. iv. 8. 27 for Krêtan pedes-
trianism. Cock-fighting and quail-
fighting were popular pastimes in
Hellas. Themistokles seems to
have thought that the spectacle of
the game-cock's indomitable pug-
macity afforded a good education,
as in his time public exhibitions
were established by law at Athens.
Note the nominative ἀλέκτωρ in-
stead of ἀλέκτορος τιμά, on the
principle of *comparatio compendi-
aria,* cf. Ol. i. 7. The coins of
Himera bore the figure of a cock
which was sacred to Asklêpios (cf.
v. 19) and to Athêne (Pausan. vi.
26) and may have had reference to
the name 'Ιμέρα=ἡμέρα according
to Plato. The bird may have been
the *totem* or tribal symbol of an
influential section of the settlers.

15 ἀκλεὴς τιμὰ κατεφυλλορόησεν ποδῶν,
  εἰ μὴ στάσις ἀντιάνειρα Κνωσίας σ' ἄμερσε πάτρας.
  νῦν δ' Ὀλυμπίᾳ στεφανωσάμενος   25
  καὶ δὶς ἐκ Πυθῶνος Ἰσθμοῖ τ', Ἐργότελες,
  θερμὰ Νυμφᾶν λουτρὰ βαστάζεις, ὁμιλέων παρ' οἰκ-
      είαις ἀρούραις.

15. 'Your rewards for speed of foot would have shed their leaves and left no renown.' Even if τιμὰ be rendered 'glory,' 'credit,' 'prowess,' the fact that the first outward 'symbol' thereof was a crown makes κατεφυλλορόησε (a word probably coined by Pindar) appropriate. The Krêtans for some cause unknown did not compete often in the great games of Greece.

17. στεφανωσάμενος.] Cf. Ol. vii. 81.

18. τ'.] This couples Ἰσθμοῖ to ἐκ Πυθῶνος, δὶς applying to each, cf. Ol. iii. 8, vii. 82.

19. The Nymphs are said to have produced the hot springs of Himera for Hêrakles at Athêne's request. The bird of Asklêpios very likely symbolised the healing virtue of these springs.

βαστάζεις.] 'Thou dost exalt the Nymphs' hot springs, dwelling hard by no alien fields.' Ergoteles may have found Krêtans settled at Himera. For βαστ. cf. χρὴ κωμάζοντα χαρίτεσσι βαστάσαι, Isth. iii. 8.

OLYMPIA XIII.

ON THE VICTORIES OF XENOPHON OF KORINTH IN THE SHORT FOOT-RACE AND THE QUINQUERTIUM.

INTRODUCTION.

THE two victories specially commemorated in this difficult ode were gained B.C. 464. Considering that Xenophon had just won two Olympian victories—a very distinguished success—very little is said about him; so that I think the ode was composed for a public commemoration by the Oligaethidae of all their victories on the occasion of this crowning triumph (see *v.* 49). It is generally supposed to have been sung on the victor's public entrance into Korinth on his return from Olympia. Xenophon's family, the Oligaethidae, were oligarchs, and contributed members to the Korinthian γερουσία. From *vv.* 9, 10 it has been inferred that the commonalty had been making some unsuccessful attempts to overthrow the oligarchical constitution. The rhythm is Lydian and Aeolian.

ANALYSIS.

vv.

1—5. While praising the victor's family, thrice victorious at Olympia, the poet will recognise the merits of the men of Korinthos,

6—10. Where the Hôrae, Good-government, Justice and Peace, dwell and keep down popular discontent.

11, 12. The poet's noble theme shall be boldly and honestly treated.

13—23. Praise of the Korinthians for athletic prowess, inventive faculty, musical taste and warlike spirit.

24—29. Prayer to Zeus to preserve the people and to receive graciously Xenophon's Kômos.

29—34. Enumeration of his victories—

35—40. Of his father's victories—

40—46. Of his relatives' victories.

47, 48. Moderation is best in everything.

49—62. Praise of the ancestral heroes of Korinth, Sisyphos, Mêdea, Glaukos.

63—92. Myth of Bellerophon.

93—95. The poet checks his mythical digression with a metaphor from javelin throwing.

96—113. Enumeration of victories of the Oligaethidae introduced by a reference to *vv.* 40—46. [The previous mention of Pythian victories, *v.* 43, is here forgotten, and they are mentioned *v.* 106.]

114, 115. Prayer to Zeus that the success of the family may continue and that they may be respected and prosperous.

There seems to be a striving after obscurity in this ode, *vv.* 18—22 containing three questions which are almost riddles. This peculiarity may be due to Pindar's deliberately accommodating himself to Korinthian taste.

Στρ. α΄.

Τρισολυμπιονίκαν
ἐπαινέων οἶκον ἄμερον ἀστοῖς,
ξένοισι θὲ θεράποντα, γνώσομαι

1. The epithet is justified by Xenophon's two victories, *vv.* 29, 30, and the single success of his father, Thessalos, *vv.* 35, 36. It is used in extension of the predicate, cf. Ol. vii. 15.

2. ἀστοῖς.] The word seems here to mean the commonalty as distinguished from the aristocratic families.

3. γνώσομαι.] 'I shall recognize Korinth the prosperous, portal of Poteidan of the Isthmos, as glorious in her youth.' The article introduces a constant epithet of Korinth (cf. Thuk. i. 13), which city, says the poet, will henceforth be rather associated in his mind with the epithet ἀγλαόκουρον. The future tense perhaps led to the causative interpretation of the Schol. εἰς ἀνάμνησιν ἀνάξω, cf. Ol. vi. 89. Don. renders 'I will make known, I will celebrate.' For the respective positions of γνώσομαι and ἀγλαόκουρον, cf. Ol. vii. 15. The first element of the compound has its special bearing shown by νικαφόρον ἀγλαΐαν, *v.* 14. As this is the only passage of Pindar where

τὰν ὀλβίαν Κόρινθον, Ἰσθμίου
5 πρόθυρον Ποτειδᾶνος, ἀγλαόκουρον.   5
ἐν τᾷ γὰρ Εὐνομία ναίει, κασιγνήτα τε, βάθρον πο-
      λίων, ἀσφαλὴς
Δίκα καὶ ὁμότροπος Εἰράνα, ταμίαι ἀνδράσι πλού-
      του,   10
χρύσεαι παῖδες εὐβούλου Θέμιτος·

MSS. give Ποτειδᾶν, as do a majority of the best here, we must conclude that the Poet purposely gave the Korinthian form of the name. See Essay on Dialect.

6. ἀσφαλής.] Most editors read ἀσφαλὲς with comma after instead of before. I follow MSS.; as βάθρον needs no epithet and ὁμότροπος seems to refer to an expressed attribute of Δίκα. Note that only Justice and Peace are the *foundation* of cities, Good-government being raised on these. There is a similar separation of Εὐνομία from the other two sisters in the interesting fragment (Frag. Adesp. 140, Bergk), Κλωθὼ Λάχεσίς τ' εὐώλενοι | κοῦραι νυκτός, | εὐχομένων ἐπακούσατ', οὐράνιαι χθόνιαί τε δαίμονες· | ὦ πανδείμαντοι, πέμπετ' ἄμμιν | ῥοδόκολπον Εὐνομίαν λιπαροθρόνους τ' ἀδελφάς, Δίκαν | καὶ στεφανηφόρον Εἰράναν. | πόλιν τε τάνδε βαρυφρόνων λελάθοιτε συντυχιᾶν. There ῥοδόκολπον is an epithet of Spring, cf. Isth. III. 36. I think that this is part of a hymn on the occasion of the resettlement of a colony under the auspices of Delphi. Hence the *two* Fates, cf. Paus. x. 24. From *v.* 17 we gather that these three 'dispensers of wealth to men, golden daughters of well-counselling Themis' are the Ὧραι of Hēsiod, *Theog.* 901 sqq. Δεύτερον ἠγάγετο λιπαρὴν Θέμιν, ἣ τέκεν Ὧρας | Εὐνομίην τε Δίκην τε καὶ Εἰρήνην τεθαλυῖαν, | αἵτ' ἔργ' ὠρεύουσι καταθνητοῖσι βροτοῖσι. The

seasons, goddesses of the orderly divisions of the year, are naturally daughters of the goddess of universal order and right, who again is the mother of the personifications of the three kinds of moral and social order. These then got the name Ὧραι as being children of the mother of the Ὧραι. The attempted derivation of Ὧραι from ὠρ-ενειν (ὥρα) shows that the poet was puzzled at the not very obvious connection between the moral and physical ideas thus confused in the later mythology. Ὧρα is connected with our 'year,' ὥρα with our 'ware' 'ward.' Note that ταμίαι is from ταμία not ταμίας. The diphthong -αι is elided in scansion, or the ι is slurred, or there is an unusual aphaeresis or synezesis. The only certain instance cited of elision of the nom. plur. diphthong is Hom. *Il.* XI. 272, ὀξεῖ' ὀδύναι, while the instances of slurred vowels are usually either after a long syllable or before a naturally short syllable; but cf. Ol. XI. [X.] 70. The newer MSS. scanned the last syllable of ταμίαι and altered the corresponding lines throughout the ode accordingly. Hermann follows them with two or three modifications of his own (*Opusc.* vol. VIII. p. 122—124).

7. ὁμότροπος.] 'Of like character' to Δίκα, i. e. equally averse from violence and contention and equally safe and trustworthy.

’Αντ. α’.

ἐθέλοντι δ’ ἀλεξεῖν
10 Ὕβριν, Κόρου ματέρα θρασύμυθον.
ἔχω καλά τε φράσαι, τόλμα τέ μοι
εὐθεῖα γλῶσσαν ὀρνύει λέγειν. 15
ἄμαχον δὲ κρύψαι τὸ συγγενὲς ἦθος.
ὔμμιν δέ, παῖδες Ἀλάτα, πολλὰ μὲν νικαφόρον ἀγ-
λαΐαν ὤπασαν

10. Cf. the oracle of Bakis, Herod. VIII. 77, δῖα Δίκη σβέσσει κρατερὸν Κόρον, Ὕβριος υἱόν. There is some MS. support for the Aldine reading θρασύθυμον: but the text helps the transition from political to poetical moderation. This Κόρος is that of Ol. II. 95, Nem. x. 20, the disgust others feel, there unjustly at success, here more justly at arrogance; while elsewhere it is surfeit or satiety felt by the successful or prosperous, which is the parent of Ὕβρις, Theognis 153, τίκτει τοι κόρος ὕβριν, ὅταν κακῷ ὄλβος ἕπηται | ἀνθρώπῳ, καὶ ὅτῳ μὴ νόος ἄρτιος ᾖ, cf. Solon Frag. 8.

11. Cf. Ol. IX. 80—82.

12. εὐθεῖα.] The Scholl. Vett. are divided as to whether this is fem. sing. or neut. plur. acc. The position of the first τε seems conclusive in favour of the latter, so that καλὰ φράσαι be balanced by εὐθεῖα λέγειν. For the form εὐθεῖα, cf. οὖρον εὐκλεῖα, Nem. VI. 30, πνοιᾶς, Ol. III. 31. The iota is probably a clerical method based on false analogy of representing the pronouncing of F as a vowel, cf. Epic θείειν, πλείειν, Curt. §§ 506, 507. Render 'I have a noble theme to rehearse and boldness prompts my tongue to give it straightforward utterance.' The epithet εὐθεῖα applied to τόλμα is otiose unless it be taken to mean 'just,' 'honest' in any sense of the terms except 'straightforward,' a resort quite unsupported by Pindaric usage, in which the physical meaning of εὐθύς seems never to be lost sight of. Moreover simply to speak of glorious deeds scarcely needed justice and boldness, but to make the greater part of an ode a straightforward enumeration of great achievements was obviously a bold undertaking both on the score of the skill required and the risk of Κόρος involved. The next verse is a plea in justification of running this risk.

13. κρύψαι.] For inf. cf. Ol. VII. 25. Dissen takes τὸ σύγγενες ἦθος to refer to Pindar who delights in difficulties. There may be a side glance in this direction, but I take the direct bearing to be on what follows, the δὲ of v. 14 introducing the particular instance of the general principle.

14. ὔμμιν.] Dat. commodi whether or no it be remote object of ὤπασαν. I take it with both clauses, and make ἀρεταῖς the indirect object of ὤπασαν rather than a dat. modi with ὑπερελθόντων.

παῖδες Ἀλάτα.] The Dorians of Korinth or the Korinthians generally are loosely called sons of the Herakleid founder or hero king Alêtes. But this designation makes it probable that the Oligaethidae considered themselves of Herakleid extraction.

15 ἄκραις ἀρεταῖς ὑπερελθόντων ἱεροῖς ἐν ἀέθλοις,   20
   πολλὰ δ᾽ ἐν καρδίαις ἀνδρῶν ἔβαλον

'Επ. α᾽.

'Ωραι πολυάνθεμοι ἀρχαῖα σοφίσμαθ᾽. ἅπαν δ᾽ εὑ-
   ρόντος ἔργον.
   ταὶ Διωνύσου πόθεν ἐξέφανεν   25

15. ὑπερελθόντων.] It is better
to take this genitive as governed by
ἀρεταῖς than as absolute. Either
the last element of the compound
νικαφόρον is quiescent or it means
'brought by victory' instead of the
usual 'bringing, winning victory,'
cf. Isth. I. 22, στεφάνων νικαφόρων.
Render 'offered festivity of victory
to your achievements as first prize-
men when ye have surpassed in
sacred games.' Dissen makes ὑπερ-
ελθόντων depend on ἀγλαΐαν 'of
such as have surpassed.'

16. ἀνδρῶν.] Still the Korinth-
ians, but only the fullgrown men,
to whom inventive success is con-
fined, while youths and boys can
win prizes in games.

17. ἀρχαῖα.] Equivalent to an
adverbial phrase with ἔβαλον. The
idiom is common enough when the
adjective agrees with the subject
(Madv. § 86 a, Rem.), and for an
exact parallel cf. Soph. Oed. Kol.
441, ἤλαυνέ μ᾽ ἐκ γῆς χρόνιον, Ol.
XIV. 11.

ἅπαν.] 'To an (original) inven-
tor is due every result (of his dis-
covery).' i.e. in any craft an
original discoverer or inventor
should have the credit of subse-
quent improvements on his dis-
covery.

18, 19. 'Whence appeared the
Graces of Dionysos in connection
with the bull-driving dithyramb?'
The answer to this question is
Arion of Mêthymna, who according
to Hêrodotos, I. 23, was said by
the Korinthians to have first
composed and given its name to

the Dithyramb at Korinth. Two
Scholl. Vett. on this passage of
Pindar tell us that Arion first
instituted the κύκλιος χορὸς and
arranged it. This statement pro-
bably means that he introduced
regular choral singing in addition
to the chant which accompanied
the dance in ring round the altar
of Dionysos, and which judging
from the Fragment of Archilochos
(77 [38], 'Ὡς Διωνύσοι᾽ ἄνακτος
καλὸν ἐξάρξαι μέλος | οἶδα διθύραμ-
βον, οἴνῳ συγκεραυνωθεὶς φρένας,)
was probably trochaic tetrameter,
cf. Arist. Poet. I. iv. A Schol.
Vet. tells us that Pindar ascribes
the first invention of the Dithy-
ramb to Naxos in his Hyporchê-
mata, to Thebes in his first Dithy-
ramb and to Korinth here. Now
this statement as regards this pas-
sage is not strictly accurate, so that
there is room for suspecting that
Pindar did not contradict himself.
He may have regarded the inven-
tion of the orchestric dithyramb or
cyclic dance as due to Naxos, the
old poetic dithyramb to Thebes
and the Doric dithyramb in the
later limited sense to Arion. The
poetic dithyramb in the old com-
prehensive sense is the vocal per-
formance including the utterances
of the satyric chorus and the germ
of the Doric dithyramb too. Com-
bining these statements with that
of Suidas that Arion was τραγικοῦ
τρόπου εὑρετὴς 'inventor of a tragic
(Satyric ?) style' and with that of
Aristotle, Problem. XIX. 15, δι᾽ ὅτι
οἱ διθύραμβοι, ἐπειδὴ μιμητικοὶ ἐγέ-

σὺν βοηλάτᾳ Χάριτες Διθυράμβῳ;

τοῦτο, οὐκ ἔτι ἔχουσιν ἀντιστρόφους, πρότερον δ' εἶχον, we may infer that Arion separated the less solemn performances of the Satyric chorus with flute accompaniment from the Dithyramb, which received at his hands the accompaniment of the Doric cithern and became a recital of some tragic episode, dispensing with division into strophe and antistrophe. I suspect some reaction against the recitative character of the Doric dithyramb is alluded to in Pindar, Frag. 54 A, [47], πρὶν μὲν εἶρπε σχοινοτένειά τ' ἀοιδὰ διθυράμβων | καὶ τὸ σὰν κίβδαλον ἀνθρώποισιν ἀπὸ στομάτων. By πρὶν the period before Lasos of Hermionê is probably meant. I give this long note and the next because Don. and K. O. Müller seem not to have made enough of the literary importance of this passage and the Scholia thereon. The suggestion which I now venture to make, that tragedy borrowed its form from the Satyric chorus, its matter from the Doric dithyramb, will perhaps clear up some of the perplexities which hamper the question of the origin of the drama.

19. βοηλάτᾳ.] Don. suggests that this epithet refers to the symbolical identification of Dionysos with the bull. He is supported by the Elean hymn given by Plutarch, Qu. Gr. 36, ἐλθεῖν ἥρω Διόνυσε, | ἅλιον ἐς ναὸν ἀγνὸν | σὺν χαρίτεσσιν ἐς ναὸν | τῷ βοέῳ ποδὶ θύων. | Ἄξιε ταῦρε Ἄξιε ταῦρε. Cookesley rightly points out that φάνηθι ταῦρος, Eur. Bacch. 1017 (P.) (cf. 920, 1159) taken with the context refers generally to Dionysos' power of self-transformation, but the other two passages show that in the play Dionysos did put on a taurine semblance. Plutarch asks with respect to the hymn, πότερον ὅτι καὶ βουγενῆ προσαγορεύουσιν καὶ

ταῦρον ἔνιοι τὸν θεόν; this general statement suggests that he did not interpret this passage of Pindar in this way, else he would probably have quoted it. I prefer the explanation of the Schol. Vet. referring it to the prize for the dithyramb being a bull, which is supported by Simonides, Frag. 145 [202], ἐξ ἐπὶ πεντήκοντα, Σιμωνίδη, ἥραο ταύρους | καὶ τρίποδας, πρὶν τόνδ' ἀνθέμεναι πίνακα· | τοσσάκι δ' ἱμερόεντα διδαξάμενος χορὸν ἀνδρῶν | εὐδόξου Νίκας ἀγλαὸν ἅρμ' ἐπέβης. This clearly refers to dithyrambs, as is shown by Frags. 147 [203], 148 [205]. I think it is very probable that by the epithet the poet implies that the prize of a bull was first given for the Arionic dithyramb. This supposition hangs very well with that of his having separated the specific dithyramb (παλαία τραγῳδία of the Orchomenian Inscr.) from the lighter satyric dances and songs. That a more valuable prize should be instituted when tyrants such as Periander and Kleisthenes patronised the Dionysiac worship is a priori probable. The γρῖφος of Simonides, Frag. 172 [230], from Athênaeos x. p. 456 c, seems to refer to Arion and therefore the word βουφόνον supports my view. The riddle is as follows:

Μιξονόμου τε πατὴρ ἐρίφου καὶ σχέτ-
    λιος ἰχθὺς
πλησίον ἡρείσαντο καρήατα· παῖδα δὲ
    νυκτὸς
δεξάμενοι βλεφάροισι, Διωνύσοιο ἄ-
    νακτος
βουφόνον οὐκ ἐθέλουσι τιθηνεῖσθαι
    θεράποντα.

Athênaeos gives two explanations: one that a work of art representating a τράγος and δελφὶς is meant while Διων. βου. θερ. is the dithyramb. I think that there is a play on νομὸς and νόμος in Μιξονόμου and that the τράγος is a Satyr

20 τίς γὰρ ἱππείοις ἐν ἔντεσσιν μέτρα,
   ἢ θεῶν ναοῖσιν οἰωνῶν βασιλέα δίδυμον

asleep on a Dolphin, either representing Arion or suggested by the
well-known legend.

Χάριτες.] For these attendants
of Dionysos see the Elean hymn
quoted above, Simonides, Frag.
148 [205] 10; while for the meaning 'songs' cf. Isth. III. 8, χρὴ δὲ
κωμάζοντ' ἀγαναῖς χαρίτεσσιν βασ
τάσαι. The poet probably had in
mind both meanings.

20. τίς γάρ.] As in the formula
τί γάρ;—the particle assumes that
the expected answer is given to
the preceding question and claims
it still more confidently for the
next. 'Aye and who invented artificial paces in horse riding and
driving, or on gods' temples placed
the twin eagles? Korinth. And
therein flourishes sweetly-breathing Song, and therein Ares with
her young warriors' deadly spears.
Supreme wide-ruling (Zeus) of
Olympia become unenvious for all
time of my verses, Father Zeus,
and while ruling this people with
unharmful sway, keep steady the
favouring gale of Xenophon's destiny, and accept at his hands the
customary festive-celebration of his
crowns.'

μέτρα.] Böckh explains 'justus
modulus, rectaque dimensio fraenorum ac commoda ratio.' Don. after
Heyne renders 'who added to the
harness of horses the means of
guiding them?'; citing Aesch.
Choeph. 796, where however μέτρον
seems to mean 'limit,' and Pind.
Frag. 84 [74], Ἀκτὶς Ἀελίου....
πολύσκοπ' ἐμαῖς θέαις μέτρ' ὀμμάτων,
Böckh's correction of ἐμῆς θεῷ μ'
ἄτερ ὀμμάτων. The suggestion is
therefore really unsupported. Moreover it makes the prep. ἐν needless.
I hold that μέτρα means the results
of the bridle, 'measures,' 'artificial
paces,' thus coming near to the

prosody meanings, as Böckh's explanation, though less forced than
Heyne's, is tame and at variance
with the subsequent account of the
revelation of the bridle to Bellerophon. According to the Schol.
Vet. Didymos referred the line to
the invention of the potter's wheel
by Hyperbios of Korinth, which led
to the invention of measures of
capacity by Pheidon. But according to one account the ἔντεα
are 'wheels,' according to another
'measures,' τὰ Φειδώνεια ἀγγεῖα,
ἱππείοις standing for Ἀργείοις.
More absurd attempts to force an
author's language into conformity
with other traditions relating to
his theme will not easily be found.

21. The ἀκρωτήριον or ornament on the top angle of the pediment was often an eagle and
hence was called ἀετός, cf. Arist.
Av. 1110, τὰς γὰρ ὑμῶν οἰκίας ἐρέ
ψομεν πρὸς ἀετόν, Paus. III. 17, ἡ δὲ
πρὸς δυσμὰς ἔχει τῶν στοῶν ἀετοὺς
τε δύο τοὺς ὄρνιθας καὶ ἴσας ἐπ'
αὐτοῖς Νίκας. Pliny, N. H. xxxv.
43, speaking of the inventions of
Dibutades of Sikyon at Korinth,
says Hinc et fastigia templorum
orta. Mr Simcox, on Tac. Hist. III.
71, confuses the sustinentes fastigium aquilae with the ἀετοί, fastigia. It is probable that the
pediment from being finished off
with an ἀετὸς got called ἀέτωμα
and that the latter word was rendered aquila by Latin architects.
From the passage of Pliny above
mentioned, I infer that Pindar
speaks of the ἀκρωτήριον as representing the ornamentation of the
entablature generally, which ornamentation was originally clay-work.
Fergusson's opinion is that the
employment of sculpture was the
essential feature of the Doric style
of architecture.

ἐπέθηκ'; ἐν δὲ Μοῖσ' ἀδύπνοος,   30
ἐν δ' Ἄρης ἀνθεῖ νέων οὐλίαις αἰχμαῖσιν ἀνδρῶν.
                                         Στρ. β'.

ὕπατ' εὐρυανάσσων
25 Ὀλυμπίας, ἀφθόνητος ἔπεσσιν   35
γένοιο χρόνον ἅπαντα, Ζεῦ πάτερ,
καὶ τόνδε λαὸν ἀβλαβῆ νέμων
Ξενοφῶντος εὔθυνε δαίμονος οὖρον·
δέξαι δέ οἱ στεφάνων ἐγκώμιον τεθμόν, τὸν ἄγει πεδίων
    ἐκ Πίσας,   40
30 πενταέθλῳ ἅμα σταδίου νικῶν δρόμον· ἀντεβόλησεν
τῶν ἀνὴρ θνατὸς οὔπω τις πρότερον.
                                          Ἀντ. β'.

δύο δ' αὐτὸν ἔρεψαν
πλόκοι σελίνων ἐν Ἰσθμιάδεσσιν   45

22. ἐπέθηκε.] I take this verb to be used with *zeugma.*

Μοῖσ'.] This refers to the poetic and musical taste displayed at Korinth in Pindar's day, not as Dissen thinks to Eumělos, Aeson and Korinthian poets of all ages; since that topic has already been dismissed *vv.* 18, 19 with the allusion to Korinth's most renowned poet. The suppression of the object to ἐν is noteworthy.

24. εὐρύ.] A Scholiast, observing the impropriety of applying 'widely' to 'ruling over' a limited district renders this word μεγάλως κραταιῶς. However the true government of Ὀλυμπίας is ὕπατε Ὀ. Ζεῦ πάτερ, cf. Aesch. *Ag.* 492 (P.), ὑπατός τε χώρας Ζεύς.

26. γένοιο.] Cf. Pyth. II. 72, note.

27. ἀβλαβῆ.] Extension of the predicative participle νέμων.

28. For metaphor cf. Aesch. *Pers.* 603, ὅταν δ' ὁ δαίμων εὐροῇ, πεποιθέναι | τὸν αὐτὸν ἀεὶ δαίμον' οὐριεῖν τύχης. *Septem c. Theb.* 702,

δαίμων...ἴσως ἂν ἔλθοι θελεμωτέρῳ πνεύματι, Ol. VII. 95. Render ἐγκώμιον τεθμὸν as if τέθμιον κῶμον, cf. Ol. VII. 88.

29. οἱ.] Cf. Pyth. IV. 23.

30. πενταέθλῳ.] Simonides enumerates the games of the quinquertium, most probably in their order, thus—Ἴσθμια, καὶ Πυθοῖ Διοφῶν ὁ Φίλωνος ἐνίκα | ἅλμα, ποδωκείην, δίσκον, ἄκοντα, πάλην.

ἀντεβόλησεν.] MSS. Rec. read οὐκ ἀντ. The phrase is modest, suggesting 'luck' rather than 'merit.' Cf. Frag. 14. [16.] ἐν ἔργμασι δὲ νικᾷ τύχα, | οὐ σθένος. It is not certain whether Xenophon was the first to win two prizes at once at Olympia or to win these particular prizes; but the latter is most likely.

33. σελίνων.] According to Schol. Rec. wreaths of dried parsley were given in addition to wreaths of pine leaves at the Isthmian games. Wreaths of green parsley were given at the Nemean games. These two festivals were originally *epita-*

φανέντα· Νέμεά τ' οὐκ ἀντιξοεῖ·
35 πατρὸς δὲ Θεσσαλοῖ' ἐπ' Ἀλφεοῦ
ῥεέθροισιν αἴγλα ποδῶν ἀνάκειται,
Πυθοῖ τ' ἔχει σταδίου τιμὰν διαύλου τ' ἀελίῳ ἀμφ' ἑνί,
μηνός τέ οἱ   50
τωὐτοῦ κρανααῖς ἐν Ἀθάναισι τρία ἔργα ποδαρκὴς
ἀμέρα θῆκε κάλλιστ' ἀμφὶ κόμαις,   55

Ἐπ. β'.

40 Ἑλλώτια δ' ἑπτάκις· ἐν δ' ἀμφιάλοισι Ποτειδᾶνος
τεθμοῖσιν

phit, on which account parsley,
a plant sacred to the gods of the
underworld, was used. Sisyphos is
said, Frag. 2. [1.], to have founded
the Isthmian games ἀποφθιμένῳ
Μελικέρτᾳ.

34. ἀντιξοεῖ.] Apparently a vb.
of Pindar's coinage from ἀντίξοος
which I take to mean literally
'scraping against,' i.e. rubbing or
planing the wrong way so as to
roughen instead of smoothing.
Render 'and Nemea showeth no
unkindly mood.' Probably Nemea
is here the tutelary nymph. The
form Νέμεά is Aeolic, cf. Κύκνειά,
Ol. xi. [x.] 15, πάτριά (?), Ol. vi. 62.

36. αἴγλα.] 'Is glory from his
feet treasured up.' For αἴγλα, cf.
Pyth. iii. 73, viii. 96; and for
the phrase, cf. τιμὰ ποδῶν, Ol. xii.
15. For ἀνάκειται, cf. Isth. iv. [v.]
17, τὶν δ' ἐν Ἰσθμῷ διπλόα θάλλοισ'
ἀρετά, | ...κεῖται, Ol. x. 8, Pyth. vi.
6—9.

37. The stadium race was 202¼
yards and the δίαυλος δρόμος was
double that, round the καμπτήρ
and back to the starting-place.
The δολιχοδρομία is variously stated
as either six or twenty-four times
the length of the stadium.

ἀμφ'.] Cf. Suidas, ἀμφὶ ἔτει·
ἐν αὐτῷ τῷ ἔτει.

μηνὸς τωὐτοῦ.] The month Mu-
nychion when the Pythian games

were held and at Athens the Del-
phinian, Munychian and Diâsian
games.

38. τρία.] According to the
Schol. Vet. he won in the δίαυλος,
ὁπλιτικὸς and στάδιος δρόμοι.

ἔργα.] Cf. Ol. vii. 14 note. If
the crowns were such as those
described Nem. vii. 78, 79, of gold
ivory and coral, they might well be
called ἔργα.

ποδαρκὴς ἀμέρα.] 'A day of foot-
racing.' Cf. Pyth. v. 31, ποδαρκέων
δρόμων τέμενος.

Ἑλλώτια.] i.e. ἔργα. With this
clause the last clause from ἔργα
should be mentally repeated. A-
thêne Hellôtia or Hellôtis was
probably a moon-goddess connected
with the old elemental worship
whence came the title Σέλλοι, Ἑλ-
λήν, προσέληνοι. She was wor-
shipped at Korinth, and at the end
of her festival, in which Athênaeos
tells us there was a huge wreath of
myrtle carried in procession, there
was a λαμπαδοδρομία.

40. ἐν δ'.] 'And in respect of
Poteidan's ordinances (held) be-
tween two seas—' i.e. the Isth-
mian games—'will more lasting
lays attend Terpsias and Eritimos
as well as his (Thessalos') father
Ptoeodôros.' I am inclined to
take μακρότεραι as extending the
predicate, in fact adverbially, mean-

Πτοιοδώρῳ σὺν πατρὶ μακρότεραι
Τερψίᾳ θ᾽ ἕψοντ᾽ Ἐριτίμῳ τ᾽ ἀοιδαί.　　　　60
ὅσσα τ᾽ ἐν Δελφοῖσιν ἀριστεύσατε,
ἠδὲ χόρτοις ἐν λέοντος, δηρίομαι πολέσιν
45 περὶ πλήθει καλῶν. ὡς μὰν σαφὲς
οὐκ ἂν εἰδείην λέγειν ποντιᾶν ψάφων ἀριθμόν.　　65
　　　　　　　　　　　　　　　　　　　Στρ. γ΄.

ἕπεται δ᾽ ἐν ἑκάστῳ
μέτρον· νοῆσαι δὲ καιρὸς ἄριστος.
ἐγὼ δὲ ἴδιος ἐν κοινῷ σταλεὶς
50 μῆτίν τε γαρύων παλαιγόνων　　　　70
πόλεμόν τ᾽ ἐν ἡρωΐαις ἀρεταῖσιν
οὐ ψεύσομ᾽ ἀμφὶ Κορίνθῳ, Σίσυφον μὲν πυκνότατον
παλάμαις ὡς θεόν,
καὶ τὰν πατρὸς ἀντία Μήδειαν θεμέναν γάμον αὐτᾷ, 75

ing further in time than the prizes and material records of the last sentence. Cf. Pyth. VI. 7—14. It is however generally taken to mean 'longer lays,' i.e. recounting a longer list of victories. The citations by which Dissen supports this rendering, viz. Pyth. VIII. 30, IX. 77, Nem. IV. 33, Schneidewin, Pyth. IV. 247, Nem. X. 45, Isthm. V. 56, prove to demonstration that Pindar felt that, however voluminous the theme, the song must never be long. I am strongly tempted, as were Mommsen, Böckh, and Hartung who yielded, to make Ptoeodôros father to Terpsias and Eritimos; but the Scholl. agree that Terpsias was brother to Ptoeodôros, Eritimos being Terpsias' son or grandson. MSS. read τέρψιες θ᾽...ἐρίτιμοι, an ingenious corruption. Böckh and Dissen read ἕσποντ᾽, taking ἐν = at.

45. περί.] Cf. Pyth. II. 59, περὶ τιμᾷ.

46. Cf. Ol. II. 98.

47. ἕπεται.] 'In every matter

a mean is involved, and the right moment is the best object of knowledge.' The exact point of time at which the golden mean is reached is καιρός, which is therefore not quite synonymous with μέτρον. For νοῆσαι cf. Ol. VII. 26. Böckh explains 'aptus et conveniens certus unicuique rei modus est.' Cf. Hor. Est modus in rebus.

49. 'But I having in my private capacity embarked on a voyage of public interest and by making mention of the craft and warrior-worth of her men of yore shall in respect of heroic excellences say truly of Korinth that, &c.' For ἐν ἀρεταῖς, cf. Ol. VI. 7, Nem. III. 32. I incline to think that v. 49 means 'engaged to sing nominally on behalf of an individual victor, really on behalf of his family.'

52. παλάμαις.] For dat. of manner, cf. Ol. I. 112. Σί-συφ-ο-ς is connected with σοφός and sap-iens.

53. Μήδειαν.] Note the order. Such an insertion of the proper

ναἲ σώτειραν Ἀργοῖ καὶ προπόλοις.

'Αντ. γ'.

55 τὰ δὲ καί ποτ᾽ ἐν ἀλκᾷ
πρὸ Δαρδάνου τειχέων ἐδόκησαν
ἐπ᾽ ἀμφότερα μαχᾶν τέμνειν τέλος,   80
τοὶ μὲν γένει φίλῳ σὺν Ἀτρέος
Ἑλέναν κομίζοντες, οἱ δ᾽ ἀπὸ πάμπαν
60 εἴργοντες· ἐκ Λυκίας δὲ Γλαῦκον ἐλθόντα τρόμεον Δα-
ναοί. τοῖσι μὲν   85
ἐξεύχετ᾽ ἐν ἄστεϊ Πειράνας σφετέρου πατρὸς ἀρχὰν
καὶ βαθὺν κλᾶρον ἔμμεν καὶ μέγαρον·

'Επ. γ'.

ὃς τᾶς ὀφιώδεος υἱόν ποτε Γοργόνος ἦ πόλλ᾽ ἀμφὶ
κρουνοῖς   90

name between the article and participle is not very rare. Not only did Mêdeia sojourn at Korinth but Aeêtes was said to have been K. of Korinth before he went to Kolchis. The Schol. cites Eumêlos for the legend. One of Mêdeia's sons was supposed to be Thessalos; so perhaps she was regarded as an ancestress of Xenophon's family, cf. v. 35.

θεμέναν.] The middle voice is of course appropriate to the independent action of Mêdeia. Higher powers are said τιθέναι γάμον.

55. τὰ δὲ καί.] Cf. Ol. IX. 95. 'And on the other hand too erst in respect of prowess before Dardanos' walls they gat credit for deciding the issue of fights in favour of either side.' I am doubtful whether ἐν ἀλκᾷ may not be adverbial, cf. Ol. II. 16, ἐν δίκᾳ. For the formula τὰ δὲ καί, cf. Ol. IX. 95.

56. ἐδόκησαν.] For the signification cf. Pyth. VI. 40. I cannot think that Don.'s 'they were thought,' 'they had the reputa-

tion,' conveys the proper force of the Aorist.

57. Cf. Eurip. Herakl., 755, μέλλω τᾶς πατριώτιδος γᾶς, | μέλλω περὶ τῶν δόμων | ...κίνδυνον πολιῷ τεμεῖν σιδάρῳ, Hor. Epp. I. XVI. 42, Quo multae magnaeque secantur judice lites, id. Sat. I. x. 15.

58. φίλῳ.] Agamemnon himself commanded the Korinthian contingent, cf. Hom. Il. II. 569—577.

59. κομίζοντες.] Cf. Pyth. I. 52.

60. ἀπό-είργοντες.] Note that this is an ordinary present and gets its object from τοὶ μέν.

61. The allusion has been held to be to Glaukos' speech, Hom. Il. VI. 144 sqq., though, as Prof. Paley points out, there are discrepancies. The father of the Homeric Glaukos is Hippolochos son of Bellerophon while Pindar's Glaukos is Bellerophon's son.

62. βαθύν.] Either 'rich' cf. Pyth. II. 1 note, or for βαθυλείμονα. μέγαρον.] Strabo, VIII. 6, mentions extensive ruins of the Sisypheion built of white stone.

63. κρουνοῖς.] i.e. Of Peirêne.

Πάγασον ζεῦξαι ποθέων ἔπαθεν,
65 πρίν γέ οἱ χρυσάμπυκα κούρα χαλινὸν
Παλλὰς ἤνεγκ', ἐξ ὀνείρου δ' αὐτίκα
ἦν ὕπαρ, φώνασε δ'· Εὕδεις, Αἰολίδα βασιλεῦ;
ἄγε φίλτρον τόδ' ἵππειον δέκευ,   95
καὶ Δαμαίῳ νιν θύων ταῦρον ἀργᾶν πατρὶ δεῖξον.

                                                    Στρ. δ'.

70 κυάναιγις ἐν ὄρφνᾳ   100
κνώσσοντί οἱ παρθένος τόσα εἰπεῖν
ἔδοξεν· ἀνὰ δ' ἔπαλτ' ὀρθῷ ποδί.
παρκείμενον δὲ συλλαβὼν τέρας,
ἐπιχώριον μάντιν ἄσμενος εὗρεν,
75 δεῖξέν τε Κοιρανίδᾳ πᾶσαν τελευτὰν πράγματος, ὥς
       τ' ἀνὰ βωμῷ θεᾶς   105
κοιτάξατο νύκτ' ἀπ' ἐκείνου χρήσιος, ὥς τέ οἱ αὐτὰ
Ζηνὸς ἐγχεικεραύνου παῖς ἔπορεν   110

                                                    'Αντ. δ'.

δαμασίφρονα χρυσόν.
ἐνυπνίῳ δ' ᾇ τάχιστα πιθέσθαι
80 κελήσατό νιν, ὅταν δ' εὐρυσθενεῖ
καρταίποδ' ἀναρύῃ Γεαόχῳ,

66. Cf. κάκρινα πρῶτος ἐξ ὀνειρά
των ἁ χρὴ | ὕπαρ γενέσθαι, Aesch.
Prom. V. 493 (P.).
69. Δαμαίῳ.] The myth and
cult of Athêne Chalinitis, Pausan.
II. 4, or Hippia, v. 82, seems to have
flourished at Korinth side by side
with the older Korinthian and
Attic myths of Poseidon, the horse-
tamer as well as the creator of horses.
Poseidon may however have ap-
plied the use of the goad to horses.
πατρί.] Bellerophon, nominally
son of Glaukos (the elder), was
really son of Poseidon, cf. Il. VI.
191. Because black bulls are of-
fered to Poseidon, Od. III. 6, the
scholl. explain ἀργᾶντα 'conspicuous

for size,' Gl. λιπαρόν, cf. βόες ἀργοί,
Il. XXIII. 30; but red bulls are
offered Pyth. IV. 205, which at
once disposes of all objection to the
simple meaning 'white.'
74. μάντιν.] Polyeidos father
of Euchênor, Il. XIII. 663, son of
Koeranos.
78. 'The golden spirit-tamer,'
cf. v. 29; i.e. the bridle.
79. ᾇ.] So best mss. for ὡς, cf.
Ol. VI. 23.
81. καρταίποδ'.] The Schol. Vet.
says this is Delphic for a bull.
Was it Delphic influence which
produced the Hesiodic descriptive
names πέντοςος, φερέοικος, &c.?
ἀναρύῃ.] So best mss. But some

θέμεν Ἱππίᾳ βωμὸν εὐθὺς Ἀθάνᾳ.   115
τελεῖ θεῶν δύναμις καὶ τὰν παρ᾽ ὅρκον καὶ παρὰ ἐλπίδα
    κούφαν κτίσιν.
ἦτοι καὶ ὁ καρτερὸς ὁρμαίνων ἔλε Βελλεροφόντας,   120
85 φάρμακον πραὺ τείνων ἀμφὶ γένυι,

Ἐπ. δ᾽.

ἵππον πτερόεντ᾽· ἀναβὰς δ᾽ εὐθὺς ἐνόπλια χαλκωθεὶς
    ἔπαιζεν.
σὺν δὲ κείνῳ καὶ ποτ᾽ Ἀμαζονίδων
αἰθέρος ψυχρᾶς ἀπὸ κόλπων ἐρήμου   125
τοξόταν βάλλων γυναικεῖον στρατόν,
90 καὶ Χίμαιραν πῦρ πνέοισαν καὶ Σολύμους ἔπεφνεν.
διασωπάσομαί οἱ μόρον ἐγώ·   130

and the Schol. Vet. have αὐερύη, cf. Il. 1. 459. Old lexicons give ἀναρύειν σφάζειν.

88. ' Now the power of the Gods maketh that (achievement) which one would vow to be impossible and never expect to perform, an easy achievement.' The meaning of τὰν (Query should we substitute τῶν?) παρ᾽ ὅρκον is shown by Archil. Frag. 74, [31], χρημάτων ἀέλπτων οὐδέν ἐστιν οὐδ᾽ ἀπώμοτον, οὐ δὲ θαυμάσιον where ἀέλπτον refers to the future generally, ἀπώμοτον to the immediate future, θαυμάσιον to the present. Until we understand the greater comprehensiveness of ἐλπὶς there seems to be an anticlimax. Aeschylos several times uses κτίζω in a general sense; cf. Pyth. v. 83.

85. φάρμακον.] This carries on the idea of φίλτρον, v. 68.

86. ἐνόπλια.] 'He went through exercises in full armour.' Cookesley says 'He performed the Pyrrhic dance' after a Schol. But if so, we are bound to suppose he danced on Pêgasos' back, which would surely have astonished that steed.

88. ψυχρᾶς.] For gender cf. Ol. i. 6. The epithet applies to the cold of the Skythian mountains and steppes.

ἐρήμου.] Used as a substantive according to Mommsen. Hermann proposes ἐρήμων. Mr Paley suggests that ἐρήμου is the imperfect of ἐρημόω. To say however that Pindar would not use ἐρήμου as fem. is to generalise from one instance, Ol. i. 6, and I see no objection to the two epithets, ἐρήμου definitive and ψυχρᾶς descriptive, 'from the hollows of the cold waste of air.' For Pindar's use of two adjectives without a conjunction cf. Pyth. ix.8. Gray's 'desert air' surely means the air of a desert place and does not illustrate this phrase. Cookesley cites Romeo and Juliet, Act ii. Sc. 2, 'the bosom of the air.'

90. καὶ Χ.] The rareness of the conjunctives καί—καί, which as Mommsen says couple opposites so as to make up one idea, prompts to render this first καὶ 'so' i.e. καὶ βάλλων ἀπὸ κόλπων, &c.

91. διασωπάσομαι.] Cf. σεσωπαμένον, Isthm. i. 63. So Apollôn. Rhod. 1. 685, has βώσεσθε for βιώσεσθε. For Bellerophon's fate, cf. Il. vi. 201.

τὸν δ' ἐν Οὐλύμπῳ φάτναι Ζηνὸς ἀρχαῖαι δέκονται.

Στρ. ε΄.

ἐμὲ δ' εὐθὺν ἀκόντων
ἱέντα ῥόμβον παρὰ σκοπὸν οὐ χρὴ
95 τὰ πολλὰ βέλεα καρτύνειν χεροῖν.   135
Μοίσαις γὰρ ἀγλαοθρόνοις ἑκὼν
Ὀλιγαιθίδαισίν τ' ἔβαν ἐπίκουρος.
Ἰσθμοῖ τά τ' ἐν Νεμέᾳ παύρῳ γ' ἔπει θήσω φανέρ'
        ἀθρό', ἀλαθής τέ μοι   140
ἔξορκος ἐπέσσεται ἐξηκοντάκι δὴ ἀμφοτέρωθεν
100 ἀδύγλωσσος βοὰ κάρυκος ἐσλοῦ.

Ἀντ. ε΄.

τὰ δ' Ὀλυμπίᾳ αὐτῶν
ἔοικεν ἤδη πάροιθε λελέχθαι·   145
τά τ' ἐσσόμενα τότ' ἂν φαίην σαφές·
νῦν δ' ἔλπομαι μέν, ἐν θεῷ γε μὰν

93. Cf. Ol. II. 89, Pyth. I. 44.
'But I casting my javelins straight
with a whirl by the mark must not
ply my many darts with might of
my two hands.' This metaphor
suggests that Xenophon had ex-
celled in the javelin-hurling in the
quinquertium. I have tried to
show that as distance counted in
the javelin-hurling the competitors
must have had to hurl past, and no
doubt within a certain distance of
a mark. So here the poet does not
say that he must not take bad
shots, but that he must not hurl
too often, i. e. he must not dilate
upon the ancient glories of Korinth.
95. καρτύνειν.] Cf. Apollôn.
Rhod. II. 332, ἀλλ' εὖ καρτύναντες
ἑαῖς ἐνὶ χερσὶν ἐρετμά.
χεροῖν.] The dual seems to be
emphatic and to support my view,
as the ἄκων appears to have been
thrown with one hand.
96. The praises of the Oligae-

thidae which had been broken off
at v. 46 are now resumed.
98. '—as to their victories at
Isthmos and at Nemea. In brief
phrase will I publish them all to-
gether, and as a true sworn-witness
there shall support me (heard) quite
sixty times at both places the
sweet-tongued voice of a worthy
herald.'
θήσω.] Cf. Pyth. I. 40, Ol. VII. 6.
100. ἀδύγλωσσος.] The excep-
tional admission of a short quan-
tity before γλῶσσα suggests that
the form was originally κλωκγα
probably the sounder connected
with κρώξω, crocio.
102. i. e. vv. 1, 29—31, 35.
103. 'Of those to come when
they come will I tell clearly; for
now am I cherishing hopes, how-
beit in God's hands is the issue;
but if the family good hap keep on
we will leave this (τέλος) to Zeus
and Ares to work out.'

105 τέλος· εἰ δὲ δαίμων γενέθλιος ἕρποι,
  Δὶ τοῦτ' Ἐνυαλίῳ τ' ἐκδώσομεν πράσσειν. τὰ δ' ὑπ'
    ὀφρύϊ Παρνασία   150
ἐν Ἄργεῖ θ' ὅσσα καὶ ἐν Θήβαις· ὅσα τ' Ἀρκάσιν
  [ἀνάσσων]
μαρτυρήσει Λυκαίου βωμὸς ἄναξ·

                              Ἐπ. ε'.

Πέλλανά τε καὶ Σικυὼν καὶ Μέγαρ', Αἰακιδᾶν τ' εὐ-
  ερκὲς ἄλσος,
110 ἅ τ' Ἐλευσὶς καὶ λιπαρὰ Μαραθών,   155
  ταί θ' ὑπ' Αἴτνας ὑψιλόφου καλλίπλουτοι
  πόλιες, ἅ τ' Εὔβοια. καὶ πᾶσαν κατὰ   160
Ἑλλάδ' εὑρήσεις ἐρευνῶν μάσσον' ἢ ὡς ἰδέμεν.
  ἄνα, κούφοισιν ἐκνεῦσαι ποσίν·

---

105. For δαίμων cf. v. 28.
106. Ἐνυαλίῳ.] Cf. v. 23.
τὰ δ'.] This list contains no
principal predicate. Perhaps we
should have a comma after Εὔβοια,
v. 112, and govern this τὰ and in
fact the whole enumeration by
εὑρήσεις, v. 114.
107. There is some uncertainty
about this verse, and ἀνάσσων is
clearly corrupt. We can best go-
vern ὅσσα by μαρτυρήσονται βωμοί,
understood from the next verse.
For ἀνάσσων Hermann has pro-
posed first Ἀρκὰς ἀνάσσων, then ὅσα
δ' Ἀρκάσι μάσσω, Mommsen Ἀρ-
κάσιν ἄσσον. I would read Ἀρκάσιν
ἄεθλα. In old uncials εθ is very
much nearer to σσ than it looks in
print. The corruption is due pro-
bably to the neighbouring endings
-νασία, ἄναξ, ἄλσος.
109. According to my canons
as to καὶ-τε in Pindar we must
have a comma after Μέγαρ', the
three places mentioned first in the
verse forming a class as having
each Apolline games, in which

Xenophon had doubtless been
victor. In the next line Eleusis
and Marathon naturally go closely
together. Argos and Thebes are
coupled Ol. ix. 68, Hêraklean myths
connecting them.
The games at Argos were Hêraea,
Hekatombaea, at Thebes Hêrak-
laea, Iolaia, at Pellêne Theoxenia,
Hermaea, at Sikyon Pythia, at
Megara Diokleia, Alkathoia, Pythia,
Nemea, in Aegina Aeakia, at Eleusis
Dêmêtria, Eleusinia, at Marathon
Hêrakleia, at Syrakuse Isthmia,
in Euboea, Geraestia, Amarynthia.
113. μάσσον'.] 'Too many for
eye to view.'
114, 115.] These two verses have
caused much trouble. MSS. give
ἀλλά κ. ἐ. π. Ζ. τέλει ἀ. διδούς.
The text is Böckh's. According to
Kayser and the Schol. Vet. the
poet is to swim out of his ode.
Generally, the Oligaethidae are to
'swim through life'. However, for
the infinitive, cf. Pyth. I. 68.
Authority is wanted for ἄνα the
vocative of ἄναξ standing before

115 Ζεῦ τέλει᾽, αἰδῶ δίδοι καὶ τύχαν τερπνῶν γλυκεῖαν.

and away from another vocative.
Kayser takes ἄνα to be for ἀνάστηθι.
I would suggest ἅμα κούφοισιν εἰσαιεὶ
ποσίν, Ζεῦ τέλει᾽, αἰδῶ, κ.τ.λ. αἰδῶ for
αἰδοίαν χάριν. For ἅμα becoming

ἀλλά, cf. Ol. i. 104, and if this
word and τέλει᾽ got altered a verb
would inevitably be substituted for
εἰσαιεί.

OLYMPIA XIV.

ON THE VICTORY OF ASOPIKOS OF ORCHOMENOS IN THE SHORT FOOT-RACE OF BOYS.

INTRODUCTION.

Asôpikos won, B.C. 476. This ode almost takes the form of a hymn to the Graces, and was sung by a chorus of boys, probably in their great temple on the banks of the Kêphisos and the Kôpaic lake. The rhythm is Lydian (*v.* 17) with Aeolian measures.

ANALYSIS.

vv.

1—11. Invocation of the Graces as Queens of Orchomenos, patronesses of the Minyae, dispensers of all blessings to men and gods.

12—15. Invocation of them severally by name.

15—18. The poet came to celebrate in Lydian measures an Olympian victory of Minyeia gained by Thalia's help.

18—22. Request that Echo will bear the news to Asôpikos' father Kleodâmos in Hades.

Στρ. α′.

Καφισίων ὑδάτων λαχοῖσαι, αἵτε ναίετε καλλίπωλον
ἕδραν,

1. The lake Kôpais or Kêphissis, as well as the river Kêphisos is meant. For the gen. after ἕδραν cf. Ol. II. 9.

λαχοῖσαι.] Don. and Böckh read λαχοῖσαν, to avoid the parêchêsis. But it is probable that the diphthong sounded differently before a con-

ὦ λιπαρᾶς ἀοίδιμοι βασίλειαι
Χάριτες Ὀρχομενοῦ, παλαιγόνων Μινυᾶν ἐπίσκοποι,　5
κλῦτ᾽, ἐπεὶ εὔχομαι· σὺν γὰρ ὕμμιν τά τε τερπνὰ καὶ
5 τὰ γλυκέα γίνεται πάντα βροτοῖς,
εἰ σοφός, εἰ καλός, εἴ τις ἀγλαὸς ἀνήρ.　　　　10
οὐδὲ γὰρ θεοὶ σεμνᾶν Χαρίτων ἄτερ
κοιρανέοισιν χοροὺς οὔτε δαῖτας· ἀλλὰ πάντων ταμίαι
ἔργων ἐν οὐρανῷ, χρυσότοξον θέμεναι παρὰ　　　15
10 Πύθιον Ἀπόλλωνα θρόνους,
ἀέναον σέβοντι πατρὸς Ὀλυμπίοιο τιμάν.

Στρ. β'.

ὦ πότνι᾽ Ἀγλαΐα φιλησίμολπέ τ᾽ Εὐφροσύνα, θεῶν
κρατίστου　　　　　　　　20
παῖδες, ἐπακοοῖτε νῦν, Θαλία τε
ἐρασίμολπε, ἰδοῖσα τόνδε κῶμον ἐπ᾽ εὐμενεῖ τύχᾳ
15 κοῦφα βιβῶντα· Λυδίῳ γὰρ Ἀσώπιχον ἐν τρόπῳ　25

sonant and a vowel. For the allot-
ment of the world among the gods,
cf. Ol. vii. 54 sqq.

2. λιπαρᾶς.] Cf. Pyth. ii. 3.

3. Χάριτες.] These are the
graces of Hêsiod, Theog. 905—911,
64—67, with whom are associated
ἔρος and ἵμερος. The graces of
Sparta were two, Klêta and Phaênna.
These would seem to represent
Aglaia whose name suggests that
at first she was especially the be-
stower of victory, cf. vv. 7, 12, Ol. ii.
50.

4. τε-καί.] For this strong form
of conjunction cf. Ol. i. 79. It is
often found when words which are
almost synonymous, or at any rate
the meanings whereof overlap, are
joined. The repetition of the article
increases and emphasises the com-
prehensiveness of the phrase.

6. σοφός.] 'Skilled in song.'
ἀγλαός.] 'Victorious (in games),'
cf. Ol. xiii. 5, 14.

7. οὐδὲ γάρ.] 'Yea, not even.'
mss. give οὔτε. The text is Bergk's.

σεμνᾶν.] For the epithet cf. Eur.
Hel. 1341, σεμναὶ χάριτες.

8. κοιρανέοισιν.] The mss. reading
κοιρανέοντι does not scan unless we
elide ἐλθέ, though mss. give it in
full, before Ἀχοῖ which in Hes.
Scut. Herc. had an initial digamma,
cf. Ol. iii. 1, sqq. note, ἠχή.

11. ἀέναον.] For the adverbial
use, cf. Ol. xiii. 17.

13. ἐπακοοῖτε νῦν.] So Momm-
sen. mss. give ἐπάκοοι νῦν. Don.
and Böckh adopt Hermann's first
correction ἐπάκοος γένευ; but the
singular is very awkward. Bergk
proposed ἐπακοοῖτέ νυν.

14. ἰδοῖσα.] Refers to Θαλία
alone, or at least especially; be-
cause she is ἐρασίμολπε, a stronger
term than φιλησίμολπε.

15. Λυδίῳ.] So mss.; and though
the ι is superfluous we need not
alter; cf. Ol. ii. 4, xiii. 91.
Ἀσώπιχον.] This is a diminutive
from Ἀσωπός, most probably for
Ἀσώπισκος.

ἐν τρόπῳ.] For ἐν introducing an

ἔν τε μελέταις ἀείδων ἔμολον,
οὕνεκ' Ὀλυμπιόνικος ἀ Μινύεια
σεῦ ἔκατι· μελανοτειχέα νῦν δόμον
Φερσεφόνας ἐλθέ, Ἀχοῖ, πατρὶ κλυτὰν φέροισ' ἀγγε-
　　λίαν,　　　　　　　　　　　　　　　　　　30
20 Κλεόδαμον ὄφρ' ἰδοῖσ', υἱὸν εἴπῃς, ὅτι οἱ νέαν
　κόλποις παρ' εὐδόξου Πίσας
　ἐστεφάνωσε κυδίμων ἀέθλων πτεροῖσι χαίταν.

adverbial phrase of manner, cf. Ol.
II. 16.

16. μελέταις.] I believe this
word means 'training of the chorus'
though it is generally taken to
mean 'song,' 'strain.' Render
'chanting a carefully practised Ode
in Lydian mode on Asôpikos.'

17. Μινύεια.] Most mss. give
the Aeolic form, but editors gene-
rally read Μινυεία. It is not easy
to say who this tutelary deity of
Orchomenos is likely to have been;
but the name Tritogeneia in Minyan
genealogy suggests Athêne. It may
be only a personification of the
territory of Orchomenos.

18. σεῦ ἔκατι.] This looks as if
it referred especially to Thalia;
whereas we might expect the victory
to be attributed to Aglaia. But,
though the special functions of the
sisters may have been originally
distinct, they were confused in
Pindar's time, and the connection
of victory with ἀγλαὸς is not invari-
able in Pindar, e.g. Ol. III. 6, ἀγ-
λαόκωμον, and is peculiar to him.
There was an initial digamma to

ἔκατι akin to ἑκών, ἕκηλος and the
Skt. √ vaç wish.

19. Ἀχοῖ.] The connection of
Echo with the underworld is ob-
vious, cf. Soph. El. 1066 (Jebb), and
she is mythically connected with
Orchomenos by her passion for
Narkissos son of Kêphisos. For the
sentiment cf. Ol. VIII. 81.

κλυτάν.] Here κλυτὸς may mean
'loud' as κλυτὰ μῆλα, Od. IX. 308.
Dissen thinks this part of the ode,
as being an indirect address to the
dead, was sung louder than the
rest.

20. υἱόν.] The subject of the de-
pendant made the object of the
principal clause, cf. Madv. § 191,
Pyth. IX. 112.

22. ἐστεφάνωσε.] The active is
justified by it being said to be in
his father's honour that he crowned
his locks; but though usually care-
ful to use the middle voice to ex-
press reflexive action, Pindar does
not do so invariably, cf. φέρε, Ol. IX.
98, στεφανωθείς, Ol. IV. 11, ἔπραξε,
Pyth. II. 40.

PYTHIAN ODES.

PYTHIA I.

ON THE VICTORY OF HIERO, TYRANT OF SYRAKUSE, (PROCLAIMED AS OF AETNA), WITH THE FOUR-HORSE CHARIOT.

INTRODUCTION.

CHRONOLOGY.

The ode was sung at a banquet at Syrakuse (*v.* 38).
The rhythm is Dorian.

ANALYSIS.

vv.

1—12. The celebrated invocation of the cithern. [Under the recital of its power over violence, represented by the thunderbolt, Zeus' eagle and Ares, there doubtless lies an admonition to Hiero to be mild in his conduct, which is taken up (*v.* 94).]

12—14. The poet contrasts the detestation in which music is held by those whom Zeus hates.

15—20. He introduces Typhôs and Mount Aetna;

21—28. Describes an eruption: whence he

29—33. Passes easily to the city Aetna, its founder Hiero and his Pythian victory.

33—40. Good wishes for the new city.

41, 42. Gnômê attributing human excellence to the gods.

43—57. Praise of Hiero, who is compared to Philoktêtes.

58—60. The Muse is asked to celebrate the victory at the palace of Deinomenos, Hiero's son, king of Aetna.

61—66. For him Hiero established Aetna with Dorian institutions, the origin and early influence of which are indicated.

67—80. An invocation to Zeus Teleios introduces mention of Hiero's victories.

81—84. Deprecation of over-praise as likely to disgust the citizens.

85—98. Exhortation to honourable ambition in spite of envy, to justice, truth, liberality, gentleness.

99, 100. Gnômê on good fortune and fame, a combination of which is the highest blessing.

$$\Sigma\tau\rho.\ a'.$$

Χρυσέα φόρμιγξ, Ἀπόλλωνος καὶ ἰοπλοκάμων

1. Χρυσέα.] Apollo's cithern is golden, Hes., *Scut. Herc.* 201, seven-stringed and played with a golden plectrum, Nem. v. 22, περικαλλής, *Il.* i. 604; but the epithet is not necessarily ideal; as φόρμιγγες were often of metal, and very costly, cf. δαιδαλέα, Pyth. iv. 296. It is just possible that the epithet suggests the high fee due to the poet, cf. *v.* 90.

φόρμιγξ.] The φόρμιγξ or κίθαρις

σύνδικον Μοισᾶν κτέανον· τᾶς ἀκούει μὲν βάσις ἀγ-
λαΐας ἀρχά,
πείθονται δ' ἀοιδοὶ σάμασιν,   5
ἀγησιχόρων ὁπόταν προοιμίων ἀμβολὰς τεύχῃς ἐλελι-
ζομένα.
5 καὶ τὸν αἰχματὰν κεραυνὸν σβεννύεις
ἀενάου πυρός. εὕδει δ' ἀνὰ σκάπτῳ Διὸς αἰετός,
ὠκεῖαν πτέρυγ' ἀμφοτέρωθεν χαλάξαις,   10
'Αντ. α'.
ἀρχὸς οἰωνῶν, κελαινῶπιν δ' ἐπί οἱ νεφέλαν

was an advance upon the λύρα with
its tortoise-shell soundingboard,
having its horns hollow in con-
tinuation of the sounding-board.
ἰοπλοκάμων.] Greek violets (με-
λάνια) are much nearer black than
ours: so that the epithet means
'black-haired;' cf. ἰοβόστρυχον Εὐά-
δναν, Ol. VI. 30, though the ἰα of
ib. 55 (ἴων ξανθαῖσι καὶ παμπορφύ-
ροις ἀκτῖσι βεβρεγμένος ἁβρὸν σῶμα
['Ίαμος]) are λευκόϊα, 'pansies.'
2. σύνδικον.] Most commenta-
tors render 'common treasure of,'
cf. ἔνδικος χάρις, Pyth. v. 97. I pre-
fer Heyne's 'that takest part with,'
cf. Ol. IX. 98, σύνδικος δ' αὐτῷ
'Ιολάου τύμβος εἰναλία τ' 'Ελευσὶς
ἀγλαΐαισιν, 'the tomb of Iolâos
(i. e. the Iolâian games at Thebes)
is witness to his (Epharmostos')
victories.' Also cf. (δόνακες) πιστοὶ
χορευτᾶν μάρτυρες, Pyth. XII. 27.
The cithern by its accompaniment
aided the celestial singers in re-
commending their theme to the
gods, just as a backer at a trial
aids his principal in recommending
his cause to the judges. The sense
of 'backer,' 'witness for,' attached
to σύνδικος long before the techni-
cal meaning 'advocate.'
3. ἀοιδοί.] Clearly not bards,
whose hymns are ἀναξιφόρμιγγες,
Ol. II. 1, but the chorus.
4. ἀμβολὰς τεύχῃς.] Equiv. to

ἀναβάλλῃ, cf. Ar. Pax, 831, Arist.
Rhet. III. 9. 1.
ἐλελιζομένα.] 'Made to vibrate.'
The word is frequentative in form,
with prosthetic ε, from a √ LIG,
and thus connected with Skt. lin-
gâmi, I bend, and not with ἑλίσσω
as Buttman, approved by Donald-
son, suggests.
5. αἰχματάν.] Generally taken
as an adj. 'pointed,' but κεραυνὸν
may be personified here.
6. ἀενάου.] For genitive of ma-
terial cf. ἄνθεμα χρύσου, Ol. II. 72,
Pyth. IV. 71, 206. The epithet may
be a touch of Pythagoreanism.
ἀνὰ σκάπτῳ Διός.] Cf. Soph.
Fr. 766, ὁ σκηπτοβάμων αἰετὸς κύων
Διός. Pheidias placed an eagle on
the sceptre of his Olympian Zeus.
It was a regular ornament of scep-
tres as appears from Aristoph. Aves,
508—510, ἦρχον δ' οὕτω σφόδρα
τὴν ἀρχὴν ὥστ' εἴ τις καὶ βασι-
λεύοι | ἐν ταῖς πόλεσιν τῶν 'Ελλήνων,
'Αγαμέμνων ἢ Μενέλαος, | ἐπὶ τῶν
σκήπτρων ἐκάθητ' ὄρνις, μετέχων ὅτι
δωροδοκοίη.
ὠκεῖαν.] Epithet introduced for
the sake of contrast. cf. v. 72.
7. ἀρχὸς οἰωνῶν.] Cf. οἰωνῶν
βασιλέα δίδυμον, Ol. XIII. 21, of the
αἰετοὶ or ἀκρωτήρια of a temple roof
on the top angles of the front and
the back.

ἀγκύλῳ κρατί, γλεφάρων ἁδὺ κλᾶιστρον, κατέχευας
ὁ δὲ κνώσσων   15
ὑγρὸν νῶτον αἰωρεῖ, τεαῖς
10 ῥιπαῖσι κατασχόμενος. καὶ γὰρ βιατὰς Ἄρης, τρα-
χεῖαν ἄνευθε λιπὼν
ἐγχέων ἀκμάν, ἰαίνει καρδίαν   20
κώματι, κῆλα δὲ καὶ δαιμόνων θέλγει φρένας, ἀμφί τε
Λατοίδα σοφίᾳ βαθυκόλπων τε·Μοισᾶν.

'Επ. α'.

ὅσσα δὲ μὴ πεφίληκε Ζεύς, ἀτύζονται βοὰν   25
Πιερίδων ἀίοντα, γᾶν τε καὶ πόντον κατ' ἀμαιμάκετον,
15 ὅς τ' ἐν αἰνᾷ Ταρτάρῳ κεῖται, θεῶν πολέμιος,   30

8. γλεφάρων.] Phonetic analogy
shows this form to be earlier than
βλεφάρων. The √ βλεπ < √ γλεπ
is probably a secondary form of
√ GLA seen in γλήνη, γλαυκός.

9. ὑγρόν.] Donaldson makes
this adjective mean 'bent or curved
generally, cf. Theokr. xxv. 206,
κέρας ὑγρόν;' but the horn in this
passage is a bow, so that the sense
'elastic' does better. He compares
the use of mollis, which is not 'an
assimilation of mobilis,' but for mol-
duis*, for mardus*, cf. Skt. mridu-s.

10. ῥιπαῖσι.] This word denotes
throbbing, pulsating movements
and sounds as of fire, winds, waves
(Pyth. iv. 195, Frag. 205, πόντου ρ.),
the hum of a teazing gnat (ἐν δ'
ὀνείρασιν | λεπταῖς ὑπαὶ κώνωπος
ἐξεγειρόμην | ῥιπαῖσι θωύσσοντος,
Aesch. Agam. 891). Donaldson says
it is used of smell, Frag. 143,
'Ανδροδάμαντα δ' ἐπεὶ φῆρες ὅδεν
ῥιπὰν μελιαδέος οἴνου. Surely the
throbbing produced by vinous ex-
citement is meant.

κατασχόμενος.] Cf. Madv. § 83 a,
Plato Phaedr. 238 D, 244 E, Hom.
Od. xiii. 2, κηληθμῷ δ' ἔσχοντο.

12. κῆλα.] For metaphor cf.
v. 44, Ol. i. 111, ii. 83, ix. 5—12,
xiii. 93—95.

δαιμόνων.] These are either
heroes in bliss or simply the dead
in Pindar's Isles of the Blessed.

ἀμφί.] 'By,' 'owing to,' cf. ἐμᾷ
ἀμφὶ μαχανᾷ, Pyth. viii. 34, infra
v. 80.

βαθυκόλπων.] Equiv. to βαθυζώ-
νων. In this style, appropriate to
matrons, and hence to goddesses,
the robe was arranged so as to
fall in loose folds over the girdle,
and conceal the figure, cf. Ol. vi.
31.

13. ἀτύζονται.] Plutarch reads
thus Qu. Symp. ix. 14. 6; while
the best mss. give ἀτύζεται against
the metre. This is probably an
early alteration made quite un-
necessarily, as we find ἐντὶ βέλη,
Ol. ii. 84. ἀλλα ἔβαν, Ol. viii. 12,
τὰ φάνεν, Ol. xi. 85. Πομφόλυξαν
δάκρυα, Pyth. iv. 121. Do not
then say with Cookesley, 'ὅσσα
i. e. ὅσους.'

14. ἀμαιμάκετον.] Lobeck Path.
Serm. Gr. viii. iv. § 3 shows from
the accentuation that the ἀ-is inten-
sive. The form μακ- seems to be
a secondary development of √ MA,
whence μαίομαι, μαιμάω. Cf. Hes.
Sc. H. 207.

15. ὅς τ'.] Note the transition
from the general to the particular.

Τυφὼς ἑκατοντακάρανος· τόν ποτε
Κιλίκιον θρέψεν πολυώνυμον ἄντρον· νῦν γε μὰν
ταί θ' ὑπὲρ Κύμας ἁλιερκέες ὄχθαι
Σικελία τ' αὐτοῦ πιέζει στέρνα λαχνάεντα· κίων δ'
    οὐρανία συνέχει,   35
20 νιφόεσσ' Αἴτνα, πάνετες χιόνος ὀξείας τιθήνα·

                    Στρ. β'.
τᾶς ἐρεύγονται μὲν ἀπλάτου πυρὸς ἁγνόταται   40
ἐκ μυχῶν παγαί· ποταμοὶ δ' ἀμέραισιν μὲν προχέοντι
    ῥόον καπνοῦ

αἰνᾷ.] Pindar is peculiar in making Τάρταρος, Ἰσθμὸς feminine.

16. Τυφώς.] The concrete mythical representative of volcanic activity. Plato rightly connects the name with τύφω (for θυπ-ω, a secondary from √ θυ), Phaedr. 230 A.

17. Κιλίκιον ἄντρον.] So Homer, Il. II. 781, γαῖα δ' ὑποστενάχιζε Διὶ ὥς τερπικεραύνῳ | χωομένῳ, ὅτε τ' ἀμφὶ Τυφωέϊ γαῖαν ἱμάσσῃ | Εἰν Ἀρίμοις ὅθι φασὶ Τυφωέος ἔμμεναι εὐνάς. Pindar says Τυφὼς Κίλιξ, Pyth. VIII. 16.

νῦν γε μάν.] 'Now however the hill-ranges behind Kyme that front the sea—'

18. ὑπέρ.] Used of comparatively high ground near but not on the coast. Nem. VII. 65, Thuk. I. 46, Herod. IV. 18. In the last passage it means apparently no more than 'more inland than.' The high ground behind Cumae would appear to abut on the sea, when seen from vessels out at sea. Strabo alludes to this passage when remarking that from Cumae to Sicily the channel is volcanic, Pithecusa and the Liparae islands marking the course of the fiery caverns.

19. κίων οὐρανία.] Cf. Aesch. P. V. 349, κίον' οὐρανοῦ τε καὶ χθονὸς | ὤμοις ἐρείδων. Pindar seems

to generalize the myth of Atlas, Od. I. 53, and to regard any cloud-capped mountain of distinguished height as a pillar of heaven.

20. πάνετες τιθήνα.] 'Year-long cherisher of keen-cold snow,' cf. ἀτενὲς ἴκελοι, Pyth. II. 77.

χιόνος ὀξείας.] Cf. gelu acutum, Hor. Od. I. 9. 3, acris hiems, I. 4. 1. Euripides has χιονότροφον (Κιθαιρῶνα), Phoen. 803, and χιονοθρέμμονας σκοπίας, Helen. 1323.

21. The eruption described in this splendid passage took place B.C. 479, three years before Aetna was founded, and only five before the date of this ode.

ἁγνόταται.] Here the idea of purification attached to fire and sulphur may be combined with that of intense brilliance, cf. Theokr. XXIV. 95, καθαρῷ δὲ πυρώσατε δῶμα θεείῳ, and Tibullus I. 9. 36, purae fulminis viae. The epithet may be Pythagorean.

22. The poet tells us what is seen by day and night respectively. Differences in the course of the eruption would not be regulated by the alternation of day and night. The contrast is complete. The black masses of rock on the ruddy torrent exactly balance the lurid flashes seen by day amid the dark smoke. αἴθων' (v. 23) = 'flame-straked.'

F.   9

αἴθων·· ἀλλ' ἐν ὄρφναισιν πέτρας
φοίνισσα κυλινδομένα φλὸξ ἐς βαθεῖαν φέρει πόντου
πλάκα σὺν πατάγῳ.   45
25 κεῖνο δ' Ἀφαίστοιο κρουνοὺς ἑρπετὸν
δεινοτάτους ἀναπέμπει· τέρας μὲν θαυμάσιον προσιδ-
ἔσθαι, θαῦμα δὲ καὶ παριόντων ἀκοῦσαι,   50
                                                                Ἀντ. β'.

οἷον Αἴτνας ἐν μελαμφύλλοις δέδεται κορυφαῖς
καὶ πέδῳ, στρωμνὰ δὲ χαράσσοισ' ἄπαν νῶτον ποτι-
κεκλιμένον κεντεῖ.   55
εἴη, Ζεῦ, τὶν εἴη ἀνδάνειν,

23. 'But in the night-gloom the ruddy flame-torrent as it rolls bears to the sea stretched far below (dark) rocks with crashing din.'

24. βαθεῖαν.] In the simple sense of 'deep' it is a strange epithet for πλάκα, 'a flat surface.' I take it to denote the distance of the sea below the heights.

25. ἑρπετόν.] Cf. Hes. Theog. 824. He has hands and feet, ἐκ δέ οἱ ὤμων | ἦν ἑκατὸν κεφαλαὶ ὄφιος δεινοῖο δράκοντος.

26. καὶ παριόντων.] '—yea and 'tis a marvel even for men when passing by to hear what a creature is pent between the dark-wooded crests of Aetna and its base; while the bed furrows and galls all his back as he lies prostrate.' The schol., Paley and Myers render 'to hear from passers by' (the mountain). Now if a sight is wonderful, a faithful description of it is so likely to be wonderful that the καὶ does not seem to have any force according to this interpretation. Moreover the mention of travellers' accounts is not in keeping with the bold strokes of this consummate piece of word-painting. The passage from Diodôros, I. 36, cited by Heyne to support the old view,

really tends to upset it; τοῖς μὲν ἰδοῦσιν θαυμαστὸν φαίνεται, τοῖς δ' ἀκούσασι παντελῶς ἄπιστον. Here παντ. ἀπ. is stronger than θαυμαστόν; while Pindar's θαῦμα is weaker than τέρας θαυμάσιον. I think the second limb of the phrase properly takes up the emphatic σὺν πατάγῳ. That the din was audible when the lava streams were not in sight may be inferred from Plin. N. H. III. 14, Favilla Tauromenium et Catinam usque pervenit, fragor vero ad Maronem et Gemellos colles. For gen. abs., cf. Ol. IX. 35; for the inf., Ol. VII. 25.

27. μελαμφύλλοις.] Oedipus calls Kolônos γῆ μελάμφυλλος, v. 483; cf. Arist. Thesm. 997, μ. τ' ὄρη δάσκια. It is an epithet of woody places rather than of trees, and suggests the dark shadows and deep blue haze which masses of trees exhibit rather than a special colour of foliage.

28. πέδῳ.] Don.'s 'plain of Sicily' is not clear. Sicily is on Typho's breast (v. 19), so that this πέδον is the floor of the Tartarean hollows under Sicily.

29. εἴη.] For ellipse of pronoun cf. Pyth. II. 83, Isthm. v. 7, Frag. 104 [236].

30 ὃς τοῦτ᾽ ἐφέπεις ὄρος, εὐκάρποιο γαίας μέτωπον, τοῦ
        μὲν ἐπωνυμίαν
    κλεινὸς οἰκιστὴρ ἐκύδανεν πόλιν
    γείτονα, Πυθιάδος δ᾽ ἐν δρόμῳ κάρυξ ἀνέειπέ νιν ἀγ-
        γέλλων Ἱέρωνος ὑπὲρ καλλινίκου   60

                                                        Ἐπ. β'.
ἄρμασι. ναυσιφορήτοις δ᾽ ἀνδράσι πρῶτα χάρις   65
    ἐς πλόον ἀρχομένοις πομπαῖον ἐλθεῖν οὖρον· ἐοικότα
        γὰρ
35 καὶ τελευτᾷ φερτέρου νόστου τυχεῖν.   ὁ δὲ λόγος
    ταύταις ἐπὶ συντυχίαις δόξαν φέρει   70
    λοιπὸν ἔσσεσθαι στεφάνοισί νιν ἵπποις τε κλυτὰν
    καὶ σὺν εὐφώνοις θαλίαις ὀνυμαστάν.
    Λύκιε καὶ Δάλου ἀνάσσων Φοῖβε, Παρνασοῦ τε κράναν
        Κασταλίαν φιλέων,   75
40 ἐθελήσαις ταῦτα νόῳ τιθέμεν εὔανδρόν τε χώραν.

32. Πυθιάδος.] Cf. τὰν Ὀλυμπιά-
δων ἐν δρόμοις Πέλοπος, Ol. I. 94.
34. ἐοικότα.] For plur. cf. Pyth.
II. 81, ἀδύνατα δ᾽ ἔπος ἐκβαλεῖν κρα-
ταῖον ἐν ἀγαθοῖς δόλιον ἀστῶν, Ol. I.
52 ἐμοὶ δ᾽ ἄπορα γαστρίμαργον μακά-
ρων τιν᾽ εἰπεῖν τυχεῖν, Pyth. IV. 247,
μακρά μοι νεῖσθαι κατ᾽ ἀμαξιτόν. For
aor. where fut. seems more natural,
cf. βαλεῖν, v. 44; Goodwin, § 23, 2,
n. 2.

36. 'And the notion induces a
belief in consideration of this good
hap that Aetna will hereafter be
renowned for wreaths won by horses
and notable in connection with
banquets gladdened by minstrelsy.'

37. Read στεφάνοισί νιν ἵπποις
τε (Heyne, Böckh). Don. prefers
στεφάνοισι σύν. With ὀνομαστὰν
σύν is right, but with κλυτὰν awk-
ward: cf. Pyth. IX. 72, πόλιν κλει-
νὰν ἀέθλοις. Its insertion in the
first phrase is probably due to the
conjecture of a copyist after the
dropping out of the second ιν.

40. ταῦτα νόῳ τιθέμεν.] 'To make
the place thus famous and happy in
her sons:' ταῦτα refers to the adjec-
tives κλυτάν and ὀνομαστάν. Cf.
Cope's Ar. Rhet. II. 12, 6 (Shilleto's
Adv.) καὶ φιλότιμοι μέν εἰσι μᾶλλον
ἢ φιλόνικοι, ...καὶ ἄμφω ταῦτα μᾶλλον
ἢ φιλοχρήματοι. For double con-
struction of τιθέμεν, if we render
'do this and make,' cf. Eur. Phoen.
951, πικρὸν δ᾽ Ἀδράστῳ νόστον Ἀργεί-
οισί τε | θήσει κλεινάς τε Θήβας.
One objection to Don.'s reading of
v. 37 and the including (Λύκιε—
τιθέμεν) in a parenthesis is that we
have τε following καὶ in a way
which hardly falls in with Pindar's
Method, cf. v. 42. I cannot give
the objections to my view better than
by quoting Don.'s note. He says
'that the subject of the sentence,
to which the epithets κλυτάν, ὀνο-
μαστάν, and εὔανδρον refer, is χώ-
ραν, which is placed emphatically
at the end, like τιμάν in P. IV. 108.
It seems impossible to take εὔανδρόν·

Στρ. γ'.

ἐκ θεῶν γὰρ μαχαναὶ πᾶσαι βροτέαις ἀρεταῖς,　80
καὶ σοφοὶ καὶ χερσὶ βιαταὶ περίγλωσσοί τ' ἔφυν.
ἄνδρα δ' ἐγὼ κεῖνον

τε χώραν with ταῦτα νόῳ τιθέμεν, as Böckh and Dissen have done. Böckh construes the passage according to this collocation as follows: ταῦτα καὶ τὴν εὔανδρον χώραν τιθέμεν ἐν νόῳ, *haec tibi vota cordi sunt, cordi sit Aetna urbs.* Dissen interprets it as follows: *memineris prima hac victoria omen a te felix datum esse aliorum decorum (h. e. ταῦτα), et viris egregiis regionem florere, ideoque dignam coronis esse.* It would be difficult to say which of these two versions is the farther removed from the probable meaning of the poet. I cannot agree with Hermann (*Opuscul.* VII. p. 115), that there is any thing harsh in this parenthetical address to the god of the Pythian games, nor do I think that there is any impropriety in the poet's addressing Apollo here as the god of Lycia and Delos, and also as the Pythian god: least of all would I suppose, as Hermann does, that the poet had written the preceding lines, and the following strophe, and then inserted this parenthesis merely for want of something better. Horace addresses Apollo in the same stanza as the Castalian, Lycian, and Delian god (*Carm.* III. 4, 61): .

Qui rore puro *Castaliae* lavat
Crines solutos, qui *Lyciae* tenet
　　Dumeta, *natalemque* sylvam,
　　　Delius et *Patareus* Apollo.

Pindar utters these prayers to Apollo, not merely as the Pythian god, but also with reference to the other functions of this deity; and therefore invokes him by his other epithets. In a note subsequently added Hermann writes as follows: "Videor meliorem viam reperisse

duce Scholiasta, qui quum postrema sic interpretetur, ἐθελήσαις ταῦτα δ εὔχομαι τῷ σῷ νόῳ πράττειν καὶ συμπεραίνειν καὶ εὔανδρον ἀποτελεῖν τὴν χώραν, credo eum posita plena interpunctione post ὀνομαστὰν legisse ἐθελήσαις ταῦτα νόῳ τιθέμεν εὐανδροῦν τε χώραν. In quo si non falsus sum, addendum lexicis erit . εὐανδρόω" (*Opuscul.* VII. p. 115, note 9). Although this would be better than to interpret the passage as Böckh and Dissen have done, it appears to me unnecessary to introduce any alteration of the last words. We should expect the middle form τίθεσθαι instead of τιθέμεν, but the active is supported by such phrases as ζυγὸν αὐχένι θέντες, "placing the yoke upon their own necks" (*Epigr. apud Demosth. de Coron.* p. 322), and κόμας ἀνδήσαντες (*P.* X. 40).'

41. μαχαναί.] The sense here is more general than 'means,' being 'aught conducive to' the result in question, and embracing circumstances, natural powers, opportunities, and so forth. The word is not found in Pindar in the sense of 'device,' unless it be in Pyth. VIII. 78, where I prefer however to render ὀρθοβούλοισι μαχαναῖς 'capacities for sound counsel,' cf. ποτανᾷ μαχανᾷ, Nem. VII. 22, which is to be interpreted by comparison of Pyth. VIII. 34, IX. 92, 'power of making winged.' The fundamental meaning is *power* possessed, conferred, or educed. From the radical element MAGH come Germ. *möglich*, 'possible,' 'practicable,' Engl. '*may*,' '*might*.'

42. σοφοί.] Cf. Ol. I. 9, Pyth. I. 12, Nem. VII. 23.

περίγλωσσοί τε.] Böckh, Dissen,

αἰνῆσαι μενοινῶν ἔλπομαι
μὴ χαλκοπάραον ἄκονθ' ὡσείτ' ἀγῶνος βαλεῖν ἔξω
παλάμᾳ δονέων, 85
45 μακρὰ δὲ ῥίψαις ἀμεύσασθ' ἀντίους.

and Donaldson refer to Cicero *Brut.* c. xii. § 46, to show that the Sicilians applied themselves to oratory before Korax and Tisias made their treatises. They failed to see that 'antea' refers back to *Haec igitur aetas prima Athenis perfectum prope oratorem tulit'* (i.e. *Periclem*), § 45. It is however presumable that natural gifts of speech were at the time of the composition of this ode, B.C. 474, enjoyed and prized by those who were soon to institute the *art* of Rhetoric. Don. construes as if there were καί...καί ...καί instead of καί...καί...τε, 'poets, warriors, or orators.' The two classes mentioned are poets and successful statesmen: cf. Pyth. v. 104—107, Frag. 110. After καί, τε is not coordinate, but the idea coupled by the τε goes more closely with that coupled by the immediately previous καί than with the idea that precedes this καί. In other words the couple formed by the τε may be regarded as one general idea expressed as two particular ideas. Cf. Ol. viii. 8, xii. 18, Pyth. iv. 148, Pyth. x. 4, Nem. iii. 60, ἀλαλὰν Λυκίων τε καὶ Φρυγῶν Δαρδάνων τε,—the connection between the two latter tribes being more intimate than that of either with the first mentioned tribe, Nem. iv. 8, Κρονίδᾳ τε Δὶ καὶ Νεμέᾳ Τιμασάρχου τε πάλᾳ,—'and Timâsarchos' wrestling at Nemea,' ib. 75, Οὐλυμπίᾳ τε καὶ Ἰσθμοῖ Νεμέᾳ τε,—here Olympia stands apart as of superior dignity, the special interest attached to Νεμέᾳ being sufficiently indicated by its position. Mommsen makes a pause before the word coupled by τε to show that there is a closer connection between

the first and second than between either and the last. He could scarcely maintain this view in the face of Pyth. xi. 60—62, Ἰόλαον.... καὶ Κάστορος βίαν, σέ τε, ἄναξ Πολύδευκες, υἱοὶ θεῶν, where υἱοὶ only applies to the two latter persons who are thus closely connected by the poet's construction as well as by their brotherhood.

44. δονέων.] 'Making it quiver,' with the ῥόμβος of a strenuous cast; cf. Ol. xiii. 94. From Nem. vii. 70, ἀπομνύω μὴ τέρμα προβὰς ἄκονθ' ὥστε χαλκοπάρᾳον ὄρσαι θοὰν γλῶσσαν, I am led to suggest that ἀγῶνοι βαλεῖν ἔξω παλάμᾳ δονέων may mean 'hurl, making my cast out of the competition' (having stepped over the line, τέρμα προβάς). As distance was a point in the javelin throwing (cf. Isth. ii. 85, μακρὰ δισκήσαις ἀκοντίσσαιμι) as well as direction, 'outside the ring' would be a crooked throw, not one *beyond* the mark; so that it is hard to believe that any competitor would make such a very bad shot as to go over (why not into?) the spectators, whereas irrelevant speech might well be compared to a false throw which is declared 'out of the competition,' and so not allowed to count.

45. ἀντίους.] Especially Simonides and Bakchylides (Schmidt). This ode was composed for a reguler competition.

ἀμεύσασθαι.] The form ἀμεύεσθαι for ἀμέϝεσθαι is a parallel form to ἀμείβεσθαι. For such variation of the radical vowel in Gk. cf. αὐδή for αϝαδη by ἀείδω, √√ΫΑΔ, ΫΙΔ, ἔλσας &c. by εἰλύω, ἴλιγγος, δέξαι, Herod., by δεῖξαι.

εἰ γὰρ ὁ πᾶς χρόνος ὄλβον μὲν οὕτω καὶ κτεάνων
δόσιν εὐθύνοι, καμάτων δ' ἐπίλασιν παράσχοι. 90

Ἀντ. γ΄.

ἦ κεν ἀμνάσειεν, οἵαις ἐν πολέμοιο μάχαις
τλάμονι ψυχᾷ παρέμειν', ἀνίχ' εὑρίσκοντο θεῶν παλά-
μαις τιμάν,
οἵαν οὕτις Ἑλλάνων δρέπει, 95
50 πλούτου στεφάνωμ' ἀγέρωχον. νῦν γε μὰν τὰν Φιλο-
κτήταο δίκαν ἐφέπων
ἐστρατεύθη· σὺν δ' ἀνάγκᾳ μιν φίλον
καί τις ἐὼν μεγαλάνωρ ἔσανεν. φαντὶ δὲ Λαμνόθεν
ἕλκει τειρόμενον μεταμείβοντας ἐλθεῖν 100

46. χρόνος.] For χρόνος=life-time, cf. Ol. I. 115; for καμάτων ἐπίλασιν παράσχοι, cf. Ol. I. 97, VIII. 7; Nem. IX. 44, where victory in the games is said to bring forget-fulness of pains generally; but here we must understand an allusion to Hiero's stone.
οὕτω.] 'As now.'
47. MSS. ἦ κεν ἂν μν. Böckh, ἦ κεν ἀμν. as in Pyth. IV. 54, Φοῖβος ἀμνάσει. Here the absorption of να is needless, so I propose ἦ κ' ἀναμν.
48. εὑρίσκοντο.] 'When he and his were gaining.'
49. δρέπει.] Cf. Ol. I. 13, Pyth. IV. 130, but mid. Nem. II. 9. Curtius connects the root with δράσσομαι; but Pott takes it to be a secondary form of √δερ.
50. ἀγέρωχον.] Always epithet of persons in the Iliad and Odyssey but not so in Pindar. The deriva-tion is uncertain.
νῦν, κ.τ.λ.] 'This time however he went to war after Philoktêtes' fashion; but a certain one though so haughty was constrained to fawn on him for his friendship.
δίκαν.] Don. is not right as to the proper signification of δίκη being ' an equivalent.' Curtius

rightly refers it to √DIK 'point out'; whence δείκνυμι, Skt. diçâmi, Lat. dico. Observe that δείκνυμι=Germ. weisen, while δίκην (adverbially)= nach Weise. It is characteristic of a people whose religion entered deeply into their daily life to con-ceive 'right,' 'justice' as direction.
51. σὺν δ' ἀνάγκᾳ.] Cf. Pyth. IX. 96, σὺν δίκᾳ.
φίλον.] Clearly an extension of the predicate: cf. v. 92. Momm-sen reads νόσου from the Schol. Vet.
52. τις.] The magistrates of Cu-mae.
μεταμείβοντας.] Substituted from Hesych. Suid. Zonar. by Böckh for μεταλλάσσοντας or μεταλάσσον-τας. Wakefield's μετανάσσοντας, a suggested fut. from ναίω, has no authority for its form, nor would the sense be appropriate. For pres. part. where fut. might be expected, cf. Ol. XIII. 56, τοὶ μὲν γένει φίλῳ σὺν Ἀτρέος Ἑλέναν κομί-ζοντας 'being for carrying back:' so Pyth. IV. 106 ἱκόμαν οἴκαδ' ἀρχαίαν κομίζων πατρὸς ἐμοῦ...τιμάν. The mid. is used in the sense 'remove oneself' Pyth. III. 96, ἐκ προτέρων μεταμειψάμενοι καμάτων.

'Επ. γ'.

ἥρωας ἀντιθέους Ποίαντος υἱὸν τοξόταν·
ὃς Πριάμοιο πόλιν πέρσεν, τελεύτασέν τε πόνους
    Δαναοῖς,   105
55 ἀσθενεῖ μὲν χρωτὶ βαίνων, ἀλλὰ μοιρίδιον ἦν.
οὕτω δ' Ἱέρωνι θεὸς ὀρθωτὴρ πέλοι
τὸν προσέρποντα χρόνον, ὧν ἔραται, καιρὸν διδούς. 110
Μοῖσα, καὶ πὰρ Δεινομένει κελαδῆσαι
πίθεό μοι ποινὰν τεθρίππων· χάρμα δ' οὐκ ἀλλότριον
    νικαφορία πατέρος.   115
60 ἄγ' ἔπειτ' Αἴτνας βασιλεῖ φίλιον ἐξεύρωμεν ὕμνον·
                        Στρ. δ'.

τῷ πόλιν κείναν θεοδμάτῳ σὺν ἐλευθερίᾳ
Ὑλλίδος στάθμας Ἱέρων ἐν νόμοις ἔκτισσε· θέλοντι
    δὲ Παμφύλου   120
καὶ μὰν Ἡρακλειδᾶν ἔκγονοι

55. 'Though making his way with crippled frame: yea, but 'twas fate's decree.'

56. We may gather from this sentence that Hiero was contemplating the capture of some city in Italy, perhaps on the invitation of some friendly state.

θεός.] One short syllable as τεὸν in Praxilla, ἀλλὰ τεὸν οὔποτε θυμὸν ἐνι στήθεσσιν ἔπειθον: Pindar several times neglects iota; so perhaps here he used θιὸς or σιός.

57. καιρόν.] Cf. Ol. II. 54, ὁ μὰν πλοῦτος ἀρεταῖς δεδαιδαλμένος φέρει τῶν τε καὶ τῶν καιρόν.

58. Δεινομένει.] Hiero's son, named as usual after Hiero's father.

59. τοινάν.] Cf. καμάτων μεγάλων π. Nem. I. 70. εὐχὰς ἀγαθὰς, ἀγαθῶν ποινὰς, Aesch. Supp. 620.

60. ὕμνον.] The next strophe is specially meant.

61. ''Tis for him that Hiero founded your city with heaven-reared freedom according to the laws of Hyllos' rule.'

κείναν.] This word seems to prove that the ode was sung at Syrakuse.

62. ἐν.] Cf. Pyth. IV. 59.

Παμφύλου, κ.τ.λ.] He mentions only two Dorian tribes, one dynastic, the Hērakleidae, or Hyllaeans, the other seeming to stand for the two non-dynastic tribes. By the particle μὰν Pindar recognises the non-Dorian character of the (Achaean) Hērakleidae, but not, what is very probable, that the Pamphylii were immigrants of divers tribes into the northern Dorian seats by Pindos and that Aegimios himself was an Ionian. Probably the Dymānes were the original Perrhaebian Dorians, though it is uncertain whether the name Dorian existed before the admixture of the other two elements.

ὄχθαις ὕπο Ταϋγέτου ναίοντες αἰεὶ μένειν τεθμοῖσιν
ἐν Αἰγιμιοῦ
65 Δωριεῖς. ἔσχον δ' Ἀμύκλας ὄλβιοι   125
Πινδόθεν ὀρνύμενοι, λευκοπώλων Τυνδαριδᾶν βαθύ-
δοξοι γείτονες, ὧν κλέος ἄνθησεν αἰχμᾶς.

'Αντ. δ'.

Ζεῦ τέλει', αἰεὶ δὲ τοιαύταν 'Αμένα παρ' ὕδωρ   130

64. ναίοντες.] Clearly 'though
dwelling' is right. The poet im-
plies that if they will carry these
institutions so far from Aegimios'
home as Amyklae they will carry
them anywhere. He is tracing the
νόμοι Ὑλλίδος στάθμας and their
origin to show their stability.
Dymas seems to be regarded as
Aegimios' eldest son; so perhaps
Pindar regards the acceptance of
the Dorian statutes by the Dymâ-
nes as matter of course, and illus-
trates their applicability to the
new town Aetna, by mentioning
the willing adhesion of the younger
Dorian tribes.

65. Δωριεῖς.] So mss. Hermann
and Böckh read Δωρίοις.

ἔσχον.] Generally rendered 'they
dwelt': but cf. Ol. ii. 9, ἱερὸν
ἔσχον οἴκημα ποταμοῦ, Σικελίας τ'
ἔσαν ὀφθαλμός. According to Isthm.
vi. 14, the Theban Aegidae took
Amyklae for the Dorians. As the
seizure of Amyklae was said to
be and probably was the first step
towards the Dorization of Lakônia,
it is needless to imagine with
Dissen an allusion to Amyklaean
colonists of Aetna. See Curtius,
Hist. of Greece (Ward) Bk. ii. c. i.
p. 185.

65. ὄλβιοι.] Proleptic. 'Now
they gat Amyklae to their pros-
perity.'

66. λευκοπώλων.] Pindar clear-
ly does not agree with Virgil as
to white horses: color deterrimus

albis, Georg. iii. 82. Plato's good
horse in the myth, Phaedros, p.
253 D, is λευκὸς ἰδεῖν, and I ven-
ture to think that if white horses
were not then prized in Greece
Plato had in mind the legendary
royal steeds of Pindar and other
poets. The Tyndaridae, the Dios-
kuroi, lived and were buried at
Therapnae on the left bank of the
Eurôtas.

βαθύδοξοι.] This is surely more
than 'famous'; but cf. βαθυπόλεμος,
Pyth. ii. 1. Perhaps it may be
rendered 'of mysterious fame.' The
first part of the compound seems
to have reference to the 'secluded,
impenetrable and secret character'
of the Spartan community. Cf.
Curtius, Hist. of Greece (Ward) Bk.
ii. ch. i. p. 203.

ὧν κ.τ.λ.] 'While the renown of
their warrior host burst into blos-
som.' Or is the aor. frequenta-
tive?

αἰχμᾶς.] Cf. Ol. vii. 19.

67. 'Zeus, universal consum-
mator, (it is my prayer) that true
report of men may for ever award
such a distinguished lot to citizens
and kings by Amenas' stream.'
For the accusative and inf. ex-
pressing an entreaty cf. Ol. xiii.
114, ἄνα, κούφοισιν ἐκνεῦσαι ποσὶν
Ζεῦ τέλει· αἰδῶ δίδοι καὶ τύχαν
τερπνῶν γλυκεῖαν (Böckh for ἀλλά...
τέλει...δίδους), Pyth. ii. 24, and Mad-
vig, § 168 a. 1, 2.

αἶσαν ἀστοῖς καὶ βασιλεῦσιν διακρίνειν ἔτυμον λόγον
ἀνθρώπων.
σύν τοι τίν κεν ἀγητὴρ ἀνήρ,
70 υἱῷ τ᾽ ἐπιτελλόμενος, δᾶμον γεραίρων τράποι σύμ-
φωνον ἐς ἀσυχίαν.   135
λίσσομαι νεῦσον Κρονίων, ἄμερον
ὄφρα κατ᾽ οἶκον ὁ Φοίνιξ ὁ Τυρσανῶν τ᾽ ἀλαλατὸς
ἔχῃ, ναυσίστονον ὕβριν ἰδὼν τὰν πρὸ Κύμας·   140
'Επ. δ᾽.

οἷα Συρακοσίων ἀρχῷ δαμασθέντες πάθον,
ὠκυπόρων ἀπὸ ναῶν ὅς σφιν ἐν πόντῳ βάλεθ᾽ ἁλικ-
ίαν,   145
75 'Ελλάδ᾽ ἐξέλκων βαρείας δουλίας.   ἀρέομαι

68. διακρίνειν.] Lit. 'distinguish
such a lot for citizens, &c.' Unless
ἔτυμος λόγος ἀνθρώπων be regarded
as a judge who awards not the lot
but the credit for, or the character
of having such a lot. Cf. Ol. VIII.
6, Nem. VII. 59.
71. ἄμερον κατ᾽ οἶκον ἔχῃ.] i. e.
κατέχῃ ἁ. οἶ. Cf. Pyth. II. 9. Render,
'that the Phoenician and Tyrrhē-
nian warriors may keep to their
homes peaceably, after seeing their
bold attack before Cumae causing
lamentation on their ships for their
grievous plight when vanquished
by the ruler of the Syrakusans.'
72. ἀλαλατός.] A very bold
metaphor, and not translateable.
ναυσίστονον.] A literal rendering
is supported by Aesch. Persae, 428,
οἰμωγὴ δ᾽ ὁμοῦ | κωκύμασιν κατεῖχε
πελαγίαν ἅλα.
ὕβριν.] Don. and Myers render
'loss' 'calamity.' Diodōros, XI.
51, omits to mention the Phoeni-
cians (Carthaginians) in his ac-
count of Hiero's victory off Cumae.
75. 'Ελλάδ᾽.] Magna Graecia.
For the comprehensive use of
'Ελλάς, cf. Thuc. I. 12, end.
From αἰρέομαι to ἀοιδοῖς, v. 94,

difficulties are frequent. I there-
fore translate : 'I shall win from
Salamis the gratitude of the Athe-
nians as my reward, but at Sparta
I shall tell of the battle before
Kithaeron, at which two places the
Persians armed with crooked bows
suffered sore, but on the well-
watered banks of Himeras (I shall
win reward) by giving tribute of
song to the sons of Deinomenes
which they earned by valour upon
their foes' defeat. If thou utter
what is in season, gathering up in
small compass the heads of many
themes, less cavil of men doth fol-
low. For surfeit blunts with dis-
gust the alacrity of expectation,
but for citizens what they hear
grieveth their secret soul, especi-
ally in respect to the merits of
others. Nathless, since envy is
better than pity, remit not noble
pursuits. Steer thy people with
the helm of justice and forge thy
speech on an anvil free from aught
false. If even some light flash of
talk is passing it is of great import
as from thee. Thou art a steward
of a great estate. There be many
trustworthy witnesses to thy good or

πὰρ μὲν Σαλαμῖνος 'Αθαναίων χάριν
μισθόν, ἐν Σπάρτᾳ δ' ἐρέω πρὸ Κιθαιρῶνος μάχαν, 150
ταῖσι Μήδειοι κάμον ἀγκυλότοξοι.
παρὰ δὲ τὰν εὔυδρον ἀκτὰν 'Ιμέρα παίδεσσιν ὕμνον
Δεινομένεος τελέσαις,
80 τὸν ἐδέξαντ' ἀμφ' ἀρετᾷ, πολεμίων ἀνδρῶν καμόντ-
ων.   155
                                                   Στρ. ε'.
καιρὸν εἰ φθέγξαιο, πολλῶν πείρατα συντανύσαις

evil. Abide in a temper that bear-
eth fair blossom if thou hast any
pleasure in ever being kindly
spoken of, and chafe not too much
at expense; but like a pilot let out
thy sail to the wind. Be not be-
guiled, my friend, by self-seeking
complaisance. Only the loud-sound-
ing of praise after death proclaims
the manner of life of the departed
both to chroniclers and bards.'

ἀρέομαι.] I follow Paley and
Schneidewin. Dissen renders 'Tol-
lo ad Salaminem Atheniensium tan-
dem iis mercedem Spartae unam
pugnam ad Cithaeronem pro Himer-
ensi vero proelio Din. filii hymnum
solvens, h. s. ita tamen ut pro Him.
proe. Din. filios canam.' But μισ-
θὸν applies better to the Poet than
to the Athenians, and Pindar uses
αἴρομαι 'I win, gain' in four other
passages, but not once in the sense
'to exalt.'

76. πὰρ μὲν Σαλαμῖνος.] This
may be 'by Salamis,' as Dissen
renders. For the genitive, cf. Pyth.
x. 62, φροντίδα τὰν πὰρ ποδός.
However for this phrase, cf. Pyth.
III. 60. Soph. Antig. 966, 1123 (?)
are closer parallels.

78. ταῖσι.] This is generally
slurred over as though relative to
μάχαν. It is a dative of place re-
ferring to Κιθαιρῶνος and Σαλαμῖνος.

79. τελέσαις.] Donaldson takes
this for optative. As ταῖσι refers
back to Σαλαμῖνος, it facilitates the

reference of the participle to ἀρέο-
μαι. Böckh's emendation ἐρέων
for ἐρέω v. 77, removes all diffi-
culty. The difference of tense be-
tween the two participles is cor-
rect, as the latter refers definitely
to the present ode. I think Donald-
son's supposed change from first
to second person is harsh.

'Ιμέρα.] Cf. Herod. vii. 165.
παίδεσσιν.] Cf. Simonides, Frag.
45. Φημὶ Γέλων' 'Ιέρωνα πολύζηλον
Θρασύβουλον, | παῖδας Δεινομένευς
τοὺς τρίποδας θέμεναι, | βάρβαρα
νικήσαντας ἔθνη, πολλὴν δὲ παρασ-
χεῖν | σύμμαχον Ἕλλησιν χεῖρ' ἐς
ἐλευθερίην.

80. ἀμφ'.] Cf. supra v. 12.
81. καιρόν.] It is not easy to
decide whether this is adverbial or
for τὰ καίρια, φθέγξαι καιρὸν being
parallel to κελαδῆσαι ποινάν.

φθέγξαιο.] Here the poet ad-
dresses himself.

πείρατα.] It is unfortunate that
scholars cannot agree how to ren-
der, Il. xiii. 359, τοὶ δ' ἔριδος κρα-
τερῆς καὶ ὁμοίου πολεμοῖο | πεῖραρ
ἐπαλλάξαντες ἐπ' ἀμφοτέροισι τάνυσ-
σαν, | ἄρρηκτόν τ' ἀλυτόν τε, τὸ
πολλῶν γούνατ' ἔλυσεν: else it might
illustrate the phrase before us, the
analysis of which is not easy. It
may be a metaphor drawn from the
handling of ropes, but we cannot
trace it, and again πείρατα may
simply mean 'the issues' 'the end'
apart from any such metaphor.

ἐν βραχεῖ, μείων ἔπεται μῶμος ἀνθρώπων. ἀπὸ γὰρ
   κόρος ἀμβλύνει   160
αἰανὴς ταχείας ἐλπίδας·
ἀστῶν δ' ἀκοὰ κρύφιον θυμὸν βαρύνει μάλιστ' ἐσλοῖσιν
   ἐπ' ἀλλοτρίοις.
85 ἀλλ' ὅμως, κρέσσων γὰρ οἰκτιρμοῦ φθόνος,
   μὴ παρίει καλά. νώμα δικαίῳ πηδαλίῳ στρατόν.
   ἀψευδεῖ δὲ πρὸς ἄκμονι χάλκευε γλῶσσαν   165
                                 Ἀντ. ε'.

εἴ τι καὶ φλαῦρον παραιθύσσει, μέγα τοι φέρεται   170
   πὰρ σέθεν. πολλῶν ταμίας ἐσσί· πολλοὶ μάρτυρες
   ἀμφοτέροις πιστοί.
   εὐανθεῖ δ' ἐν ὀργᾷ παρμένων,
90 εἴπερ τι φιλεῖς ἀκοὰν ἀδεῖαν αἰεὶ κλύειν, μὴ κάμνε
   λίαν δαπάναις·   175

συντανύσας.] 'Having brought together by stretching' is the literal meaning of the word, but the process is not familiar except in archery. Now the drawing of a bow does not suggest comprehension, or compression, which we clearly want here. We must therefore consider συντανύω to have been formed as the correlative to ἐκτανύω and ἐκτείνω, the verbal element becoming quite subordinate to the preposition, and so seeming to acquire a sense opposite to its original meaning.

82. μείων.] Cf. Ol. I. 35, ἔστι δ' ἀνδρὶ φάμεν ἐοικὸς ἀμφὶ δαιμόνων καλά· μείων γὰρ αἰτία. It is implied that μῶμος and αἰτία are inevitable.

83. αἰανής.] This epithet is applied to κόρον, Isthm. III. 2.

84. Cf. ἴσχει τε γὰρ ὄλβος οὐ μείονα φθόνον. ὁ δὲ χαμηλὰ πνέων ἄφαντον βρέμει, Pyth. XI. 29.

85. Cf. Herod. III. 52, φθονέεσθαι κρέσσον ἐστὶν ἢ οἰκτείρεσθαι.

86. νώμα κ.τ.λ.] For the comparison of a state with a ship or

fleet, cf. Pyth. VIII. 98.

ἀψευδεῖ, κ.τ.λ.] Cf. Ol. VI. 82, δόξαν ἔχω τιν' ἐπὶ γλώσσᾳ ἀκόνας λιγυρᾶς. Cic. de Oratore, III. 30, § 121, non enim solum acuenda nobis neque procudenda lingua est, sed onerandum complendumque pectus maximarum rerum et plurimarum suavitate, copia, varietate. The general sense is 'form your habit of speech with a regard to truth before everything.' The metaphor is intelligible as a whole but will not bear dissection.

87. παραιθύσσει.] Active in Ol. XI. 73, συμμαχία θόρυβον παραιθυξε μέγαν, 'his fellow-warriors sent along a mighty wave of cheers.'

μέγα.] i.e. μέγα ἐστὶ φερόμενον. Cf. Plat. Theaet. 148 E, ἀκούων τὰς παρὰ σοῦ ἀποφερομένας ἐρωτήσεις.

88. ἀμφοτέροις.] Cf. Dem. Fals. Leg. p. 411, ἀκριβῆ τὴν παρ' ἑαυτοῦ εἰς ἑκάτερα αἴσθησιν.

90. μὴ κάμνε.] For sentiment cf. Isth. V. 10, εἰ γάρ τις ἀνθρώπων δαπάνᾳ τε χαρεὶς | καὶ πόνῳ πράσσει θεοδμάτους ἀρετάς, κ.τ.λ.

ἐξίει δ' ὥσπερ κυβερνάτας ἀνὴρ
ἱστίον ἀνεμόεν. μὴ δολωθῆς, ὦ φίλος, εὐτραπέλοις
κέρδεσσ'· ὀπιθόμβροτον αὔχημα δόξας   180

'Επ. ε'.

οἷον ἀποιχομένων ἀνδρῶν δίαιταν μανύει
καὶ λογίοις καὶ ἀοιδοῖς. οὐ φθίνει Κροίσου φιλόφρων
ἀρετά.
95 τὸν δὲ ταύρῳ χαλκέῳ καυτῆρα νηλέα νόον   185
ἐχθρὰ Φάλαριν κατέχει παντᾷ φάτις.
οὐδέ μιν φόρμιγγες ὑπωρόφιαι κοινωνίαν
μαλθακὰν παίδων ὀάροισι δέκονται.   190

91. ἐξίει.] This metaphor occurs with regard to hospitality, Isthm. II. 40, οὐδέ ποτε ξενίαν οὖρος ἐμπνεύσαις ὑπέστειλ' ἱστίον ἀμφὶ τράπεζαν, which Donaldson renders unsatisfactorily : 'nor did the favouring breeze which blew around his hospitable table desist from blowing so as to compel him to furl his sails.' Rather 'nor did the wafting wind though blowing fresh about his hospitable board induce him to furl his sail.' The timid mariner furls his sails if the breeze freshens, but a calm does not compel the furling in any case. Those who compare Soph. Aj. 659, δεινῶν δ' ἄημα πνευμάτων ἐκοίμισε | στένοντα πόντον, should go on ἐν δ' ὁ παγκρατὴς ὕπνος | λύει πεδήσας, which illustrates their interpretation of ἐμπνεύσας ὑπέστειλ' ἱστίον.
92. ὦ φίλος.] We perhaps should render, 'Be not allured, my friend, by (desire for) shifty gains.' mss. ὦ φίλε κέρδεσιν εὐτραπέλοις. Hermann read φίλος, cf. Nem. III. 76. The Oxford Edition read εὐτρ. κέρδεσσ'. But a schol. explains τῇ ἐχθροτάτῃ φιλοκερδείᾳ, which suggests that ὦ φίλε is due to a gloss, and that κέρδεσιν εὐτρ. is right, two long syllables being lost before ὀπιθόμβροτον. For sentiment cf.

Pyth. II. 74—78 according to Don. who explains κέρδεσσ' as referring to the cunning arts of flatterers. It is true that this word means 'wiles,' 'arts' in Homer, but here the context suggests the commoner meaning.
αὔχημα.] Cf. Ol. IX. 38.
94. λογίοις.] On this word see my monograph 'On the First Ages of Written Greek Literature,' published by the Cambridge Philosoph. Soc. 1868. Cf. Nem. VI. 31, παροιχομένων γὰρ ἀνέρων ἀοιδοὶ καὶ λόγοι τὰ καλά σφιν ἔργ' ἐκόμισαν.
95. ταύρῳ καυτῆρα.] For constr. cf. Madv. § 45 b, Rem.
νηλέα νόον] Perhaps 'As being ruthless of soul'; though cf. Pyth. IV. 184, IX. 23 for an adj. qualifying a subst. simply, with another subst. or adj. used for a subst. (with article) in apposition.
96. Cf. ὁ δ' ὄλβιος ὃν φᾶμαι κατέχοντ' ἀγαθαί, Ol. VII. 10.
97. 'Nor do citherns in vaulted halls admit him to gentle communion in the choral songs of boys.'
κοινωνίαν.] Cognate accus., cf. Eur. Iph. Aul. 1181, δέχομαι σε δέξιν ἥν σε δέξασθαι χρεών.
98. ὀάροισι.] Dative after κοινωνίαν. The word is probably for ϜαϜαρος a reduplicated form (Curtius)

τὸ δὲ παθεῖν εὖ πρῶτον ἀέθλων· εὖ δ' ἀκούειν δευτέρα
μοῖρ'· ἀμφοτέροισι δ' ἀνὴρ
100 ὃς ἂν ἐγκύρσῃ καὶ ἕλῃ, στέφανον ὕψιστον δέδεκται. 195

connected with εἴρηκα from √VAR
'speak.' However the δ- might be
for sa, sam, 'together' as in ὅπα-
τρος, ὅξυξ.

99. For sentiment cf. Nem. IX.
46, εἰ γὰρ ἅμα κτεάνοις πολλοῖς ἐπί-

δοξον ἄρηται | κῦδος, οὐκέτ' ἔστι πόρ-
σω θνατὸν ἔτι σκοπιᾶς ἄλλας ἐφάπ-
τεσθαι ποδοῖν.

δευτέρα μοῖρα.] Cf. οὐ πάνυ μοίρας
εὐδαιμονίσαι | πρώτης, Soph. Oed.
Col. 144.

PYTHIA II.

ON A VICTORY (NOT PYTHIAN) GAINED BY HIERO TYRANT OF SYRAKUSE WITH THE FOUR-HORSE CHARIOT.

INTRODUCTION.

THIS ode is not Pythian, but celebrates a victory gained (B.C. 477), either at the Theban Iolâia or Hêrakleia, or else at the Panathênaea.

It was sung in Ortygia (*v.* 6) and sent by a private passenger on some merchant vessel before the Kastoreion, the processional song of victory (*vv.* 67—71).

The rhythm is Aeolian.

CHRONOLOGY.

	B.C.
HIERO became tyrant of Syrakuse	478
Anaxilaos of Rhegium died	476

Therefore the intervention by which Hiero earned the gratitude of the Lokrians (*v.* 19) fell between these two dates. Though the expressions in *vv.* 18—20 lead one to infer that the event was recent when the ode was written, it would appear that the Lokrian state was not so grateful as the Lokrian maid, else why is Ixion's message to men introduced *v.* 24? Possibly they were not content with deliverance, but wished Hiero to help them to take vengeance on Anaxilas, which to one who felt that needless war was baneful might well seem to savour of ingratitude. Commentators seem not to have observed the covert recommendation of a peaceful unambitious policy throughout the ode. Note especially the likening of Hiero to Kinyras (*vv.* 15—17), the mention of Rhadamanthys (*v.* 73), and the sentiments expressed *vv.* 63, 66. Pindar's rivals were apparently of the war party, as I infer especially from *vv.* 52, 53, 59—61. This hypothesis gives the unity which we look for in a lyric composition without imputing to Pindar, as Böckh does, the imprudence and bad taste of alluding to Hiero's designs on his brother Polyzêlos' wife Dâmareta, daughter of Thêro and widow of Gelo, who left a son by her. The comparison of the Lokrians, descendants of slaves and their mistresses, to Ixion is singularly appropriate. Are *vv.* 46—48 aimed at them?

	B.C.
Simonides of Keos born	556
Went to Hiero's court	477

His nephew Bakchylides was probably introduced by him.

Now the best authorities give B.C. 450 as the '*floruit*' of Bakchylides, and Professor Jebb in his Remarks on Professor Mahaffy's Review of 'The Attic Orators' (p. 26) says : 'As to Bakchylides being the rival of Pindar, that notion rests on the statement of two scholia, that in Pind. Olymp. II. 156, Pindar alludes to Bakchylides. But this will hardly do, for the second Olympian refers to 476 B.C., and Bakchylides the nephew of Simonides could scarcely on any view have been so prominent at so early a date.'

Professor Jebb overlooks the scholia on Pyth. II., Bergk's 5th Fragment of Bakchylides, and the fact that Simonides' nephew if 40 years younger than his uncle, would be nearly 40 B.C. 477. It seems to me that Bakchylides might very well be a calumniator of Pindar, and a competitor so far as Hiero's and Thêro's commissions were concerned. Probably he was amongst the ἄντιοι of Pyth. I. 45, B.C. 474. Bakchylides celebrated Pherenikos' Olympian victory, 482 B.C. The presumption is in favour of the mention of the horse not being long after the victory. All this notwithstanding, I do not accept Professor Mahaffy's correction 'Bakchylides *floruit*, B.C. 470.' The phrase most naturally applies to his reputation in Greece, with which the appreciation of him in Sicily should not be confounded. From the sneer at μαθόντες, Ol. II. 87, we may infer that Pindar's detractors were comparatively slow in maturing their skill. Simonides *floruit* B.C. 489, when we know he was 66 years old at least, and there is no need for supposing the nephew to have been more than 67 years of age, B.C. 450, while he may have been much younger.

	B. C.
Simonides died	465
Bakchylides *floruit*	450

ANALYSIS.

vv.

1—4. Dedication of ode to Syrakuse, mighty in war.

4—12. Mention of Hiero's victory with the four-horse chariot, in winning which the warrior maiden Artemis assisted him.

13, 14. Different men praise different kings.

15—17. Kyprian songs celebrate Kinyras out of gratitude for his good works.

18—20. So the Lokrian maiden praises Hiero for her deliverance from the evils of war.

21—41. The myth of Ixion, inculcating the duty of gratitude and of moderation in desires.

42—48. The offspring of Ixion and Nephele.

49—52. God accomplishes all his designs, and is the dispenser of glory and humiliation.

52—56. Calumny must be avoided, as the difficulties of Archilochos warn us.

56—58. Riches and good fortune are praised. Riches Hiero has and military power.

58—61. It is idle to say that in wealth and honour any Hêllen of former time surpassed Hiero. [Some one would appear to have tried to stimulate Hiero to some enterprise by suggesting that he should emulate the glory of some warrior of days gone by.]

62—67. Hiero had won renown in war as a youth, while his wise counsels in maturer years afford the poet ἀκίνδυνον ἔπος of praise.

67—71. Hail. This ode is sent by private opportunity. Give a cordial welcome to the Kastoreion (which will follow).

72—75. Advice to follow Rhadamanthys' example in not encouraging flatterers.

76—85. Denunciation of slanderers and their impotent malice.

86. Plain-spokenness is best under any form of government.

86—end. Envy reproved and contentment commended.

Στρ. α΄.

Μεγαλοπόλιες ὦ Συράκοσαι, βαθυπολέμου
τέμενος Ἄρεος, ἀνδρῶν ἵππων τε σιδαροχαρμᾶν δαι-
μόνιαι τροφοί,   5
ὔμμιν τόδε τᾶν λιπαρᾶν ἀπὸ Θηβᾶν φέρων
μέλος ἔρχομαι ἀγγελίαν τετραορίας ἐλελίχθονος,
5 εὐάρματος Ἱέρων ἐν ᾇ κρατέων
τηλαυγέσιν ἀνέδησεν Ὀρτυγίαν στεφάνοις,   10
ποταμίας ἕδος Ἀρτέμιδος, ἆς οὐκ ἄτερ

1. **Μεγαλοπόλιες**] Literally, no
doubt, 'consisting of, including,
mighty πόλεις,' i.e. Ortygia and
Achradine, without counting the
suburbs Tychê and Neâpolis. As
an epithet of Athens it may mean
'with mighty akropolis.' With a
city's name in the singular it is a
substantive, as the appellative
Megalopolis.

βαθυπολέμου] 'Lord of inveter-
ate war.' Literally 'possessed of a
highly-piled store of wars.'

2. **σιδαροχαρμᾶν.**] 'Fighting in
iron mail.' Prof. Paley, Dissen and
others take -χάρμας as 'delighting
in,' a rendering which seems to me
aesthetically inferior to, and less
classical than the other. Horses
can hardly be said to delight in
iron, so that either my rendering
must be accepted or ἀνδρῶν ἵππων
τε taken as a hendiadys. According
to analogy the form appears to be
akin to χάρμη rather than an inde-
pendent derivative from the √χαρ.
Now, although χάρμη means 'suc-
cessful struggle' Ol. ix. 86, and
though there are analogies for the
meanings 'delight' and 'battle'
attaching to the same word, yet
there is no trace of the simple
meaning 'delight' belonging to
χάρμη. We have here then an
early notice of the armour for
horses described by Xenophon in
the last chapter of his περὶ ἱππι-
κῆς.

δαιμόνιαι] 'By grace divine.' For
my rendering cf. ἴστω γὰρ ἐν τούτῳ
πεδίλῳ δαιμόνιον πόδ' ἔχων, Ol. vi. 8,
cf. ἔκτεινε Λᾶον μόριμος υἱός, Ol. ii.
38, θεύμοροι νίσσονται κατ' ἀνθρώπους
ἀοιδαί, Ol. iii. 10. Cf. also Ol. ix.
110.

3. **λιπαρᾶν.**] Cf. Λιπαρᾶν τε
Θηβᾶν μέγαν σκόπελον, Frag. 178
[289]. Always in Pindar ' gleam-
ing,' 'bright' especially of cities.
With λ. κόσμον, Ol. viii. 82, of the
Olympic crown, cf. τηλαυγέσιν στε-
φάνοις just below; while λ. γήραϊ,
Nem. vii. 99, is 'sleek old age.'

φέρων] Here and in v. 62 the
poet speaks of himself as going to
Syrakuse, though in v. 68 we are
told that the ode was sent. How-
ever he does not in this verse
'identify himself' with his ode.

4. **ἐλελίχθονος.**] 'Thirling.' It
seems to be for ἐλελιξίχθονος, cf.
Pyth. i. 4. Cf. θεμισκρέων for θεμισ-
τοκρέων, κελαινεφὴς for κελαινονεφής.

6. **τηλαυγέσιν.**] Either because
borne aloft in the στεφανηφορία or
because displayed in conspicuous
places.

7. **ποταμίας.**] The worship of Ar-
temis Alpheiôa was conveyed from
Elis to Ortygia. Many cults united
under the name Artemis, as is
shown by her various functions and
appellatives. The Lydian Arte-
mis seems to have taken the place
of sundry Aryan elemental deities
and local nymphs, as for instance

F.   10

κείνας ἀγαναῖσιν ἐν χερσὶ ποικιλανίους ἐδάμασσε πώ-
λους.　　　　　　　　　　　　　　　　　　　15
　　　　　　　　　　　　　　　　　　　　　'Αντ. α'.

ἐπὶ γὰρ ἰοχέαιρα παρθένος χερὶ διδύμα
10 ὅ τ' ἐναγώνιος 'Ερμᾶς αἰγλάεντα τίθησι κόσμον, ξεστὸν
　　ὅταν δίφρον　　　　　　　　　　　　　　　20
ἔν θ' ἅρματα πεισιχάλινα καταζευγνύῃ
σθένος ἵππιον, ὀρσοτρίαιναν εὐρυβίαν καλέων θεόν.
ἄλλοις δέ τις ἐτέλεσσεν ἄλλος ἀνὴρ
εὐαχέα βασιλεῦσιν ὕμνον ἄποιν' ἀρετᾶς.　　　25
15 κελαδέοντι μὲν ἀμφὶ Κινύραν πολλάκις
φᾶμαι Κυπρίων, τὸν ὁ χρυσοχαῖτα προφρόνως ἐφίλασ'
'Απόλλων,　　　　　　　　　　　　　　　30
　　　　　　　　　　　　　　　　　　　　'Επ. α'.

ἱερέα κτίλον 'Αφροδίτας· ἄγει δὲ χάρις φίλων ποί-
νιμος ἀντὶ ἔργων ὀπιζομένα.

---

of Arethusa. As a huntress she is
brought into connection with rivers,
mountains, horses and wild beasts.
Hunting is a natural pursuit for the
death-bringer, and this function
is appropriate to a moon goddess,
as in all probability she was pri-
marily.

ᾶς οὐκ ἄτερ.] As Λατοῦς ἱπποσόα θυγάτηρ, Ol. III. 26.

9. χερὶ διδύμα.] 'With both her
hands' is Dissen's interpretation;
though I suspect it means that the
hand of the goddess moves with
the hand of the mortal groom as
its double. Render ' her hand
with his.' Observe ἰοχέαιρα, cf.
μητίονται, v. 92.

11. ἐν θ' ἅρματα.] Here and in
v. 86 ἐν is Aeolic for ἐς, which is
from ἐνς i. e. ἐν + a casual suffix ς:
cf. ἐξ by ἐκ, though without dis-
tinction of meaning. The ἅρμα
was everything except the body
(δίφρος). For position of prep. cf.
v. 59.

12. σθένος ἵππιον.] Cf. σθένος
ἡμιόνων, Ol. VI. 22.

17. κτίλον.] As Kinyras is said
to have been the inventor of copper
mining, the hammer, anvil, tongs,
lever and of tiles (Plin. Nat. Hist.
VII.), κτίλον may well mean 'civi-
lized' rather than 'domesticated.'
Don. refers to Il. II. 548, where
we are told of Athêne and Erech-
theus, κὰδ δ' ἐν 'Αθήνης εἷσε, ἑῷ ἐνὶ
πίονι νηῷ, and Hes. Theog. 988 τόν ῥα
νέον τέρεν ἄνθος ἔχοντ' ἐρικυδέος ἥβης
| παῖδ ἀταλὰ φρονέοντα φιλομμειδὴς
'Αφροδίτη | ὦρτ' ἀνερειψαμένη, καί μιν
ζαθέοις ἐνὶ νηοῖς | νηοπόλον νύχιον
ποιήσατο, δαίμονα δῖον—of Phaë-
thon, son of Kephalos and Eos.

ἄγει.] 'For they are moved by
gratitude that giveth him reverence
in requital for kindly deeds.' For
ellipse of object cf. Pyth. IV. 70,
Plato Gorgias 484 B and Nem. VII.
23, σοφία δὲ κλέπτει παράγοισα μύθοις.

ποίνιμος.] So Spiegel for MSS.
ποίτινος or ποί τινος. T. Mommsen

σὲ δ', ὦ Δεινομένειε παῖ, Ζεφυρία πρὸ δόμων   35
Λοκρὶς παρθένος ἀπύει, πολεμίων καμάτων ἐξ ἀμα-
χάνων
20 διὰ τεὰν δύναμιν δρακεῖσ' ἀσφαλές.
θεῶν δ' ἐφετμαῖς Ἰξίονα φαντὶ ταῦτα βροτοῖς   40
λέγειν ἐν πτερόεντι τροχῷ
παντᾷ κυλινδόμενον·
τὸν εὐεργέταν ἀγαναῖς ἀμοιβαῖς ἐποιχομένους τίνεσθαι.

Στρ. β'.

25 ἔμαθε δὲ σαφές. εὐμενέσσι γὰρ παρὰ Κρονίδαις   45
γλυκὺν ἑλὼν βίοτον, μακρὸν οὐχ ὑπέμεινεν ὄλβον,
μαινομέναις φρεσὶν
Ἥρας ὅτ' ἐράσσατο, τὰν Διὸς εὐναὶ λάχον   50
πολυγαθέες· ἀλλά νιν ὕβρις εἰς ἀνάταν ὑπεράφανον
ὦρσεν· τάχα δὲ παθὼν ἐοικότ' ἀνὴρ
30 ἐξαίρετον ἕλε μόχθον. αἱ δύο δ' ἀμπλακίαι   55
φερέπονοι τελέθοντι· τὸ μὲν ἥρως ὅτι

πότ τινος. The Schol. explains ἀμειπτική. For ποίνη in good sense cf. Pyth. I. 59, Nem. I. 70.

18. Δεινομένειε παῖ.] Cf. Τελαμώνιε π. Soph. *Aj.* 134, Λητᾴα κόρη, Soph. *El.* 570, Pyth. VIII. 19, Ξενάρκειον υἱόν.

πρὸ δόμων.] 'Before her door.' The daughters of the people are meant, not the ladies of the gynaekonitis.

20. δρακεῖσ'.] 'Having assumed an expression of security.' Myers' 'So that her eyes are not afraid for anything' needs a present tense. Cookesley suggests that it is a pres. from δράκημι. Cf. λεόντων ὡς Ἀρη δεδορκότων, Aesch. *Sept. c. Theb.* 53, ὁρῶντ' ἀλκάν, Ol. IX. 111; for the adjective cf. δριμὺ βλέπειν, Aristoph. *Ran.* 562, Hes. *Sc. H.* 160, δεινὸν δερκομένη.

23. ταυτᾷ.] 'Round and round.'

24. ἐποιχομένους.] Cf. οἰχνέοντές σφε, Pyth. V. 80, ὅτι πλείσταισι βρότων | ξενίαις αὐτοὺς ἐποίχονται,

τραπέζαις, Ol. III. 40, 'because the Emmemidae do honour to (or 'visit them with') the Tyndaridae with more hospitable boards than all mortals beside.' In the last quotation the ἐπ- will bear a sense of reciprocity, in the present passage still more so.

24. τίνεσθαι.] For inf. cf. Pyth. I. 68.

26. μακρόν.] Proleptic; cf. Pyth. I. 51. Aesch. *Persae* 298, ἄνανδρον τάξιν ἠρήμου θανών.

27. λάχον.] Cf. γάμου μέρος λαχοῦσα, Soph. *Antig.* 918.

28. αὐάταν.] The first syllable is short as in Pyth. III. 24, so that T. Mommsen writes ἀϝάταν. The word is connected with ἄδω, οὐτάω ὠτειλή, from √VAN or VĀ, 'harm.'

29. ἀνήρ.] Emphatic. He had presumed as if a God.

30. δ'.] Epexegetic.

31. μὲν—τε (v. 33).] Cf. Pyth. XI. 1, Frag. 53 [45]. 11, γόνον ὑπάτων

ἐμφύλιον αἷμα πρώτιστος οὐκ ἄτερ τέχνας ἐπέμιξε
θνατοῖς,

’Αντ. β′.

ὅτι τε μεγαλοκευθέεσσιν ἔν ποτε θαλάμοις   60
Διὸς ἄκοιτιν ἐπειρᾶτο. χρὴ δὲ κατ’ αὐτὸν αἰεὶ παντὸς
ὁρᾶν μέτρον.

35 εὐναὶ δὲ παράτροποι ἐς κακότατ’ ἀθρόαν   65
ἔβαλόν ποτε καὶ τὸν ἵκοντ’· ἐπεὶ νεφέλᾳ παρελέξατο,
ψεῦδος γλυκὺ μεθέπων, ἄιδρις ἀνήρ·
εἶδος γὰρ ὑπεροχωτάτᾳ πρέπεν οὐρανιᾶν   70
θυγατέρι Κρόνου· ἄντε δόλον αὐτῷ θέσαν
40 Ζηνὸς παλάμαι, καλὸν πῆμα. τὸν δὲ τετράκναμον
ἔπραξε δεσμόν,

’Επ. β′.

ἑὸν ὄλεθρον ὅγ’· ἐν δ’ ἀφύκτοισι γυιοπέδαις πεσὼν
τὰν πολύκοινον ἀνδέξατ’ ἀγγελίαν.   75

πατέρων μελπέμεν γυναικῶν τε Καδ-
μειᾶν ἔμολον, Soph. Phil. 1056,
ἐπείπερ ἐστι μὲν | Τεῦκρος παρ’ ὑμῖν
...ἐγώ θ’, κ.τ.λ., Eur. Or. 1317, πάλιν
κατάστηθ’ ἡσύχῳ μὲν ὄμματι | χροῷ τ’
ἀδήλῳ τῶν δεδραμένων πέρι, Ol. ιν. 15.
32. Cf. πρωτοκτόνοισι προστρο-
παῖς ’Ιξίονος, Aesch. Eum. 718.
ἐμφύλιον αἷμα.] Cf. αἷμα συγγε-
νές, Eur. Suppl. 148.
34. χρὴ δέ, κ.τ.λ.] Here we
have a concise statement of the
Pythagorean doctrine of the rela-
tive ethical mean formulated by
Aristotle, Nik. Eth. II.
35. Cf. ἑτέρῳ λέχεῖ δαμαζομέναν
ἐννυχοι πάραγον κοῖται, Pyth. XI. 24.
36. I have followed Don. read-
ing ἔβαλόν ποτε καὶ τὸν ἵκοντ’ (τὸν
ἵκ.=τὸν προσίκτορα, cf. Aesch. Eum.
435) notwithstanding ἵ for regular
ἷ. After most mss. Benedict reads
ἔβαλον ποτὶ καὶ τὸν ἵκοντ’=καὶ τὸν
ποθίκοντα, T. Mommsen ἔβαλον, π.
κ. τ. ἱ.=καὶ ὃν ποθίκοντο ‘e’en whom
they approach.’ Böckh read first

ἑ. ποτὶ κοῖτον ἱκόντ’, and afterwards
ἑ. ποτε καὶ τὸν ἑκόντ’ after Bothe.
As to the last conjecture Don.
regards it as only tolerable on the
very questionable hypothesis that
Pindar alludes to Hiero’s criminal
design on his sister-in-law Dâma-
reta, widow of Gelo, wife of Poly-
zêlos, and her son by Gelo. The
story of Ixion scarcely suits the
supposed allusion, which would be
moreover imprudent and out of
harmony with the tone of the Ode.
ἵκω (which is only in the Middle
Voice used absolutely with the
meaning ‘come as a suppliant’ in
Homer) ἱκνέομαι, ἱκανός, ἵκμενος, οἶκος,
προϊκτης, προϊσσομαι, προῖξ are from
the √ΙΚ ‘to go to for shelter.’
Don.’s version is somewhat shaken
by ἀπροσίκτων ἐρώτων, Nem. XI. 48.
Render, ‘for a union leading him
from his purpose cast into manifold
trouble even the suppliant.’
40. καλὸν πῆμα.] Hes. Theog.
585, καλὸν κακόν.

ἄνευ οἱ Χαρίτων τέκεν γόνον ὑπερφίαλον,
μόνα καὶ μόνον, οὔτ' ἐν ἀνδράσι γερασφόρον οὔτ' ἐν
θεῶν νόμοις·   80
τὸν ὀνύμαξε τράφοισα Κένταυρον, ὃς
45 ἵπποισι Μαγνητίδεσσιν ἐμίγνυτ' ἐν Παλίου   85
σφυροῖς, ἐκ δ' ἐγένοντο στρατὸς
θαυμαστός, ἀμφοτέροις
ὁμοῖοι τοκεῦσι, τὰ ματρόθεν μὲν κάτω, τὰ δ' ὕπερθε
πατρός.

                                                                Στρ. γ΄.

θεὸς ἅπαν ἐπὶ ἐλπίδεσσι τέκμαρ ἀνύεται,   90
50 θεός, ὃ καὶ πτερόεντ' αἰετὸν κίχε, καὶ θαλασσαῖον
παραμείβεται
δελφῖνα, καὶ ὑψιφρόνων τιν' ἔκαμψε βροτῶν,   95
ἑτέροισι δὲ κῦδος ἀγήραον παρέδωκ'. ἐμὲ δὲ χρεὼν
φεύγειν δάκος ἀδινὸν κακαγοριᾶν.
εἶδον γὰρ ἑκὰς ἐὼν ταπόλλ' ἐν ἀμαχανίᾳ

ἔπραξε.] Equivalent to ἐπράξετο, cf. Isthm. iv. 7, ἔν τ' ἀγωνίοις ἀέθλοις ποθεινὸν κλέος ἔπραξεν, Ol. xiv. 22.
41. ἀγγελίαν.] The message is given v. 24.
42. 'Without blessing of the Graces did she bear to him a monstrous offspring, sole of her kind and it the same.'
ὑπερφίαλον.] From √φυ; cf. δρία by δρῦς, σίαλος 'a fat hog' by σῦς.
43. νόμοις.] Dissen renders 'where the laws of gods have force,' comparing Cum semel infernas intrarant funere leges, Prop. iv. 11, 3. It means rather 'the customary worship of the Gods.'
48. τὰ ματρόθεν.] 'Having the parts derived from their dams netherward, but their upper parts from the sire.' Note the inversion of the phrase in the second clause.
49. Cf. τοῖσι τέλειον ἐπ' εὐχᾷ κωμάσομαί τι παθὼν ἐσλόν, Pyth. ix.

89. Render 'God accomplishes every end upon conceiving it.'
51. τινα.] 'Many a one.' Cf. καί τινα σὺν πλαγίῳ | ἀνδρῶν κόρῳ στείχοντα τὸν ἐχθρότατον | φᾶσέ νιν δώσειν μόρῳ, Nem. i. 64. Where τινὰ ἀνδρ. τὸν ἐχθ. clearly means 'some (or many) of the most hateful.'
52. ἐμὲ δέ, κ.τ.λ.] 'But 'tis meet that I avoid the excessive bite of evil-speaking. For I have seen, though far removed in time, chiding Archilochos generally in distress through battening on grievous abuse of his enemies. But to have wealth together with destiny's fair lot of wisdom is best. Thou manifestly hast it so as to display it with liberal soul.' 'Wisdom' means, as usual in Pindar, 'the minstrel's talent and lore.'
54. ἑκὰς ἐών.] Archilochos flourished B.C. 688—620.

55 ψογερὸν Ἀρχίλοχον βαρυλόγοις ἔχθεσιν   100
πιαινόμενον· τὸ πλουτεῖν δὲ σὺν τύχᾳ πότμου σοφίας
ἄριστον.

'Αντ. γ.

τὺ δὲ σάφα νιν ἔχεις, ἐλευθέρᾳ φρενὶ πεπαρεῖν,   105
πρύτανι κύριε πολλᾶν μὲν εὐστεφάνων ἀγυιᾶν καὶ
στρατοῦ. εἰ δέ τις
ἤδη κτεάτεσσί τε καὶ περὶ τιμᾷ λέγει   110
60 ἕτερόν τιν' ἂν Ἑλλάδα τῶν πάροιθε γενέσθαι ὑπέρτερον,
χαύνᾳ πραπίδι παλαιμονεῖ κενεά.
εὐανθέα δ' ἀναβάσομαι στόλον ἀμφ' ἀρετᾷ
κελαδέων. νεότατι μὲν ἀρήγει θράσος   115
δεινῶν πολέμων· ὅθεν φαμὶ καὶ σὲ τὰν ἀπείρονα δόξαν
εὑρεῖν,

'Επ. γ'.

65 τὰ μὲν ἐν ἱπποσόαισιν ἄνδρεσσι μαρνάμενον, τὰ δ' ἐν
πεζομάχαισι· βουλαὶ δὲ πρεσβύτεραι   120

---

56. πιαινόμενον.] Cf. 'I will feed fat the ancient grudge I bear him,' *Merchant of Venice*, Act I. sc. 3.

τὸ πλουτεῖν, κ.τ.λ.] I follow Dissen and Donaldson. For double genitive cf. Pyth. IX. 89. But Prof. Paley gives, after Böckh, 'But the being wealthy with such luck as fate sends us is wisdom's best gift.' Again Tafelius takes σοφίας with πλουτεῖν citing Hes. *W. and D.* 453, Ἀνὴρ φρένας ἀφνειός, Soph. *Antig.* 683, θεοὶ φύουσιν ἀνθρώποις φρένας, | πάντων ὅς ἐστι χρημάτων ὑπέρτατον. Again σοφίας ἄριστον might be 'better far than poetic talent.' Cf. Pyth. V. 58.

For sentiment cf. Bakchylides Frag. 1, ὄλβιος, ὧτινι θεὸς μοῖράν τε καλῶν ἔπορεν | σύν τ' ἐπιζήλῳ τύχᾳ ἀφνειὸν βιοτὰν διάγειν.

57. πεπαρεῖν.] Only found here and in Hêsychios. It is probably connected with *appareo*.

58. εὐστεφάνων.] Cf. Ἰλίῳ μέλλοντες ἐπὶ στέφανον τεῦξαι, Ol. VIII. 32, and ἐϋστεφάνῳ ἐπὶ Θήβῃ, Hes. *Theog.* 978. Is it 'well enwalled'?

59. περί.] Pindar uses περί with dat. with δηριόμαι, μάρναται, ἁμιλλᾷ, so here we must supply a participle signifying 'contending.' For position cf. v. 11, Ol. VII. 12, Pyth. v. 67, VIII. 99.

62. στόλον.] Cookesley after Dissen takes this to be cognate acc. 'voyage.' However the meaning 'prow' is preferable.

ἀμφί.] Cf. ἀμφὶ παλαίσμασιν φόρμιγγ' ἐλελίζων, Ol. IX. 13.

63. θράσος πολέμων.] Cf. τόλμαν καλῶν Nem. VII. 59. For gen. cf. Pyth. v. 106.

ἀρήγει.] Probably ἀρηγ<ἀργ<ἀρκ akin to ἀρκέω, ἀλαλκεῖν. The root is secondary from √AR 'join, fit,' Curt. No. 488.

64. εὑρεῖν.] Attic εὑρέσθαι.

ἀκίνδυνον ἐμοὶ ἔπος σὲ ποτὶ πάντα λόγον
ἐπαινεῖν παρέχοντι. χαῖρε· τόδε μὲν κατὰ Φοίνισσαν
        ἐμπολὰν   125
μέλος ὑπὲρ πολιᾶς ἁλὸς πέμπεται·
τὸ Καστόρειον δ᾽ ἐν Αἰολίδεσσι χορδαῖς ἑκὼν
70 ἄθρησον χάριν ἑπτακτύπου
    φόρμιγγος ἀντόμενος.   130
γένοι᾽, οἷος ἐσσὶ μαθών· καλός τοι πίθων, παρὰ παισὶν
    αἰεὶ

66. ἀκίνδυνον.] Does this mean 'suggesting no risks'? See Introductory remarks.

σέ.] So Böckh for ῥα. He reads ποτὶ σὲ for ποτὶ ῥα; but he does not adduce a parallel for the position of the pronoun between a preposition and its noun. The pronoun would be more likely to drop out after σ than after ι. If ἔτοσε ποτι were left the second ε would be crossed out as redundant and ῥα subsequently appended for the sake of scansion.

67. χαῖρε.] 'Commences the postscript of the ode,....the Kastoreion or song of victory was subsequently sent when the procession returned from Thebes. This Kastoreion was the ἱππικὸς νόμος, cf. Isthm. I. 14—17, Ol. I. 100.' (Don.)

69. ἐν.] Cf. Ol. v. 19, VII. 12, Nem. III. 79, Isth. IV. 27.

ἑκών, κ.τ.λ.] Cf. ἐκόντι τοίνυν πρέπει νόῳ τὸν εὐεργέταν ὑπαντιάσαι Pyth. v. 41. Cookesley fails to see the opposition between τόδε μὲν μέλος and τὸ Καστόρειον δέ, and consequently differs from Don. Render 'But on the Kastoreion in Aeolian mode look kindly, greeting it in honour of the seven-toned cithern.'

70. ἑπτακτύπου.] Cf. Φόρμιγγ᾽ ἑπτάγλωσσον, Nem. v. 24.

72. 'Be true to thyself having learnt what manner of man thou art. With children, mark ye, an ape is pretty, ever pretty. But

Rhadamanthys hath attained welfare, because to him was allotted thought's fruit (experience) irreproachable, nor doth his mind within him take delight in dishonesty such as by flatterers' arts ever waiteth on man. The whisperings of calumny are an irresistible evil both to listener and accused, altogether like the temper of foxes. But to the beast of gain how forsooth is this gainful in the issue? For as though the rest of the tackle hath toil of fishery in the depths, I like a cork above the net am undipped in brine. It is impossible for a guileful citizen to utter openly a word so that it have weight among nobles; nevertheless of a surety fawning upon all he weaveth in every way crooked plots. I have no part with him in impudence. Be it mine to befriend my friend. But upon my foe, as though a foe, like a wolf I will run suddenly, treading now here now there in crooked ways. For under every constitution a man of straightforward speech comes to the fore, at a tyrant's court or where the headlong commons, or when the wise have care of the state. One must not contend with God who at times upholds their interests, otherwhile again would give high honour to others. But not even this soothes the soul of the envious, but dragging as it were at an overweighted

Στρ. δ΄.

καλός. ὁ δὲ 'Ραδάμανθυς εὖ πέπραγεν, ὅτι φρενῶν
ἔλαχε καρπὸν ἀμώμητον, οὐδ᾽ ἀπάταισι θυμὸν τέρπεται
  ἔνδοθεν,   135
75 οἷα ψιθύρων παλάμαις ἕπετ᾽ αἰεὶ βροτῷ.
  ἄμαχον κακὸν ἀμφοτέροις διαβολιᾶν ὑποφαύτιες,   140
  ὀργαῖς ἀτενὲς ἀλωπέκων ἴκελοι.

scale they inflict a painful galling sore on their own heart, ere they attain all that they are devising in their thoughts. For it availeth to bear a yoke lightly after taking it upon the neck. But to kick, mark ye, against the goad is a slippery course. Be it mine to please the noble and to be their associate.'

γένοι'.] Paley says 'As in Ol. XIII. 26, γ. must here stand for εἴης.' The passage is ἀφθόνητος ἔπεσσιν γένοιο ἅπαντα χρόνον Ζεῦ πάτερ. Now χρόνον ἅπαντα may go closely with ἀφθόνητος, and γένοιο = 'become.' So here the poet's advice is confined to a particular case and Don.'s 'continue to be' is wrong. No doubt such an injunction though stated particularly may apply generally. Note that οἷος ἐσσὶ goes with both verb and participle. For phrase cf. Od. VII. 312, τοῖος ἐὼν οἷός ἐσσι, τά τε φρονέων ἅ τ᾽ ἐγώ περ.

καλόι.] For repetition cf. κῆμέ γὰρ ἐκ τώντρω σύνοφρυς κόρα ἐχθὲς ἰδοῖσα—τὰς δαμάλας παρελεῦντα, καλὸν, καλὸν ἦμεν ἔφασκεν Theokr. VIII. 72, Λυσανίη σὺ δὲ ναιχὶ καλὸς, καλός, Kallim. Epigr. 30, καλὸς μὲν γάρ ἐστι, καλός, ὦ μῆτερ, Alkiphr. Ep. III. The ape seems to have been called Καλλίας at Athens.

πίθων.] Cf. Archilochos Frag. 89. In Babrios' Fables 564, πίθωνα is used ὑποκοριστικῶς of a young ape (Schneidewin). By πίθηκος is figured 'a wheedler,' cf. Aristoph. Vesp., ὑπό τι μικρὸν ἐπιθήκισα, Thesm. 1133, Equites 887.

73. φρενῶν καρπόν.] Cf. Nem. x. 12, φρενῶν καρπὸν εὐθείᾳ συνάρμοξεν δίκᾳ.

75. οἷα.] For neuter plural instead of agreement with antecedent cf. Ol. I. 14, ἀγλαΐζεται δὲ καὶ μουσικᾶς ἐν ἀώτῳ οἷα παίζομεν, Pyth. VI. 21 ὀρθὰν | ἄγεις ἐφημοσύναν τά ......φαντὶ Φιλύρας υἱὸν παραινεῖν; Hom. Hymn. Merc. 66. Cookesley wrongly 'As delight (τὸ τέρπεσθαι being understood in τέρπεται) is given to (lit. 'follows') a man, &c.'

76. διαβολιᾶν.] Observe διάβ. ὑποφαύτιες.] MSS. ὑποφατιες (2 ὑποφάντιες). Böckh conjectures the text; cf. πιφαύ-σκω. The allusion is to the slanders of Bakchylides, though Hermann thought it was to the ὑπακουσταὶ and ποταγωγίδες 'listeners' and 'spies' whom Aristotle, Politics v. 11, says Hiero employed. Plutarch, however, ascribes their introduction to Dionysios. That διαβ. ὑποφ. = διάβολοι is shown by ἴκελοι, cf. ψιθύρων = ψιθυριστῶν v. 75.

77. Cf. Aristoph. Vesp. 1241, οὐκ ἔστιν ἀλωπεκίζειν οὐδ᾽ ἀμφοτέροισι γίγνεσθαι φίλον. 'It does not do to play the fox (be a calumniator and enemy to both parties in a quarrel) nor to be friendly to both sides.' This is a part which may be undertaken in all good faith, but is impossible to play. The οὐδ᾽ shows the second line is somewhat in opposition to ἀλωπεκίζειν.

ἀτενές.] Used adverbially = παντελῶς, cf. πάνετες τιθήνα, Pyth. I. 20.

κερδοῖ δὲ τί μάλα τοῦτο κερδαλέον τελέθει;
ἅτε γὰρ εἰνάλιον πόνον ἐχοίσας βαθὺ   145
80 σκευᾶς ἑτέρας, ἀβάπτιστός εἰμι, φελλὸς ὡς ὑπὲρ ἕρκος,
ἅλμας.

'Αντ. δ'.

ἀδύνατα δ' ἔπος ἐκβαλεῖν κραταιὸν ἐν ἀγαθοῖς
δόλιον ἀστόν· ὅμως μὰν σαίνων ποτὶ πάντας, ἀγὰν
πάγχυ διαπλέκει.   150
οὔ οἱ μετέχω θράσεος. φίλον εἴη φιλεῖν·
ποτὶ δ' ἐχθρὸν ἅτ' ἐχθρὸς ἐὼν λύκοιο δίκαν ὑποθεύ-
σομαι,   155
85 ἄλλ' ἄλλοτε πατέων ὁδοῖς σκολιαῖς.
ἐν πάντα δὲ νόμον εὐθύγλωσσος ἀνὴρ προφέρει,
παρὰ τυραννίδι, χὠπόταν ὁ λάβρος στρατός,   160
χὦταν πόλιν οἱ σοφοὶ τηρέωντι. χρὴ δὲ πρὸς θεὸν
οὐκ ἐρίζειν,

78. κερδοῖ.] MSS. κέρδει (1 κέρ-
δοι). Huschke read the text. κερδὼ
is connected with κέρδη 'wiles.' Pro-
bably 'trick, wile' is the original
signification of κέρδος, and the re-
sulting 'gain' the derivative mean-
ing.
  τοῦτο.] i.e. 'to slander.'
  79. εἰνάλιον πόνον.] Cf. Theokr.
XXI. 39, δειλινὸν ὡς κατέδαρθον ἐν
εἰναλίοισι πόνοισι.
  80. For metaphor of a cork cf.
παῖδες γὰρ ἀνδρὶ κληδόνες σωτήριοι |
θανόντι. φελλοὶ δ' ὡς ἄγουσι δίκτυον
| τὸν ἐκ βυθοῦ κλωστῆρα σώζοντες
λίνου, | Aesch. Choëph. 505. I think
that the poet means that he keeps
up his own reputation and that of
poets generally, though other poets
are trying to drag him down. The
net is the band of contemporary
poets; the heavy parts are those of
poor and precarious repute who try
to drag down the cork, Pindar.
  81. ἀδύνατα.] For Plur. cf. Pyth.
I. 84.

82. ἀστόν.] Cf. βασιλεὺς πραΰς
ἀστοῖς, οὐ φθονέων ἀγαθοῖς, Pyth. III.
71.
  ἀγάν.] MSS. ἄγαν, which will
not scan. Böckh gives ἀγὰν =
σπεῖραν, περίκλασιν, καμπήν, Schol.
on Aratos Phaen. 668, ἀγὴ ὄφιος.
  διαπλέκει.] For signification cf.
Aeschines in Ctesiphont. p. 442,
ἀντιδιαπλέκει πρὸς τοῦτο εὐθύς. The
metaphor is from the twists and
turns of wrestlers.
  83. εἴη.] For omission of per-
sonal pronoun, cf. Pyth. I. 29.
  84. For sentiment, cf. Isthm. II.
66, χρὴ δὲ ἔρδοντα μαυρῶσαι τὸν
ἐχθρόν. Archil. Frag. 65 (Bergk),
ἐν δ' ἐπίσταμαι μέγα | τὸν κακῶς
με δρῶντα δεινοῖς ἀνταμείβεσθαι κα-
κοῖς.
  86. ἐν.] For ἐς, cf. v. 11.
  88. For sentiment, cf. Theognis
687, οὐκ ἔστιν θνητοῖσι πρὸς ἀθανά-
τους μαχέσασθαι | οὐδὲ δίκην εἰπεῖν·
οὐδένι τοῦτο θέμις.

’Επ. δ'.

ὃς ἀνέχει ποτὲ μὲν τὰ κείνων, τότ' αὖθ' ἑτέροις ἔδωκεν
　　　μέγα κῦδος.　ἀλλ' οὐδὲ ταῦτα νόον　　　　　　　165
90 ἰαίνει φθονερῶν· στάθμας δέ τινος ἑλκόμενοι
περισσᾶς ἐνέπαξαν ἕλκος ὀδυναρὸν ἑᾷ πρόσθε καρδίᾳ,
πρὶν ὅσα φροντίδι μητίονται τυχεῖν.　　　　　　　170
φέρειν δ' ἐλαφρῶς ἐπαυχένιον λαβόντα ζυγὸν
ἀρήγει· ποτὶ κέντρον δέ τοι
95 λακτισδέμεν τελέθει
　　ὀλισθηρὸς οἶμος.　ἁδόντα δ' εἴη με τοῖς ἀγαθοῖς ὁμι-
　　λεῖν.　　　　　　　　　　　　　　　　　　　175

89. μὲν—αὖθ'.] Cf. οὗτος μὲν δὴ
ἄεθλος ἀάατος ἐκτετέλεσται. | νῦν αὖτε
σκοπὸν ἄλλον ὃν οὔπω τις βάλεν ἀνὴρ
| εἴσομαι, Od. xxii. 5.
κείνων.] The poet's rivals.
ταῦτα.] i.e. getting their turn of
exaltation.
90. στάθμας κ.τ.λ.] 'Dragging at a
measuring line' is not satisfactory;
on the other hand στάθμα is not
found to mean 'weight,' σταθμός.
The genitive follows analogy of
verbs meaning 'hold' 'grasp.'
Cookesley should not say that ἐπὶ
can be understood.　I cannot agree
with Don. that στάθμη always means

a 'standard' 'measuring line' else-
where in Pindar.　It seems to be
=to γραμμή, the line across the
stadium at the starting or (Pyth.
ix. 118) winning place, in Nem. vi.
7, καίπερ ἐφαμερίαν οὐκ εἰδότες οὐδὲ
μετὰ νύκτας ἄμμε Πότμος | οἵαν τιν'
ἔγραψε δραμεῖν ποτὶ στάθμαν.
91. ἕλκος.] Here we have a
play on the word ἑλκόμενοι.
94. Cf. Aesch. Prom. Vinct. 322,
οὔκουν ἐμοί γε χρώμενος διδασκάλῳ
πρὸς κέντρα κῶλον ἐκτενεῖς ὁρῶν ὅτι
τραχὺς μόναρχος οὐδ' ὑπεύθυνος κρατεῖ,
and Agam. 1624, πρὸς κέντρα μὴ
λάκτιζε μὴ παίσας μογῇς.

PYTHIA III.

ON VICTORIES OF A RIDING HORSE PHERENIKOS, WON
BY HIERO, TYRANT OF SYRAKUSE.

INTRODUCTION.

THIS ode celebrates victories of the horse Pherenikos, who won
the Pythian prize, B.C. 486 and 482; but the appellative Αἰτναῖος
(*v.* 69) proves this ode to be later than B.C. 476: therefore it must
have been composed either B.C. 474 or 470. I incline (after Dissen)
to the former of these dates, that of the first Pythian ode, in which
Hiero's illness is mentioned. The tyrant probably knew then that
his disease was incurable, though he did not die until B.C. 467,
probably in the prime of life, as Pindar says he was young at the
time of the battle of Himera, B.C. 480.

A horse Pherenikos won at the Olympic games, B.C. 472. If it
be the same horse that won at Pytho, he must have been decidedly
"aged" at the time of his Olympian victory, viz. at least 15 years
old, unless the received dates of the Pythian victories are quite
wrong. Mr Abraham Moore suggests that there may have been
more than one Pherenikos in Hiero's stud, see my note on Ol. I. 18.
If not, commentators ought to do the animal the justice of pointing
out his extraordinary retention of vigour[1]. Mr E. Myers would put
the victory (he ignores the scholia entirely) B.C. 474, and the ode a
good deal later than the victory. The language of the ode would
suit the close of Hiero's life best; but it may be conjectured that he
rallied unexpectedly after his illness in 474. If this ode had been
composed after the Olympian victory, B.C. 472, there would very

---

[1] Pliny, *Nat. Hist.* XI. 64, gives about sixteen years as old age for
horses. At this time, sixteen years is old for well-kept horses that work;
though stud horses live to twenty-five or thirty.

probably have been mention thereof, and again, the victory with the chariot won B.C. 474, would probably have received notice, unless the ode had been composed before the Pythian games in that year. An ode intended for an anniversary was probably finished before the festival began. The rhythm is Aeolian.

ANALYSIS.

vv.

1—7. A wish that Cheiron, the instructor of Asklêpios, were still living.

8—46. The myth of the sin and doom of Asklêpios' mother, Korônis, and of his miraculous birth;

47—53. Enumeration of his cures;

54—60. His presumption in raising a man from death for a reward, and the blasting by lightning of himself and his patient.

61, 62. Deprecation of a desire for immortal life, and advice to make full use of practicable resources.

63—67. If possible, the Poet would prevail on Cheiron to train another healer,

68—76. And would have come to Hiero, who is a model ruler, with two blessings, health and a Kômos' ode for Pherenikos' Pythian victories[1].

77—79. He will pray for Hiero to Rhea, who with Pân is worshipped just before his door.

80—82. Introduction of the proverb "The immortals assign to mortals two ills for every single blessing."

82, 83. The ignoble bear ills badly, the noble gracefully.

84—86. Destiny has attached to Hiero the highest prosperity.

86—103. The instability of happiness illustrated by the celestial marriages and subsequent troubles of Pêleus and Kadmos.

103—106. One ought to enjoy present blessings, as prosperity is transitory.

107—111. The poet will make the best of his circumstances, but if

---

[1] This language may allude to an intended visit which he made, B.C. 473.

ᴉe would secure fame for

(types of longevity) owe excellence long-lived—

ᴈd and prayers promised ᴉis advice and his mythi-g life. The general tone ; Olympian. The intro-usceptible of any certain ·efers to the conduct of a ᷓ be dismissed as fanciful d in mind the mistakes, by those who consulted led to tell of its origin ·, as well as to the god of the mention of Asklêpios' that Hiero had been led ·erhaps that near Himera; . of Olympos by showing ᴀ this inferior member of even the god of healing ᴵ did his mother. A story propriate to the subject of ᴀt among the extant odes ne to the second Pythian other to Korônis.

Στρ. α'.

Ἤθελον Χείρωνά κε Φιλυρίδαν,
εἰ χρεὼν τοῦθ' ἀμετέρας ἀπὸ γλώσσας κοινὸν εὔξασθαι
ἔπος,

2. ἀπὸ γλώσσας.] 'Openly.' Cf. Ol. vi. 13, Ἀγησία, τίν δ' αἶνος ἑτοῖ-μος, ὃν ἐν δίκᾳ | ἀπὸ γλώσσας Ἀδρασ-τος μάντιν Οἰκλείδαν ποτ' ἐς Ἀμφιάρη-ον | φθέγξατ'; so that ἀμετέρας is a sort of enallage for ἡμᾶς.

κοινόν.] Schneidewin after one

Schol. explains κοινῶς λεγόμενον ἐν τῷ βίῳ, cf. Pyth. v. 101, λεγόμενον ἐρέω. But I think Prof. Paley is right in rendering 'the common prayer of all,' i.e. of the citizens generally.

ζώειν τὸν ἀποιχόμενον,
Οὐρανίδα γόνον εὐρυμέδοντα Κρόνου, βάσσαισί τ' ἄρ-
　χειν Παλίου Φῆρ' ἀγρότερον　　　　　　　　5
5 νόον ἔχοντ' ἀνδρῶν φίλον· οἶος ἐὼν θρέψεν ποτὲ　10
τέκτονα νωδυνίας ἅμερον γυιαρκέος Ἀσκληπιόν,
ἥρωα παντοδαπᾶν ἀλκτῆρα νούσων.

　　　　　　　　　　　　　　　　　Ἀντ. α'.

τὸν μὲν εὐΐππου Φλεγύα θυγάτηρ,
πρὶν τελέσσαι ματροπόλῳ σὺν Ἐλειθυίᾳ, δαμεῖσα
　χρυσέοις　.　　　　　　　　　　　15
10 τόξοισιν ὑπ' Ἀρτέμιδος,
εἰς Ἀΐδα δόμον ἐν θαλάμῳ κατέβα, τέχναις Ἀπόλ-
　λωνος. χόλος δ' οὐκ ἀλίθιος　　　　　20
γίνεται παίδων Διός. ἁ δ' ἀποφλαυρίξαισά μιν
ἀμπλακίαισι φρενῶν, ἄλλον αἴνησεν γάμον, κρύβδαν
　πατρός　　　　　　　　　　　25
πρόσθεν ἀκειρεκόμᾳ μιχθεῖσα Φοίβῳ·

　　　　　　　　　　　　　　　　　Ἐπ. α'.

15 καὶ φέροισα σπέρμα θεοῦ καθαρόν,
οὐκ ἔμειν' ἐλθεῖν τράπεζαν νυμφίαν,

4. Φῆρ'.] The Φ is Aeolic for
θ. With θήρ cf. Lat. *fera*, Eng.
'deer.' Render 'centaur.'
ἀγρότερον.] It is doubtful whether
the suffix was originally the com-
parative *tara*, cf. ἀγροτήρ, ἀγρό-
τειρα.
5. νόον ἀνδρῶν φίλον.] For the
gen. cf. φίλαν ξένων ἄρουραν, Nem.
ix. 8. It is perhaps best to regard
φίλον νόον as equivalent to a com-
pound substantive φιλονοία.
6. νωδ. γυιαρκέος.] The mss.
give the sing., but the metre sug-
gests the plur. which Böckh reads,
but cf. χόρον, Pyth. ix. 114.
Ἀσκληπιόν.] Probably connect-
ed with σκέλλω, σκληρός, σκληφρός
'lean,' with α privative.
τελέσσαι.] Cf. ἔτεκεν δ' ἀνίκα

Μοῖραι | τέλεσαν ταυροκέρων θεὸν,
Eur. *Bacch.* 104, so ἀντείλας Διόνυ-
σον, Isth. vi. 5.
χρυσέοις.] A constant epithet of
things pertaining to deities.
11. ἐν θαλάμῳ.] 'In her cham-
ber.' This implies that she fell
sick and died, but was not stricken
with sudden death.
13. αἴνησεν.] Cf. λέκτρ' ἐπήνεσα,
Eur. *Or.* 1672, Pyth. iv. 222.
14. ἀκειρεκόμᾳ.] v. l. ἀκερσε-
κόμᾳ, which is found in the Frag.
of Hésiod on this legend.
15. καθαρόν.] Involving no de-
filement or disgrace as did her
illicit union with the Arkadian
Ischys son of Elatos.
16. ἔμειν' ἐλθεῖν.] Heyne and
Dissen—'endure to go to marriage

οὐδὲ παμφώνων ἰαχὰν ὑμεναίων, ἅλικες   30
οἷα παρθένοι φιλέοισιν ἑταῖραι
ἑσπερίαις ὑποκουρίζεσθ᾽ ἀοιδαῖς· ἀλλά τοι
20 ἤρατο τῶν ἀπεόντων· οἷα καὶ πολλοὶ πάθον.   35
ἔστι δὲ φῦλον ἐν ἀνθρώποισι ματαιότατον,
ὅστις αἰσχύνων ἐπιχώρια παπταίνει τὰ πόρσω,
μεταμώνια θηρεύων ἀκράντοις ἐλπίσιν.   40

Στρ. β΄.

ἔσχε τοιαύταν μεγάλαν ἀυάταν
25 καλλιπέπλου λῆμα Κορωνίδος. ἐλθόντος γὰρ εὐνάσθη
ξένου
λέκτροισιν ἀπ᾽ Ἀρκαδίας.   45
οὐδ᾽ ἔλαθε σκοπόν· ἐν δ᾽ ἄρα μηλοδόκῳ Πυθῶνι τόσσ-
αις ἄιεν ναοῦ βασιλεὺς

feasts,' comparing πάντες ἠντιάσθε θεοὶ γάμου, Il. XXIV. 62. The poet clearly means that, like Kreüsa in Euripides' *Ion*, Korônis would have married after her child by Apollo was born. If ἐλθεῖν be considered awkward with τράπεζαν it may be regarded as almost redundant, it being often superfluously added to μένω in Epic poems. It might then be rendered 'waited for the marriage feast,' but I prefer 'waited to go to the marriage feast'—taking ἐλθεῖν only with τράπεζαν and governing ἰαχὰν by ἐμεῖν.

17. 'Nor for the sound of the full hymenaeal chorus and its pleasantries which maiden companions of the bride's own age love to utter in song at eventide.'

παμφώνων.] Cf. Ol. VII. 12. The Hymenaeos was accompanied by flutes to which this epithet is confined by Pindar.

18. οἷα.] Cf. Ol. I. 16, Pyth. II. 75, VI. 21.

19. ὑποκουρίζεσθαι.] Gen. 'to call by pet names' or 'to give a flattering term to anything.' Hêsychios gives κουριζομέναις· ὑμεναιουμέναις. This probably gives the

original sense of the verb. The Hymenaeal songs contained covert allusions to coarse topics as well as endearments of the bride, and by consequence 'to call or speak in the fashion of *young people* who serenade a bride' includes the meaning we require here and those more commonly conveyed.

20. For sentiment cf. δυσέρωτας εἶναι τῶν ἀπόντων, Thuk. VI. 13, Nem. III. 30.

21. 'For there is a class amongst men most foolish, of those who think their native estate beneath them, and cast glances at what is afar, pursuing a bootless quest with impracticable hopes. Such a strong infatuation did the passionate Korônis conceive.'

22. παπταίνει.] Cf. μήκετι πάπταινε πόρσιον, Ol. I. 114.

23. θηρεύων.] Cf. κερδέων δὲ χρὴ μέτρον θηρευέμεν, Nem. XI. 47.

24. ἔσχε.] Cf. Pyth. I. 65, *infra v.* 89.

ἀυάταν.] The first two syllables are short, cf. Pyth. II. 28.

25. ξένου.] Ischys.

27. 'But she escaped not the ken of the watchful one, for though

Λοξίας κοινᾶνι παρ' εὐθυτάτῳ γνώμαν πιθὼν   50
πάντα ἴσαντι νόῳ· ψευδέων δ' οὐχ ἅπτεται, κλέπτει
· τέ μιν
30 οὐ θεὸς οὐ βροτὸς ἔργοις οὔτε βουλαῖς.

'Αντ. β'.

καὶ τότε γνοὺς 'Ίσχυος Εἰλατίδα   55
ξεινίαν κοίταν ἄθεμίν τε δόλον, πέμψεν κασιγνήταν
μένει
θύοισαν ἀμαιμακέτῳ

he was at the time at Pytho rich in offerings of sheep, the king of the shrine, Loxias, perceived it in his most infallible consciousness, having convinced his judgment by his all-knowing intelligence.'

σκοπόν.] Cf. τοξοφόρον Δάλου θεοδμάτας σκοπόν, Ol. VI. 59.

μηλοδόκῳ.] Admission to the adyton could only be got after sacrifice of living victims, cf. ἐπὶ δ' ἀσφάκτοις μήλοισι δόμων μὴ πάριτ' ἐς μυχόν, Eurip. Ion, 229.

τόσσαις.] Aeolic 1st Aor. part. = in sense to τυχών, cf. Pyth. IV. 25, x. 33. The best way of explaining the -σσ- is to compare θέσσαν for ἔθεσαν, ὁμόσσαι for ὁμόσαι, and to assume a √το from √ΤΑ the primary form from which √√ΤΑΚ ΤΥΚ τεκ-εῖν, τυχ-εῖν are developed.

28. πιθών.] Böckh and Dissen read γνώμᾳ comparing γνώμᾳ πεπιθὼν πολυβούλῳ, Isth. III. 90. Don. also compares πιθήσας, Pyth. IV. 109. The MSS give πεπιθών against the metre. A gloss however gives πείσας. Hermann, Mommsen and others read γνώμαν. I was once inclined to read πιθὼν as present to πιθήσας though not found elsewhere, as the false reading πεπιθών seems at first sight to point to γνώμᾳ rather than γνώμαν; but on the other hand it is not satisfactory to make γνώμᾳ identical with νόῳ; and it may be that πιθὼν was altered by

a critic who took νόῳ as an objective instead of a modal dative. The Scholiast says that γνώμαν πεπιθὼν = τὴν πρόγνωσιν (acc. of respect) ...πεισθεὶς ὑπὸ τοῦ κοινωνοῦ αὐτοῦ νοῦ. This is much the same as my rendering. The phrase is explanatory of the obscure phrase κοινᾶνι παρ' εὐθυτάτῳ 'in concert with his infallible confidant.' Pindar's language emphatically rejects the Hesiodic legend that a crow was Apollo's informant. Schn. considers κοιν. παρ' εὐθ., to be in special contrast to the crow, called comes obscurus tripodum, Stat. Theb. III. 506. The reading and rendering I choose are the most emphatic on this view. Hesiod (Frag. 225 Goettl.) says a crow told Apollo; Pindar says Apollo persuaded himself; so that the active form πιθὼν is forcible. Does πιθὼν imply that for all his omniscience Apollo was loth to believe the teaching? For the use of παρά cf. Dem. Phil. IV. 136, ταῦτα τοίνυν ἔκαστον εἰδότα καὶ γιγνώσκοντα παρ' αὐτῷ δεῖ μὰ Δὶ' οὐ γράψαι κελεύειν πόλεμον...τὸν τὰ βέλτιστα ἐπὶ πᾶσι δικαίοις συμβουλεύοντα.

29. ψευδέων.] Cf. σὲ (Φοῖβον), τὸν οὐ θεμιτὸν ψεύδει θιγεῖν, Pyth. IX. 42.

31. καὶ.] 'So,' 'accordingly.'

32. ξεινίαν κοίταν.] 'Her couching with the stranger Ischys.'

ἐς Λακέρειαν, ἐπεὶ παρὰ Βοιβιάδος κρημνοῖσιν ᾤκει
παρθένος· δαίμων δ᾽ ἕτερος   60
35 ἐς κακὸν τρέψαις ἐδαμάσσατό νιν, καὶ γειτόνων
πολλοὶ ἐπαῦρον, ἀμᾷ δ᾽ ἔφθαρεν· πολλὰν δ᾽ ὄρει πῦρ
ἐξ ἑνὸς   65
σπέρματος ἐνθορὸν ἄϊστωσεν ὕλαν.

                                                          Ἐπ. β΄.

ἀλλ᾽ ἐπεὶ τείχει θέσαν ἐν ξυλίνῳ
σύγγονοι κούραν, σέλας δ᾽ ἀμφέδραμεν
40 λάβρον Ἀφαίστου, τότ᾽ ἔειπεν Ἀπόλλων· Οὐκέτι   70
τλάσομαι ψυχᾷ γένος ἀμὸν ὀλέσσαι
οἰκτροτάτῳ θανάτῳ, ματρὸς βαρείᾳ σὺν πάθᾳ.
ὡς φάτο· βάματι δ᾽ ἐν πρώτῳ κιχὼν παῖδ᾽ ἐκ νεκροῦ   75
ἅρπασε· καιομένα δ᾽ αὐτῷ διέφανε πυρά.

34. παρθένος.] 'In her unwed-
ded state.' The application of this
term to a pregnant female is illus-
trated by the Spartan Παρθενίαι.
ᾤκει refers either to the time of
Artemis' mission (best), or to the
action of the δαίμων ἕτερος, when
Korônis was already φέροισα σπέρμα
θεοῦ καθαρόν.
ἕτερος.] Schol. quotes Kallima-
chos Frag. 119, οὐ πάντες ἀλλ᾽ οὓς
ἔσχεν ἅτερος δαίμων. Cf. Nem. VIII.
3, τὸν μὲν ἀμέροις ἀνάγνας χερσὶ
βαστάζεις ἕτερον δ᾽ ἑτέραις, Plut. de
Isid. et Osir., οἱ δὲ τὸν μὲν ἀμείνονα
θεὸν τὸν δ᾽ ἕτερον δαίμονα καλοῦσιν; in
prose without the opposite expres-
sed, Plato Phaed. 114 E. Here the
opposite is implied as Apollo is the
god of truth, whom a power prompt-
ing to deceit led her to offend. We
must not render δαίμων 'fortune,'
'doom' with Cookesley and Myers.
36. ἐπαῦρον.] Schol. quotes
Πολλάκι καὶ σύμπασα πόλις κακοῦ
ἀνδρὸς ἀπηύρα, Hes. W. and D. 238.
Cf. Eur. Suppl. 223—227. The
gen. after ἐπαῦρον is suppressed.
The αὐρ of ἀπαυράω ἐπαυρίσκομαι is
most likely for αϝαρ. (ἀπούρας for

ἀποϝαρας) from √ϝΑΡ 'take' whence
ἐλ-εῖν, αἱρέω for ϝαργω, or for ϝαρϳω
(denom. vb. from lost nominal
stem ϝαρϳο-).]
πολλὰν δ᾽.] Observe the abrupt
introduction of a simile. The mss.
give δ᾽ἐν. I retain δ᾽ = 'for.' Schol.
quotes Euripides (Frag. of Ino),
μικροῦ γὰρ ἐκ λαμπτῆρος Ἰδαῖον λέπας
πρήσειεν ἄν τις. The expression is
doubtless proverbial.
37. σπέρματος.] Cf. αἰθοίσας σπ.
φλογός, Ol. VII. 48; so semina flammae.
38. τείχει.] This use is interest-
ing as it corresponds to the Skt. dêhî
'mound,' 'rampart,' Zend √diz 'to
heap up' (Curt. No. 145). Boisson-
ade's suggestion of τεύχει is unne-
cessary.
41. ὀλέσσαι.] mss. give ὀλέσαι.
The right reading may be ὀλέσθαι.
42. ματρός, κ.τ.λ.] Poetically
expressed for σὺν ματρὶ βαρέως πα-
θούσῃ.
43. πρώτῳ.] Aristarchos writes
τριτάτῳ suggested as the Schol.
says by Il. XIII. 20, τρὶς μὲν ὀρέξατ᾽
ἰὼν (Ποσειδῶν) τὸ δὲ τέτρατον ἵκετο
τέκμωρ.
44. διέφανε.] The Schol. tells

F.   11

45 καὶ ῥά μιν Μάγνητι φέρων πόρε Κενταύρῳ διδάξαι   80
πολυπήμονας ἀνθρώποισιν ἰᾶσθαι νόσους.

Στρ. γ΄.

τοὺς μὲν ὧν, ὅσσοι μόλον αὐτοφύτων
ἑλκέων ξυνάονες, ἢ πολιῷ χαλκῷ μέλη τετρωμένοι   85
ἢ χερμάδι τηλεβόλῳ,

50 ἢ θερινῷ πυρὶ περθόμενοι δέμας ἢ χειμῶνι, λύσαις
ἄλλον ἀλλοίων ἀχέων   90
ἔξαγεν· τοὺς μὲν μαλακαῖς ἐπαοιδαῖς ἀμφέπων,
τοὺς δὲ προσανέα πίνοντας, ἢ γυίοις περάπτων πάν-
τοθεν
φάρμακα, τοὺς δὲ τομαῖς ἔστασεν ὀρθούς·

us that the fire parted and left a gap; lit. 'blazed on both sides.'

47. 'Those then who came afflicted with natural sores or with their limbs wounded by polished bronze or far-hurled stone or with bodies wasted by summer heat or wintry cold he loosed and rescued from their divers pangs. Some by treatment with soothing spells, and others by gracious draughts or wrapping their limbs all about with simples, and others by use of the knife, he set up whole and sound. But even skill lieth in the bonds of greed. Even him gold displayed in the palms did lead seduced by a splendid fee to bring back from death a man already enthralled thereby: and therefore Kronos' son with his hands shot through them both and quickly destroyed the breath of their breasts, for the levin bolt in a moment dealt them death. One must seek from the deities what is befitting mortal minds, knowing what is before our feet, and of what estate we are. Yearn not, dear heart, for the life of the immortals, but make the most of the conditions for practicable achievements which befall.'

τοὺς μὲν ὦν.] Taken up and divided into τοὺς μὲν v. 51, τοὺς δὲ

v. 53, which is explanatory of the general distribution ἄλλον ἀλλ. v. 50.

51. Observe the variety of construction ἀμφέπων...πίνοντας...περάπτων...τομαῖς. The poet divides the healing art into three departments, those of incantation, medicine and surgery; we must not then render φάρμακα 'amulets,' or ' charms,' though περιάμματα bears these meanings as well as that of πλάσματα to which φάρμακα is here equivalent. For the use of incantations cf. Tib. I. vv. 9—12: Ille ego, quum tristi morbo defessa iaceres | te dicor votis eripuisse meis; | ipseque te circum lustrari sulfure puro | carmine quum magico praecinuisset anus. Porphyry tells us that Pythagoras κατεκήλει δὲ ῥυθμοῖς καὶ μέλεσι καὶ ἐπῳδαῖς τὰ ψυχικὰ πάθη καὶ τὰ σωματικά. See also Welcker kl. Schrif. III. p. 64 sqq.

52. περάπτων.] For Aeolic extrusion of ι, cf. περόδοις, Nem. XI. 40.

53. ἔστασεν ὀρθούς.] Cf. v. 96. Dissen does not seem to see that ἔστασεν ὀρθοὺς applies to the three previous clauses, and that τομαῖς is equivalent to τέμνων. He compares the transition δρέπων μέν...

Ἀντ. γ'.

ἀλλὰ κέρδει καὶ σοφία δέδεται.　　　95

55 ἔτραπεν καὶ κεῖνον ἀγάνορι μισθῷ χρυσὸς ἐν χερσὶν
φανεὶς
ἄνδρ' ἐκ θανάτου κομίσαι
ἤδη ἁλωκότα· χερσὶ δ' ἄρα Κρονίων ῥίψαις δι' ἀμ-
φοῖν ἀμπνοὰν στέρνων καθέλεν　　　100
ὠκέως, αἴθων δὲ κεραυνὸς ἐνέσκιμψεν μόρον.　　　105
χρὴ τὰ ἐοικότα πὰρ δαιμόνων μαστευέμεν θναταῖς
φρασίν,
60 γνόντα τὸ πὰρ ποδός, οἵας εἰμὲν αἴσας.

Ἐπ. γ'.

μή, φίλα ψυχά, βίον ἀθάνατον
σπεῦδε, τὰν δ' ἔμπρακτον ἄντλει μαχανάν.　　　110
εἰ δὲ σώφρων ἄντρον ἔναι' ἔτι Χείρων, καί τί οἱ
φίλτρον ἐν θυμᾷ μελιγάρυες ὕμνοι
65 ἁμέτεροι τίθεν· ἰατῆρά τοί κέν μιν πίθον　　　115

ἀγλαΐζεται δέ, Ol. I. 14, which is
quite different.
54. There may be a side glance
at the necessity for poets taking
payment into consideration. Cf.
Isth. II. 1—11.
δέδεται.] Cf. δέδεται γὰρ ἀναιδεῖ
ἐλπίδι γυῖα, Nem. XI. 45.
55. Plato censures this passage
Rep. III. p. 408. Virgil gives the
legend Aen. VII. 764—774. He
says Hippolytos was the man re-
stored to life.
56. κομίσαι.] Cf. ὦ Μέγα, τὸ δ'
αὖτις τεὰν ψυχὰν κομίξαι οὔ μοι δυνα-
τόν, Nem. VIII. 44.
59. θναταῖς.] Dissen, misled by
ὄντας δὲ θνητοὺς θνητὰ καὶ φρονεῖν
χρέων, Eur. Alc. 809, renders θν.
φρασὶ modesta mente. The Doric
φρασὶ seems to be on the analogy
of ἀνδράσι, πατράσι, &c. For senti-
ment cf. θνατὰ θνατοῖσι πρέπει, Isth.
IV. 16, Frag. 33.
60. τὸ πὰρ ποδός.] Here is sup-

posed to be a rare instance of παρὰ
with gen.='at': cf. Pyth. I. 76,
X. 62. If, however, the phrase=
'our immediate future' the idea
of motion from is not abandoned.
Cf. φόνου παρποδίου νεφέλαν, Nem.
IX. 38.
οἵας εἰμὲν αἴσας.] Observe the
change from third person singular
in γνόντα to first pers. plur. For
constr. cf. ἄλλοτε ἄλλων ἐστὶ λόγων,
Plato Gorg. 482 A, Madv. § 54 b
Rem. 1.
61. ψυχά.] In spite of the
Schol. I think Hiero is addressed,
judging by the context. The ten-
derness is suitable to the theme.
ἀθάνατον.] Condition as well as
duration seems to be signified.
62. σπεῦδε.] Cf. μηκέτι μακρο-
τέραν σπεύδειν ἀρετάν, Isth. III. 31,
ξυνὸν γὰρ τοῦτο πᾶσι ἀγαθὸν σπεύδε-
ται, Herod. VII. 53.
μαχανάν.] Cf. Pyth. I. 41.

καὶ νῦν ἐσλοῖσι παρασχεῖν ἀνδράσιν θερμᾶν νόσων
ἤ τινα Λατοΐδα κεκλημένον ἢ πατέρος.
καί κεν ἐν ναυσὶν μόλον Ἰονίαν τέμνων θάλασσαν   120
Ἀρέθουσαν ἐπὶ κράναν παρ' Αἰτναῖον ξένον,

                                                    Στρ. δ'.

70 ὃς Συρακόσσαισι νέμει βασιλεὺς
    πραῢς ἀστοῖς, οὐ φθονέων ἀγαθοῖς, ξείνοις δὲ θαυ-
        μαστὸς πατήρ.   125
    τῷ μὲν διδύμας χάριτας,
    εἰ κατέβαν ὑγίειαν ἄγων χρυσέαν κῶμόν τ' ἀέθλων
        Πυθίων αἴγλαν στεφάνοις,   130
    τοὺς ἀριστεύων Φερένικος ἔλεν Κίρρᾳ ποτέ·
75 ἀστέρος οὐρανίου φαμὶ τηλαυγέστερον κείνῳ φάος   135
    ἐξικόμαν κε βαθὺν πόντον περάσαις.

                                                    Ἀντ. δ'.

    ἀλλ' ἐπεύξασθαι μὲν ἐγὼν ἐθέλω
    Ματρί, τὰν κοῦραι παρ' ἐμὸν πρόθυρον σὺν Πανὶ
        μέλπονται θαμὰ

66. θερμᾶν.] Feverish symp-
toms would probably set in occa-
sionally though Hiero's ailment was
stone.
67. ἢ πατέρος.] As there is no re-
cord of Zeús having been father of
any other healer than Apollo we
must suppose the poet to have for-
gotten the impropriety of imagining
Cheiron to be turning Apollo in-
to a physician: of course it is a
high compliment to Hiero to bring
Apollo in.
68. Ἰονίαν.] The southern part
of the Adriatic, and the sea between
Greece and the part of Italy south
of the Iapygian promontory. Cf.
Thuk. I. 24, Ἐπίδαμνος ἐστι πόλις ἐν
δεξιᾷ ἐσπλέοντι τὸν Ἰόνιον κόλπον,
36, τῆς τε γὰρ Ἰταλίας καὶ Σικελίας
καλῶς · παραπλοῦ (Κέρκυρα) κεῖται.
Pindar would voyage by the Korin-
thian Gulf and Kerkyra, thence

crossing βαθὺν πόντον (v. 76) to the
south coast of Iapygia.
69. Αἰτναῖον.] See Introduc-
tion.
71. ἀστοῖς.] Cf. Pyth. I. 68, II.
82.
73. στεφάνοις.] The plur. has
its proper force, or rather is proba-
bly for the dual, see Introd.
74. ποτέ.] The time of the last
victory was at least eight years
back.
77. ἐπεύξασθαι.] Note the force
of the preposition—'to add to my
ode a prayer.'
78. Ματρί.] Rhea or Kybele.
Pindar cherished the cult of these
Phrygian deities as a member of a
flute-playing family, the flute being
an importation from Phrygia.
κοῦραι.] These or among these
may have been Pindar's daughters
Prôtomache and Eumêtis.

σεμνὰν θεὸν ἐννύχιαι. 140

80 εἰ δὲ λόγων συνέμεν κορυφάν, Ἱέρων, ὀρθὰν ἐπίστα,
μανθάνων οἶσθα προτέρων·

ἓν παρ᾽ ἐσλὸν πήματα σύνδυο δαίονται βροτοῖς 145
ἀθάνατοι. τὰ μὲν ὦν οὐ δύνανται νήπιοι κόσμῳ φέρειν,
ἀλλ᾽ ἀγαθοί, τὰ καλὰ τρέψαντες ἔξω.

Ἐπ. δ΄.

τὶν δὲ μοῖρ᾽ εὐδαιμονίας ἕπεται. 150

85 λαγέταν γάρ τοι τύραννον δέρκεται,
εἴ τιν᾽ ἀνθρώπων, ὁ μέγας πότμος. αἰὼν δ᾽ ἀσφαλὴς
οὐκ ἔγεντ᾽ οὔτ᾽ Αἰακίδᾳ παρὰ Πηλεῖ
οὔτε παρ᾽ ἀντιθέῳ Κάδμῳ· λέγονται μὰν βροτῶν 155
ὄλβον ὑπέρτατον οἳ σχεῖν, οἵτε καὶ χρυσαμπύκων

90 μελπομενᾶν ἐν ὄρει Μοισᾶν καὶ ἐν ἑπταπύλοις 160

80. 'Since, Hiero, thou hast knowledge so as to understand the point of sayings, thou dost learn and know from men of yore.'

μανθάνων.] Proverbs are abiding monitors, so that translators need not make the tense past. For genitive after it cf. Eur. *Rhes.* 129, μαθόντες ἐχθρῶν μηχανὰς κατασκόπου | βουλευσόμεσθα, Soph. *Ant.* 723.

82. νήπιοι.] The notion of low birth is perhaps included.

83. τὰ καλά, κ.τ.λ.] Clearly a proverbial expression. I cannot agree with Don. that it is borrowed from the custom of turning *old* clothes. The Schol. is not responsible for the *old*. Aristides (A.D. 117—180) quotes the passage à propos of beggars wearing rags, but saying that they have good clothes at home. I take Pindar's allusion to be to the practice which doubtless prevailed among Greeks who studied their personal appearance of hiding stains or rents (which might befall the newest robes) by arranging the folds. This interpretation suits the phrase κόσμῳ φέρειν excellently.

85. δέρκεται.] Cf. Ol. VII. 11, ἄλλοτε δ᾽ ἄλλον χάρις ἐποπτεύει, Isth. I. 39, Pyth. v. 52.

86. εἴ τιν᾽.] For phrase cf. Ol. I. 56, εἰ δέ τιν᾽ ἄνδρα θνατὸν Ὀλύμπου σκοποὶ—ἐτίμασαν, ἦν Τάνταλος οὗτος.

Πότμος.] The θεὸς of Ol. I. 106, cf. Πότμος ἄναξ, Nem. IV. 42.

αἰὼν δ᾽.] 'But a life free from reverse befel neither Aeakos' son Pêleus nor godlike Kadmos; yet they are said to have gotten bliss higher than all mortals beside, in that they even heard the golden-snooded Muses sing (the one) in M. Pêlion (the other) in seven-gated Thebes when (the latter) took to wife cow-eyed Harmonia and the former Thetis far-famed daughter of sage Nêreus.'

89. σχεῖν.] Cf. Pyth. I. 65, supra v. 24.

90. ἐν ὄρει.] Pêlion, cf. Nem. VII. 22.

καί.] Note the conjunctive where we might expect a disjunctive phrase ὁ μὲν ἐν ὄρει, ὁ δὲ ἐν Θήβαις, and also the suppression of ὁ μὲν in the next line.

ἄϊον Θήβαις, ὁπόθ' Ἁρμονίαν γᾶμεν βοῶπιν,
ὁ δὲ Νηρέος εὐβούλου Θέτιν παῖδα κλυτάν.

Στρ. ε΄.

καὶ θεοὶ δαίσαντο παρ' ἀμφοτέροις,   165
καὶ Κρόνου παῖδας βασιλῆας ἴδον χρυσέαις ἐν ἕδραις,
   ἕδνα τε
95 δέξαντο· Διὸς δὲ χάριν
ἐκ προτέρων μεταμειψάμενοι καμάτων ἔστασαν ὀρθὰν
   καρδίαν. ἐν δ' αὖτε χρόνῳ   170
τὶν μὲν ὀξείαισι θύγατρες ἐρήμωσαν πάθαις
εὐφροσύνας μέρος αἱ τρεῖς· ἀτὰρ λευκωλένῳ γε Ζεὺς
   πατὴρ   175
ἤλυθεν ἐς λέχος ἱμερτὸν Θυώνᾳ.

Ἀντ. ε΄.

100 τοῦ δὲ παῖς, ὅνπερ μόνον ἀθανάτα
τίκτεν ἐν Φθίᾳ Θέτις, ἐν πολέμῳ τόξοις ἀπὸ ψυχὰν
   λιπὼν   180
ὦρσεν πυρὶ καιόμενος
ἐκ Δαναῶν γόον. εἰ δὲ νόῳ τις ἔχει θνατῶν ἀλαθείας
   ὁδόν, χρὴ πρὸς μακάρων   185
τυγχάνοντ' εὖ πασχέμεν. ἄλλοτε δ' ἀλλοῖαι πνοαὶ
105 ὑψιπετᾶν ἀνέμων. ὄλβος οὐκ ἐς μακρὸν ἀνδρῶν ἔρ-
   χεται,
ἄπλετος εὖτ' ἂν ἐπιβρίσαις ἕπηται.   190

---

94. χρυσέαις.] Cf. ἐν θρόνοις Κάδμοιο κούραις, Ol. II. 22. The two passages together suggest that the thrones of Kadmos' palace were celebrated.
95. Διός, κ.τ.λ.] 'And by grace of Zeus they passed out of former troubles and raised up their souls from misery.'
96. μεταμειψάμενοι.] Cf. Ol. XII. 12.
98. αἱ τρεῖς.] Ino, Autonoe and Agave.
99. Θυώνᾳ.] Semele.

103. ἀλαθείας ὁδόν.] Cf. Isth. II. 10. Here 'the usual course of real events' as opposed to 'the forecasts of flatterers' is signified.
104. τυγχάνοντ'.] Equiv. to εὐτυχοῦντα, cf. Ol. II. 51, τὸ δὲ τυχεῖν πειρώμενον ἀγωνίας παραλύει δυσφρο-νᾶν.
εὖ πασχέμεν.] For sense cf. Nem. I. 32, ἀλλ' (ἔραμαι) ἐόντων εὖ τε πα-θεῖν καὶ ἀκοῦσαι φίλοις ἐξαρκέων and Theogn. 108, τῶν αὐτοῦ κτεάνων εὖ πασχέμεν.
105. 'Men's bliss cometh not

σμικρὸς ἐν σμικροῖς, μέγας ἐν μεγάλοις
ἔσσομαι· τὸν δ' ἀμφέποντ' αἰεὶ φρασὶν
δαίμον' ἀσκήσω κατ' ἐμὰν θεραπεύων μαχανάν.
110 εἰ δέ μοι πότμον θεὸς ἁβρὸν ὀρέξαι,   195
ἐλπίδ' ἔχω κλέος εὑρέσθαι κεν ὑψηλὸν πρόσω.
Νέστορα καὶ Λύκιον Σαρπηδόν', ἀνθρώπων φάτις,
ἐξ ἐπέων κελαδεννῶν, τέκτονες οἷα σοφοὶ   200
ἅρμοσαν, γινώσκομεν. ἁ δ' ἀρετὰ κλειναῖς ἀοιδαῖς
115 χρονία τελέθει. παύροις δὲ πράξασθ' εὐμαρές.   205

for long, whensoever it attendeth
them in measure exceeding full.'
106. ἄπλετος.] I think this form
should be separated from ἁπλᾱ́-
τος and connected with πίμπλημι.
Hesych. explains it as πολύς. Cf.
Isth. III. 29, ἀπλέτου δόξας, Soph.
Trach. 981, ἀλλ' ἐπί μοι μελέῳ |
βάρος ἄπλετον ἐμμέμονε φρήν. For
sentiment cf. ὁ μέγας ὄλβος οὐ μόνι-
μος ἐν βρότοις, Eur. Or. 340, Ol. II.
36, Pyth. VII. 20. The mss. give
ὃς πολύς, of which the πολύς is
clearly a gloss substituted for the
true reading.
ἐπιβρίσαις.] Lit. 'after having
weighed them down.'
107. σμικροῖς.] 'Small will I be
when small my state, great when
it is great.' The Schol. and Photius
understand this of persons. I fol-
low Dissen, who compares Eur. El.
407, ἐν σμικροῖς ὤν, because his in-
terpretation suits the context very
much better than the other.
108. τὸν ἀμφέποντ'.] 'The for-
tune that from time to time at-
tendeth me will I revere in my
heart, doing it service with all my
power.'

111. εὑρέσθαι.] By munificence
to poets.
πρόσω.] Best taken with ὑψηλὸν
which is proleptic, cf. ἀτενὲς ἴκελοι,
Pyth. II. 77.
112. The poet seems to imply
that fame is independent of longe-
vity. It would appear that Hiero
knew that his life was drawing to a
close when this ode was composed.
This view gives deep significance
to the latter part from v. 86.
112. φάτις.] Acc. Plur. for φά-
τιας. Cf. fabula, Hor. Epod. XI.
10.
113. τέκτονες.] Cf. κεκρότηται
χρυσέα κρηπὶς ἱεραῖσιν ἀοιδαῖς | οἷα
τειχίζομεν ἤδη ποικίλον | κόσμον αὐ-
δάεντα λόγων, Frag. 206, and Milton's
'build the lofty rhyme.' Don.
quotes Kratinos in Schol. on Aris-
toph. Equites 527, τέκτονες εὐπαλά-
μων ὕμνων.
114. ἁ δ', κ.τ.λ.] 'By glorious
(qy. glorifying?) songs is excellence
made lasting. But few find it easy
to win them.' For sentiment cf.
Ol. IV. 10, X. (XI.) 4—10, XI. (X)
91—93, Nem. IV. 6, ῥῆμα δ' ἐργμά-
των χρονιώτερον βιοτεύει.

PYTHIA IV.

ON THE VICTORY OF ARKESILAS IV. KING OF KYRENE, WITH THE FOUR-HORSE CHARIOT.

INTRODUCTION.

COMPOSED at Thebes (v. 299) for recitation at Kyrêne, in the same year as, but probably before Pyth. v. which celebrates the same victory (won B.C. 466), apparently at the instance of Arkesilas' banished kinsman Dâmophilos, possibly on his commission. A divided duty may have been the cause of the poet's allowing himself so large a freedom of digression i.e. from v. 4 to v. 63, and from v. 68 to v. 262, which last is partly applicable to the quarrel between Arkesilas and Dâmophilos, while the allegory vv. 263—269, the advice vv. 270—276 bear on Dâmophilos' banishment. Further from vv. 277—279 it may reasonably be inferred that Dâmophilos, who had been staying at Thebes, was concerned in the transmission of the ode. He may have provided and himself taught an especially good messenger who was in his turn to teach the chorus. Yet more from v. 279 to v. 299, the end, the praises and hopes of Dâmophilos are sung. Altogether on the assumption that Arkesilas asked for and paid for the ode himself the poet cannot be acquitted of unfairness, and of running a serious risk of doing this friend more harm than good.

The rhythm is Dorian.

ANALYSIS.

vv.

1—3. The muse is invoked to celebrate Arkesilas' victory at Pytho,

4—8. Where was delivered the oracle which sent Battos to found Kyrêne.

9—12. And brought about at length the fulfilment of Mêdeia's prophecy.

This ode is the finest extant specimen of Pindar's poetry. It comprises a masterpiece of Lyric, as opposed to Epic, narrative in the story of the Argonauts. The length of the digression scarcely needs explanation, so skilfully is it introduced, and so clearly is the bearing of the Minyan expedition on the founding of Kyrêne kept in view. It has been suggested that the relations between Pelias and Iâson are intended to suggest an analogy between those of Arkesilas and Dâmophilos: but if so, Pindar must have felt confident that Arkesilas' vanity would keep him blind to such an insulting comparison. Rather, let us consider that the interview between Pelias and Iâson, brought in without any motive beyond that of artistic propriety, chanced to afford an example for Arkesilas' imitation, and gave occasion for a general sentiment applicable to the enmity which had subsisted between Arkesilas and Dâmophilos (vv. 145, 146). Dissen is doubtless right in the suggestion that the noble moderation of Iâson in vindicating his undoubted rights was put forth as an example for Arkesilas to follow, while at the same time the character ascribed to Iâson seems to have been suggested to the poet by that of Dâmophilos. Perhaps vv. 158, 159 covertly inculcate the duty of restoring an exile to his home.

$$Στρ. α'.$$

Σάμερον μὲν χρή σε παρ' ἀνδρὶ φίλῳ
στᾶμεν, εὐΐππου βασιλῆϊ Κυράνας, ὄφρα κωμάζοντι
　　σὺν 'Αρκεσίλᾳ,
Μοῖσα, Λατοίδαισιν ὀφειλόμενον Πυθῶνί τ' αὔξῃς
　　οὖρον ὕμνων,　　　　　　　　　　　　　　　5
ἔνθα ποτὲ χρυσέων Διὸς αἰητῶν πάρεδρος
5 οὐκ ἀποδάμου 'Απόλλωνος τυχόντος ἱέρεα
χρῆσεν οἰκιστῆρα Βάττον καρποφόρου Λιβύας, ἱερὰν　10
　　νᾶσον ὡς ἤδη λιπὼν κτίσσειεν εὐάρματον

1. **Σάμερον.**] Probably not for
τάμερον but compounded with the
pronominal element *sa*, which we
have in ὁ, ἡ, οἱ, αἱ, while the Attic used
ta. The neuter accusative termi-
nation corresponds to the Sanskrit
method of forming adverbs from
substantives with a prepositional or
adverbial prefix, cf. ἀντίβιον by ἀντι-
βίην, ὑπέρβιον.

3. **Λατοίδαισιν.**] Cf. Nem. ix. 4,
διδύμοις παίδεσσιν (Λατοῦς)...Πυθῶνος
αἰπεινᾶς ὁμοκλάροις ἐπόπταις. Clear-
ly then Dissen is right in explain-
ing the word to mean Apollo and
Artemis, who, with their mother,
presided over the Pythian games.

Πυθῶνί τ'.] Cf. infra, v. 66, Nem.
iv. 9, Κρονίδᾳ τε Δὶ καὶ Νεμέᾳ.

αὔξῃς.] There is no need to ren-
der 'raise and send abundantly.'
Rather, 'freshen the gale of songs.'

οὖρον.] Cf. εὔθυν' ἐπὶ τοῦτον ἐπέων
ὦ Μοῖσ' ἄγ' οὖρον | εὐκλεῖα, Nem. vi.
29, where εὐκλεῖα is for εὐκλεϜα acc.
sing.; see also Ol. ix. 47.

4. **αἰητῶν.**] So one ms.; the
rest αἰετῶν. These were represen-
tations of the eagles said to have
been sent from east and west to
determine by their meeting the
centre of the earth, which adorned
the ὀμφαλὸς or white hemispherical
stone in the adytum at Delphi.
Remember that Apollo was the in-
terpreter of the will of Zeus, cf.

Aesch. Eum. 19, Διὸς προφήτης ἐστὶ
Λοξίας πατρός.

5.· Cf. Pyth. iii. 27. It appears
that the responses delivered at
Delphi varied in correctness accord-
ing as the God was supposed to be
present or absent, for instance, at
his other special haunts Dêlos and
Patara.

ἱέρεα.] Scans as a dactyl. The
best mss. give this Aeolic form;
others ἱερέα. Böckh and Don. read
ἱρέα.

6. **χρῆσεν.**] 'Declared Battos
colonist of fruitful Libya that leav-
ing the sacred isle he should at
length found a city famed for good-
ly chariots, &c.'

ἱερὰν νᾶσον.] Thêra. The epithet
refers to the number of deities there
worshipped.

7. **ὡς κτίσσειεν.**] Dissen and
Prof. Paley take this phrase as final.
'That he should found' should
after a *verbum declarandi* of course
be ὡς κτίσοι. For the construction
cf. ὡς ἂν κτίσαιεν, Ol. vii. 42. The
poet seems to have wavered between
the senses of 'declaring' and 'or-
dering' in χρῆσεν. ἤδη is explained
by vv. 9, 10. Prof. Paley renders
'at once'; but he did not obey
'at once' according to Hêrodotos,
iv. 155, 157. For the words of the
oracle cf. infra, v. 69.

πόλιν ἐν ἀργινόεντι μαστῷ,

'Αντ. α'.

καὶ τὸ Μηδείας ἔπος ἀγκομίσαιθ'   15
10 ἑβδόμᾳ καὶ σὺν δεκάτᾳ γενεᾷ Θήραιον, Αἰήτα τό ποτε
ζαμενὴς
παῖς ἀπέπνευσ' ἀθανάτου στόματος, δέσποινα Κόλχων.
εἶπε δ' οὕτως
ἡμιθέοισιν 'Ιάσονος αἰχματᾶο ναύταις·   20
Κέκλυτε, παῖδες ὑπερθύμων τε φωτῶν καὶ θεῶν·
φαμὶ γὰρ τᾶσδ' ἐξ ἁλιπλάκτου ποτὲ γᾶς 'Επάφοιο
κόραν   25
15 ἀστέων ῥίζαν φυτεύσεσθαι μελησίμβροτον
Διὸς ἐν 'Άμμωνος θεμέθλοις.

'Επ. α'.

ἀντὶ δελφίνων δ' ἐλαχυπτερύγων ἵππους ἀμείψαντες
θοάς,   30
ἀνία τ' ἀντ' ἐρετμῶν δίφρους τε νωμάσοισιν ἀελλό-
ποδας.

8. ἀργινόεντι.] So most MSS.
This is defended by the proper
names 'Αργῖνον, 'Αργινοῦσαι. Her-
mann, Böckh, Don. read ἀργήεντι
for the Triclinian ἀργήεντι.
μαστῷ.] Cf. Pyth. IX. 57, ὄχθος
ἀμφίπεδος, of Kyrêne. 'And should
revive by fulfilment for Thêra in
the seventeenth generation the ut-
terance of Mêdeia.' Her prophecy
was delivered at Thêra (v. 42) on
the way from Lake Tritônis to Lêm-
nos.
10. Θήραιον.] The position re-
quires that it should be taken as an
extension of the predicate. Battos
or Aristoteles was the 17th in de-
scent from Euphêmos, and he made
Thêra μεγαλᾶν πολίων ματρόπολιν
(v. 20).
ζαμενής.] 'Inspired.' Cf. Pyth.
IX. 39, ζαμενὴς κένταυρος, where
the context suits the metaphysical
meaning.

14. 'Επάφοιο κόραν.] Note the
confusion between the thing per-
sonified and the personification;
see Essay on Style.
15. ἀστέων ῥίζαν.] Cf. Pyth. IX.
8. The cities were Apollônia,
Barka, Hesperides against which
Arkesilas was organising an expe-
dition, and Teuchira.
φυτεύσεσθαι.] 'shall have plant-
ed in her.'
16. 'Near the foundations of
the temple of Zeus Ammon' (cf.
Ol. VI. 16). Or 'on foundations
sacred to Zeus Ammon,' whose
oasis and temple were in Libya not
very far from Kyrêne. The Schol.
says that the whole district was
sacred to this God.
18. δίφρους τε.] 'And instead
of oars reins of storm-footed chariot-
teams, (them) they shall speed.'
The conjunction is generally ig-
nored and only ἀνία taken with

κεῖνος ὄρνις ἐκτελευτάσει μεγαλᾶν πολίων
20 ματρόπολιν Θήραν γενέσθαι, τόν ποτε Τριτωνίδος ἐν
    προχοαῖς   ·35
λίμνας θεῷ ἀνέρι εἰδομένῳ γαῖαν διδόντι
ξείνια πρῴραθεν Εὔφαμος καταβὰς
δέξατ'· αἴσιον δ' ἐπί οἱ Κρονίων Ζεὺς πατὴρ ἔκλαγξε
    βροντάν·   40
                           Στρ. β'.

ἁνίκ' ἄγκυραν ποτὶ χαλκόγενυν
25 ναΐ κρημνάντων ἐπέτοσσε, θοᾶς Ἀργοῦς χαλινόν. δώ-
    δεκα δὲ πρότερον

ἀμείψαντες. But the reins of riding horses cannot be regarded as instead of oars, while the reins of chariots may be with propriety; so that here we have hendiadys.

19. ὄρνις.] ‘Ominous token;’ i. e. the clod, cf. Ar. Αv. 719, ὄρνιν τε νομίζετε πάνθ' ὅσαπερ περὶ μαντείας διακρίνει.

20. Τριτωνίδος ἐν προχοαῖς λίμνας.] The Argonauts somehow went eastward from the Phasis to the ocean stream, the eastern part of which is no doubt a mixture of the Caspian Sea and the Persian Gulf, and to the Red Sea (v. 251) which seems to be included under the term Ὠκεανός, v. 26. Thence they carried the ship for twelve days to Lake Tritônis over land. Thus it is possible that in this version of the return, which differs materially from that of Apollônios Rhodios, the Nile's western mouth is called Lake Tritônis, it being nearer to Kyrêne than the Palus Tritonis, which used to communicate with the Lesser Syrtis. On the other hand the poet's ἐρυθρὸς πόντος may be used in the large Hêrodotean sense applying to all the sea between India and Africa, and, the shape of Africa not being known,

the overland passage may have been imagined as across the West of Africa to the Lake near the Lesser Syrtis. This variety of the legend might well arise after the circumnavigation of Africa achieved by order of Psammêtichos. The next place on their route which Pindar mentions was Thêra then called Kallistê, which they reached some time after their departure from Libya. Pindar ignores their intermediate wanderings about Italy and Kerkyra. Other accounts tell of a visit to Lêmnos before the arrival at Kolchis.

21. θεῷ.] For dat. with δέκομαι ‘to receive as a compliment or favour,’ cf. δέξαι δέ οἱ στεφάνων ἐγκώμιον τεθμόν, Ol. XIII. 29, infra v. 37.

22. ξείνια.] See vv. 34—37.

23. αἴσιον.] Extension of predicate. ‘And thereupon, Father Zeus Kronos' son sent a thunder-clap as a sanction.’

25. ἐπέτοσσε.] Cf. Pyth. III. 27, x. 33, where it takes acc. ῥέξουσας, so that ποτικρημνάντων is gen. abs. without pronoun; cf. Pyth. VIII. 43, 85, I. 26.

χαλινόν.] Cf. Eur. Hec. 539, Λῦσαί τε πρύμνας· καὶ χαλινωτήρια | νεῶν δὸς ἡμῖν.

ἀμέρας ἐξ Ὠκεανοῦ φέρομεν νώτων ὕπερ γαίας ἐρή-
μων   45
εἰνάλιον δόρυ, μήδεσιν ἀνσπάσσαντες ἀμοῖς.
τουτάκι δ᾽ οἰοπόλος δαίμων ἐπῆλθεν, φαιδίμαν   50
ἀνδρὸς αἰδοίου πρόσοψιν θηκάμενος· φιλίων δ᾽ ἐπέων
30 ἄρχεται, ξείνοις ἅτ᾽ ἐλθόντεσσιν εὐεργέται
δεῖπν᾽ ἐπαγγέλλοντι πρῶτον.   55
                            Ἀντ. β΄.

ἀλλὰ γὰρ νόστου πρόφασις γλυκεροῦ
κώλυεν μεῖναι. φάτο δ᾽ Εὐρύπυλος Γαιαόχου παῖς
ἀφθίτου Ἐννοσίδα
ἔμμεναι· γίνωσκε δ᾽ ἐπειγομένους· ἂν δ᾽ εὐθὺς ἁρπάξαις
ἀρούρας   60
35 δεξιτερᾷ προτυχὸν ξένιον μάστευσε δοῦναι.
οὐδ᾽ ἀπίθησέ νιν, ἀλλ᾽ ἥρως ἐπ᾽ ἀκταῖσιν θορών,
χειρί οἱ χεῖρ᾽ ἀντερείσαις δέξατο βώλακα δαιμονίαν. 65
πεύθομαι δ᾽ αὐτὰν κατακλυσθεῖσαν ἐκ δούρατος
ἐναλία βᾶμεν σὺν ἅλμᾳ
                            Ἐπ. β΄.

40 ἐσπέρας ὑγρῷ πελάγει σπομέναν. ἦ μάν νιν ὤτρυνον
θαμὰ   70

26. νώτων.] Cf. infra v. 228,
Ol. vii. 87, ὦ Ζεῦ πάτερ, νώτοισιν
Ἀταβυρίου μεδέων.
29. φιλίων, κ.τ.λ.] 'And he be-
gan a friendly address in such terms
as the kindly disposed use when first
proffering hospitality to strangers
on their arrival.'
30. ἄρχεται.] A minority of
MSS. read ἄρχετο. The present gives
variety.
32. ἀλλὰ γάρ.] 'But (we declined
to stay) for.'
33. Εὐρύπυλος.] The mythical
king of the district.
Ἐννοσίδα.] This is most proba-
bly not for Ἐννοσιγαῖος as is gene-
rally said. The change of γ to δ is
rare. The Attic form δᾶ and the

Theokritean δάν, which have been
supposed to be for γᾶ, γάν, are pro-
bably for δγᾶ, δγᾶν and equivalent
to Ζῆν or Ζῆνα, cf. Curt. Ἐννοσίδα
is probably for Ἐννοσίδγα < Ἐννοσι-
γαο formed from the stem Ἐννοσι-
(for ἐνϝοσι 'a shaking' from the
√ϝοθ whence ὠθέω) and the suffix
-γα.
36. ἀπίθησέ νιν.] 'Nor did he
(Eurypylos) fail to persuade him
(Euphemos).' Hermann reads the
dat. ἱν = οἱ. Perhaps 'nor did he
(Euphêmos) disobey him (Eurypy-
los)' is to be defended by εὐμενέοντες
ἀνέψιον, infra v. 127.
37. οἱ.] Cf. supra v. 21.
βώλακα.] The receiving of earth
was a token of sovereignty.

λυσιπόνοις θεραπόντεσσιν φυλάξαι· τῶν δ' ἐλάθοντο
φρένες·
καί νυν ἐν τᾷδ' ἄφθιτον νάσῳ κέχυται Λιβύας   75
εὐρυχόρου σπέρμα πρὶν ὥρας. εἰ γὰρ οἴκοι νιν βάλε
πὰρ χθόνιον
Ἄιδα στόμα, Ταίναρον εἰς ἱερὰν Εὔφαμος ἐλθών,
45 υἱὸς ἱππάρχου Ποσειδάωνος ἄναξ,   80
τόν ποτ' Εὐρώπα Τιτυοῦ θυγάτηρ τίκτε Καφισοῦ
παρ' ὄχθαις·

Στρ. γ'.

τετράτων παίδων κ' ἐπιγεινομένων
αἷμά οἱ κείναν λάβε σὺν Δαναοῖς εὐρεῖαν ἄπειρον.
τότε γὰρ μεγάλας   85
ἐξανίστανται Λακεδαίμονος Ἀργείου τε κόλπου καὶ
Μυκηνᾶν.
50 νῦν γε μὲν ἀλλοδαπᾶν κριτὸν εὑρήσει γυναικῶν
ἐν λέχεσιν γένος. οἵ κεν τάνδε σὺν τιμᾷ θεῶν   90
νᾶσον ἐλθόντες τέκωνται φῶτα κελαινεφέων πεδίω

41. θεραπόντεσσιν.] For the meaning of the word cf. *v.* 287. The dative is natural after ὤτρυνον in the rare sense 'urgently commanded.' Mêdeia is the subject to ὤτρυνον.

43. πρὶν ὥρας.] 'Before the full time.' Its final disposition ought to have been later and at Taenaros.

46. This verse gives a reason for Pindar being glad to celebrate Euphêmos and his descendants.

49. ἐξανίστανται.] Prof. Paley seems to adopt ἐξανίσταντ' ἄν in his translation though he has not published this reading. One ms. gives -αντο. Dissen after the Schol. explains -ανται as the *praesens propheticum*. As it was, descendants of Euphêmos joined with Thêras in colonizing Thêra. Not, however, as Dissen says, in the fourth generation. For the Minyans who colonized Thêra had married Spartiâte women according to Hêrodo-

tos, while the Dorian conquest of Lakedaemon was in the fifth generation from Hêrakles the contemporáry of Euphêmos. Now Argos colonized Rhodes ; Lakedaemon, Knidos; Epidauros (Mykênae?) Cos; so that I think Pindar means that some of the original settlers of the Dorian Hexapolis would have gone to Libya at the time of the Dorian migration from Peloponnêsos. The Hêrakleidae were Danai. 'The blood of the fourth generation descended from him' is the fifth generation, during which the Dorian migration might be supposed to have happened. ἐξανίστανται then may be retained as a prophecy of that migration and rendered 'there will be migrations from.'

50. ἀλλοδαπᾶν.] Lêmnian.

52. φῶτα.] Battos.

κελαινεφέων.] For κελαινονεφέων, Cf. Curt. 509 note.

δεσπόταν· τὸν μὲν πολυχρύσῳ ποτ' ἐν δώματι   95
Φοῖβος ἀμνάσει θέμισσιν

'Αντ. γ'.

55 Πύθιον ναὸν καταβάντα χρόνῳ
ὑστέρῳ νάεσσι πολεῖς ἀγαγὲν Νείλοιο πρὸς πῖον
τέμενος Κρονίδα.
ἦ ῥα Μηδείας ἐπέων στίχες. ἔπταξαν δ' ἀκίνητοι
σιωπᾷ   100
ἥρωες ἀντίθεοι πυκινὰν μῆτιν κλύοντες.

ὦ μάκαρ υἱὲ Πολυμνάστου, σὲ δ' ἐν τούτῳ λόγῳ   105
60 χρησμὸς ὤρθωσεν μελίσσας Δελφίδος αὐτομάτῳ
κελάδῳ·
ἅ σε χαίρειν ἐς τρὶς αὐδάσαισα πεπρωμένον
βασιλέ' ἄμφανεν Κυράνᾳ,   110

'Επ. γ'.

δυσθρόου φωνᾶς ἀνακρινόμενον ποινὰ τίς ἔσται πρὸς
θεῶν.

---

54. ἀμνάσει.] For ἀναμνάσει.
θέμισσιν.] Cf. Δελφοὶ θεμιστῶν
ὕμνων μάντιες 'Απολλωνίδαι, Pind.
Frag. 174 [204].
55. καταβάντα.] 'Stepping down
from the threshold into;' cf. κατ'
οὐδοῦ βάντα, Hom. Od. IV. 680.
56. ἀγαγέν.] So most MSS.
Doric infinitive. Others ἀγαγεῖν.
'To lead members in ships to the
rich precinct near the Nile of the
Son of Kronos.'
Νείλοιο.] The Schol. takes N.
with Κρονίδα, quoting Αἰγύπτοιο
Διϊπετέος ποταμοῖο, Od. IV. 581 and
Αἰγύπτιε Ζεῦ Νεῖλε, Parmeno. The
first quotation proves nothing, as
Διϊπετὴς is a general epithet of
rivers, and the other Hermann
rightly explains to mean qui Aegyp-
tiis Jupiter es. For Νείλοιο τέμενος
cf. οἴκημα ποταμοῦ, Ol. II. 10.
57. ἔπταξαν.] Cf. σιγῇ πτῆξειαν
ἄφωνοι, Soph. Aj. 171.
59. υἱέ.] Battos.

ἐν.] Cf. ἐν τοῖς ὁμοίοις νόμοις ποιή-
σαντες τὰς κρίσεις, Thuk. I. 77, Pyth.
I. 62. 'Thee in accordance with
this rede did the oracular answer
of the Delphic bee with cry un-
sought glorify. For she, after a
thrice-uttered salutation, revealed
thee as the destined king of Kyrêne
when thou wast asking what release
from stuttering speech shall there
be from the gods.' Hêrodotos omits
the salutation (IV. 155), but gives
the oracle, Βαττ' ἐπὶ φωνὴν ἦλθες·
ἄναξ δέ σε Φοῖβος 'Απόλλων | ἐς Λι-
βύην πέμπει μηλοτρόφον οἰκιστῆρα.
60. ὤρθωσεν.] Cf. τόνγε Θεμισ-
τίου ὀρθώσαντες οἶκον τάνδε πόλιν |
θεοφιλῆ ναίοισι, Isth. V. 65.
μελίσσας.] The prophetess is so
named because honey was the
special food of inspired persons.
The Schol. quotes ταῖς ἱεραῖς μελίσ-
σαις τέρπεται; Cf. Ol. VI. 47.
63. ποινά.] Schol. ἀμοιβὴ ἢ
λύσις. The intermediate meaning

ἢ μάλα δὴ μετὰ καὶ νῦν, ὥτε φοινικανθέμου ἦρος ἀκμᾷ,
65 παισὶ τούτοις ὄγδοον θάλλει μέρος Ἀρκεσίλας·   115
τῷ μὲν Ἀπόλλων ἅ τε Πυθὼ κῦδος ἐξ ἀμφικτιόνων
    ἔπορεν
ἱπποδρομίας. ἀπὸ δ' αὐτὸν ἐγὼ Μοίσαισι δώσω   120
καὶ τὸ πάγχρυσον νάκος κριοῦ· μετὰ γὰρ
κεῖνο πλευσάντων Μινυᾶν, θεόπομποί σφισιν τιμαὶ
    φύτευθεν.

                                        Στρ. δ'.

70 τίς γὰρ ἀρχὰ δέξατο ναυτιλίας;
    τίς δὲ κίνδυνος κρατεροῖς ἀδάμαντος δῆσεν ἅλοις;
    θέσφατον ἦν Πελίαν   125
    ἐξ ἀγαυῶν Αἰολιδᾶν θανέμεν χείρεσσιν ἢ βουλαῖς
    ἀκάμπτοις.

between 'punishment,' 'fine' and 'release' is 'quittance.' Schol. ἡ ποινὴ ἀπολύσεως ἕνεκεν γίνεται. However compensation may be intended. Cf. Pyth. ii. 17. For the story cf. Herod. iv. 155.

64. φοινικανθέμου.] Cf. Isth. iii. 36, νῦν δ' αὖ(ἡ τῶν Κλεωνυμιδῶν ἑστία) μετὰ χειμέριον ποικίλων μηνῶν ζόφον χθὼν ὥτε φοινικέοισιν ἄνθησεν ῥόδοις | δαιμόνων βουλαῖς.

65. ὄγδοον μέρος.] The seventh in descent from Battos, the eighth Kyrênaean descendant of Euphêmos. Cf. τρίτον κασιγνητᾶν μέρος, Pyth. xii. 11.

66. As the Amphictyons founded and presided at the Pythian games, Ἀμφικτυόνων was read till Böckh altered it. Cf. Nem. vi. 40, Isth. iii. 26, Nem. x. 19.

69. φύτευθεν.] Cf. δαίμων φυτεύει δόξαν ἐπήρατον, Isth. v. 12.

70. δέξατο.] Lat. excepit eos. For suppression of object cf. Pyth. ii. 17. 'What origin of their seafaring befell?'

71. This verse seems best explained by supposing an allusion to the version of the legend of

Promêtheus followed by Aeschylos, see esp. Prom. Vinct. 64, ἀδαμαντίνου νῦν σφηνὸς αὐθάδη γνάθον | στέρνων διαμπὰξ πασσάλευ' ἐρρωμένως, here applied in a metaphorical sense of course. Orelli on Saeva necessitas | clavos trabales et cuneos manu | gestans aëna, Hor. Od. i. xxxv. 17 (cf. iii. xxiv. 5), quotes this passage of Pindar, and also τῶνδ' ἐφήλωται τορῶς γόμφος διαμπάξ, Aesch. Suppl. 945. The last passage refers to the custom of nailing up metal plates on which laws &c. were inscribed in temples (Paley). The emblems of Horace suggest fixedness; but, as Orelli, I think rightly, explains, the idea is derived from their use in architecture. Hence, neither quotation applies to this passage. The idea of necessity is imported by the Schol. The true interpretation is 'What was the peril to which they were immoveably devoted, on which their hearts were fixed?' Render, 'What perilous quest held them fast with stout nails of adamant?' For gen. of material cf. Pyth. i. 21.

72. ἐξ.] For ἐκ introducing the

ἦλθε δέ οἱ κρυόεν πυκινῷ μάντευμα θυμῷ,   130
πὰρ μέσον ὀμφαλὸν εὐδένδροιο ῥηθὲν ματέρος·
75 τὸν μονοκρήπιδα παντῶς ἐν φυλακᾷ σχεθέμεν μεγάλᾳ,
εὖτ' ἂν αἰπεινῶν ἀπὸ σταθμῶν ἐς εὐδείελον   135
χθόνα μόλῃ κλειτᾶς Ἰωλκοῦ,

'Αντ. δ'.

ξεῖνος αἴτ' ὢν ἀστός. ὁ δ' ἄρα χρόνῳ
ἵκετ' αἰχμαῖσιν διδύμαισιν ἀνὴρ ἔκπαγλος· ἐσθὰς δ'
ἀμφότερόν μιν ἔχεν,   140
80 ἅ τε Μαγνήτων ἐπιχώριος ἁρμόζοισα θαητοῖσι γυίοις,
ἀμφὶ δὲ παρδαλέᾳ στέγετο φρίσσοντας ὄμβρους·
οὐδὲ κομᾶν πλόκαμοι κερθέντες ᾤχοντ' ἀγλαοί,   145
ἀλλ' ἅπαν νῶτον καταίθυσσον. τάχα δ' εὐθὺς ἰὼν
σφετέρας
ἐστάθη γνώμας ἀταρμύκτοιο πειρώμενος   150

agent cf. Soph. *Ant.* 210, 294, Thuk.
I. xx. 3 (Shilleto). Perhaps it would
be more correct to say 'author'
than 'agent.'

Αἰολιδᾶν.] Both Iâson's parents
were grandchildren of Aeolos.

73. πυκινῷ.] 'Wary.' In most
cases in Homer πυκινὸς applies to
one who has dangers to avoid.

78. ὁ δ', κ.τ.λ.] 'He came ac-
cordingly at last, a hero to marvel
at for his twin spears, and raiment
in two fashions covered him, both
that of the Magnêsian land close
fitting to his admirable limbs, while
by a leopard's skin over all he was
made proof against chilling showers.'
Prof. Paley renders φρίσσοντας
'hurtling,' cf. *horrida grando*, Verg.
Georg. 1. 449, where I think *horrida*
may mean 'causing to shiver or
shudder.' As in Pyth. vi. 10—12
Pindar compares ὄμβρος to an army,
he may here intend a metaphor
from serried ranks of spears. As
to which meaning is best δίχα μοι
νόος ἀτρέκειαν εἰπεῖν.

79. διδύμαισιν.] Cf. *Il.* iii. 18.

The dative should be taken with
ἔκπαγλος. In art we find warriors
represented with two spears, some-
times of unequal size.

81. So Paris, *Il.* iii. 17. For
δὲ after τε cf. τί δ' ἔρδων φίλος | σοί
τε,...Κρονίδα, φίλος δὲ Μοίσαις Ἐυ-
θυμίᾳ τε μέλων εἴην τοῦτ' αἴτημί σε,
Frag. 132 [127], Pyth. xi. 30.

φρίσσοντας.] A Schol. explains
φρίσσειν ποιοῦντας, and quotes μαι-
νομένοιο Διωνύσοιο, *Il.* vi. 132, i.e.
μανιοποιοῦ Δ.; so χλωρὸν δέος, *Il.*
vii. 479, αἰδοία χάρις, Ol. vi. 76,
χερὶ κούφᾳ, Pyth. ix. 11.

83. καταίθυσσον.] 'Fell waving
down all his back.' For construc-
tion cf. Pyth. v. 10. His long hair
indicates that he was a Greek in
spite of his strange attire, and so
καρηκομόων. On the dedication of
the hair to River Gods, Mother
Earth or Apollo, see Prof. Paley's
note on Aesch. *Choëph.* 6, *Il.* xxiii.
144—146.

84. ἀταρμύκτοιο.] We must assume
a stem ταρμ-υκ- (cf. κηρ-υκ-) from
the root of τρέμω. Mss. generally

85 ἐν ἀγορᾷ πλήθοντος ὄχλου.

Ἐπ. δ'.

τὸν μὲν οὐ γίνωσκον· ὀπιζομένων δ' ἔμπας τις εἶπεν
  καὶ τόδε·
Οὔ τί που οὗτος Ἀπόλλων, οὐδὲ μὰν χαλκάρματός
  ἐστι πόσις   155
Ἀφροδίτας· ἐν δὲ Νάξῳ φαντὶ θανεῖν λιπαρᾷ
Ἰφιμεδείας παῖδας, Ὦτον καὶ σέ, τολμάεις Ἐφιάλτα
  ἄναξ.
90 καὶ μὰν Τιτυὸν βέλος Ἀρτέμιδος θήρευσε κραιπνόν, 160
ἐξ ἀνικάτου φαρέτρας ὀρνύμενον,
ὄφρα τις τᾶν ἐν δυνατῷ φιλοτάτων ἐπιψαύειν ἔραται.

                          Στρ. ε'.

τοὶ μὲν ἀλλάλοισιν ἀμειβόμενοι   165
γάρυον τοιαῦτ'· ἀνὰ δ' ἡμιόνοις ξεστᾷ τ' ἀπήνᾳ προ-
  τροπάδαν Πελίας
95 ἵκετο σπεύδων· τάφε δ' αὐτίκα παπτάναις ἀρίγνωτον
  πέδιλον
δεξιτερῷ μόνον ἀμφὶ ποδί. κλέπτων δὲ θυμῷ   170
δεῖμα προσέννεπε· Ποίαν γαῖαν, ὦ ξεῖν', εὔχεαι
πατρίδ' ἔμμεν; καὶ τίς ἀνθρώπων σε χαμαιγενέων
  πολιᾶς   175

ἀταρβακτ.; one however ἀταρβυκτ.
and μ and β are easily confused
(cf. Ol. i. 58, ix. 8). Hesych. gives
ταρμύξασθαι· φοβηθῆναι.

89. Otos and Ephialtes were ce-
lebrated for beauty (cf. Hom. Od.
xi. 305), and owed their death to
Artemis as well as did Tityos who
was renowned for great stature.

92. 'That men may be fain to
aspire to loves that are within their
capacity.'

ἔραται.] Subjunct. The second
syllable is long.

95. τάφε.] For σθαπ- for σταπ
secondary of √STA, cf. stup-eo.

98. From θαρσήσαις, v. 101, we
should infer that Pelias astonished
and took aback Iâson, and that
therefore this verse is insulting.
χαμαιγενὴς means lit. 'born on the
ground' and cannot be equivalent
to γηγενής. Cookesley well contrasts
διογενεῖς applied to kings. Again
πολιᾶς can scarcely suggest that he
was τηλύγετος. Pelias in the inso-
lent bluster of sudden terror asks
Iâson in effect 'what low old hag
brought you forth?' An insult is
meant by asking who his *mother*
was. Iâson tells him who his
father was.

ἐξανῆκεν γαστρός; ἐχθίστοισι μὴ ψεύδεσιν
100 καταμιάναις εἰπὲ γένναν.

'Αντ. ε'.

τὸν δὲ θαρσήσαις ἀγανοῖσι λόγοις
ὧδ' ἀμείφθη· Φαμὶ διδασκαλίαν Χείρωνος οἴσειν. ἄν-
τροθε γὰρ νέομαι   180
πὰρ Χαρικλοῦς καὶ Φιλύρας, ἵνα Κενταύρου με κοῦραι
θρέψαν ἀγναί.

εἴκοσι δ' ἐκτελέσαις ἐνιαυτοὺς οὔτε ἔργον   185
105 οὔτ' ἔπος εὐτράπελον κείνοισιν εἰπὼν ἱκόμαν
οἴκαδ', ἀρχαίαν κομίζων πατρὸς ἐμοῦ, βασιλευομέναν
οὐ κατ' αἶσαν, τάν ποτε Ζεὺς ὤπασεν λαγέτᾳ   190
Αἰόλῳ καὶ παισί, τιμάν.

'Επ. ε'.

πεύθομαι γάρ νιν Πελίαν ἄθεμιν λευκαῖς πιθήσαντα
φρασὶν
110 ἁμετέρων ἀποσυλᾶσαι βιαίως ἀρχεδικᾶν τοκέων·   195
τοί μ', ἐπεὶ πάμπρωτον εἶδον φέγγος, ὑπερφιάλου
ἀγεμόνος δείσαντες ὕβριν, κᾶδος ὥσείτε φθιμένου
δνοφερὸν   200

99. ἐξανῆκεν.] Similarly used
Eur. *Ion*, 1000, ὃν πρῶτον ὑμῶν πρό-
γονον ἐξανῆκε γῆ.
102. διδασκαλίαν.] Cf. Pyth. vi.
19.
οἴσειν.] Clearly a present here.
Is οἴσω when future in sense pre-
sent in form like εἶμι, ἔδομαι, φάγο-
μαι? Observe the verbal οἰσ-τέος.
105. εὐτράπελον.] So one м.л.
The rest, ἐντρ. Heyne from Schol.
ἐκτρ. Should we read οὔτε ἔπος
τραπελόν, 'shifty'?
εἰπών.] Observe the zeugma—
'having neither (wrought) a (deceit-
ful) deed nor spoken a deceitful
word.'
106. κομίζων.] Present in fu-
ture sense, cf. Pyth. i. 52.
109. 'For I hear that lawless
Pelias in obedience to mad thoughts

forcibly despoiled thereof my pa-
rents the owners by prime right.'
λευκαῖς.] Clearly connected with
λύσσα Att. λύττα for λυκγα. This
Pindaric use is all that is wanted to
confirm this explanation of λύσσα.
Hesych. gives λευκῶν πραπίδων·
κακῶν φρενῶν. Hermann thinks
Pindar imitates φρεσὶ λευγαλέῃσι
πιθήσας, Hom. *Il.* ix. 119, but if the
Homeric adjective suggested λευ-
καῖς it can only have been by the
sound λευ- and λευκὸς must have
been known to the poet in the sense
of 'mad.'
110. ἀρχεδικᾶν.] Cf. ἀρχέπλου-
τος, Soph. *El.* 72. Perhaps it
means 'possessed of ancient juris-
diction' as δικασπόλοι. The other
rendering assumes an unusual
meaning for δίκη.

12—2

ἐν δώμασι θηκάμενοι, μίγα κωκυτῷ γυναικῶν
κρύβδα πέμπον σπαργάνοις ἐν πορφυρέοις,
115 νυκτὶ κοινάσαντες ὁδόν, Κρονίδᾳ δὲ τράφεν Χείρωνι
δῶκαν.   205
                                                                        Στρ. ϛ΄.

ἀλλὰ τούτων μὲν κεφάλαια λόγων
ἴστε. λευκίππων δὲ δόμους πατέρων, κεδνοὶ πολῖται,
φράσσατέ μοι σαφέως·
Αἴσονος γὰρ παῖς ἐπιχώριος οὐ ξείναν ἱκοίμαν γαῖαν
ἄλλων.   210

113. μίγα.] Cf. μίγδ' ἄλλοισι
θεοῖσι, Il. VIII. 437.
115. νυκτί.] Cf. sua narret
Ulixes | quae sine teste gerit, quorum
nox conscia sola est, Ov. Met. XIII.
15, nox conscia sacris, ib. VI. 588.
'Having made the journey under
cover of night.'
τράφεν.] Doric pres. infinitive.
For inf. cf. Ol. VI. 33.
118. ἱκοίμαν.] By some regarded
as potential. The optative with ἀν
expresses a mental conception re-
lating to future time unemphati-
cally, without ἀν emphatically. If
we choose to consider that we have
here and in all similar cases a
suppressed protasis then we must
state the case thus; in apodosis
the opt. with ἀν properly expresses
a possible or probable result of the
future fulfilment of the conditions,
without ἀν a result necessarily con-
sequent upon or included in the
fulfilment of the condition. Ob-
serve however that the expression
of an *imagined case* as opposed to
an *actual case* does not necessarily
involve the imagination of the case
as the result of conditions; so
that, though every indefinite hy-
pothesis respecting future time is
imaginative, every such imagined
case is not necessarily hypothetical.
A hypothesis is needed for the ex-
planation of such a mental con-
ception but not for its *completion*

or *analysis*. Thus then the in-
variable assumption of a suppressed
protasis is due to the easy confusion
between *explanation* and *analysis*,
the *Potential* theory to forgetting
that *imagined* as well as *potential*
is opposed to *actual*, and again to
the Teutonic auxiliaries 'can,'
'could,' 'may,' 'might,' used to
supply the loss of a mood of men-
tal conception. Now potentiality
is no doubt very frequently an at-
tribute of what is mentally con-
ceived, but is not essential to it nor
necessarily implied any more than
is obligation. For example οὐκ ἂν
μεθείμην τοῦ θρόνου, Aristoph. Ran.
830, *I will not give up the throne*,
is literally *I have a conception of
not being likely to give up the
throne*, while Pindar's οὐχ ἱκοίμαν
is literally *I have a conception of
not coming*, the omission of ἂν ex-
cluding the possibility of an alter-
native, which is suggested by its
presence, and thus giving emphasis,
as does its omission in apodosis
with a past tense of the indicative
(Goodwin § 49, 2, note *a*). For
omission of ἂν in Pindar, cf. Pind.
Ol. III. fin. οὐ μιν διώξω· κεινὸς
εἴην..., '*I should* be foolish' ('if
I were to pursue it'—suppressed):
Pyth x. 21, θεὸς εἴη ἀπήμων κέαρ,
'a god *would* be free from pain
of heart.' See also Ol. IX. 80.
In Homer the omission of κεν, κε is

Φὴρ δέ με θεῖος Ἰάσονα κικλήσκων προσηύδα.
120 ὡς φάτο· τὸν μὲν ἐσελθόντ᾽ ἔγνον ὀφθαλμοὶ πατρίς·
ἐκ δ᾽ ἄρ᾽ αὐτοῦ πομφόλυξαν δάκρυα γηραλέων γλεφά-
ρων, 215
ἂν πέρι ψυχὰν ἐπεὶ γάθησεν, ἐξαίρετον
γόνον ἰδὼν κάλλιστον ἀνδρῶν.

Ἀντ. ϛ.

καὶ κασίγνητοί σφισιν ἀμφότεραι 220
125 ἤλυθον κείνου γε κατὰ κλέος· ἐγγὺς μὲν Φέρης κράναν
Ὑπερῆδα λιπών,
ἐκ δὲ Μεσσάνας Ἀμυθάν· ταχέως δ᾽ Ἄδματος ἵκεν
καὶ Μέλαμπος
εὐμενέοντες ἀνεψιόν. ἐν δαιτὸς δὲ μοίρᾳ 225
μειλιχίοισι λόγοις αὐτοὺς Ἰάσων δέγμενος,
ξείνι᾽ ἁρμόζοντα τεύχων, πᾶσαν ἐν εὐφροσύναν τά-
νυεν, 230
130 ἀθρόαις πέντε δραπὼν νύκτεσσιν ἔν θ᾽ ἁμέραις
ἱερὸν εὐζωᾶς ἄωτον.

Ἐπ. ϛ.

ἀλλ᾽ ἐν ἕκτᾳ πάντα λόγον θέμενος σπουδαῖον ἐξ ἀρχᾶς
ἀνὴρ 235

frequent. In Attic poetry ἄν is rarely omitted save in questions and negative clauses (esp. after οὐκ ἔσθ᾽ ὅπως, ὅστις; cf. Aesch. *Agam.* 603 [P.]) or after a comparative phrase with ἤ. Mr Nixon has pointed out to me that ἄν is occasionally omitted with the optative by Antiphon and Andokides and even Isaeos. Critics have no doubt frequently inserted the particle wrongly; e.g. Eurip. *Androm.* 929 (P.) πῶς οὖν τάδ᾽ ὡς εἴποι τις ἐξαμάρτανες;—'as one would certainly ask (if he heard you)'—corrected to πῶς οὖν ἄν εἴποι τις τάδ᾽ ἐξ.; see also Aesch. *Agam.* 535 (P.), *Choēph.* 585 (P.), Eurip. *Iph. in Aul.* 1210, 1215 (P.).

121. πομφόλυξαν.] Cf. Pyth. I.13.

124. κασίγνητοι.] Aeson's brothers.

σφισιν.] This might be a *dat. commodi*, but the order suggests that it is possessive, cf. Ol. IX. 15.

125. κείνου γε.] Cf. v. 243, and ἤθελον κείνον γε πείθεσθ᾽ ἀναξίαις ἑκόντες, Nem. VIII. 10.

Ὑπερῆδα.] A spring near Pherae. Cf. ὦ γῆ Φεραία χαῖρε, σύγγονόν θ᾽ ὕδωρ, | Ὑπέρεια κρήνη νᾶμα θεοφιλέστατον, Soph. Frag. 83.

127. ἀνεψιόν.] For acc. for dat. cf. *supra* v. 36.

129. ἁρμόζοντα.] Cf. ἁρμόδιον δεῖπνον, Nem. I. 21. Don. renders 'friendly,' 'pleasing.' The Thessalian εὐωχίαι were celebrated.

131. 'The sacred prime of good cheer.'

συγγενέσιν παρεκοινᾶθ'· οἱ δ' ἐπέσποντ'. αἶψα δ' ἀπὸ
    κλισιᾶν
ὦρτο σὺν κείνοισι, καί ῥ' ἦλθον Πελία μέγαρον·
135 ἐσσύμενοι δ' εἴσω κατέσταν· τῶν δ' ἀκούσαις αὐτὸς
    ὑπαντίασεν   240
Τυροῦς ἐρασιπλοκάμου γενεά· πραὺν δ' Ἰάσων
μαλθακᾷ φωνᾷ ποτιστάζων ὄαρον
βάλλετο κρηπῖδα σοφῶν ἐπέων· Παῖ Ποσειδᾶνος Πε-
    τραίου,   245
                                                    Στρ. ζ'.

ἐντὶ μὲν θνατῶν φρένες ὠκύτεραι
140 κέρδος αἰνῆσαι πρὸ δίκας δόλιον, τραχεῖαν ἑρπόντων
    πρὸς ἐπίβδαν ὅμως·
ἀλλ ἐμὲ χρὴ καὶ σὲ θεμισσαμένους ὀργὰς ὑφαίνειν
    λοιπὸν ὄλβον.   250
εἰδότι τοι ἐρέω· μία βοῦς Κρηθεῖ τε μάτηρ
καὶ θρασυμήδεϊ Σαλμωνεῖ· τρίταισιν δ' ἐν γοναῖς   255

---

135. ὑπαντίασεν.] Cf. Pyth. v111.
11.
136. γενεά.] Pelias.
137. ποτιστάζων.] For the me-
taphor cf. Pyth. xii. 10. Render
'and Iâson, letting softly flow to-
wards him mild speech in gentle
tone, began a sage address.'
138. βάλλετο.] Cf. Pyth. vii. 3.
140. ἐπίβδαν.] Lit. 'The day
after a carouse.' I connect the
word with βδέω, βδελυρός, as being
lit. 'the consequent nausea.' Cur-
tius supposes a metathesis from
ἐπιδβα for ἐπιδϜα for ἐπι-διϜα 'the

day after,' cf. Lat. dies for divas.
There is no analogy to justify this
derivation. The stems βδε-, βδα-
I connect with the √SPU, the U
becoming Ϝ and disappearing be-
fore ε, α.
142. βοῦς.] A rare metaphori-
cal usage for 'wife' or 'mother.'
Cf. Aesch. Agam. 1126, ἄπεχε τῆι
βοὸς | τὸν ταῦρον, and Horace's
iuuenca, Od. ii. 5, 6, also his proper
name Damalis.
143. τρίταισιν.] The pedigree
was as follows:

Aeolos m. Enarea (μία βοῦς)

Krêtheus	Athamas	Sisyphos	Salmôneus	Periêres
m.			Tyro—Poseidon	
Aeson	Amythâon	Pheres	Pelias	
Iâson	Melampos	Admêtos		

ἄμμες αὖ κείνων φυτευθέντες σθένος ἀελίου χρύσεον
145 λεύσσομεν. Μοῖραι δ' ἀφίσταντ', εἴ τις ἔχθρα πέλει
ὁμογόνοις, αἰδῶ καλύψαι.   260
                                        Ἀντ. ζ'.

οὐ πρέπει νῷν χαλκοτόροις ξίφεσιν
οὐδ' ἀκόντεσσιν μεγάλαν προγόνων τιμὰν δάσασθαι.
μῆλά τε γάρ τοι ἐγὼ
καὶ βοῶν ξανθὰς ἀγέλας ἀφίημ' ἀγρούς τε πάντας,
        τοὺς ἀπούραις   265
150 ἀμετέρων τοκέων νέμεαι, πλοῦτον πιαίνων·
κού με πονεῖ τεὸν οἶκον ταῦτα προσύνοντ' ἄγαν·
ἀλλὰ καὶ σκᾶπτον μόναρχον καὶ θρόνος, ᾧ ποτε
        Κρηθεΐδας   270
ἐγκαθίζων ἱππόταις εὔθυνε λαοῖς δίκας.
τὰ μὲν ἄνευ ξυνᾶς ἀνίας

The epithet applied to Salmôneus reflects doubtless on Pelias. It may be as Böckh suggests that Arkesilas and Dâmophilos were second cousins with a common great-grandmother, but it is not necessary to establish a close parallel between them and Pelias and Iâson. See Introduction.

144. κείνων.] The gen. is as if φυτευθέντες were πεφυκότες.

χρύσεον.] By hypallage for the gen. For the phrase cf. Aesch. Eum. 746, φάος βλέπειν =' to live.'

146. καλύψαι.] The Schol. Heyne and Böckh render the inf. as consecutive, Hermann would read αἰδοῖ and explains non probant Parcae si quod inter cognatos odium est id prae pudore et reverentia celare. Itaque aperte loquar. Dissen renders Parcae secedunt... ...ad suum pudorem "occultandum; Don. 'the Fates stand apart......in order that they' may 'not witness anything so shameful.' I suppose he would render literally ' to hide

from themselves the shameful spectacle,' to which version Dissen's is preferable. For inf. cf. v. 187, Pyth. x. 17, Ol. i. 9.

149. καὶ...τε.] The τε shows that the fields are the pastures of the herds, while the sheep presumably browsed on open hillsides; or the fields are ploughed by the cattle. Cf. Pyth. i. 42.

151. 'And it grieves me not that these provide thy house beyond measure.'

πονεῖ.] For this rare transitive sense cf. Anakr. xl. 14, εἰ τὸ κέντρον πονεῖ τὸ τῆς μελίττης. For ταῦτα προσύνοντα =τὸ ταῦτα προσύνειν, cf. Ol. ix. 104, Pyth. vi. 32.

152. σκᾶπτον...θρόνος.] Dissen explains the nominative as absolute used for emphasis, and compares Plat. Theaetet. 173 D, but it is easy to supply the verb from the former clause, and τὰ μὲν v. 154 does not seem to be resumptive. I therefore place a full stop after δίκας.

Ἐπ. ζ'.

155 λῦσον ἄμμιν, μή τι νεώτερον ἐξ αὐτῶν ἀναστήῃ κα-
κόν.   275
    ὡς ἄρ' ἔειπεν, ἀκᾷ δ' ἀνταγόρευσεν καὶ Πελίας.
    Ἔσομαι
    τοῖος· ἀλλ' ἤδη με γηραιὸν μέρος ἁλικίας   280
    ἀμφιπολεῖ· σὸν δ' ἄνθος ἥβας ἄρτι κυμαίνει· δύνασαι
        δ' ἀφελεῖν
    μᾶνιν χθονίων. κέλεται γὰρ ἐὰν ψυχὰν κομίξαι
160 Φρίξος ἐλθόντας πρὸς Αἰήτα θαλάμους   285
    δέρμα τε κριοῦ βαθύμαλλον ἄγειν, τῷ ποτ' ἐκ πόντου
        σαώθη

Στρ. η'.

    ἔκ τε ματρυιᾶς ἀθέων βελέων.
    ταῦτά μοι θαυμαστὸς ὄνειρος ἰὼν φωνεῖ. μεμάντευμαι
        δ' ἐπὶ Κασταλίᾳ,   290
    εἰ μετάλλατόν τι. καὶ ὡς τάχος ὀτρύνει με τεύχειν
    ναῒ πομπάν.

155. ἀναστήῃ.] Most MSS. read
-στησῃ: Kayser suggests -στῇ σοι.
The Schol. recognises -σταίη and
-στήσῃ. For the admissibility of
the optative, cf. Goodwin § 44, 2,
note 2. He views it as a mere
irregularity of construction: but
I think it may convey a less defi-
nite notion of the realisation of the
purpose than does the subjunctive.
In this passage then it would be
more polite as being less threaten-
ing than ἀναστήῃ. However as the
point is doubtful I defer to the
weight of editorial authority.
158. σόν, κ.τ.λ.] 'While thy
bloom of youth is just at the full
swell.'
159. μᾶνιν.] Illustrated by Aesch.
Eum. 767, αὐτοὶ γὰρ ἡμεῖς ὄντες
ἐν τάφοις τότε | τοῖς τἀμά παρβαί-
νουσι νῦν ὁρκώματα | ἀμηχάνοισι πρά-
ξομεν δυσπραξίαις, κ.τ.λ.

κομίξαι.] Schol. ὅτι δὲ τὰς ψυχὰς
ἀνεκαλοῦντο τῶν ἐπὶ ταῖς ἀλλοδαπαῖς
ἀποιχομένων καὶ Ὅμηρος δηλοῖ, Od.
IX. 64—66. Upon solemn invoca-
tion the soul of one who died at
sea or in a foreign land accom-
panied its countrymen to its native
land.
162. ματρυιᾶς.] Ino, or ac-
cording to Pindar Dēmodike, to
Pherekydes Themisto, to Sopho-
kles Nephele (Schol.).
164. εἰ μετάλλατόν τι.] 'In case
there were aught worth enquiry.'
Cf. Ol. VI. 62. A dream was not to
be depended upon; but Pelias being
uneasy asked the oracle in the first
instance whether or no the dream
were worth acting upon as a pre-
liminary to enquiring what was to
be done. Either the poet puts it
shortly or the oracle anticipated
the second question.

165 τοῦτον ἄεθλον ἑκὼν τέλεσον· καί τοι μοναρχεῖν
καὶ βασιλευέμεν ὄμνυμι προήσειν. καρτερὸς 295
ὅρκος ἄμμιν μάρτυς ἔστω Ζεὺς ὁ γενέθλιος ἀμφοτέροις.
σύνθεσιν ταύταν ἐπαινήσαντες οἱ μὲν κρίθεν· 300
ἀτὰρ Ἰάσων αὐτὸς ἤδη

'Αντ. η'.

170 ὤρνυεν κάρυκας ἐόντα πλόον
φαινέμεν παντᾷ. τάχα δὲ Κρονίδαο Ζηνὸς υἱοὶ τρεῖς
ἀκαμαντομάχαι
ἦλθον Ἀλκμήνας θ' ἑλικοβλεφάρου Λήδας τε, δοιοὶ
δ' ὑψιχαῖται 305
ἀνέρες, Ἐννοσίδα γένος, αἰδεσθέντες ἀλκάν,
ἔκ τε Πύλου καὶ ἀπ' ἄκρας Ταινάρου· τῶν μὲν
κλέος 310
175 ἐσλὸν Εὐφάμου τ' ἐκράνθη σόν τε, Περικλύμεν' εὐ-
ρυβία.
ἐξ Ἀπόλλωνος δὲ φορμικτὰς ἀοιδᾶν πατὴρ
ἔμολεν, εὐαίνητος Ὀρφεύς. 315

'Επ. η'.

πέμπε δ' Ἑρμᾶς χρυσόραπις διδύμους υἱοὺς ἐπ' ἄτρυτον
πόνον
τὸν μὲν Ἐχίονα, κεχλάδοντας ἥβᾳ, τὸν δ' Ἔρυτον.
ταχέως δ'

τεύχειν ναῖ τομπάν.] Cf. Hom.
Od. x. 18. 'To make ready a ship
for the restoration.'
165. μον. καὶ βασιλ.] Cf. Hes.
Theog. 883, βασιλευέμεν ἠδὲ ἀνάσ-
σειν.
168. κρίθεν.] Equivalent to δι-
εκρίθησαν.
172. ὑψιχαῖται.] Equivalent to
Thukydides' ἀκρόκομοι. The sons
of Poseidon might be expected to
follow eastern fashions such as the
top-knot which Thuk. tells us was
Ionian, though he wrongly supposed
it originated in Attika instead of
Asia Minor.

173. αἰδεσθέντες.] Don. 'in their
valour continually inspired by a
sense of honour,' quoting Il. xv.
561. Cf. ib. v. 529, and Ol. vii.
44. Dissen: 'fearing their valour,
using it with moderation.' Mr H.
A. Birks neatly renders 'chivalrous
as strong.' Schneid. agrees with
Don. I incline to the supposition
that they were youths as yet untried
in daring ventures and so 'bash-
fully diffident of their valour.'
179. κεχλάδοντας.] Though the
Schol. explains πληθύοντας, I take
the sense found in Skt. hlâdê,
'I rejoice.' 'Swelling' does not suit

180 ἀμφὶ Παγγαίου θέμεθλα ναιετάοντες ἔβαν·   320
   καὶ γὰρ ἑκὼν θυμῷ γελανεῖ θᾶσσον ἔντυνεν βασιλεὺς
     ἀνέμων
   Ζήταν Κάλαΐν τε πατὴρ Βορέας, ἄνδρας πτεροῖσιν 325
    νῶτα πεφρίκοντας ἄμφω πορφυρέοις.
   τὸν δὲ παμπειθῆ γλυκὺν ἡμιθέοισιν πόθον ἔνδαιεν Ἥρα
                               Στρ. θ΄.

185 ναὸς Ἀργοῦς, μή τινα λειπόμενον
   τὰν ἀκίνδυνον παρὰ ματρὶ μένειν αἰῶνα πέσσοντ', ἀλλ'
    ἐπὶ καὶ θανάτῳ   330
   φάρμακον κάλλιστον ἑᾶς ἀρετᾶς ἄλιξιν εὑρέσθαι σὺν
    ἄλλοις.

κρόταλα, Frag. 57 Β. [48]: 'sound-
ing merrily' does, cf. Ol. IX. 2.
For the order which the Schol.
says Alkman most frequently uses
are quoted Κάστωρ τε, πώλων ταχέων
δμητῆρες ἱππόται σοφοί, καὶ Πολυδεύ-
κης κυδρός, Alkm. Frag. 12 [3], Il.
v. 774. The previous υἱούς makes
this passage less peculiar.

180. Pindar's selection of heroes
for mention is thus explained:
Hêrakles and the Dioskuroi as
Dorian heroes were naturally wor-
shipped in the Dorian colony
Kyrênê, where also Apollo, Posei-
don and Hermes were especially
honoured. The Boreades from
Pangaeon in the extreme north
are opposed to Euphêmos from the
extreme south.

184. 'Hêra 'twas who enkindled
in the demigods that all-persuad-
ing sweet desire for ship Argo, that
none should be left behind and
stay in his mother's house leading
in luxury the life from peril free,
but should e'en at hazard of death
win with other his compeers a
most noble elixir in his prowess.
So when the flower of mariners
came to Iolkos Iâson numbered
them and withal gave praise to
each, and for him a seer enquiring

of God by flight of birds and sacred
lots, Mopsos to wit, right willingly
gave the signal to embark. And
when they had slung the anchor
above the beak their leader on the
prow took in his hands a golden
goblet and called upon Zeus, father
of Uranos' seed, who hath for lance
the lightning, and on beats of waves
and winds to hie them on swiftly,
and on nights and tracks over the
main, and on days to be favorable
and fortune of return-home kindly.'

186. αἰῶνα.] Generally mascu-
line in Pindar: the fem. τὰν is sig-
nificant.

πέσσοντ'.] Lit. 'coddling,' which
originally means 'parboiling.' Cf.
Ol. I. 82, τί κέ τις ἀνώνυμον | γῆρας
ἐν σκότῳ καθήμενος ἕψοι μάταν.

187. φάρμακον.] Don. 'A sea-
soning or relish even for death it-
self in his own glory and renown,'
see New Crat. § 175. I cannot
accept this. The 'elixir compound-
ed of his prowess' is renown, which
enables him to say non omnis mo-
riar. Cf. ἀλλὰ θεοὶ γὰρ ἀνηκέσ-
τοισι κακοῖσι | ὦ φίλ', ἐπὶ κρατερὴν
τλημοσύνην ἔθεσαν | φάρμακον, Ar-
chiloch. Frag. 9 [48] 5, Pyth. XI. 55
—58. The use of ἐπὶ proposed by
Don. is not properly supported. In

ἐς δ' Ἰαωλκὸν ἐπεὶ κατέβα ναυτᾶν ἄωτος,	335
λέξατο πάντας ἐπαινήσαις Ἰάσων. καί ῥά οἱ
190 μάντις ὀρνίχεσσι καὶ κλάροισι θεοπροπέων ἱεροῖς
Μόψος ἄμβασε στρατὸν πρόφρων· ἐπεὶ δ' ἐμβόλου 340
κρέμασαν ἀγκύρας ὕπερθεν,

'Αντ. θ'.

χρυσέαν χείρεσσι λαβὼν φιάλαν
ἀρχὸς ἐν πρύμνᾳ πατέρ' Οὐρανιδᾶν ἐγχεικέραυνον
Ζῆνα, καὶ ὠκυπόρους	345
195 κυμάτων ῥιπὰς ἀνέμων τ' ἐκάλει, νύκτας τε καὶ πόντου
κελεύθους,
ἄματά τ' εὔφρονα καὶ φιλίαν νόστοιο μοῖραν·
ἐκ νεφέων δέ οἱ ἀντάϋσε βροντᾶς αἴσιον	350
φθέγμα· λαμπραὶ δ' ἦλθον ἀκτῖνες στεροπᾶς ἀπο-
ρηγνύμεναι.
ἀμπνοὰν δ' ἥρωες ἔστασαν θεοῦ σάμασιν	355
200 πιθόμενοι· κάρυξε δ' αὐτοῖς

'Επ. θ'.

ἐμβαλεῖν κώπαισι τερασκόπος ἀδείας ἐνίπτων ἐλπίδας·
εἰρεσία δ' ὑπεχώρησεν ταχεῖαν ἐκ παλαμᾶν ἄκορος. 360
σὺν Νότου δ' αὔραις ἐπ' Ἀξείνου στόμα πεμπόμενοι
ἤλυθον· ἔνθ' ἁγνὸν Ποσειδάωνος ἔσσαντ' εἰναλίου
τέμενος,
205 φοίνισσα δὲ Θρηϊκίων ἀγέλα ταύρων ὑπᾶρχεν	365

the passages he cites we have one good thing added to another good thing, while here it is not so.
191. Observe the anachronism. Beaks and anchors are post-Homeric, cf. Il. i. 436, ἐκ δ' εὐνὰς ἔβαλον. The εὐναί were heavy stones attached to the prow by ropes and let down on each side to keep the ship's head off shore, while the πρυμνήσια were tied to something on shore (Paley).
194. ὠκυπόρους.] Proleptic, cf.

Pyth. i. 51; as also is εὔφρονα, v. 196.
199. ἔστασαν.] Poetic use of ἵστημι with nomen actionis instead of a special verb, so with βοήν, Aesch., μῆνιν, Soph., ἐλπίδα, βοήν, κραυγήν, ἰαχήν, Eurip.
202.] εἰρεσία.] 'And the blade-eddies from under their speeding palms went back unceasingly.'
205. As Hieron, where Phrixos' sons had built the altar, was in Asia Minor, Θρηϊκίων is for Βιθυνίων.

καὶ νεόκτιστον λίθων βωμοῖο θέναρ.

ἐς δὲ κίνδυνον βαθὺν ἱέμενοι δεσπόταν λίσσοντο ναῶν,

Στρ. ί.

συνδρόμων κινηθμὸν ἀμαιμάκετον   370
ἐκφυγεῖν πετρᾶν.   δίδυμοι γὰρ ἔσαν ζωαί, κυλινδέ-
σκοντό τε κραιπνότεραι

210 ἢ βαρυγδούπων ἀνέμων στίχες· ἀλλ' ἤδη τελευτὰν
κεῖνος αὐταῖς

ἡμιθέων πλόος ἄγαγεν. ἐς Φᾶσιν δ' ἔπειτεν   375
ἤλυθον, ἔνθα κελαινώπεσσι Κόλχοισιν βίαν
μῖξαν Αἰήτᾳ παρ' αὐτῷ. πότνια δ' ὀξυτάτων βελέων 380
ποικίλαν ἴϋγγα τετράκναμον Οὐλυμπόθεν

215 ἐν ἀλύτῳ ζεύξαισα κύκλῳ

'Αντ. ί.

μαινάδ' ὄρνιν Κυπρογένεια φέρεν
πρῶτον ἀνθρώποισι, λιτάς τ' ἐπαοιδὰς ἐκδιδάσκησεν
σοφὸν Αἰσονίδαν·   385
ὄφρα Μηδείας τοκέων ἀφέλοιτ' αἰδῶ, ποθεινὰ δ' Ἑλλὰς
αὐτὰν

Herodotos, vii. 75, tells us that the Bithynians were from Thrace.

206. λίθων.] Gen. of material cf. Soph. *El.* 19 (Jebb), *supra v.* 71: only two mss. give λίθων, two λίθον, one λίθοιο, the rest λίθινον. I prefer to take λίθων with θέναρ, the hollow on the top of the altar to hold the offerings, which might be in a stone whatever the body of the altar was made of.

209.] Prof. Paley suggests that the Symplêgades may have been a mythical reminiscence of icebergs.

212. κελαινώπεσσι.] Cf. Herod. ii. 104, where he mentions the dark skin and swarthy hair of the Kolchoi as a proof that they were Egyptians said to have belonged to the host of Sesôstris.

βίαν μῖξαν.] Cf. ἐπιμίξαις Αἰθιοπεσσι χεῖρας, 'having engaged hand to hand with Aethiopians,' Nem. iii. 61, Hom. *Il.* iv. 456, xxi. 469.

213. πότνια.] Cf. πότνια θηρῶν, Hom. *Il.* xxi. 470.

214. ἴϋγγα.] Cf. Theokr. ii., Nem. iv. 135, ἴϋγγι δ' ἕλκομαι ἦτορ. The bird was tied by wings and legs to the four spokes and turned with the wheel as a love-charm.

216. μαινάδ'.] 'Maddening.' Cf. *supra v.* 81.

217. λιτάς.] Adj. Cf. Ol. vi. 132. σοφόν.] Proleptic.

218. ποθεινὰ δ' Ἑλλάς.] 'And yearning for Hellas with persuasion's lash might goad her heart-afire. So she quickly revealed the ways of performing the feats set by her father, and she compounded with oil antidotes against severe pains, and gave him to anoint him-

ἐν φρασὶ καιομέναν δονέοι μάστιγι Πειθοῦς.   390
220 καὶ τάχα πείρατ᾽ ἀέθλων δείκνυεν πατρωΐων·
σὺν δ᾽ ἐλαίῳ φαρμακώσαισ᾽ ἀντίτομα. στερεᾶν ὀδυνᾶν
δῶκε χρίεσθαι. καταίνησάν τε κοινὸν γάμον   395
γλυκὺν ἐν ἀλλάλοισι μῖξαι.

Ἐπ. ι'.

ἀλλ᾽ ὅτ᾽ Αἰήτας ἀδαμάντινον ἐν μέσσοις ἄροτρον σκίμ-
ψατο
225 καὶ βόας, οἳ φλόγ᾽ ἀπὸ ξανθᾶν γενύων πνέον καιο-
μένοιο πυρός,   400
χαλκέαις δ᾽ ὁπλαῖς ἀράσσεσκον χθόν᾽ ἀμειβόμενοι·
τοὺς ἀγαγὼν ζεύγλᾳ πέλασσεν μοῦνος. ὀρθὰς δ᾽ αὔ-
λακας ἐντανύσαις   405
ἤλαυν᾽, ἀνὰ βωλακίας δ᾽ ὀρόγυιαν σχίζε νῶτον
γᾶς. ἔειπεν δ᾽ ὧδε· Τοῦτ᾽ ἔργον βασιλεύς,
230 ὅστις ἄρχει ναός, ἐμοὶ τελέσαις ἄφθιτον στρωμνὰν
ἀγέσθω,   410

Στρ. ια'.

κῶας αἰγλᾶεν χρυσέῳ θυσάνῳ.
ὡς ἄρ᾽ αὐδάσαντος ἀπὸ κρόκεον ῥίψαις Ἰάσων εἷμα
θεῷ πίσυνος
εἷχετ᾽ ἔργου· πῦρ δέ νιν οὐκ ἐόλει παμφαρμάκου ξείνας
ἐφετμαῖς,   415
σπασσάμενος δ᾽ ἄροτρον, βοέους δήσαις ἀνάγκας

self withal, and they plighted troth to each other to tie the mutual bond of sweet wedlock.'

219. μάστιγι.] Cf. Tib. i. 5. 3, *namque agor ut per plana citus sola uerbere turben | Quem celer assueta uersat ab arte puer*, Hor. Od. iii. 26. 11, *Regina sublimi flagello | Tange Chloën semel arrogantem*, Tib. i. 8. 6.

Πειθοῦς.] Alkaeos made Peitho the daughter of Aphrodite.

221. ἀντίτομα.] Cf. Aesch. *Agam.* 16, ὕπνου τόδ᾽ ἀντίμολπον ἐν τέμνων

(Prof. Kennedy's emend. for ἐντέμνων ἄκος).

222. καταίνησαν.] Καταινέω, 'I betroth,' is used of the parent, Eur. *Iph. in Aul.* 695, cf. *Or.* 1092 (Paley). For κοινὸν...μῖξαι, cf. Pyth. ix. 13.

225. γενύων scans as a dissyllable, πνέον as a monosyllable.

233. ἐόλει.] This is the plup. not the imp. (Buttmann) of √Ϝελ whence εἷλω 'press.' mss. read αιολλει against metre. 'For the fire had not forced him back.'

234. ἀνάγκας.] Most mss. read

235 ἔντεσιν αὐχένας ἐμβάλλων τ' ἐριπλεύρῳ φυᾷ
κέντρον αἰανὲς βιατὰς ἐξεπόνησ' ἐπιτακτὸν ἀνὴρ 420
μέτρον. ἴυξεν δ' ἀφωνήτῳ περ ἔμπας ἄχει
δύνασιν Αἰήτας ἀγασθείς.

'Αντ. ιά.

πρὸς δ' ἑταῖροι καρτερὸν ἄνδρα φίλας 425
240 ὤρεγον χεῖρας, στεφάνοισί τέ μιν ποίας ἔρεπτον, μειλι-
χίοις τε λόγοις

ἀγαπάζοντ'. αὐτίκα δ' 'Αελίου θαυμαστὸς υἱὸς δέρμα
λαμπρὸν

ἔννεπεν, ἔνθα νιν ἐκτάνυσαν Φρίξου μάχαιραι· 430
ἤλπετο δ' οὐκέτι οἱ κεῖνόν γε πράξασθαι πόνον.

κεῖτο γὰρ λόχμᾳ, δράκοντος δ' εἴχετο λαβροτατᾶν
γενύων, 435
245 ὃς πάχει μάκει τε πεντηκόντορον ναῦν κράτει,
τέλεσαν ἂν πλαγαὶ σιδάρου.

'Επ. ιά.

μακρά μοι νεῖσθαι κατ' ἀμαξιτόν· ὥρα γὰρ συνάπτει·
καί τινα 440
οἶμον ἴσαμι βραχύν· πολλοῖσι δ' ἄγημαι σοφίας ἑτέ-
ροις.

βοέοις, a few ἀνάγκαις, both of which
T. Mommsen adopts, taking ἔντεσι
as *dativus termini*. The reading in
the text is the simplest. For gen.
cf. ἀνάγκας χερσί, Nem. VIII. 3,
δόμους ἀβρότατος, Pyth. XI. 34, στο-
λίδα τρυφᾶι, Eurip. *Phoen.* 1491.
237. 'And Aeëtes cried out,
though his agony choked speech in
amazement at his power.' Note the
dat. of attendant circumstances.
240. ἔρεπτον.] Here for ἔρεφον.
242. ἔνθα, κ.τ.λ.]. Poetic for
'where Phrixos had flayed and hung
it out.'
243. πράξασθαι.] Hermann reads
πράξεσθαι used passively, needless-
ly, for οἱ means 'at Pelias' bidding,'

but the accomplishment was de-
cidedly for Iâson's benefit, and
therefore the middle voice is appro-
priate.
244. δράκοντος, κ.τ.λ.] Lit. 'It
was clinging to the most ravening
jaws of a dragon.'
245. πεντηκόντορον.] Of this
description was the ship Argo, so
that the comparison is full of point.
247. μακρά.] For plur. cf. Pyth.
I. 34, Nem. IV. 71.
ὥρα γὰρ συνάπτει.] '(Yet return
I must) for the time is drawing in.'
I follow Böckh. Hermann ren-
ders *jam tempus est.*
248. ἄγημαι.] 'I am a (recog-
nised) leader in minstrelsy.'

κτεῖνε μὲν γλαυκῶπα τέχναις ποικιλόνωτον ὄφιν,
250 ὦ ᾽ρκεσίλα, κλέψεν τε Μήδειαν σὺν αὐτᾷ, τὰν Πελίαο
　　φόνον　　　　　　　　　　　　　　　　　445
ἔν τ᾽ Ὠκεανοῦ πελάγεσσι μίγεν πόντῳ τ᾽ ἐρυθρῷ
Λαμνιᾶν τ᾽ ἔθνει γυναικῶν ἀνδροφόνων·
ἔνθα καὶ γυίων ἀέθλοις ἐπέδειξαν κρίσιν ἐσθᾶτος
　　ἀμφίς,　　　　　　　　　　　　　　　450
　　　　　　　　　　　　　　　Στρ. ιβ΄.

καὶ συνεύνασθεν. καὶ ἐν ἀλλοδαπαῖς
255 σπέρμ᾽ ἀρούραις τουτάκις ὑμετέρας ἀκτῖνας ὄλβου
　　δέξατο μοιρίδιον
ἆμαρ ἢ νύκτες· τόθι γὰρ γένος Εὐφάμου φυτευθὲν
　　λοιπὸν αἰεὶ　　　　　　　　　　　455
τέλλετο· καὶ Λακεδαιμονίων μιχθέντες ἀνδρῶν
ἤθεσιν ἔν ποτε Καλλίσταν ἀπῴκησαν χρόνῳ　　460

250. σὺν αὐτᾷ.] Dissen, 'with her own assistance.' There is slight ms. authority for αὐτῷ, i.e. δέρματι. I would suggest σύνευνον 'for his bride,' cf. Ol. ι. 88, regarding σὺν αὐτᾷ as a correction for συνάπτει repeated from v. 247.

φόνον.] Cf. φόνον ἔμμεναι ἡρώεσσιν, Il. xvi. 44.

252. The poet skips the passage of Africa which he had already told of and takes up the Argonauts at Lêmnos whither they were led by the attraction of the games instituted by Hypsipyle to celebrate the funeral of Thoas her father.

253. mss. ἐπεδείξαντο κρίσιν. Hermann -αντο κρῖμ', Böckh. -αντ' ἀγών'. Pauw. -αν κρίσιν γ'; but the γ is unnecessary as ιν may be scanned long perhaps, cf. Pyth. iii. 6. The Pindaric evidence as to the use of active or middle is exactly balanced. It is not certain whether γυίων κρίσιν go together—'means of judging of their limbs' or γυίων ἀέθλοις, 'athletic games.' The latter construction is well supported by

Pyth. ix. 119, σὺν δ᾽ ἀέθλοις ἐκέλευσεν διακρῖναι ποδῶν. Of course the Argonauts would not be able to take part in horse-races.

ἀμφίς.] Buttmann (Lexil. ιι. 216) renders 'without raiment.' However ἀμφί takes the gen. of the prize, Pyth. ix. 105, though the dat. Ol. ix. 90. ἀμφίς : ἀμφί :: εἰς : ἐν :: ἐξ : ἐκ. These Lêmnian games are mentioned Ol. iv. 20—24, where the wreath is mentioned, but no other prize. For a garment as prize cf. Ol. ix. 97. Thuk. i. 6 is against early stripping at games as far as the διάζωμα is concerned : still 'without raiment' might mean the absence of the χλαῖνα (κρόκεον εἷμα, v. 232) and be significant in connection with the καὶ συνεύνασθεν.

255. ὑμετέρας.] Cf. Ol. xi. [x.] 6.

μοιρίδιον.] Generally taken with σπέρμα; but it clearly goes with ἆμαρ, 'fatalis dies, an noctes.'

257. Cf. Herod. iv. 145.

258. Καλλίσταν.] Thêra, whither the descendants of Euphêmos and Malake emigrated from Lakônia.

νᾶσον· ἔνθεν δ' ὔμμι Λατοίδας ἔπορεν Λιβύας πεδίον
260 σὺν·θεῷ τιμαῖς ὀφέλλειν, ἄστυ χρυσοθρόνου
    διανέμειν θεῖον Κυράνας   465

                                  'Αντ. ιβ'.

    ὀρθόβουλον μῆτιν ἐφευρομένοις.

    γνῶθι νῦν τὰν Οἰδιπόδα σοφίαν· εἰ γάρ τις ὄζους
      ὀξυτόμῳ πελέκει

    ἐξερείψαι κεν μεγάλας δρυός, αἰσχύνοι δέ οἱ θαητὸν
      εἶδος,   470

---

260. τιμαῖς.] Cf. supra v. 51.

261. Κυράνας.] For her mythic history cf. Pyth. ix.

262. 'Having found out an upright policy for it;'—i. e. for the government of Kyrêne.

263—end.] 'Learn now the wisdom of Oedipus.

'If one were haply to lop off the branches of a mighty oak and mar its admirable form, even though its fruit fail, yet it gives proof itself if ever at last it come to a winter fire, or (if), having left bare its own place, together with upright pillars in a master's house, supported thereon, it bears a slavish burden in alien halls.

'But thou art a most timely healer and Paeon honoureth the light thou sheddest. Needs must apply a gentle hand when tending an ulcerous wound. For to shake a state is easy even for men of little worth, but to settle it again on its base is right hard unless God suddenly become guide to the rulers. Now for this service are the people's thanks fully expressed to thee. Deign then to give all earnest care to happy Kyrêne.

'Of the sayings of Homer this too lay to heart and cherish—he said that a good messenger conferreth the greatest honour on every affair. So the muse is glorified by correct delivery of an ode. Further know Kyrêne and the most renowned

palace of Battos the just heart of Dâmophilos. For he, as a youth amongst boys, but in counsels as an elder when he hath attained a life of a hundred years, deprives the evil tongue of loud speech and hath learnt to loathe an insolent, not quarrelling with the well-born nor delaying the accomplishment of any purpose. For opportunity, so far as men command it, hath a brief limit. Well hath he discerned it and is attentive to it as a willing servant, not as a drudge. Now they say that this is most distressing, when knowing good to abide perforce away therefrom. Even so yon Atlas struggles against heaven's weight now afar from fatherland and treasures: but the Titans deathless Zeus set free. In course of time as the breeze falls there are shiftings of sails. Well, he is confident that somewhile, his baneful malady exhausted, he will see his home, and near Apollo's fount applying himself to boon companionship will ofttimes give up his heart to youthful mirth, and fingering his daintily-wrought cithern amongst song-loving fellow-townsmen will attain unto peace, bringing woe to no man while himself unharmed by the citizens. So would he tell how fair a source of immortal verse he discovered for Arkesilas when lately entertained at Thebes.'

264—269. The construction is

265 καὶ φθινόκαρπος ἐοῖσα διδοῖ ψᾶφον περ' αὐτᾶς,
εἴ ποτε χειμέριον πῦρ ἐξίκηται λοίσθιον,
ἢ σὺν ὀρθαῖς κιόνεσσιν δεσποσύναισιν ἐρειδομένα   475
μόχθον ἄλλοις ἀμφέπει δύστανον ἐν τείχεσιν,
ἐὸν ἐρημώσαισα χῶρον.

Ἐπ. ιβ'.

270 ἐσσὶ δ' ἰατὴρ ἐπικαιρότατος, Παιάν τέ σοι τιμᾷ
φάος.   480
χρὴ μαλακὰν χέρα προσβάλλοντα τρώμαν ἕλκεος
ἀμφιπολεῖν.
ῥάδιον μὲν γὰρ πόλιν σεῖσαι καὶ ἀφαυροτέροις·   485
ἀλλ' ἐπὶ χώρας αὖτις ἕσσαι δυσπαλὲς δὴ γίνεται,
ἐξαπίνας
εἰ μὴ θεὸς ἀγεμόνεσσι κυβερνατὴρ γένηται.

275 τὶν δὲ τούτων ἐξυφαίνονται χάριτες.   490
τλᾶθι τᾶς εὐδαίμονος ἀμφὶ Κυράνας θέμεν σπουδὰν
ἄπασαν.

Στρ. ιγ'.

τῶν δ' Ὁμήρου καὶ τόδε συνθέμενος
ῥῆμα πόρσυν'· ἄγγελον ἐσλὸν ἔφα τιμὰν μεγίσταν
πράγματι παντὶ φέρειν·   495
αὔξεται καὶ Μοῖσα δι' ἀγγελίας ὀρθᾶς. ἐπέγνω μὲν
Κυράνα

somewhat confused by the running together of two hypothetical sentences which is effected by substituting καὶ ἐοῖσα for ἂν εἴη, with a disjunctive particle after διδοῖ, which is the verb of the apodosis to εἴ ποτε ἐξίκηται ...ἢ...ἀμφέπει. Observe κεν in protasis; see Goodwin § 50. 2, note 2; also εἰ with subj. see Goodwin § 50. 1, note 2 (δ). This is Doric as well as Homeric, and is found, though rarely, in Attic.
For the indicative ἀμφέπει see Goodwin § 51, note 8. The variation denotes that a particular danger of subjugation by Persia was in the poet's mind.
The allegory is to be thus interpreted;—the oak is the state of Kyrênê; the lopped branches are banished nobles; the fire is insurrection; the master's house is the Persian empire.
268. ἀμφέπει.] Cf. κάλλιστον ὄλβον ἀμφέπων, Isth. III. 77.
278. The nearest correspondence is ἐσθλὸν καὶ τὸ τέτυκται ὅτ' ἄγγελος αἴσιμα εἰδῇ, Il. xv. 207.
279. Before the days of writing for literary purposes of course everything depended on the accuracy of

280 καὶ τὸ κλεεννότατον μέγαρον Βάττου δικαιᾶν
Δαμοφίλου πραπίδων. κεῖνος γὰρ ἐν παισὶν νέος, 500
ἐν δὲ βουλαῖς πρέσβυς ἐγκύρσαις ἑκατονταετεῖ βιοτᾷ,
ὀρφανίζει μὲν κακὰν γλῶσσαν φαεννᾶς ὀπός, 505
ἔμαθε δ' ὑβρίζοντα μισεῖν,

Ἀντ. ιγ'.

285 οὐκ ἐρίζων ἀντία τοῖς ἀγαθοῖς,
οὐδὲ μακύνων τέλος οὐδέν. ὁ γὰρ καιρὸς πρὸς
ἀνθρώπων βραχὺ μέτρον ἔχει.
εὖ νιν ἔγνωκεν· θεράπων δέ οἱ, οὐ δράστας ὀπαδεῖ.
 φαντὶ δ' ἔμμεν 510
τοῦτ' ἀνιαρότατον, καλὰ γινώσκοντ' ἀνάγκᾳ
ἐκτὸς ἔχειν πόδα. καὶ μὰν κεῖνος Ἄτλας οὐρανῷ 515
290 προσπαλαίει νῦν γε πατρῴας ἀπὸ γᾶς ἀπό τε κτεάνων·
λῦσε δὲ Ζεὺς ἄφθιτος Τιτᾶνας. ἐν δὲ χρόνῳ
μεταβολαὶ λήξαντος οὔρου 520

Ἐπ. ιγ'.

ἱστίων. ἀλλ' εὔχεται οὐλομέναν νοῦσον διαντλήσαις
ποτὲ
οἶκον ἰδεῖν, ἐπ' Ἀπόλλωνός τε κράνᾳ συμποσίας ἐφέπων
295 θυμὸν ἐκδόσθαι πρὸς ἥβαν πολλάκις, ἔν τε σοφοῖς 525
δαιδαλέαν φόρμιγγα βαστάζων πολίταις ἀσυχίᾳ θιγέμεν,
μήτ' ὦν τινι πῆμα πορών, ἀπαθὴς δ' αὐτὸς πρὸς
ἀστῶν· 530
καί κε μυθήσαιθ', ὁποίαν Ἀρκεσίλᾳ
εὗρε παγὰν ἀμβροσίων ἐπέων, πρόσφατον Θήβᾳ ξενωθείς.

the messenger who was sent to train the chorus. See *Essay on Pindar and his Poetry*.
286. πρόϲ.] Wrongly rendered 'among.'
289. ἐκτόϲ.] Sc. καλῶν; cf. ὅστις ϲημάτων ἔξω πόδα | ἔχει, Aesch. *Prom. V.* 263.
294. κράνᾳ.] Kyre the fountain of Kyrēne.
295. Cf. τίς ἐρασμίην τρέψας

θυμὸν ἐς ἥβην ὀρχεῖται; Anakreon 18, Pyth. vi. 48. Hence we may read ψυχὴν διδόντες ἡδονῇ, Aesch. *Pers.* 841.
296. θιγέμεν.] Takes the dat. Pyth. viii. 24, ix. 43, Nem. iv. 35, νουμηνίᾳ θιγέμεν, 'to touch upon the day of the new moon.'
299. It is not improbable that Dâmophilos had composed a poem on the Argonauts which Pindar had made use of in this ode.

PYTHIA V.

ON THE VICTORY OF ARKESILAS IV. KING OF KYRENE
WITH THE FOUR-HORSE CHARIOT.

INTRODUCTION.

THIS ode commemorates the same victory as Pyth. IV., won B.C.
466. It was probably composed after Pyth. IV., but soon after the
victory to be sung on the public reception of the horses and cha-
rioteer Karrhôtos (*vv.* 40, 41), in the great Paved Street of Kyrêne
(*vv.* 84—87), probably at the time of the Karneia (*vv.* 73—76). This
Karrhôtos was brother to Arkesilas' wife. Mommsen thinks Pindar
was present at Kyrêne; but the end of Pyth. IV. is against the sup-
position, unless we suppose that Pyth. IV. was sent immediately
after the victory, and that Pindar went later with Karrhôtos and
Euphêmos who took the horses to Pytho and stayed in Greece col-
lecting troops for an expedition against Hesperides.

The rhythm is Aeolian and the ode is probably a Kastoreion
(*v.* 9), see also Pyth. II. 67.

ANALYSIS.

vv.
1—4. Wealth combined with merit availeth much.
5—10. Arkesilas attains to wealth and good fame by Kastor's
aid.
11, 12. The noble bear heaven-sent power better than others.
13. Arkesilas walketh in justice, and is attended by great
prosperity;

vv.

14—18. In that he is king of mighty cities,

19—21. And has just now won the chariot-race at Pytho.

21—23. Exhortation to give God the glory,

24—39. And to love Karrhôtos the charioteer who kept the chariot safe, and dedicated it at Pytho.

40, 41. It is right to give a hearty welcome to your benefactor.

42—49. Karrhôtos is blessed by being the theme of song for his dexterity in keeping his chariot safe during a general upset.

50. No one is, nor will be, free from trouble ;

51—53. But the ancient prosperity of Battos attends his family in varying degree.

53—58. From him lions were made to flee by Apollo,

59—65. The god of healing, music and poetry, and of the Delphic oracle,

65—68. By means of which he settled the Hêrakleids and Dorians in Peloponnêsos.

68—76. The poet claims descent from Aegidae who won renown at Sparta and went to Thêra whence they received the Karneia which festival connects the poet's family with Kyrêne (which festival they celebrate at Kyrene to its honour).

77—82. There the Antênoridae are worshipped, having been adopted as heroes by the followers of Aristoteles.

83—89. He beautified Kyrêne in honour of the exiles, and after death became a revered hero.

90—97. Arkesilas' royal ancestry though dead hear his song of victory.

97—100. His chorus ought to laud Apollo for the victory.

100—109. Praise of Arkesilas for sense, eloquence, courage, strength and success in games and musical competitions.

109—116. Prayer that his prosperity may be lasting and that he may win at Olympia.

The idea that success and prosperity are to be attributed to the favour of a deity runs through the whole ode. The introduction of the Antênoridae is to be explained by their being in some way connected with the breeding of horses at Kyrêne (*v.* 79).

Στρ. α'.

Ὁ πλοῦτος εὐρυσθενής,
ὅτάν τις ἀρετᾷ κεκραμένον καθαρᾷ
βροτήσιος ἀνὴρ πότμου παραδόντος αὐτὸν ἀνάγῃ
πολύφιλον ἐπέταν.
5 ὦ θεόμορ' Ἀρκεσίλα,
σύ τοί νιν κλυτᾶς
αἰῶνος ἀκρᾶν βαθμίδων ἄπο
σὺν εὐδοξίᾳ μετανίσεαι   10
ἔκατι χρυσαρμάτου Κάστορος·

1. 'Far-reaching is the potency
of wealth, whene'er a mortal man
on Destiny bestowing it combined
with honest merit may have led it
home as a right welcome hench-
man. O Arkesilas, whose lot hath
come from God, thou verily, from
the first steps of thy renowned life
pursuest it, and good fame withal,
by the help of Kastor of the golden
car, who after a wintry storm shed-
deth beams of calm upon thy happy
hearth.'

2. ἀρετᾷ.] As elsewhere in the
ode a long syllable corresponds to
the two short syllables of ἀρετᾷ
Hermann proposed ὀργᾷ. But Ol.
II. 10, 53, and the quotation of the
Schol.(Kallimachos, οὔτ' ἀρετῆς ἄτερ
ὄλβος ἐπίσταται ἄνδρας δέξειν, | οὔτ'
ἀρετὴ ἀφένοιο, Sappho, ὁ πλοῦτος
ἄνευ ἀρετᾶς οὐκ ἀσινὴς πάροικος), sup-
port the text. The epithet καθαρᾷ
is illustrated by Ol. IV. 16. In Pin-
dar ἀρετᾷ often means 'excellence,'
'distinction;' so that it is not ne-
cessarily 'pure,' 'disinterested.'

3. ἀνάγῃ.] This verb is used of
'bringing home' a mistress or guest,
Il. III. 48, Od. III. 272, IV. 534.
For the personification of wealth
see Prof. Paley's note on Aesch.
Agam. 1303.

4. πολύφιλον.] The Scholl.
interpret also 'making' or 'bringing

many friends' which is certainly
analogous to the use of πολύξενος,
Ol. I. 93.

5. θεόμορ'.] The reading of mss.
θεόμοιρ' is not to be absolutely re-
jected as it might scan ‿ ‒, cf. Pyth.
I. 56. θεο- is Πότμος, cf. Ol. I. 106.

6. νιν.] i.e. πλοῦτον ἀρετᾷ κεκρα-
μένον καθαρᾷ.

7. The metaphor of the second
sentence does not quite fall in with
that of the first. For, as Arkesilas
had always had wealth, it was his
ἐπέτας, after whom he could not
strictly be said to go. The solution
of the difficulty is that αὐτὸν, v. 3,
means realized wealth, νιν, v. 6, pro-
spective wealth, or we may say that
the personification is dropped and
that the νιν is the wealth which Ar-
kesilas kept seeking and acquiring
owing to the God of wealth being
an inmate of his house. In ἀκρ.
βαθ. ἄπο we have a metaphor ap-
propriate to a dweller in a grand
palace or on an acropolis, who
would begin a journey by descend-
ing steps. Life is here regarded as
a journey as in v. 13. The meta-
phor in Lucr. II. 1123, gradus aetatis
scandere adultae, is quite different.

9. This refers partly to success
in chariot-races, partly to com-
merce, Kastor being the god of ma-
riners as well as a charioteer. Dis-

10 εὐδίαν ὃς μετὰ χειμέριον ὄμβρον τεὰν καταιθύσσει
    μάκαιραν ἑστίαν.

'Αντ. α΄.

σοφοὶ δέ τοι κάλλιον   15
φέροντι καὶ τὰν θεόσδοτον δύναμιν.
σὲ δ' ἐρχόμενον ἐν δίκᾳ πολὺς ὄλβος ἀμφινέμεται·
τὸ μέν, ὅτι βασιλεὺς
15 ἐσσὶ μεγαλᾶν πολίων·   20
    ἔχει συγγενὴς
    ὀφθαλμὸς αἰδοιότατον γέρας,
    τεᾷ τοῦτο μιγνύμενον φρενί·

sen thinks success in war rather than in commerce is meant, but it is doubtful whether Arkesilas found war lucrative. He derived great wealth from the silphium trade. Don., whom I follow, supports his view by quoting Homer's hymn, v. 6, σωτῆρας τέκε παῖδας ἐπιχθονίων ἀνθρώπων | ὠκυπόρων τε νεῶν, and Theokritos (Idyll xxii. 6). There was a temple of the Dioskuroi on the Σκυρωτὴ πλατεῖα at Kyrêne.

10. Here an allusion to recent seditions at Kyrêne is introduced. The idea of motion towards in καταιθύσσει explains the acc. ἑστίαν. In Pyth. IV. 83 the acc. of motion over is found with καταιθυσσον.

11. σοφοί.] The word is here used in the sense of 'noble' as by Theognis, cf. Pyth. II. 88.

12. καὶ τὰν θεόσδοτον.] The καὶ shows that the poet considers prosperity harder to bear becomingly than adversity. The τὰν refers to θεόμορ, v. 5. It almost means 'such as yours.' The form θεόσδοτος is puzzling. I agree with Curtius in the derivation of θεὸς from a root θες, and advance the strong argument against the roots DIV or DHI that the radical vowel in such a Greek form would be ι or οι not ε(ι); yet

I think he should not have explained θέσφατος as for θεσοφατος without discussing θεόσδοτος (Hes. and Pind.). The σ seems to have been inserted by poets for metrical reasons, perhaps on false analogy from insertions of σ in conjugation, or from its presence in διόσδοτος.

13. ἐρχόμενον.] Cf. Ol. I. 115.
ἐν δίκᾳ.] Cf. Ol. II. 16.

15. i. e. of the pentapolis of Kyrêne.

16—18. 'It is the eye which regardeth thy family that keeps this most majestic honour associated with thy wisdom.' Don. renders συγγενὴς ὀφθαλμὸς 'your innate excellence;' Hermann 'the family glory' gentile lumen, with τοῦτο γέρας in apposition and ἐπεὶ for ἔχει. Neither rendering seems solemn enough to justify the abrupt parenthesis nor have they sufficient support. As below ὄμμα='protection' (cf. Aesch. Pers. 170, P.); so here ὁ συγγενὴς πότμος is called ὀφθαλμός, cf. Pyth. III. 85, Isth. I. 39, Ol. VII. 11. τεᾷ φρενὶ=τὶν φρονίμῳ ὄντι; Prof. Paley renders 'in your mind' saying 'μιγνύμενον seems to represent κεκραμένον ἀρετᾷ.'

For ὀφθαλμὸς='glory,' 'flower' cf. Ol. II. 10, VI. 16.

μάκαρ δὲ καὶ νῦν, κλεεννᾶς ὅτι   25
20 εὖχος ἤδη παρὰ Πυθιάδος ἵπποις ἑλὼν δέδεξαι τόνδε
    κῶμον ἀνέρων,

                       Ἐπ. α'.

Ἀπολλώνιον ἄθυρμα. τῷ σε μὴ λαθέτω   30
Κυράναν γλυκὺν ἀμφὶ κᾶπον Ἀφροδίτας ἀειδόμενον,
παντὶ μὲν θεὸν αἴτιον ὑπερτιθέμεν·
φίλει δὲ Κάρρωτον ἔξοχ' ἑταίρων·
25 ὃς οὐ τὰν Ἐπιμαθέος ἄγων   35
ὀψινόου θυγατέρα Πρόφασιν Βαττιδᾶν
ἀφίκετο δόμους θεμισκρεόντων·
ἀλλ' ἀρισθάρματον
ὕδατι Κασταλίας ξενωθεὶς γέρας ἀμφέβαλε τεαῖσιν
    κόμαις   40

                       Στρ. β'.

30 ἀκηράτοις ἀνίαις
    ποδαρκέων δυώδεκ' ἂν δρόμων τέμενος.   45
κατέκλασε γὰρ ἐντέων σθένος οὐδέν· ἀλλὰ κρέμαται,
ὁπόσα χεριαρᾶν

20. For εὖχος ἑλὼν cf. Ol. XI. 63.

21. Ἀπολλώνιον ἄθυρμα.] 'Apollo's delight.' So Anakreon calls the rose Ἀφροδίσιον ἄθυρμα, Pindar calls roses ἄνθε' Ἀφροδίσια, Nem. VII. 53; but the words are generally explained differently. It is on account of the rose gardens of the district of Kyrêne that it is called Aphrodite's garden.

τῷ, κ.τ.λ.] 'Wherefore, let there not escape thee when thou art hymned at Kyrêne in the sweet garden of Aphrodite, the maxim 'set a god o'er everything as the author.' I. e. give Apollo the glory.

25. ἄγων, κ.τ.λ.] 'Bringing Excuse, daughter of Afterthought, that is wise too late'—means of course getting defeated, and trying to explain away the failure. There is a touch of quiet humour about the phrase. For the Personification cf. Ol. VII. 44.

27. θεμισκρεόντων.] For θεμιστοκρεόντων.

31. ποδαρκέων.] Gen. plur. adj. The Scholl. and Mommsen take it for a participle and read δώδεκα δρόμων (δωδεκαδρόμων) taking τέμενος as acc. of motion over. For the adj. cf. Ol. XIII. 37, Soph. El. 699, ἱππικῶν ὠκύπους ἀγών.

32. 'For he gat no damage at all to his strong equipage; but there is hung up (ἀνάκειται) all the dainty handiwork of skilled craftsmen with which he passed the Krisaean hill into the level in the valley of the god.' I. e. which he brought from Krisa to the course in the valley between this hill and Delphi.

τεκτόνων δαίδαλ' ἄγων
35 Κρισαῖον λόφον
ἄμειψεν ἐν κοιλόπεδον νάπος   50
.θεοῦ· τό σφ' ἔχει κυπαρίσσινον
μέλαθρον ἀμφ' ἀνδριάντι σχεδόν,
Κρῆτες ὃν τοξοφόροι τέγεϊ Παρνασίῳ καθέσσαν τὸν
μονόδροπον, φυτόν.   55

                        'Αντ. β'.

40 ἑκόντι τοίνυν πρέπει
νόῳ τὸν εὐεργέταν ὑπαντιάσαι.
'Αλεξιβιάδα, σὲ δ' ἠΰκομοι φλέγοντι Χάριτες.   60
μακάριος, ὃς ἔχεις
καὶ πεδὰ μέγαν κάματον
45 λόγων φερτάτων
μναμήϊον· ἐν τεσσαράκοντα γὰρ   65
πετόντεσσιν ἀνιόχοις ὅλον
δίφρον κομίξαις ἀταρβεῖ φρενί,

34. δαίδαλ'.] mss. give δαιδάλματ', probably from a gloss, but whether for δαίδαλ' or some less obvious word we cannot be sure.

36. ἐν.] For ἐς, cf. Pyth. II. 11.

37. τό, κ.τ.λ.] 'Wherefore there doth possess it the shrine of cypress wood hard by the figure which bow-bearing Krētans dedicated in the fane on Parnāsos, that one cut in a single piece, a block of natural growth.' mss. read καθέσσαντο, μον. φυτόν, which gives a simpler construction, but does not scan. The article makes the phrase impressive which it should be. No doubt it was a compliment to have given the Kyrēnaic shrine a place near the sacred monument of the Krētan foundation of the oracle, and for this reason the poet mentions it. 'Höck thinks it was one of the works of art attributed to Daedalus, who may have been supposed to pare and polish the rude forms of trees into some approximate resemblance to the human shape.'—Don. Some take φυτὸν as an adjective.

41. ὑπαντιάσαι.] This verb is used absolutely Pyth. IV. 135, and with dat. Pyth. VIII. 11 where the sense is 'advancing to oppose.' The pronoun σε is omitted, cf. Pyth. I. 29, and τὸν εὐεργ. = 'your benefactor.' For the sentiment cf. Pyth. II. 69.

42. 'Αλεξιβιάδα.] Karrhōtos the charioteer, brother-in-law to Arkesilas.

φλέγοντι.] Cf. Ol. IX. 22, Isth. VI. 23, φλέγεται δ' ἰοβοστρύχοισι Μοίσαις. Φλέγω is intrans. Ol. II. 72, Nem. VI. 39.

46. 'For with undaunted mind didst thou bring in thy car unhurt among (those of) forty fallen charioteers.' The prep. ἐν goes closely with ὅλον, not with κομίξαις. Cf. πᾶν δ' ἐπίμπλατο | ναυαγίων Κρισαῖον ἱππικῶν πέδον, Soph. El. 730.

ἦλθες ἤδη Λιβύας πεδίον ἐξ ἀγλαῶν ἀέθλων καὶ πα-
τρωίαν πόλιν.   70

                                                    Ἐπ. β'.

50 πόνων δ' οὔ τις ἀπόκλαρός ἐστιν οὔτ' ἔσεται·
    ὁ Βάττου δ' ἔπεται παλαιὸς ὄλβος ἔμπαν τὰ καὶ τὰ
    νέμων,
    πύργος ἄστεος ὄμμα τε φαεννότατον   75
    ξένοισι. κεῖνόν γε καὶ βαρύκομποι
    λέοντες περὶ δείματι φύγον,
55 γλῶσσαν ἐπεί σφιν ἀπένεικεν ὑπερποντίαν·
    ὁ δ' ἀρχαγέτας ἔδωκ' Ἀπόλλων   80
    θῆρας αἰνῷ φόβῳ,
    ὄφρα μὴ ταμία Κυράνας ἀτελὴς γένοιτο μαντεύμασιν.

                                                    Στρ. γ'.
    ὃ καὶ βαρεῖαν νόσων   85

49. ἀγλαῶν.] Moschopulos' ex-
cellent emendation for ἀγαθῶν.
Mommsen's objection, that ἀγλαὸς
qualifies victories not contests, does
not apply here, as ἀγλαῶν suggests
'in which thou wast victorious.'
Surely a past contest may in this
sense be called 'victorious' outright
though 'glorious' suggests the idea
of victory quite enough. However,
Mommsen reads ἀγαθέων, an epithet
of Pytho, not used 'de Pythiis.'

50. This statement is slightly
at variance with that of Ol. XI. (X.)
22, if πόνων means the troubles at-
tending competition in games.
Hermann thinks it refers to some
private trouble of Karrhôtos. This
is unnecessary, cf. Pyth. x. 21.

51. 'But it is Battos' ancient
prosperity that is in attendance
bringing albeit chequered fortune.'
For the sentiment cf. Ol. II. 35—
37. For τὰ καὶ τὰ cf. Ol. VII. 22.

52. πύργος.] Lit. 'a wall,' cf.
Ol. VIII. 38. For metaphor cf. Ol.
II. 6, ἔρεισμ' Ἀκράγαντος, of Thêro.
ὄμμα.] Dissen renders 'light,'

cf. κοινὸν φέγγος 'a light (i.e. safety)
to all,' of Aegina, Nem. IV. 12. It
seems a mistake to suppose a me-
taphor within a metaphor needless-
ly. Again φαεινὸς is a Homeric
epithet of 'eyes.' Cf. supra, v.
17.

54. περί.] Equals Lat. prae, cf.
Aesch. Pers. 696, σέβομαι δ' ἀντία
λέξαι | σέθεν ἀρχαίῳ περὶ τάρβει,
Choëph. 32, περὶ φόβῳ (see Paley's
note on v. 29). Paley compares
ἀμφὶ τάρβει, Choëph. 538, ἀμφὶ
θυμῷ, prae ira, Soph. Frag. 147,
ἀμφὶ φόβῳ, Eur. Orest. 825. Pindar
seems here to be playing the cour-
tier amusingly by telling half a tale
of which we get the other half
from Pausanias (x.15); namely that
Battos suddenly saw a lion, and
that his fright forced him to cry
out distinctly and loudly, and thus
the impediment in his speech was
cured.

58. μαντεύμασιν.] For the dat.
after ἀτελὴς γένοιτο (not after ἀτε-
λὴς) cf. Aesch. Eum. 361, θεῶν δ'
ἀτέλειαν ἐμαῖς λιταῖς ἐπικραίνειν.

60 ἀκέσματ' ἄνδρεσσι καὶ γυναιξὶ νέμει,
   πόρεν τε κίθαριν, δίδωσί τε Μοῖσαν οἷς ἂν ἐθέλῃ,
   ἀπόλεμον ἀγαγὼν
   ἐς πραπίδας εὐνομίαν,   90
   μυχόν τ' ἀμφέπει
65 μαντήιον· τῷ καὶ Λακεδαίμονι
   ἐν Ἄργει τε καὶ ζαθέᾳ Πύλῳ
   ἔνασσεν ἀλκάεντας Ἡρακλέος   95
   ἐκγόνους Αἰγιμιοῦ τε. τὸ δ' ἐμόν, γαρύοντ' ἀπὸ Σπάρτας
   ἐπήρατον κλέος,

59. Under the general statement
the particular blessings vouchsafed
to Kyrêne and the Battiadae are
implied. The healing alludes to
Battos' cure, and to the silphium
of Kyrêne.
61. For the cultivation of music
and poetry at Kyrêne cf. Pyth. IV.
295—end.
65. μαντήϊον.] So all MSS. If
rightly, the ι is not scanned. Her-
mann, ·Don. and others read μαν-
τεῖον as MSS. give καρνεῖ', v. 75, while
v. 46 the best MSS. give μυ(η)αμήϊον,
which I preserve reading v. 75
Καρνηΐ', with Böckh, though not
accepting τεᾷ, for τεᾶ. Surely it is
better to alter MSS. once where they
are certainly wrong somehow than
twice where they may be right.
One point remains. The third
syllables of this verse and v. 94 are
long, all the other corresponding
syllables are short. One solution
of this difficulty is to make the first
three syllables a separate verse in
each case with Hermann whom
Don. follows. Another and sim-
pler way is to assume the admissi-
bility of an alternative long syllable
in this place. Forms in -ηϊο- for
-εϜιο- are quite analogous to the
Pindaric βασιλῆα, -ῆϊ, -ῆες.
68. τὸ δ' ἐμόν.] 'Now they say
that the renown of my family right
dear to me is from Sparta, sprung

from whence Aegidae, my fore-
fathers, went to Thêra (not without
the sanction of Gods, but some divine
appointment was bringing a festive
gathering for many sacrifices) ;
thence having received, Apollo, thy
Karneia, we honour in the banquet
the nobly built city of Kyrêne.'
The usual rendering of τὸ ἐμὸν ἐπή-
ρατον κλέος is 'my glorious descent
(race).' This is a forced interpre-
tation of κλέος. That the chief re-
nown of the Aegidae was connect-
ed with Sparta is shown by Isth. VI.
14, 15, ἕλον δ''Αμύκλας | Αἰγεῖδαι σέθεν
(Θῆβας) ἔκγονοι μαντεύμασι Πυθίοις,
and again they were the diffusers
of the Karneia. Pindar here im-
plies that his forefathers were
Aegidae who returned to Thebes
by way of Thêra from Sparta.
From vv. 73—76 they seem to have
introduced Karneia at Thebes, but
perhaps only as a family festival.
However, if Pindar was at Kyrêne
as Mommsen supposes, we need not
refer these verses to Thebes at all,
as he might be identifying himself
with the Aegidae of Kyrêne. Don.
considers this passage to be at vari-
ance with Isth. VI. 14, 15; but does
not touch upon the possible recon-
ciliation of the two statements
which I noticed independently of
Dissen. Herod. IV. 149 tells us that
Aegidae joined in the colonization

'Αντ. γ'.

ὅθεν γεγεννναμένοι
70 ἵκοντο Θήρανδε, φῶτες Αἰγεῖδαι,   100
   ἐμοὶ πατέρες, οὐ θεῶν ἄτερ, ἀλλὰ μοῖρά τις ἄγεν·
   πολύθυτον ἔρανον
   ἔνθεν ἀναδεξάμενοι,
   Ἄπολλον, τεᾷ   105
75 Καρνήϊ᾽ ἐν δαιτὶ σεβίζομεν
   Κυράνας ἀγακτιμέναν πόλιν·
   ἔχοντι τὰν χαλκοχάρμαι ξένοι
   Τρῶες Ἀντανορίδαι· σὺν Ἑλένᾳ γὰρ μόλον, καπνω-
       θεῖσαν πάτραν ἐπεὶ ἴδον   110
'Επ. γ'.

   ἐν Ἄρει. τὸ δ᾽ ἐλάσιππον ἔθνος ἐνδυκέως
80 δέκονται θυσίαισιν ἄνδρες οἰχνέοντές σφε δωροφό-
   ροι,   115

of Thêra, and *ib.* 147 that the colo-
nists found Kadmeians in the island.
Hermann takes *vv.* 73—76 as pa-
renthetical, and takes πόλιν for ἐς
πόλιν with ἄγεν. He also proposes
violent alterations, thus *v.* 68, τὸ δ᾽
ἐμόν, γαρύεω, *v.* 69, ὅθεν κεκοιναμένοι,
v. 72 sqq. πολύθυτον ἔρανον ἔνθεν ἀνα-
δεξάμενοι, Ἄπολλον, τεᾷ, Κάρνειε, ἐν
δαιτὶ σεβιζέμεν Κυρ. ἀγακτ. πόλιν.
This ingenuity is expended because
the account of Pindar's descent
given in the text does not seem to
him credible. It is needless to as-
sume that *all* the Aegidae migrated
from Thebes to Sparta; and if some
were left there it is highly probable
that one or more of the descendants
of the emigrants should, after the
institution of the Karneia (said to
date B.C. 674) return to Thebes to
introduce to their kindred the new
rites.

72. ἔρανον.] The Karneia was
a sort of religious camp-meeting or
prolonged picnic, towards the ban-
quets of which each participator

contributed. Hence ἔρανος is pecu-
liarly appropriate.

77. ἔχοντι.] i. e. possess, as
δαίμονες ἐγχώριοι.

78. Ἀντανορίδαι.] Glaukos, A-
kamas, Hippolochos. Note occur-
rence of two names which belong
also to the Lykian Aeolids, cf. Ol.
XIII. 60. The meaning of the le-
gend is that the western Greeks
found eastern Greeks already es-
tablished in Libya. From *v.* 79 it
seems likely that Karrhôtos claim-
ed descent from these Antênoridae,
or that they were connected in
some way with the breeding of
horses at Kyrêne.

79. τὸ δ᾽.] 'That chariot-driv-
ing race was religiously welcomed
and entertained with sacrifices by
the gift-bearing men whom Aristo-
teles (Battos) had brought, opening
up a path o'er the deep sea with
swift ships.' The word ἐλάσιππον
explains the mention of the Antê-
noridae.

80. δέκονται.] Lit. 'adopted,'

τούς τ' Ἀριστοτέλης ἄγαγε ναυσὶ θοαῖς
ἁλὸς βαθεῖαν κέλευθον ἀνοίγων.
κτίσεν δ' ἄλσεα μείζονα θεῶν,   120
εὐθύτομόν τε κατέθηκεν Ἀπολλωνίαις
85 ἀλεξιμβρότοις πεδιάδα πομπαῖς
ἔμμεν ἱππόκροτον
σκυρωτὰν ὁδόν, ἔνθα πρυμνοῖς ἀγορᾶς ἔπι δίχα κεῖται
θανών   125
                          Στρ. δ'.

μάκαρ μὲν ἀνδρῶν μέτα
ἔναιεν, ἥρως δ' ἔπειτα λαοσεβής.
90 ἄτερθε δὲ πρὸ δωμάτων ἕτεροι λαχόντες ἀΐδαν   130
βασιλέες ἱεροὶ
ἐντί, μεγάλαν δ' ἀρετὰν
δρόσῳ μαλθακᾷ
ῥανθεῖσαν κώμων ὑπὸ χεύμασιν   135

'admitted;' i. e. as heroes of the colony. The present is historic as in Pyth. IV. 163, Ol. II. 23.

οἰχνέοντες.] Cf. Ol. III. 40, Pyth. VI. 4.

82. βαθεῖαν.] Cf. Pyth. III. 76, of the high seas. For the hypallage cf. Ol. XI. (x.) 5, 6.

83. ' And he made the groves of the god greater than before, and laid down a straight-cut paved road that the plain might resound with the tramp of horses in procession to Apollo for averting ills from mortals.' Beware of taking πεδιάδα closely with σκυρωτὰν ὁδόν, neglecting the order of the words.

κτίσεν.] Cf. Ol. XIII. 83, κτίσιν, for this general sense of κτίζω.

84. Böckh quotes a description of the remains of a splendid street at Kyrêne cut out of solid rock, with tombs cut out of the rock on each side. This led from the ἀγορά to Apollo's temple.

87. For Battos' tomb cf. Catull.

VII. 6, Batti ueteris sacrum sepulcrum.

90. πρὸ δωμάτων.] 'Before the royal palace.' Perhaps in the ἀγορά, for the phrase is not opposed to ἀγορᾷ but to πρυμνοῖς ἀγορᾶς.

92. μεγάλαν.] Some MSS. and editors read μεγαλᾶν, ἀρετᾶν ῥανθεισᾶν. Böckh read nominatives, making ῥανθεῖσα a predicate, which is wrong; Dissen μεγαλᾶν ἀρετᾶν ῥανθεῖσιν ὑπὸ χεύμασιν. For the construction cf. Ol. IX. 103. Render, 'but the besprinkling of a great victory with the soft dew of the outpourings of Kômos' songs they hear, I ween, with such faculty as the dead possess—a happiness to them and a glory common to them and their son Arkesilas and his rightful possession.' For sentiment cf. Ol. VIII. 78, XIV. 18.

94. For the metaphorical use of ῥαίνω cf. Pyth. VIII. 57, Isth. V. 21, ῥαινέμεν εὐλογίαις. Mommsen reads ὕμνων ὑπὸ χεύμασιν, κ.τ.λ.

95 ἀκούοντί ποι χθονίᾳ φρενί,
σφὸν ὄλβον υἱῷ τε κοινὰν χάριν
ἔνδικόν τ' Ἀρκεσίλᾳ· τὸν ἐν ἀοιδᾷ νέων πρέπει
χρυσάορα Φοῖβον ἀπύειν,   140
                                                    Ἀντ. δ'.

ἔχοντα Πυθωνόθεν
τὸ καλλίνικον λυτήριον δαπανᾶν
100 μέλος χαρίεν. ἄνδρα κεῖνον ἐπαινέοντι συνετοί.
λεγόμενον ἐρέω·   145
κρέσσονα μὲν ἀλικίας
νόον φέρβεται
γλῶσσάν τε· θάρσος δὲ τανύπτερος
105 ἐν ὄρνιξιν αἰετὸς ἔπλετο·   150
ἀγωνίας δ', ἕρκος οἷον, σθένος·
ἔν τε Μοίσαισι ποτανὸς ἀπὸ ματρὸς φίλας, πέφανταί
    θ' ἁρματηλάτας σοφός·
                                                    Ἐπ. δ'.

ὅσαι τ' εἰσὶν ἐπιχωρίων καλῶν ἔσοδοι,   155
τετόλμακε. θεός τέ οἱ τονῦν τε πρόφρων τελεῖ δύνασιν,

96. σφόν.] An Epic form, only found here in Pindar's extant works.

99. 'The recompense for cost that glorious victory gives, a dainty song.' Cf. Isth. VII. 1, λύτρον εὐδόξων καμάτων.

101. 'I will utter common talk. He cherishes wisdom beyond his years, and in speech and daring is as a broad-winged eagle amongst birds, while his might in athletic contest is as a rampart, and among the muses he learnt to soar from his mother dear, and he hath shown himself a skilful charioteer, and (to speak generally) he hath essayed all the competitions in noble accomplishments of the neighbourhood.' The qualifications for a statesman are given vv. 102—105, cf. Pyth. i. 42, those of

an accomplished citizen vv. 106—109. Commentators generally consider v. 106 to concern war, but θάρσος sufficiently disposes of this topic, and it is hard on Pindar to suppose that he coupled war and policy with an adversative particle, war and poetry with a connective. For the genitive cf. θράσος δεινῶν πολέμων, Pyth. ii. 64. The metaphor is most appropriate to boxing and wrestling. For λεγόμενον cf. Nem. iii. 52, λεγόμενον δὲ τοῦτο προτέρων ἔπος ἔχω.

108. ἔσοδοι.] Cf. Pyth. vi. 50.

109. θεός.] 'God now giveth successful effect to thy capabilities. So in all time to come, whatever (capabilities) the blessed Kronidae grant thee to possess for deeds or counsels, may an autumnal stormy blast of wind not make havoc of thy life.'

110 καὶ τὸ λοιπὸν ὅσαν κε Κρονίδαι μάκαρες

δίδοῖτ᾽ ἐπ᾽ ἔργοισιν ἀμφί τε βουλαῖς 160

ἔχειν, μὴ φθινοπωρὶς ἀνέμων

χειμερία καταπνοὰ δαμαλίζοι χρόνον.

Διός τοι νόος μέγας κυβερνᾷ

115 δαίμον᾽ ἀνδρῶν φίλων. 165

εὔχομαί νιν Ὀλυμπίᾳ τοῦτο δόμεν γέρας ἔπι Βάττου

γένει.

I would suggest τὸ νῦν γε and a comma after τετόλμακε. As the text stands neither τε is wanted. With τε, τε before it and τε-λᾶ after it, γε would stand a good chance of becoming τε, and the change of punctuation would inevitably follow.

110. ὅσαν κε.] MSS. give ἅ, which will not scan at all. Moschopulos interpolated πλεῖστα after the ἅ. Böckh and Don. give ὄπισθε, Mommsen ὁποῖα in text, ὅσ᾽ ὧν κε in notes. With a relative, which is wanted, χρόνον is a secondary accusative. Böckh has to make δόμασιν the object to διδοῖτε ἔχειν, and regard μὴ δαμαλίζοι as a final change. For final μὴ without ὄφρα, ὅπως or ὡς (Pindar only uses ἵνα = 'where') cf. Ol. IX. 60, Pyth. IV. 155, Pyth. VIII. 30. The final optative would stand here as an attraction, but it is far better to take δαμαλίζοι as a true optative. I read ὅσαν because ἐπ᾽ ἔργοισιν, κ.τ.λ. do not go well with an indefinite relative. The loss of κε before κρ is accountable and would

involve the unsettlement of the previous word.

113. The metaphor of a blighting wind is peculiarly appropriate to the locality of Kyrêne, which would be subject to the Sirocco, but the adj. χειμερία suits rather the climate of Boeotia.

χρόνον.] We have χρόνον, 'lifetime,' Ol. I. 115; but the sense we have to give here is only supported by the analogy of θέρος, ὀπώρα, ὥρα, 'crops,' 'fruits,' and perhaps by αἰὼν μόρσιμος, Ol. II. 10, where we may translate 'a fortunate lot in life.' Prof. Paley suggests χρόνῳ. I suggest φθινοπωρίδ᾽ (so that it lose its fruit) ἀνέμων χειμερίᾳ καταπνοᾷ δαμαλίζοι χρόνος.

114. κυβερνᾷ.] 'Doth pilot.' For the metaphor cf. Ol. XII. 3—5, Pyth. X. 72.

116. τοῦτο γέρας.] Victory in the chariot race. Cf. Ol. VIII. 57 for this use of the demonstrative pronoun.

ἔπι.] 'In addition,' i. e. to this Pythian victory. For the position cf. Pyth. IX. 124.

PYTHIA VI.

INTRODUCTION.

XENOKRATES, son of Aenesidâmos, brother of Thêro the tyrant, won this victory B.C. 494. I infer from the exordium that this ode was not the first composed to commemorate the victory; but it was probably made for recitation at or before a banquet at Delphi in honour of Thrasybulos, Xenokrates' son and charioteer. It is, therefore, of the same date as Pyth. xII., only Pyth. x. being earlier than these two odes. This victory is mentioned Isth. II. 18, Ol. II. 49. The ode is a very fine specimen of Pindar's art. Thrasybulos may have stayed some time in Greece before the games, as is suggested by *vv.* 22, 23, training his father's horses.

ANALYSIS.

vv.

1—18. The poet announces that he is engaged on a theme patronized by Aphrodite and the Graces, in honour of Pytho, where there stands an indestructible treasure-house of song for the victor, to proclaim his Pythian victory in the chariot-race won for his father by Thrasybulos.

19—27. Thrasybulos regards the behest of Cheiron to reverence Zeus and one's parents.

28—42. Myth of Autolykos' devotion for his father, the highest example of filial piety.

43—45. Thrasybulos comes nearest to this standard,

46—54. And is generous, prudent, accomplished, devoted to horse-training and driving, and a delightful companion.

$Στρ. a'.$

'Ακούσατ'· ἦ γὰρ ἐλικώπιδος 'Αφροδίτας
ἄρουραν ἢ Χαρίτων
ἀναπολίζομεν, ὀμφαλὸν ἐριβρόμου
χθονὸς ἐς νάϊον προσοιχόμενοι·
5 Πυθιόνικος ἔνθ' ὀλβίοισιν 'Εμμενίδαις
ποταμίᾳ τ' 'Ακράγαντι καὶ μὰν Ξενοκράτει
ἑτοῖμος ὕμνων
θησαυρὸς ἐν πολυχρύσῳ
'Απολλωνίᾳ τετείχισται νάπᾳ·

2. **ἄρουραν.**] Cf. Ol. ιχ. 27, Nem. vι. 33, Πιερίδων ἀρόταις, i. e. 'poets,' χ. 26, Μοῖσαισί τ' ἔδωκ' ἀρόσαι, where, as perhaps here, the ἄρουρα is a theme of song. In Ol. ιχ. 27 χαρίτων κᾶπον means poetry generally. Cf. also, for the connection of the Graces and Epinikian poetry, Ol. χιν. 12—14. Aphrodite might be introduced from her early association with the Graces; but Dissen may perhaps be right in referring the mention of the patroness of Erotic poetry to the youth of Thrasybulos. Aphrodite and the Graces are brought into connection with Pytho in Frag. 67 [60], Πρὸς 'Ολυμπίου Διός σε, | χρυσέα κλυτόμαντι Πυθοῖ, | λίσσομαι Χαρίτεσσί τε καὶ σὺν 'Αφροδίτᾳ | ἐν ζαθέῳ με δέξαι χορῷ δοίδιμον Πιερίδων προφάταν.

3. **ἀναπολίζομεν.**] From this word it is to be inferred that Pindar had already composed an ode in honour of Xenokrates.

ὀμφαλόν.] Here not the oracular stone, for which cf. Pyth. ιν. 4, but Delphi.

4. **ἐς νάϊον.**] The text is Hermann's, he having disposed of his former conjecture δένναον (Don.). mss. give ἐς νάον, which I suspect is an incorporated gloss. If so, it is misplaced ingenuity to attempt emendation. Comparing Pyth. ν.

80, ιι. 24, Ol. ιιι. 40, I think προσοιχόμενοι means 'honouring' rather than 'taking an imaginary journey to,' so that I object to the retention of ἐς, and conclude that a quadrisyllabic adjective, or a substantive phrase in apposition with ὀμφαλόν, is lost.

6. 'And for the River-Nymph Akragas and especially for Xenokrates.' The city was situated just above the junction of two streams, the Akragas and Hypsas, by which it was enclosed on three sides. The tutelary nymph or goddess of the town (cf. Pyth. χιι. 2) being synonymous with the River could hardly fail to be regarded as a companion of or a phase of Artemis Potamia, cf. Pyth. ιι. 7. Else the form 'Ακράγας would, as applied to a river, be masculine before the rise of the city.

7. **ἑτοῖμος.**] Cf. Ol. νι. 12.

8. **θησαυρός.**] For such a treasure-house or shrine, which in the case of a Pythian victor would be in the temple at Delphi or its precinct, cf. Pyth. ν. 37—39.

9. **τετείχισται.**] Cf. Frag. 176 (206), Pyth. ιιι. 113, Ol. νι. 1—4 for metaphor.

νάπᾳ.] The whole valley between Parnâsos and the Krisaean hill, including the flat plain at the bottom of the valley where the victory had

Στρ. β'.

10 τὸν οὔτε χειμέριος ὄμβρος ἐπακτὸς ἐλθών,
ἐριβρόμου νεφέλας
στρατὸς ἀμείλιχος, οὔτ' ἄνεμος ἐς μυχοὺς
ἁλὸς ἄξοισι παμφόρῳ χεράδι
τυπτόμενον. φάει δὲ πρόσωπον ἐν καθαρῷ

been won and the temple high above where a memorial had doubtless been consecrated.

10. 'Which neither the wintry rain-storm, coming as an invading foe, the ruthless host of the deep-roaring cloud nor the wind carries to the hollows of the sea, battered by the all-sweeping débris' (borne on the flood-water). It is not necessary to suppose with Prof. Paley that 'the figure in the poet's mind is that of a treasure-house built on a headland near an estuary.' Any building that was carried away and knocked to pieces by the flood-water of a mountain-stream might be said to be carried to the sea, even if it were situated far inland. It is not unlikely that such a fate as the poet here describes had to his knowledge befallen one of the treasuries in the precinct, which might have been carried by a temporary affluent of the Pleistos into that stream, which after a course of less than ten miles from Delphi reaches the Krisaean bay. This from its configuration might well be called ἁλὸς μυχοί, as it contains at least four smaller bays.

12. ἄνεμος.] Four mss. and Böckh give ἄνεμοι. So also the Schol. which read τυπτόμενοι (mss. -μενοι, -μενος) v. 14, and explained it τύπτοντες. The poet has expanded the idea of ὄμβρος until one feels that οὔτ' ἄνεμος is only introduced at all because of the previous οὔτε.

13. ἄξοισι.] So the best mss. Critics altered it to ἄξοι or ἄξει;

but Don. says 'the change (to ἄνεμοι) is not necessary, for singular nouns coupled by disjunctive conjunctions, especially when the copula τε forms part of the disjunctive, sometimes govern a plural verb in the Greek poets. Compare Eurip. *Alcest.* 360, καί μ' οὔθ' ὁ Πλούτωνος κύων, οὔθ' οὑπὶ κώπῃ ψυχοπομπὸς ἂν Χάρων ἔσχον.' Whereon Prof. Paley remarks, 'The plural is used because the idea is "both Charon and Cerberus together would have been unable to stop me."' So here we should render, 'nor the wind withal.' For the sentiment of this passage cf. Hor. *Od.* III. 30. 1—5.

χεράδι.] Schol. χεράς δὲ ὁ μετὰ ἰλύος καὶ λίθων συρφετός. It is rather wood and floating wreckage generally.

14. φάει.] 'But its façade in clear light shall proclaim afar, Thrasybulos, a chariot-victory in Krisa's vale, honourably spoken of by men, (a) common (glory) to thy father and his race.'

In the region of poetic fame there are no storms, according to the suggestion of the poet. For πρόσωπον cf. Ol. VI. 3. κοινὰν is the epithet of the idea conveyed by λόγοισι—θνατῶν—εὐδοξον ἁρματι—νίκαν—Κρ.—ἐν—πτυχαῖσι. Thus it comes to qualify εὐδοξον as if it were an adverb. Here we have a most striking instance of Pindar's habit of making dative cases and preposition phrases dependent on nouns. Prof. Paley alters φάει to φανεῖ, rendering 'But it shall show

15 πατρὶ τεῷ, Θρασύβουλε, κοινάν τε γενεᾷ
    λόγοισι θνατῶν
    εὔδοξον ἄρματι νίκαν
    Κρισαίαισιν ἐν πτυχαῖς ἀπαγγελεῖ.

Στρ. γ'.

    σύ τοι σχέθων νιν ἐπιδέξια χειρὸς ὀρθὰν
20 ἄγεις ἐφημοσύναν,
    τά ποτ' ἐν οὔρεσι φαντὶ μεγαλοσθενῆ
    Φιλύρας υἱὸν ὀρφανιζομένῳ
    Πηλείδᾳ παραινεῖν· μάλιστα μὲν Κρονίδαν,
    βαρύοπαν στεροπᾶν κεραυνῶν τε πρύτανιν,

its front in a clear spot,' &c. Dissen takes λόγοισι θνατῶν with ἀπαγγελεῖ. The Schol., followed by Heyne, Böckh, Dissen, Don., needlessly understands ἔχων to govern πρόσωπον. Thus Don. interprets 'the hymn with joyful, serene countenance (as befits a messenger of good news) will announce,' &c. Hermann makes ἀπαγγελεῖ govern πρόσωπον, and renders, *carmen hoc patri tuo nunciabit hilarem vultum* (i. e. exhilarabit ei vultum) *communemque genti victoriam*. The only doubt I have about my version, which is substantially that of Mr Myers, is as to whether φάει ἐν καθαρῷ may not be an adverbial phrase, 'with pure splendour,' cf. Ol. II. 63. I do not believe it can be taken as equivalent to an adjective, such as φαιδρόν, λαμπρόν. For the suppression of ἐόν, if it be thought that my version requires it, cf. Ol. IV. 10.

15. κοινάν.] Cf. Pyth. v. 96, Ol. II. 50.

19. 'Thou verily holding him on thy right hand (i. e. by incurring risk for thy father) dost keep unswervingly the behest which they say that once in the mountain Cheiron uttered in exhortation to mighty Achilles.' Heimsoeth approved by Schneidewin refers νιν

to ἐφημοσύναν. Generally νιν is thought to refer to πατρί, v. 15, and the meaning therefore to be : 'by honouring your father (i. e. by placing him on your right hand) you obey the injunctions of Cheiron.' 'That the right hand was the place of honour is clear from Frag. 112' (Πῦρ πνέοντος ἅ τε κεραυνοῦ | ἄγχιστα δεξιὰν κατὰ χεῖρα πατρὸς | ἵζεαι, of Athêne). Don. Yes, but it is the place of honour bestowed by the occupant of the highest place, and so not appropriate to this context. On the right hand also a Greek would keep one who required protection in battle, and the instance of Antilochos suggests that the metaphor here is from a battlefield. The metaphor of ὀρθὰν ἄγεις is as Prof. Paley says 'from leading a person so as to prevent him falling. Conversely χαμαὶ πίπτειν is said of things which come to nought, as in v. 37.'

ἐπιδέξια.] Cf. Theokr. xxv. 18, τεῆς ἐπιδέξια χειρός.

20. ἐφημοσύναν.] Cf. Χείρωνος ἐντολάς, Frag. 155 (167).

21. τά ποτ'.] Cf. Ol. I. 16.

22. ὀρφανιζομένῳ.] 'When separated from his parents.' Pêleus survived Achilles.

23. μάλιστα.] i. e. as the Allfather.

25 θεῶν σέβεσθαι·
ταύτας δὲ μή ποτε τιμὰς
ἀμείρειν γονέων βίον πεπρωμένον.

Στρ. δ'.

ἔγεντο καὶ πρότερον Ἀντίλοχος βιατὰς
νόημα τοῦτο φέρων,
30 ὃς ὑπερέφθιτο πατρός, ἐναρίμβροτον
ἀναμείναις στράταρχον Αἰθιόπων
Μέμνονα. Νεστόρειον γὰρ ἵππος ἅρμ' ἐπέδα
Πάριος ἐκ βελέων δαϊχθείς. ὁ δ' ἔφεπεν
κραταιὸν ἔγχος·
35 Μεσσανίου δὲ γέροντος
δονηθεῖσα φρὴν βόασε παῖδα ὅν·

Στρ. ε'.

χαμαιπετὲς δ' ἄρ' ἔπος οὐκ ἀπέριψεν· αὐτοῦ
μένων δ' ὁ θεῖος ἀνὴρ
πρίατο μὲν θανάτοιο κομιδὰν πατρός,
40 ἐδόκησέν τε τῶν πάλαι γενεᾷ

26. ταύτας.] Cf. Ol. VIII. 57,
IV. 24, Pyth. v. 116. It here = τῆς
τοῦ σέβεσθαι.
27. γονέων βίον πεπρωμένον.]
'Parents' allotted time of life.' This
injunction seems to mean 'deem
it a sacred duty to defend your
parents' life by pious devotion from
dangers which human aid can
avert.' As Xenokrates lived very
nearly twenty years after this vic-
tory, he cannot have been very old
at the time this victory was won;
so that the parallel given in the
following myth is not close.
28. Prof. Paley considers that
we have a later form of this ac-
count in Il. VIII. 90, etc., where
Diomêdes saves Nestor from Hek-
tor. This episode was given in the
Aethiopis of Arktinos.
29. νόημα τοῦτο φέρων.] Cf.
Isth. I. 40, ὁ πονήσαις νόῳ προμά-

θειαν φέρει. Render 'cherishing
this principle.' The participle goes
with βιατάς.
32. ἵππος...δαϊχθείς.] For constr.
cf. Ol. IX. 2, 103, Pyth. IV. 151, XI.
22.
36. βόασε.] Is this causative?
The participle is curious; because
otherwise we should have to turn
the phrase into φρονιμὸς γέρων δο-
ναθεὶς φρένα. For ἐκ with the pas-
sive, cf. Pyth. IV. 72.
37. χαμαιπετές.] Extension of
predicate. For the metaphor cf.
Ol. IX. 12.
40. ἐδόκησεν.] Cf. Ol. XIII. 56.
In these passages Don. (on Nem.
VII. 11) takes δοκέω = εὐδοκέω, com-
paring τυχεῖν for εὐτυχεῖν, δοκέοντα
for εὔδοξον, Nem. VII. 31, but this
view is in neither case at all cer-
tain. For τε after μέν, cf. Ol. IV.
15.

14—2

ὁπλοτέροισιν, ἔργον πελώριον τελέσαις,
ὕπατος ἀμφὶ τοκεῦσιν ἔμμεν πρὸς ἀρετάν.
τὰ μὲν παρίκει·
τῶν νῦν δὲ καὶ Θρασύβουλος
45 πατρῴαν μάλιστα πρὸς στάθμαν ἔβα,

Στρ. ς'.

πάτρῳ τ' ἐπερχόμενος ἀγλαΐαν ἔδειξεν
νόῳ δὲ πλοῦτον, ἄγων
ἄδικον οὔθ' ὑπέροπλον ἥβαν, δρέπει,
σοφίαν δ' ἐν μυχοῖσι Πιερίδων·
50 τίν τ', Ἐλέλιχθον, ὃς στάσας ἱππείας ἐσόδους,

42. 'To be supreme as regards virtue towards parents.'
45. 'Came nearest to our fathers' standard.' We need not assume that Thrasybulos had ever risked his life for his father's sake excepting in the chariot-race. To compare him to Antilochos need not be more than a forcible way of ascribing to him the character of a φιλοπάτωρ. Cf. Xen. De Venatione, chap. I. § 14, Ἀντίλοχος τοῦ πατρὸς ὑπεραποθανὼν τοσαύτης ἔτυχεν εὐκλείας ὥστε μόνος φιλοπάτωρ παρὰ τοῖς Ἕλλησιν ἀναγορευθῆναι.
46. 'And in imitation of his uncle (Théro) he is wont to display splendid hospitality; but with judgment doth he manage his wealth, not enjoying the pleasures of youth unjustly or in excess, but cultivating minstrelsy in the Pierides' retired haunts.'
ἀγλαΐαν.] Generally rendered 'glory,' 'love of glory,' and explained as referring to the victory in the chariot-race; but the topic of driving comes vv. 50, 51, and there is no reason to believe that Théro had gained a victory in any great games before this success of Xenokrates, while his hospitality is lauded, Ol. II. ad fin. Then again νόῳ δέ, κ.τ.λ. comes in much better

as qualifying indulgence in hospitality, explaining that though lavish he showed judgment and refinement. Moreover the δὲ v. 47 is awkward as a coördinate conjunction with τ' v. 50, as the old explanation assumes, though for τε— δὲ cf. Pyth. IV. 81, XI. 30.
48. οὔθ'.] For omission of the first negative cf. Pyth. X. 29, 41.
ἥβαν.] Elsewhere ‿ ‿ — correspond to these two long syllables. Hermann would read αὐάταν which he thinks gave rise to ἀπάσαν foisted in before νόῳ in the best MSS. Now they give ἀπασαν which might be for ὤπασεν, a gloss on ἔδειξεν, or inserted from remembrance of ἔδειξεν ἀπάσαν, Nem. IV. 83, or a gloss on ἀγλαΐαν. From the Schol.'s ὑπερήφανον Mommsen suggests ὑπεράφανον ἀκμάν. For the meaning given to ἥβαν cf. Pyth. IV. 295.
50. ἐσόδους.] 'Contests;' cf. Pyth. V. 108. The reading of the best MSS. is τίν τ' Ἐ., ὀργαῖς πάσαις ὃς ἱππείαν ἔσοδον. Moschopulos, εὗρές θ' ὃς ἱππείαν ἔσοδον, Böckh from a Schol. ὃς θ' εὗρεν ἱππίας ἐσόδους. Don. says 'I think that ὀργαῖς πάσαις, which is found in many of the MSS., has crept into the text from a marginal explana-

μάλα ἀδόντι νόῳ, Ποσειδᾶν, προσέχεται.
γλυκεῖα δὲ φρὴν
καὶ συμπόταισιν ὁμιλεῖν
μελισσᾶν ἀμείβεται τρητὸν πόνον.

tion of μάλα ἀδόντι νόῳ, and from the resemblance of ὀργαῖς ἐς to the reading ὅς θ' εὗρες, which is recognized by the Scholiast. With μάλα ἀδόντι νόῳ, we may compare Pyth. v. 40, 41, ἑκόντι νόῳ. The writer of the interpretation ὀργαῖς πάσαις probably referred to Isth. I. 41: εἰ δ' ἀρετᾷ κατάκειται πᾶσαν ὀργάν, which is not unlike τὶν προσέχεται πάσαις ὀργαῖς.' With this I agree, except as to the resemblance of ὀργαῖς ἐς, which is only found in interpolated MSS. We want a resemblance to ὀργαῖς—ὅς or to πάσαις ὅς. Now ὅς στάσαις might easily become ὅς στάσαις by confusion with the participle, and then ὅς πάσαις, πάσαις ὅς, especially with ὀργαῖς πάσαις in the margin. Hermann keeps ὀργαῖς ἐς ἱππίαν ἔσοδον (suopte ingenio ductus ad equestria studia) with rare conservatism; for dat. of cause cf. Ol. IX. 83; the construction is possible though awkward.

52. 'His disposition is so sweet in converse even with his companions in the drinking-bout that it surpasseth honeycomb wrought by toil of bees,' i.e. even when heated with wine he is pleasant. Or is it better to render, 'And his disposition is sweet, yea, in companionship with fellow-revellers it surpasseth,' &c.?

γλυκεῖα.] Its position enables it to go with ὁμιλεῖν and ἀμείβεται.

53. ὁμιλεῖν.] For inf. cf. Ol. VII. 26, Aristoph. Nubes 1069, οὐδ' ἡδὺς ἐν τοῖς στρώμασιν τὴν νύκτα παννυχίζειν.

54. ἀμείβεται.] Cf. Pyth. I. 45, II. 50, VII. 19.

PYTHIA VII.

ON THE VICTORY OF MEGAKLES OF ATHENS WITH THE FOUR-HORSE CHARIOT.

INTRODUCTION.

MEGAKLES the Alkmaeonid, for whose Pythian victory B.C. 490 this ode was written, was son of Hippokrates, and nephew and son-in-law to Kleisthenes the Athenian reformer. Hêrodotos (VI. 131) mentions a Megakles, son of Hippokrates, and grandson of Megakles, the successful suitor for the hand of Agariste, daughter of Kleisthenes, tyrant of Sikyon. He also mentions Kleisthenes the reformer, and could scarcely have omitted to mention it if he too had had a son Megakles who had been of sufficient importance to be twice ostrakized (Lysias κατ' 'Αλκιβιάδου, p. 143). The only reason for supposing that Kleisthenes had a son Megakles is the statement of Isokrates (περὶ τοῦ ζεύγους, p. 351) that Kleisthenes was πρόπαππος to Alkibiades, which he was if Alkibiades' maternal grandfather Megakles married his cousin, a daughter of Kleisthenes. It may then be regarded as certain that our Megakles had not a cousin of the same name. Again if Alkibiades' maternal grand*father* were son of Kleisthenes he would be second cousin once removed to his guardian Perikles, while it is more likely that Perikles should have been guardian to his cousin's son than to a more distant relative. I therefore give the following interesting pedigree :

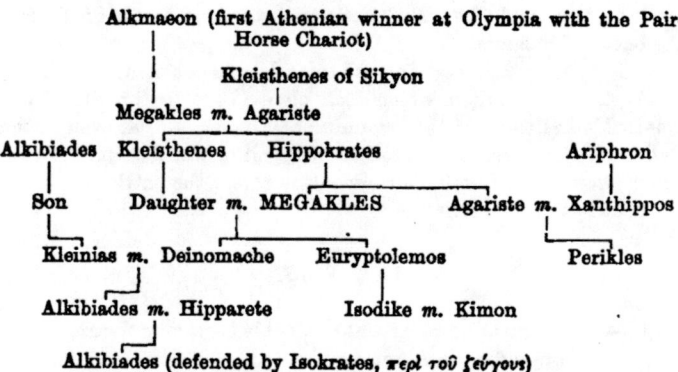

Alkmaeon (first Athenian winner at Olympia with the Pair-Horse Chariot)

Kleisthenes of Sikyon

Megakles *m.* Agariste

Alkibiades Kleisthenes Hippokrates Ariphron

Son Daughter *m.* MEGAKLES Agariste *m.* Xanthippos

Kleinias *m.* Deinomache Euryptolemos Perikles

Alkibiades *m.* Hipparete Isodike *m.* Kimon

Alkibiades (defended by Isokrates, περὶ τοῦ ζεύγους)

Curtius says—*History of Greece* (Ward's Translation) Bk. III. ch. I. p. 264—'Such a man as Pindar could take no part in the enthusiasm of the Wars of Liberation, and could shortly after the battle of Marathon sing the glories of an Athenian without giving one word to that great day.' Now Pindar did take part in the enthusiasm in question, cf. Pyth. I. 75—78, Frag. 54 [46]. As to his not mentioning the battle of Marathon; in the first place, the ode is very short. In the next place Hêrodotos (VI. 115) tells us that the Alkmaeonidae were accused of signalling to the Persians by a bright shield to sail round Sunion, and seize the city before the army got back from Marathon[1]; and again the priesthood at Delphi was inclined to Mêdism. We should not then expect any mention of Marathon in an ode composed for recitation at Delphi in honour of an Alkmaeonid. It is not likely that Pindar's personal feelings with respect to the victory of Athens and Plataeae, whose alliance was based on enmity to Thebes and Theban institutions, were very sympathetic. The spirit of national combination against the Empire of the Mêde was kindled only by the preparations of Xerxes for the invasion of Hêllas, and then only into a wavering flame, which would have been ignominiously extinguished but for Athenian intrigue.

[1] Hêrodotos' arguments against the truth of the charge are not conclusive. The fact of their having freed Athens from the Peisistratidae does not preclude the possibility of their welcoming the Persians as allies against the democratic party and Themistokles. Their close connection with the Mêdizing Delphians is collateral evidence against their loyalty.

Nothing that could be called national enthusiasm arose until after the battle of Salamis.

It is by no means certain that this ode was not composed before the battle of Marathon, which took place about the middle of the month Metageitnion or the beginning of August, so that even if the Pythian games were celebrated in Metageitnion rather than Munychion, they might have fallen some days before the battle.

The rhythm is Aeolian.

ANALYSIS.

vv.

1—4. The mention of Athens is a noble beginning for an ode on horses for the Alkmaeonidae.

5—8. No city, no family in Hellas is more distinguished.

9—12. All Hellas knows how splendidly the Alkmaeonidae built Apollo's temple at Pytho.

13—17. Enumeration of the victories of the family.

18, 19. The poet's pleasure at the new victory is alloyed by the victor's undeserved unpopularity.

20—22. Vicissitude is the invariable condition of lasting prosperity.

Στρ.

Κάλλιστον αἱ μεγαλοπόλιες ᾿Αθᾶναι
προοίμιον ᾿Αλκμανιδᾶν εὐρυσθενεῖ γενεᾷ
κρηπῖδ᾿ ἀοιδᾶν
ἵπποισι βαλέσθαι.
5 ἐπεὶ τίνα πάτραν, τίνα τ᾿ οἶκον

1. 'Athens with her mighty acropolis is the fairest opening theme for the widely influential race of Alkmaeonidae to lay as a foundation of odes for their horses.'

μεγαλοπόλιες.] Cf. Pyth. ΙΙ. 1.

2. γενεᾷ.] This dative is generally taken with βαλέσθαι. The double dative is quite admissible, cf. ῾Ηροδότῳ τεύχων τὸ μὲν ἅρματι τεθρίππῳ γέρας, Isth. I. 14; but the order of the words favours my rendering.

3. κρηπῖδ᾿.] Cf. Frag. quoted Ol. I. 16.

4. βαλέσθαι.] Cf. Pyth. IV. 138.

5. 'For what fatherland and what family, though they be my own, shall I name as more illustrious for Hellas to hear tell of?'

τίνα τ᾿.] So best mss. For elision before an initial digamma cf. Ol. IV. 9.

ναίων ὀνυμάξομαι   5
ἐπιφανέστερον
Ἑλλάδι πυθέσθαι;
                                                          Ἀντ.

πάσαισι γὰρ πολίεσι λόγος ὁμιλεῖ
10 Ἐρεχθέος ἀστῶν, Ἄπολλον, οἳ τεόν γε δόμον   10
Πυθῶνι δίᾳ
θαητὸν ἔτευξαν.
ἄγοντι δέ με πέντε μὲν Ἰσθμοῖ
νῖκαι, μία δ' ἐκπρεπὴς
15 Διὸς Ὀλυμπιάς,
δύο δ' ἀπὸ Κίρρας,
                                                          Ἐπ.

ὦ Μεγάκλεες, ὑμαί τε καὶ προγόνων.   15
νέᾳ δ' εὐπραγίᾳ χαίρω τι· τὸ δ' ἄχνυμαι,

6. ναίων.] So best mss. Böckh
and Don. ναίοντ', Mommsen αἰᾶν,
Schneidewin λαῶν or θνατῶν. The
text is generally condemned; but
I think it is defensible, without
taking ὀνυμάξομαι passively, as
Mommsen suggests. If the poet
had said ὀνυμάξεταί τις there would
be no difficulty; but by substitu-
ting the first person for the indefi-
nite third he perplexed critics. He
speaks not as a Theban and an
Aegid, but as a representative
Greek, who can imagine himself to
belong to any state and family.
Thus he can artificially express by
the text, ἥντινα πάτραν, ἥντινά τε
οἶκον ναίει, οὐκ ὀνυμάξεταί τις, κ.τ.λ.;
cf. Goodwin, § 62, note 1.
9. ὁμιλεῖ.] 'Is familiar.'
10. Ἐρεχθέος.] The name of
the hero king might well stand for
the city, but it is peculiarly appro-
priate to this context, as to him
was ascribed the invention of driv-
ing with four horses. The re-
building of the temple at Delphi
here mentioned began B.C. 548,
and was executed by the Alkmaeo-

nidae, then in exile at Delphi, with
splendid liberality, the cost far ex-
ceeding the sum for which they had
contracted with the Amphictyonic
Council to do the work.
12. θαητόν.] Extension of pre-
dicate.
13. ἄγοντι.] Turn, 'I am led
on (to sing) by,' &c.
14. ἐκπρεπής.] 'Paramount.'
This was Alkmaeon's victory, ac-
cording to Hērodotos, with four
horses; to Isokrates with a pair.
Pindar, who ought to have had
thorough knowledge on the sub-
ject, here contradicts the state-
ment of the Schol. on Aristoph.
Nubes v. 71, that Megakles the
contemporary of Peisistratos gained
three Olympian victories.
15. Ὀλυμπιάς.] For genitive cf.
note on Ol. I. 7, end.
17. ὑμαί.] 'Gained by thee and
thy coëvals,' cf. Pyth. VIII. 66.
18. τι.] The qualification indi-
cated is very slight. The joy is
very great but not absolutely un-
alloyed.

φθόνον ἀμειβόμενον τὰ καλὰ ἔργα.
20 φαντί γε μὰν οὕτω κεν ἀνδρὶ παρμονίμαν   20
θάλλοισαν εὐδαιμονίαν
τὰ καὶ τὰ φέρεσθαι.

19. ἀμειβόμενον.] 'That envy requiteth your noble deeds.' Cf. Isth. I. 52, ἄμμι δ' ἔοικε Κρόνου σεισίχθον' υἱὸν | γείτον' ἀμειβομένοις εὐεργέταν | ἁρμάτων ἱπποδρόμιον κελαδῆσαι. However, καλὰ ἔργα may be 'noble achievements' referring to the victories just enumerated (cf. Ol. IX. 85), ἀμειβόμενον meaning 'rivalling' (cf. Pyth. VI. 54), with almost the same sentiment as that of Pyth. XI. 29, ἴσχει τε γὰρ ὄλβος οὐ μείονα φθόνον.

20. 'They say however that as in your case if happiness should be flourishing abidingly for a man it would meet with varied fortune.' Prof. Paley rightly draws attention to the voice, which Dissen ignores. There is a preponderance of mss. authority in favour of πὰρ μονίμαν, with which reading οὕτω must mean 'on such conditions,' and τὰ καὶ τὰ be the subject to φέρεσθαι (passive).

τὰ καὶ τά.] Cf. Ol. II. 53. In Aristotle's Rhet. III. 17 mid., ἢ τὰ καὶ τὰ seems to mean 'or what not.' Here, as in Isth. III. 51, it is clearly euphemistic for 'bad as well as good.'

PYTHIA VIII.

ON THE VICTORY OF ARISTOMENES OF AEGINA IN THE WRESTLING MATCH.

INTRODUCTION.

ARISTOMENES, son of Xenarches, was a young scion of the noble family of the Midylidae. The Schol. says he won in the thirty-fifth (λε') Pythiad; but this must be wrong, as then, B.C. 450, Aegina had been subjugated by Athens; and it is evident from v. 98 that Aegina was free at the date of composition. Müller (*Aeginetica* p. 177) proposed λβ', and referred the allusions to the downfall of Ὕβρις to a supposed success of the Aeginetans over the Athenians (supported only by a doubtful passage of Stephanos of Byzantium) at the battle of Kekryphaleia. Müller took the old reckoning of the Pythiads, and should have read with Böckh λγ' as he meant B.C. 458. Hermann shows that the allusions are not applicable to the battle of Kekryphaleia, for, however the Aeginetans themselves fared, their allies were defeated, and the Athenians were not humbled, nor is it likely that they would be likened by Pindar to Zeus' foes the giants. He therefore, I think rightly, considers that the battle of Salamis is meant, though I am disposed to modify his view, and say that the struggle between Persia and Hellas is meant with special reference to the battle of Salamis. To the argument from general analogy, Donaldson adds the suggestion that Ὕβριν, v. 12, refers to Bakis' oracle on Xerxes (Herod. VIII. 77) δῖα Δίκη σβέσσει κρατερὸν Κόρον, Ὕβριος υἱόν. I add two more arguments in my notes on vv. 16, 98—100. As to the date of the ode, however, I am not so sure of Hermann's suggestion of the twenty-eighth Pythiad (κη') B.C. 478. He thought the Göttingen MS. gave λη', but Mommsen is positive it gives λε'. The emendation λβ', B.C. 462, is less violent, and is not open to the same objections as is the next Pythiad. At the date I suggest the great victory of Eurymedon, four years previously, and the death of Xerxes in the following year, had revived the memory of Salamis, while apprehensions of Athenian aggression had been roused by the recent reduction of Thasos. The ode was sung in Aegina, *v.* 64, after the dedication of Aristomenes' wreath, in a temple of Apollo, *vv.* 18—20.

ANALYSIS.

vv.

1—5. Invocation of Hêsychia, daughter of Dikê, who holds the keys of counsels and wars, to accept Aristomenes' Pythian victory.

6—12. She is gentle to the gentle, but overwhelms Insolence when roused to wrath.

12, 13. Porphyrion had to learn this by experience.

13—15. [Parenthetical.] Gain is best when got from the willing, but violence in the end makes even the haughtiest to fall.

16—18. Typhos and Porphyrion escaped not Hêsychia, the former being slain by Zeus, the latter by Apollo,

19, 20. Who welcomed the victor Xenarkes' son and his kômos of Dorians, when he dedicated his wreath.

21—28. Praise of Aegina for justice, excellence in games and heroic valour.

29—34. The poet must without prolixity perform his task of praising Aristomenes.

35—43. For following his uncle's example he has won the praise which Amphiarâos uttered when he beheld the Epigoni fighting at Troy;

44, 45. 'The sires' nobleness is seen in their sons.'

45—55. Amphiarâos' mention of Alkmaeon and prophecy of Adrastos' return to Argos.

56—60. The poet's indebtedness to Alkmaeon is expressed.

61—66. Apollo has given Aristomenes victory at Pytho and at home.

67—72. Prayer that the poet's ode may be appropriate, just and acceptable to the gods.

73—75. Reputation for wisdom attends success,

75—78. But 'tis not in mortals to command it. The deity gives it, sending men up and letting them drop like a player at ball.

78—80. Mention of Aristomenes' victories.

81—87. His Pythian victory and glorious return.

88—97. Reflections on the advantage of youthful success and the fleeting character of human blessings and affairs generally.

98—100. Prayer to Aegina to keep the city free in conjunction with the national heroes.

Στρ. ά.

Φιλόφρον 'Ασυχία, Δίκας
ὦ μεγιστόπολι θύγατερ,
βουλᾶν τε καὶ πολέμων
ἔχοισα κλαῖδας ὑπερτάτας   5
5 Πυθιόνικον τιμὰν 'Αριστομένει δέκευ.
τὺ γὰρ τὸ μαλθακὸν ἔρξαι τε καὶ παθεῖν ὁμῶς
ἐπίστασαι καιρῷ σὺν ἀτρεκεῖ·

'Αντ. ά.

τὺ δ' ὁπόταν τις ἀμείλιχον   10

1. 'Ασυχία.] We must not identify mythologically Hēsychia with Eirēnē, who is the sister of Dikē, Ol. xiii. 7. The term ἡσυχία is more general and less formal than εἰρήνη, cf. Nem. ix. 48.

2. μεγιστόπολι.] 'Who dost abide in mightiest cities'—and art the cause of their greatness is implied.

8, 4. 'Holding the master keys of choice between counsels and wars.' This means that the attainment or preservation of tranquillity is the ultimate object and paramount motive of just counsels and just wars, and is therefore mistress of the supreme decisions as to peace or war. We may render βουλᾶν τε καὶ πολέμων 'of peace or war,' as here both come under the common idea of 'settlement of disturbing differences.' Cf. note on

τε—καί, Ol. xiv. 5. It is natural that in the subsequent expansion of the idea of these two verses, Hēsychia should be regarded as the cause of a war undertaken to repel unjust aggression. For the metaphorical use of κλαῖδες cf. Pyth. ix. 39. The manner of its application is illustrated by Aesch. Eumen. 827, 828, where Athēne says καὶ κλῇδας οἶδα δωμάτων μόνη θεῶν | ἐν ᾧ κεραυνός ἐστιν ἐσφραγισμένος.

5. δέκευ.] For δέκευ with dat. cf. Ol. xiii. 29, Pyth. iv. 23.

6. τὸ μαλθακόν.] 'To render and accept alike the gentle treatment natural to you.' Note the force of the article. For sentiment cf. Pyth. iv. 296, 297.

7. καιρῷ σὺν ἀτρ.] 'Whenever it is strictly seasonable.'

8. 'Thou again whensoever relentless resentment is forced into

καρδίᾳ κότον ἐνελάσῃ,
10 τραχεῖα δυσμενέων
   ὑπαντιάξαισα κράτει τιθεῖς
   ὕβριν ἐν ἄντλῳ. τὰν οὐδὲ Πορφυρίων μάθεν   15
   παρ' αἶσαν ἐξερεθίζων. κέρδος δὲ φίλτατον,
   ἑκόντος εἴ τις ἐκ δόμων φέροι·

                                        'Επ. α'.

15 βία δὲ καὶ μεγάλαυχον ἔσφαλεν ἐν χρόνῳ.   20

thy heart dost sternly confront the
might of foes and plunge Insolence
in the brine.' The strong meta-
phor in ἐνελάσῃ from driving in a
nail or bolt expresses reluctance to
resort to violence and determina-
tion when once forced to resort
thereto. For Ὕβριν see Introduc-
tion.

11. ὑπαντιάξαισα.] The force of
ὑπὸ may be here almost 'calmly,'
or even 'reluctantly,' which suits
Pyth. IV. 135; but not Pyth. V. 41,
nor ὑπάντασεν, infra, v. 59. Is the
force the same in ὑπειπεῖν? The
lit. meaning of the compounds
would then be to 'take the initia-
tive in advancing to meet,' as a
superior would in welcoming an
inferior who had come into his
presence, or as confident defenders
might, to the surprise of arrogant
invaders, at the outset of an en-
gagement. This is just what the
Greeks did at the Battle of Sala-
mis.

12. ἄντλῳ.] Used metaphori-
cally for the sea in its baneful as-
pect. Cf. Ol. IX. 53, Eur. Hec.
1025, ἀλίμενόν τις ὡς εἰς ἄντλον πε-
σὼν | λέχριος ἐκπεσεῖ φίλας καρδίας, |
ἀμέρσας βίον, Hom. Od. XV. 477,
τὴν μὲν ἔπειτα γυναῖκα βάλ' Ἄρτεμις
ἰοχέαιρα, | ἄντλῳ δ' ἐνδούπησε πε-
σοῦσ' ὡς εἰναλίη κήξ.

τάν.] 'Her character even Por-
phyrion had not learnt when he
was provoking her beyond mea-
sure.'

13. κέρδος—φέροι.] For the con-

struction compare Ol. X. 4, εἴ τις
εὖ πράσσοι, τέλλεται, Pyth. I. 81,
Isth. IV. 14, πάντ' ἔχεις, | εἴ σε τού-
των μοῖρ' ἐφίκοιτο καλῶν, and supply
ἐστί. Pindar used the optative
with εἰ in protasis, with pres. ind.
in apodosis, where Attic authors
would use the subjunctive with ἐάν,
to express a general supposition in
indefinite time. He also uses the
aor. subj. in protasis with εἰ, with
pres. ind. in apodosis; apparently
when he wishes to indicate that
the general supposition has refer-
ence to a special case; cf. Pyth. IV.
266, 274, Nem. VII. 11, 16, IX. 46,
Isth. III. 59, IV. 13. These remarks
are supplementary to Goodwin § 48.
II. A, § 54. 2, § 63. 4 B. Render,
'For gain is most welcome when-
ever one gets it from the home of
a willing giver.' Hermann takes
this to refer to the tribute of land
and water given to Dareios by the
Aeginêtans and other Greeks. But
just after a glorious victory a poet
would hardly allude to a previous
humiliation. Moreover the sim-
plest explanation—'The gains of
commerce are more blessed than
the spoils of war'—applies too well
to the Aeginêtans and to the con-
text to be set aside. Hermann
thinks that the epithet μεγάλαυχον
(v. 15) would apply to Xerxes.
This is true, and it might also
glance at Pausanias and again at
the Athenians.

15. ἔσφαλεν.] The gnômic Ao-
rist.

Τυφὼς Κίλιξ ἑκατόγκρανος οὔ μιν ἄλυξεν,
οὐδὲ μὰν βασιλεὺς Γιγάντων· δμᾶθεν δὲ κεραυνῷ
τόξοισί τ' Ἀπόλλωνος· ὃς εὐμενεῖ νόῳ   25
Ξενάρκειον ἔδεκτο Κίρραθεν ἐστεφανωμένον
20 υἱὸν ποίᾳ Παρνασίδι Δωριεῖ τε κώμῳ.

                                                       Στρ. β'.

ἔπεσε δ' οὐ Χαρίτων ἑκὰς   30
ἁ δικαιόπολις ἀρεταῖς
κλειναῖσιν· Αἰακιδᾶν
θίγοισα νᾶσος· τελέαν δ' ἔχει
25 δόξαν ἀπ' ἀρχᾶς. πολλοῖσι μὲν γὰρ ἀείδεται   35
νικαφόροις ἐν ἀέθλοις θρέψαισα καὶ θοαῖς
ὑπερτάτους ἥρωας ἐν μάχαις·

                                                       Ἀντ. β'.

τὰ δὲ καὶ ἀνδράσιν ἐμπρέπει.
εἰμὶ δ' ἄσχολος ἀναθέμεν   40
30 πᾶσαν μακραγορίαν
λύρᾳ τε καὶ φθέγματι μαλθακῷ,
μὴ κόρος ἐλθὼν κνίσῃ. τὸ δ' ἐν ποσί μοι τράχον   45

16. Κίλιξ.] Cf. Pyth. ι. 16.
Perhaps the epithet is inserted to
point the allusion to the Eastern
foes of Hellas. The Kilikians faced
the Aeginêtans at Salamis.

μιν.] Either βίαν, the result of
βία on his part, or better, Hêsy-
chia, taking κέρδος—χρόνῳ as a pa-
renthesis.

17. βασιλεύς.] i.e. Porphyrion;
perhaps with an allusion to Xerxes'
title.

κεραυνῷ.] Sc. Διός.

19. Ξενάρκειον...υἱόν.] Cf. Pyth.
II. 18.

20. Παρνασίδι.] The third and
fifth syllables of the last verse of
the Epodes may be long or short,
and it is doubtful whether ποίᾳ is
an iambic or a spondee. Hermann
thinks these syllables must be long,
and so alters vv. 60, 100. mss. give

Παρνασίᾳ, which will not scan.
Böckh corrected ΠΑΡΝΑΣΙΑΙ to
ΠΑΡΝΑΣΙΔΙ.

Δωριεῖ τε κώμῳ.] 'And escorted
by a triumphal procession of Do-
rians.' The participle is taken with
κώμῳ by Zeugma.

21. 'Your island of cities where
justice dwells, from having expe-
rienced the glorious virtues of the
Aeakidae, is wont to be cast full
near to the Graces;' i.e. to meet
with praise in song.

27. ἥρωας.] e.g. Aeakos, Pêleus,
Telamon, Aias, Achilles.

28. τὰ δὲ καί.] Cf. Ol. IX. 95.

31. φθέγματι μαλθακῷ.] 'Ge-
nial vocal melody.' The epithet is
appropriate to the Aeolian style.

32. μή.] The construction is
elliptical. Sc. 'and should fear to
do so if I had leisure.' For the

ἴτω τεὸν χρέος, ὦ παῖ, νεώτατον καλῶν,
ἐμᾷ ποτανὸν ἀμφὶ μαχανᾷ.

Ἐπ. β΄.

35 παλαισμάτεσσι γὰρ ἰχνεύων ματραδελφεοὺς
Ὀλυμπίᾳ τε Θεόγνητον οὐ κατελέγχεις,   50
οὐδὲ Κλειτομάχοιο νίκαν Ἰσθμοῖ θρασύγυιον·
αὔξων δὲ πάτραν Μιδυλιδᾶν λόγον φέρεις,
τὸν ὄνπερ ποτ' Ὀϊκλέος παῖς ἐν ἑπταπύλοις ἰδὼν 55
40 υἱοὺς Θήβαις αἰνίξατο παρμένοντας αἰχμᾷ,

Στρ. γ΄.

ὁπότ' ἀπ' Ἄργεος ἤλυθον
δευτέραν ὁδὸν Ἐπίγονοι.   60
ὧδ' εἶπε μαρναμένων·
Φυᾷ τὸ γενναῖον ἐπιπρέπει
45 ἐκ πατέρων παισὶ λῆμα. θαέομαι σαφὲς   65

suppression of the idea of fearing
cf. Pyth. IV. 155.
κνίσῃ.] So best mss., though
most editors read κνίσσῃ. But
the sixth syllable of this and the
corresponding verses is according
to the best mss. as often short as
long.
τὸ δ'—μαχανᾷ.] 'But let that
which is at my feet go forward
speedily, the debt forsooth due to
thee, my son, the freshest of thy
glories, being endowed with wings
by my art.' τὸ δ' ἐν ποσί μοι is in
our idiom 'what I have in hand;'
cf. φροντίδα τὰν πὰρ ποδός, Pyth. x.
62, τὸ πὰρ ποδός, Pyth. III. 60, τὸ
πρὸ ποδὸς χρῆμα, Isth. VII. 13. For
ποτανὸν cf. Nem. VII. 22, explained
on Pyth. I. 40; for ἀμφὶ cf. Pyth.
I. 80.
37. θρασύγυιον.] The epithet is
specially appropriate to the wrest-
ling match and pankration.
38. φέρεις.] The praise is won
for the clan, hence the active is
best; cf. ἐστεφάνωσε, Ol. XIV. 22.
39. ἐν.] 'Near;' cf. Ol. VI. 16,

IX. 16. The son of Oïkles was the
dead Amphiarâos, who had an
oracle at Orôpos and another at
Potniae, from one of which he is
supposed to see and speak.
40. υἱούς.] i. e. his own son.
Alkmaeon and the sons of his
(Amphiarâos) six fellow-warriors.
παρμένοντας αἰχμᾷ.] 'Standing
their ground in battle.'
43. μαρναμένων.] Used abso-
lutely with a substantive; cf. μο-
λόντων infra v. 85, θνασκόντων Ol.
IX. 35, Pyth. IV. 25, Isth. III. 5 ζώει
δὲ μάσσων ὄλβος ὀπιζομένων.
44. φυᾷ.] Dat. of cause, cf.
Ol. IX. 83. 'By nature doth the
noble spirit derived from sires dis-
play itself in sons.'
45. παισί.] So best mss. Two
interpolated mss. give παισίν. Her-
mann reads, παῖ, σοί, because in all
the corresponding verses the fifth
syllable ends a word. For the
quantity of the sixth syllable cf.
v. 31, note on κνίσῃ. The text
gives far the best sense.

δράκοντα ποικίλον αἰθᾶς Ἀλκμᾶν ἐπ' ἀσπίδος
νωμῶντα πρῶτον ἐν Κάδμου πύλαις.

Ἀντ. γ'.

ὁ δὲ καμὼν προτέρᾳ πάθᾳ
νῦν ἀρείονος ἐνέχεται   70
50 ὄρνιχος ἀγγελίᾳ
Ἄδραστος ἥρως· τὸ δὲ οἴκοθεν
ἀντία πράξει. μόνος γὰρ ἐκ Δαναῶν στρατοῦ
θανόντος ὀστέα λέξαις υἱοῦ, τύχᾳ θεῶν   75
ἀφίξεται λαῷ σὺν ἀβλαβεῖ

Ἐπ. γ'.

55 Ἄβαντος εὐρυχόρους ἀγυιάς. τοιαῦτα μὲν
ἐφθέγξατ' Ἀμφιάρηος. χαίρων δὲ καὶ αὐτὸς
Ἀλκμᾶνα στεφάνοισι βάλλω, ῥαίνω δὲ καὶ ὕμνῳ, 80
γείτων ὅτι μοι καὶ κτεάνων φύλαξ ἐμῶν

46, 47. The serpent was emblematic of the power of prophecy. The Schol. tells us that it indicated his descent from Melampus, whose ears two serpents opened with their tongues so that he could hear the speech of animals and birds. Cf. Ol. vi. 46, 47.

48. 'And he that formerly suffered from disaster, hero Adrastos, now hath his lot determined by the declaration of a more favourable augury. But as to his own household he shall fare contrariwise.' Böckh thinks that a relation of Aristomenes had fallen at the battle of Kekryphaleia; Don. at the battle of Salamis. But Alkmaeon is a more important personage in this episode than Adrastos, who is brought in parenthetically; while Alkmaeon is the instance of the general principle stated vv. 44, 45. A propos of Aristomenes see vv. 38, 39. I think that Adrastos is introduced to illustrate the opening of the ode by showing that βία even when triumphant entails suffering.

His lot also illustrates the mixed and fleeting nature of human success and is therefore consonant with the latter part of the ode. The leader of the Aeginetan ships at Salamis may have been a Midylid and may have lost a son but the balance of probability is against the myth fitting real events so accurately.

52. μόνος.] So best mss. Hermann (Don.) μοῦνος.

53. υἱοῦ.] i. e. Aegialos.

55. Ἄβαντος.] i. e. of Argos. Abas was said to have been the twelfth king of Argos.

57. στεφάνοισι βάλλω.] Cf. Pyth. ix. 123, 124.

ῥαίνω.] Cf. Pyth. v. 93.

58—60. There seems to have been a shrine of Alkmaeon near Thebes on the road to Delphi which the poet was wont to visit as he passed. I take the aorists as frequentative. The treasuries of temples were much used by private individuals for keeping their wealth in security.

F.   15

ὑπάντασεν ἰόντι γᾶς ὀμφαλὸν παρ' ἀοίδιμον,   85
60 μαντευμάτων τ' ἐφάψατο συγγόνοισι τέχναις.

Στρ. δ'.

τὺ δ', ἐκαταβόλε πάνδοκον
ναὸν εὐκλέα διανέμων   90
Πυθῶνος ἐν γυάλοις,
τὸ μὲν μέγιστον τόθι χαρμάτων
65 ὤπασας, οἴκοι δὲ πρόσθεν ἁρπαλέαν δόσιν
πένταεθλίου σὺν ἑορταῖς ὑμαῖς ἐπάγαγες,   95
ὦναξ, ἑκόντι δὴ εὔχομαι νόῳ

'Αντ. δ'.

κατά τιν' ἁρμονίαν βλέπειν
ἀμφ' ἕκαστον ὅσα νέομαι.
70 κώμῳ μὲν ἀδυμελεῖ
Δίκα παρέστακε· θεῶν δ' ὅπιν   100

60. ἐφάψατο.] Cf. Ol. i. 86, ix.
12. Hermann reads μάντις, χρησ-
μῶν τ' ἀμφ' ἅψατο.
62. διανέμων.] Cf. Pyth. iv. 261.
66. ὑμαῖς.] i. e. of Apollo and
Artemis. The feast was the Del-
phinia at Aegina. Cf. Pyth. vii.
17.
67. 'O king! with willing mind
I pray that I may be regarding
due proportion according to any
one's merits in respect to all that
I sing about each victor.'
68. мss. give κατά τιν'. Pauw
altered to κατὰ τὶν which Böckh
and Dissen take as a dative, making
an impossible construction; Her-
mann and Don. as an accusative
= σὲ as in Korinna and Theokritos.
Don. construes 'I do not hesitate
to profess my confidence that by
thy favour, O King, I shall look
tuneful in all that I sing of every
victor.' Now I think that I have
disposed of the notion that κατὰ
δαίμονα, Ol. ix. 28, means by favour
of the deity, by which passage Don.
supports his rendering of κατά τὶν.

Again one can understand 'looking
warlike, frightened, sour, &c.;' but
what is the expression which in-
dicates and accompanies tuneful-
ness? Mommsen renders 'Precor,
o rex, ut semper in unaquaque re
(quaecumque tracto) ad congruen-
tiam (modestiam) quandam lubenti
animo circumspiciam.'
69. νέομαι.] Don. says 'the
poets often use words expressive of
motion in general, like νέομαι here,
to signify "singing" or "narration,"
comp. ἀναδραμεῖν, Ol. viii. 54.
διελθεῖν, N. iv. 72. ὁδὸς λόγων,
Ol. i. 110, and the use of the words
οἶμος, οἴμη. See also Ovid. Fast. i.
15: adnue conanti per laudes ire
tuorum. The construction is: ὅσα
νέομαι ἀμφ' ἕκαστον, "in all that
I go through, discuss, or sing,
about each individual victor:" so
κελαδέοντι ἀμφὶ Κινύραν, Pyth. ii.
15.'
71. Δίκα.] Cf. supra, vv. 1, 22,
Ol. iii. 4.
ὅπιν.] Cf. Ol. ii. 6.

ἄφθιτον αἰτέω, Ξέναρκες, ὑμετέραις τύχαις.
εἰ γάρ τις ἐσλὰ πέπαται μὴ σὺν μακρῷ πόνῳ,
πολλοῖς σοφὸς δοκεῖ πεδ' ἀφρόνων 105
    Ἐπ. δ'.

75 βίον κορυσσέμεν ὀρθοβούλοισι μαχαναῖς·
τὰ δ' οὐκ ἐπ' ἀνδράσι κεῖται· δαίμων δὲ παρίσχει,
ἄλλοτ' ἄλλον ὕπερθε βάλλων, ἄλλον δ' ὑπὸ χειρῶν. 110
· μέτρῳ κατάβαιν'· ἐν Μεγάροις δ' ἔχεις γέρας,
μυχῷ τ' ἐν Μαραθῶνος, Ἥρας τ' ἀγῶν' ἐπιχώριον
80 νίκαις τρισσαῖς, ὦ 'ριστόμενες, δάμασσας ἔργῳ· 115
    Στρ. ε'.

τέτρασι δ' ἔμπετες ὑψόθεν

72. ἄφθιτον αἰτέω.] For con-
struction cf. Nem. v. 9, 10, τάν
ποτ' εὔανδρόν τε καὶ ναυσικλυτὰν |
θέσσαντο, 'they erst prayed that
it (Aegina) might be both blessed
with warriors and famed for ships.'
74. ' To many he seems to be a
wise man amongst fools, and to be
arming his life by powers of right
counsel.'
75. κορυσσέμεν.] Cf. Isth. vii.
54.
μαχαναῖς.] Cf. Pyth. i. 41.
76. κεῖται.] Cf. Pyth. x. 71.
παρίσχει.] So. αὐτά, cf. Pyth. ii.
17, Ol. i. 40.
77, 78. 'Now tossing one up
now another, now bringing one
now another below the level of the
hands.' Don. quotes Eur. Bacch.
877 (P.), τί τὸ κάλλιον | παρὰ θεῶν
γέρας ἐν βροτοῖς | ἢ χεῖρ' ὑπὲρ κορυ-
φᾶς | ἐχθρῶν κρείσσω κατέχειν; Dis-
sen better explains the passage as
a metaphor from playing at ball,
quoting Pallad. Alexandr. in
Brunck, Analect. T. ii. p. 431,
Jacobs, Anthol. Gr. T. iii. p. 138:
Παίγνιόν ἐστι Τύχης μερόπων βίος.—
καὶ τοὺς μὲν κατάγουσα πάλιν σφαι-
ρηδὸν ἀείρει, τοὺς δ' ἀπὸ τῶν
νεφελῶν εἰς Ἀίδην κατάγει. This is
well illustrated by a coin of Terina,

showing a winged Nikê sitting with
a ball balanced on the back of her
hand and another in the air above,
for which I am indebted to Prof.
Colvin as well as for other coins
which I have mentioned.
79, 80. ἀγῶν'... δάμασσας.] Cf.
Ol. ix. 84, 85.
ἔργῳ.] Cf. Nem. i. 26.
81. 'And (at Pytho) didst thou
fall uppermost on the bodies of
four (youths) with fell intent, to
whom alike neither was a cheerful
return adjudged at the Pythian
festival nor indeed when they came
to their mothers did pleasant
laughter of bystanders rouse de-
light; but by back ways aloof from
their foes they skulk racked by
their disgrace.'
With this passage cf. Ol.
viii. 67. With vv. 81, 82, cf.
Aesch. Agam. 1145, 1146 (P.), καί
τίς σε κακοφρονῶν τίθησι δαίμων,
ὕπερθεν βαρὺς ἐμπίπτων. The simi-
larity of diction suggests indebted-
ness on one part or the other.
Now as the Pythian games fell in
the third year of the Olympiad,
while the Oresteia was exhibited
in the second, and as this diction
would come more naturally to the
composer of this ode than to the

σωμάτεσσι κακὰ φρονέων·
τοῖς οὔτε νόστος ὁμῶς
ἐπ' ἀλπνὸς ἐν Πυθιάδι κρίθη,   120
85 οὐδὲ μολόντων πὰρ ματέρ' ἀμφὶ γέλως γλυκὺς
ὦρσεν χάριν· κατὰ λαύρας δ' ἐχθρῶν ἀπάοροι
πτώσσοντι, συμφορᾷ δεδαγμένοι.   .125

                               'Αντ. έ.

ὁ δὲ καλόν τι νέον λαχὼν
ἁβρότατος ἔπι μεγάλας
90 ἐξ ἐλπίδος πέταται   130
ὑποπτέροις ἀνορέαις, ἔχων
κρέσσονα πλούτου μέριμναν. ἐν δ' ὀλίγῳ βροτῶν
τὸ τερπνὸν αὔξεται· οὔτω δὲ καὶ πιτνεῖ χαμαί,
ἀποτρόπῳ γνώμᾳ σεσεισμένον.

                               'Επ. έ.

95 ἐπάμεροι· τί δέ τις; τί δ' οὔ τις; σκιᾶς ὄναρ   135

dramatist, this resemblance is a small item of evidence against the date of this ode being so late as the thirty-third Pythiad, B.C. 458, and in favour of B.C. 462.

82. κακὰ φρονέων.] Cf. Nem. IV. 95, μαλακὰ μὲν φρονέων ἐσλοῖς | τραχὺς δὲ παλιγκότοις ἔφεδρος.

85. For οὐδὲ after οὔτε cf. Isth. II. 44, 45.

86. ἀπάοροι.] I follow Prof. Paley who quotes Od. XII. 435, ἀπήωροι δ' ἔσαν ὄζοι, 'the boughs hung far out of reach.' Don. renders 'in anxious suspense, or fear, on account of their enemies.'

88. 'While he who hath won some fresh honour in his green youth from his high hopes is borne up as on wings of manly ardour cherishing ambition loftier than the pursuit of wealth.' The elastic gait of the exultant and hopeful is contrasted with the dejected mien of the vanquished just described.

92. μέριμναν.] So MSS. except two interpolated MSS. which give τέρψιν πλούτοιο. Hermann reads μέριμηραν not elsewhere found in Pindar. For text cf. Ol. I. 108, II. 60. For sentiment cf. Nem. IX. 32, ἐντί τοι φίλιπποί τ' αὐτόθι καὶ κτεάνων ψυχὰς ἔχοντες κρέσσονας | ἄνδρες.

94. 'Shaken by a reversal of judgment' i.e. on the part of the Gods. Cf. Pyth. X. 21.

95. Dissen takes ἐπάμεροι as vocative with one Schol. The other explains τῶν ἀνθρώπων τῶν ἐφημέρων κ.τ.λ. Neither takes the first δὲ into account which shows that ἐπάμεροι is a sentence. Dissen again after the first-mentioned Schol. interprets τί δ' κ.τ.λ. Quid est magnus? quid est parvus?— reading οὔτις. But 'What is a man? What is he not? Mankind is a dream of a shadow' is preferable. We may paraphrase: 'A man is nothing. A man is anything. Mankind is unreal as a dream,

ἄνθρωπος. ἀλλ' ὅταν αἴγλα διόσδοτος ἔλθῃ,
λαμπρὸν φέγγος ἔπεστιν ἀνδρῶν καὶ μείλιχος αἰών.
Αἴγινα φίλα μᾶτερ, ἐλευθέρῳ στόλῳ   140
πόλιν τάνδε κόμιζε Δὶ καὶ κρέοντι σὺν Αἰακῷ
100 Πηλεῖ τε κἀγαθῷ Τελμῶνι σὺν τ' Ἀχιλλεῖ.   145

variable as a shadow.' The second
question is intensely pregnant. It
implies that so sudden and wild
are the freaks of fortune that
nothing is too improbable to be
predicated of that nonentity, a
man.

96. αἴγλα.] Cf. Ol. XIII. 36.

98—100. Here we seem to have
an allusion to the female figure
which the Aeginêtans said ap-
peared to them and urged them
to engage at Salamis (Herod. VIII.
84) as well as to the assistance
given by Aeakidae (ib. 83). Δὶ
is Ζεὺς Πανελλήνιος of Aegina.

ἐλευθέρῳ στόλῳ.] 'Conduct this
commonwealth on its voyage in
freedom's cause.' Apart from the
allusion to Salamis this means
simply 'support the independence
and freedom to maintaining which
the policy of Aegina is ever di-

rected.' We know that early in
B.C. 478 the Aeginêtans and Ko-
rinthians were disturbed at the re-
building of the walls of Athens.
Did Pindar already foresee danger
from this quarter to the freedom
of Aegina? After the reduction
of Naxos and Thasos, Athenian
ambition must have afforded much
stronger cause for apprehension.

99. σύν.] For the position of
that prep. cf. Pyth. II. 12. Note
that the heroes are coupled to Zeus
by καί, the Aeakids of the first and
second generations are coupled to
Aeakos by τε—τε, the brothers of
the first generation are coupled by
καί. Cf. Ol. III. 8, Pyth. I. 42.

100. κἀγαθῷ.] So Moschopulos
and Böckh; MSS. καὶ ἀγαθῷ; Ed.
Rom. πηλεῖ τε κἀρίστῳ; Hermann
πηλεῖ τ' ἐσθλῷ καὶ σὺν κ.τ.λ., but
cf. vv. 20, 60.

PYTHIA IX.

ON THE VICTORY OF TELESIKRATES OF KYRENE IN THE ARMED FOOT-RACE.

INTRODUCTION.

TELESIKRATES, the son of Karneiades (which name suggests that he was an Aegid—cf. Pyth. v. 68—76), won as ὁπλιτοδρόμος B.C. 478, which success this ode celebrates. He also won in the stadium at Delphi B.C. 470. It has been inferred from *v.* 73 that the victor had not returned to Kyrêne, where this ode was recited, but see my note on that verse and *vv.* 90, 91. From the digression about Iolâos, *vv.* 79 sqq., I infer that Telesikrates trained partly at Thebes. As to the explanation of the ode I cannot do better than quote Donaldson:

'The whole context of the ode shows that Telesicrates was about to marry some foreign damsel, whose heart he had won by the display of his strength and agility in the armed race. This appears from the legend about Apollo taking a foreign bride to Africa, after having consulted a sage adviser whether he should marry her or no; likewise, from the allusion in *v.* 99, and from the story about Alexidamus, who gained his wife by swiftness in the course. I would also explain the words καλλιγύναικι πάτρᾳ (*v.* 74) with reference to this; Telesicrates did not seek the love of a foreign damsel because there was a lack of beautiful women in Lybia; on the contrary he will take home his bride to the land of the fair. On the subject of this ode, beside the explanations of Böckh and Dissen, see Böckh, *Berlin Jahrbücher*, October, 1830, and Welcker, *Rheinisches Museum*, for 1834, p. 372, 373.'

I think it is sufficient to suppose that the poet means 'as Kyrêne's athletic prowess won for her a desirable husband, and Alexidâmos' speed won him a wife, so your achievements have won for you a bride.' It seems to me that the destined bride must have been one of the παρθενικαί of *v.* 99, i.e. a maid of Kyrêne. It would appear that Telesikrates had made some stay in Greece, as he won three prizes, both at Aegina and Megara, and that on his return he intended to celebrate his marriage. From *vv.* 89, 90 it may be inferred that Telesikrates was a great friend of Pindar's, perhaps a connection; so he may have confided to the poet his attachment to some maid to whom he was not yet betrothed. Böckh thinks that he was betrothed to a Theban damsel. This marriage question is interesting only in connection with Pindar's skill in working in a secondary subject without interfering with his primary theme.

The rhythm is a mixture of Dorian and Lydian.

ANALYSIS.

vv.

1—4. Proclamation of the victory of Telesikrates of Kyrêne.

5—65. Myth of the marriage of Apollo and Kyrêne.

5—8. Apollo carries off Kyrêne to Libya.

9—13. Aphrodite presides over their marriage.

14—18. Kyrêne's parentage.

18—25. Her hardy habits.

26—28. Apollo sees her wrestling with a lion.

29—37. He calls Cheiron to see, expresses his admiration, and asks his advice as to a union with her.

38, 39. Cheiron is amused and makes answer,

39—41. 'That neither gods nor men like to acknowledge an incipient passion.

42—49. 'So even thou, the omniscient God of truth, art dissembling and asking my advice.'

50—65. Cheiron foretells the marriage of Apollo and Kyrêne, the eventual foundation of the Kyrênaic cities, the welcoming of the bride by Libya, and the birth of the offspring of the union Aristaeos.

66—70. The poet tells the consummation of the marriage in Libya, where Kyrêne frequents a city renowned in games.

71—75. Even now Karneiades' son has won success in her honour at Pytho.

. 76—78. Great achievements afford an inexhaustible theme, but
it is best to say much in a few words ;

78, 79. For a sense of proportion is of the first importance in
everything,

79, 80. As Thebes learnt by Iolâos' conduct,

80—83. Who, after the slaughter of Eurystheus, was buried in
the tomb of Amphitryon, the Kadmeian's guest,

84—86. To whom and to Zeus Alkmêna bare twins.

87, 88. About them it is natural to make a digression and about
Dirke.

88—90. They fulfilled the poet's prayer that Telesikrates might
furnish him with another theme ;

90—92. For he had already furnished several by victories at
Aegina and Megara.

93—96. Wherefore let friend and foe, according to Nêreus' maxim,
heartily praise even a foe when he has wrought nobly
for the public good.

97—103. Telesikrates has won the admiration of maidens in the
local contests at Kyrêne.

103—125. As the ode requires an appropriate conclusion, the poet
tells how Telesikrates' ancestor, Alexidâmos, won the
daughter of Antaeos, when her suitors' claims were de-
cided by a foot-race.

Στρ. α'.

'Εθέλω χαλκάσπιδα Πυθιονίκαν
σὺν βαθυζώνοισιν ἀγγέλλων
Τελεσικράτη Χαρίτεσσι γεγωνεῖν,
ὄλβιον ἄνδρα, διωξίππου στεφάνωμα Κυράνας·   5

1. χαλκάσπιδα.] i.e. ὁπλιτοδρό-
μον. Of the χάλκεα ἔντεα, cf. Ol. IV.
22, which consisted of shield, hel-
met and greaves (Pausanias, VI.
10), the shield was the heaviest and
most important item. The oblong
shield of the ὁπλίτης was techni-
cally ὅπλον, but ἀσπις often stands
for it, as here, and φεράσπιδες σάγαι,
of the equipment of ὁπλῖται,
Aesch. Pers. 240, so ἀσπιδοδούποισιν
ὁπλίταις δρόμοις, Isth. I. 23.

2. βαθυζώνοισι.] Cf. Pyth. I. 12.
ἀγγέλλων.] A metaphor from
the heralds' office, cf. Pyth. I. 32.
3. Χαρίτεσσι.] Cf. Pyth. VI. 2.
4. στεφάνωμα.] Either 'a crowned
honour to Kyrêne' in apposition
with ἄνδρα, or with the notion of
the previous clause, cf. Ol. II. 4,
ἀκρόθινα, Ol. VII. 16, πυγμᾶς ἄποινα.
Pindar likens his Epinikian song
to a wreath, Ol. VI. 86, 87, Nem.
VII. 77—79, Isth. III. 45.

5 τὰν ὁ χαιτάεις ἀνεμοσφαράγων ἐκ Παλίου κόλπων
   ποτὲ Λατοΐδας
ἅρπασ᾿, ἔνεικέ τε χρυσέῳ παρθένον ἀγροτέραν δίφρῳ,
   τόθι νιν πολυμήλου   10
καὶ πολυκαρποτάτας θῆκε δέσποιναν χθονὸς
ῥίζαν ἀπείρου τρίταν εὐήρατον θάλλοισαν οἰκεῖν. 15.

                                  Ἀντ. α΄.

ὑπέδεκτο δ᾿ ἀργυρόπεζ᾿ Ἀφροδίτα
10 Δάλιον ξεῖνον θεοδμάτων
   ὀχέων ἐφαπτομένα χερὶ κούφᾳ·
καί σφιν ἐπὶ γλυκεραῖς εὐναῖς ἐρατὰν βάλεν αἰδῶ, 20

8. 'That she might have for home a lovely vigorous root of a third mainland;'—i.e. a root of cities (cf. Pyth. IV. 15) on a third mainland. For the hypallage cf. Ol. VIII. 68, XI. (X.) 6, Pyth. V. 82. Here perhaps as generally, when two coördinate adjectives with no conjunction or pause occur one is definitive—i.e. θάλλοισαν 'full of vigorous life,' the other descriptive. Perhaps εὐήρατον is proleptic. In Pindar's time Kyrēne was called Aphrodite's garden, but the beauty of its vegetation was also legendary. For the two adjectives cf. Ol. XIII. 88, Isth. I. 23 quoted on v. 1 supra, Isth. II. 3, 7, VII. 25, Ol. I. 59, II. 54, III. 19, IX. 91, X. 1, Pyth. IV. 214, X. 6, Nem. VII. 46. However this explanation is occasionally inapplicable, e. g. infra vv. 55, 106, λιπαρὰν εὐωνύμων ἀπ' Ἀθηναίων, Nem. IV. 19. In many cases I take adjectives with the predicates which others take in simple agreement, e.g. infra v. 13. In preferring such a construction I am influenced partly by the order and position of the words and partly by the sense obtained.

9. ὑπέδεκτο.] For the force of the prep., implying something more than a passive reception, cf. Pyth.

VIII. 11.

ἀργυρόπεζ᾿ Ἀφροδίτα.] Though I differ extensively from the exponents of the 'Dawn Theory' yet I believe that Dawn was one of the ideas which made up the complex personification Aphrodite. To this idea I refer the epithet ἀργυρόπεζα and her name which I render 'shining on the water.' The Skt. abhra is 'water' and with this is connected ἀφρός, which in the compound retains its earlier meaning. The second element I take to be for διϝετη from the √DIV 'shine' 'play.' The white light on the eastern horizon and on the sea is expressed in the epithet 'silver-footed,' while the glow of sunset suggested φοινικόπεζα for Dēmētēr (Ol. VI. 94). For she is in one of her phases an Evening Goddess.

11. ὀχέων.] Gen. of motion from, cf. Madv. § 60. 4, Soph. El. 324 (Jebb), with ὑπέδεκτο 'welcomed by taking.'

ἐφαπτ. κ.τ.λ.] 'Reaching out to him with supporting hand.' For κούφᾳ=κουφιζούσῃ cf. ὀρθᾷ χερί, Ol. XI. (X.) 4, Pyth. IV. 81, infra 36, κλιτὰν χέρα, Soph. Ant. 974, ἕλκοι ἀλαὸν ἀλαστόροισιν ἱμμάτων κύκλοις.

12. ἐρατὰν αἰδῶ.] 'Bewitching coyness.'

ξυνὸν ἁρμόζοισα θεῷ τε γάμον μιχθέντα κούρᾳ θ'
  Ὑψέος εὐρυβία·
ὃς Λαπιθᾶν ὑπερόπλων τουτάκις . ἦν βασιλεύς, ἐξ
  Ὠκεανοῦ γένος ἥρως   25
15 δεύτερος· ὅν ποτε Πίνδου κλεενναῖς ἐν πτυχαῖς
  Ναῒς εὐφρανθεῖσα Πηνειοῦ λέχει Κρείοισ' ἔτικτεν,   30
                                                        Ἐπ. α'.
Γαίας θυγάτηρ. ὁ δὲ τὰν εὐώλενον
θρέψατο παῖδα Κυράναν· ἁ μὲν οὔθ' ἱστῶν παλιμβά-
  μους ἐφίλησεν ὁδούς,
οὔτε δείπνων οἰκοριᾶν μεθ' ἑταιρᾶν τέρψιας,   35
20 ἀλλ' ἀκόντεσσίν τε χαλκέοις
φασγάνῳ . τε μαρναμένα κεράιζεν ἀγρίους
θῆρας, ἦ πολλάν τε καὶ ἀσύχιον   40
βουσὶν εἰράναν παρέχοισα πατρῴαις, τὸν δὲ σύγκοιτον
  γλυκὺν
παῦρον ἐπὶ γλεφάροις
25 ὕπνον ἀναλίσκοισα ῥέποντα πρὸς ἀῶ.
                                                        Στρ. β'.
κίχε νιν λέοντί ποτ' εὐρυφαρέτρας   45
ὀβρίμῳ μούναν παλαίοισαν

13. 'Making mutually binding on the god and the daughter of widely-ruling Hypseus the union entered into by them.'
  ἁρμόζοισα.] This word is often used of parents arranging a formal marriage for their children. The poet gives to this amour as much solemnity and dignity as possible.
  μιχθέντα.] Cf. Pyth. IV. 222, 223. So Schol.; mss. μιχθέντι.
  18. ἱστ. παλιμ. ὁδούς.] 'Pacing to and fro at the loom.' The Schol. quotes Il. I. 41, ἱστὸν ἐποιχομένην.
  19. οἰκοριᾶν.] So Moschopulos for οἰκουριᾶν (ὦν); 'nor merry junketings with stay-at-home maidens of her own age.' The full form would

be οἰκϝοριᾶν. Bergk and Mommsen read οὔτε δείπνων τέρψιας οὔθ' ἑταρῶν οἰκουριᾶν from the Schol. which apparently has repeated οὔτε by mistake for μετά.
  23. 'But, as for the (universal) bed-fellow, sweet sleep, enjoying it as it sinks for a little while on her eyelids towards dawn.' ταῦρον must be taken with ἐπὶ γλεφάροις and therefore with ῥέποντα, though were ῥέποντα, κ.τ.λ., absent it would be a secondary predicate. There seems to be a confused metaphor from weighing out money to spend.
  26. There are several notices of the early existence of lions in Europe.

ἄτερ ἐγχέων ἑκάεργος Ἀπόλλων.
αὐτίκα δ᾽ ἐκ μεγάρων Χείρωνα προσέννεπε φωνᾷ·
30 Σεμνὸν ἄντρον, Φιλυρίδα, προλιπὼν θυμὸν γυναικὸς
   καὶ μεγάλαν δύνασιν   50
θαύμασον, οἷον ἀταρβεῖ νεῖκος ἄγει κεφαλᾷ, μόχθου
   καθύπερθε νεᾶνις   55
ἦτορ ἔχοισα· φόβῳ δ᾽ οὐ κεχείμανται φρένες.
τίς νιν ἀνθρώπων τέκεν; ποίας δ᾽ ἀποσπασθεῖσα
   φύτλας

                                                  Ἀντ. β᾽.
ὀρέων κευθμῶνας ἔχει σκιοέντων,   60
35 γεύεται δ᾽ ἀλκᾶς ἀπειράντου;
ὁσία κλυτὰν χέρα οἱ προσενεγκεῖν,
ἦ ῥα καὶ ἐκ λεχέων κεῖραι μελιαδέα ποίαν;
τὸν δὲ Κένταυρος ζαμενής, ἀγανᾷ χλαρὸν γελάσσαις
   ὀφρύϊ, μῆτιν ἑὰν   65

29. προσέννεπε.] 'Addressed him and called him out from his hall.' Cf. Ol. i. 8, ix. 19.

31. οἷον—κεφαλᾷ.] The Schol. and Mommsen explain ἐπάγει τῇ ἑαυτῆς κεφαλῇ, dat. termini; but she had already invited the struggle so the tense disposes of this interpretation. Schneidewin would change κεφαλᾷ to κραδίᾳ. But 'with undaunted head' is a natural remark for a spectator to make pointing out her mien and attitude. Beware of rendering κεφαλᾷ 'soul,' 'spirit,' 'courage,' &c.

32. κεχείμανται.] For a different application of the metaphor, cf. Ol. xii. 6.

33. ἀποσπασθεῖσα.] Apollo affects to think that her situation cannot be of her own choice.

36, 37. The reading ἦ ῥα must be wrong as καὶ 'even' makes the marriage seem either less proper or desirable than the supposed 'open concubinage.' The best mss. read ἦ ῥα and three have a following comma. Differing from Don. I

maintain that a marriage was as little and as much 'open' as concubinage. Cheiron's playful rebuke does not refer to a suggestion of illicit intercourse, but to Apollo pretending to ask advice when he knew what would happen. In v. 41 εὐνᾶς only means 'betrothal,' as in Ol. vii. 6. According to Don.'s version of v. 41 the pure god Apollo proposes to do that at which gods and men are abashed, εὐνᾶς being taken to mean 'concubinage.' The ensuing remarks of Cheiron show that vv. 39—41 mean 'lovers do not like to avow their attachment when they first feel the influence of passion.' Render vv. 36, 37 then, 'Is it lawful to make her renowned by laying my hand on her and after wedlock to cull the honey-sweet flower?' For κλυτὰν 'ennobling' 'glorifying' cf. supra v. 11, κούφᾳ. For ἦ ῥα cf. Soph. Aj. 172, 177, Isth. vi. 3.

38. ζαμενής.] 'Inspired,' cf. Pyth. iv. 10.

χλαρόν.] This word is not for

εὐθὺς ἀμείβετο· Κρυπταὶ κλαΐδες ἐντὶ σοφᾶς Πειθοῦς
ἱερᾶν φιλοτάτων,   70
40 Φοῖβε, καὶ ἔν τε θεοῖς τοῦτο κἀνθρώποις ὁμῶς
αἰδέοντ’, ἀμφανδὸν ἀδείας τυχεῖν τοπρῶτον εὐνᾶς,

’Επ. β’.

καὶ γὰρ σέ, τὸν οὐ θεμιτὸν ψεύδει θιγεῖν,   75
· ἔτραπε μείλιχος ὀργὰ παρφάμεν τοῦτον λόγον. κούρας
δ’, ὁπόθεν, γενεὰν
ἐξερωτᾷς, ὦ ἄνα; κύριον ὃς πάντων τέλος   80
45 οἶσθα καὶ πάσας κελεύθους·
ὅσσα τε χθὼν ἠρινὰ φύλλ’ ἀναπέμπει, χὠπόσαι
ἐν θαλάσσᾳ καὶ ποταμοῖς ψάμαθοι
κύμασιν ῥιπαῖς τ’ ἀνέμων κλονέονται, χὤτι μέλλει,
χὠπόθεν   85
ἔσσεται, εὖ καθορᾷς.
50 εἰ δὲ χρὴ καὶ πὰρ σοφὸν ἀντιφερίξαι,

Στρ. γ’.

ἐρέω· ταύτᾳ πόσις ἵκεο βᾶσσαν
τάνδε, καὶ μέλλεις ὑπὲρ πόντου   90
Διὸς ἔξοχον ποτὶ κᾶπον ἐνεῖκαι·
ἔνθα νιν ἀρχέπολιν θήσεις, ἐπὶ λαὸν ἀγείραις
55 νασιώταν ὄχθον ἐς ἀμφίπεδον· νῦν δ’ εὐρυλείμων
πότνιά σοι Λιβύα   95

χλωρὸς which is for χλοερός; but
from the same √GHAB ‘shine.’
Curt. connects it with κέχλαδα from
a secondary form of the same root.
39. κλαΐδες.] Cf. Pyth. VIII. 4.
The meaning is ‘secret are first
dawnings of hallowed passion over
which Persuasion has control.’ For
the two genitives cf. Ol. I. 94, 95.
42. For sentiment cf. Pyth. III.
29; for dat. Pyth. IV. 296, VIII. 24,
Nem. IV. 35.
43. μείλιχος ὀργά.] ‘Your melt-
ing mood,’ ‘tender passion.’
παρφάμεν.] ‘To make this mis-
leading speech.’

50. ‘But if one must match
oneself even with the all-knowing.’
53. Libya is called the ‘special
garden of Zeus’ from the oasis of
Zeus Ammon. Don. quotes Shake-
speare, Hen. V., final chorus: ‘for-
tune made his sword | with which
the world’s best garden he achiev-
ed.’ On coins of Kyrênê Zeus had
ram’s horns.
54. θήσεις.] The future is re-
mote.
λαόν.] The Thêraeans.
55. ὄχθον ἐς ἀμφίπεδον.] Cf.
Pyth. IV. 8.
νῦν δ’.] ‘But for the present.’

δέξεται εὐκλέα νύμφαν δώμασιν ἐν χρυσέοις πρόφρων·
ἵνα οἱ χθονὸς αἶσαν
αὐτίκα συντελέθειν ἔννομον δωρήσεται,   100
οὔτε παγκάρπων φυτῶν νήποινον, οὔτ᾽ ἀγνῶτα θηρῶν.

'Αντ. γ'.

τόθι παῖδα τέξεται, ὃν κλυτὸς 'Ερμᾶς
60 εὐθρόνοις "Ωραισι καὶ Γαίᾳ   105
ἀνελὼν φίλας ὑπὸ ματέρος οἴσει.
ταὶ δ᾽ ἐπιγουνίδιον θαησάμεναι βρέφος αὐταῖς,
νέκταρ ἐν χείλεσσι καὶ ἀμβροσίαν στάξοισι, θήσονταί
τέ νιν ἀθάνατον,   110
Ζῆνα καὶ ἁγνὸν 'Απόλλων', ἀνδράσι χάρμα φίλοις
ἄγχιστον, ὀπάονα μήλων,
65 'Αγρέα καὶ Νόμιον, τοῖς δ᾽ 'Αρισταῖον καλεῖν.   115

Of the two epithets here, one qualifies the district the other the personification thereof. The third adj. in the next line goes with the predicate.

56. δώμασιν.] Cf. vv. 68, 69. The poet imagines that the temple of Kyrēne which existed in his time dated back to the mythical period referred to.

ἵνα...δωρήσεται.] i.e. ἐν Λιβύᾳ Λιβύα δωρ. The confusion of place and person is complete.

57. συντελέθειν ἔννομον.] 'To be a joint possession for her to occupy.' I venture to think that Prof. Paley is partly right in quoting Aesch. *Suppl.* 559 where ἔννομοι means 'inhabitants.' Here it seems to mean 'inhabited.' It is also rendered 'by legal right.'

58. φυτῶν.] Especially silphium.

νήποινον.] Cf. Pyth. II. 17.

60. Γαίᾳ.] Cf. v. 102.

61. ὑπό.] 'From under,' cf. Ol. VI. 43.

62. θαησάμεναι.] So Bergk for mss. θησάμεναι or θηκάμεναι. Schol.

ἐπὶ τοῖς γόνασι | θεῖσαι τὸν 'Αρισταῖον καὶ θαυμάσασαι τὸ βρέφος. Two interpolated mss. give κατθηκάμεναι (Don.).

αὐταῖς.] This is to be taken with ἐπιγουνίδιον.

63. ἐν.] Join with στάξοισι.

θήσονται.] A Schol. renders θρέψουσι. Is the word from the √θη 'suckle, suck'—'they shall nurture him to be'? I incline to think so. The mid. from √θε 'they shall make him' is not regular. We should expect θήσοισιν, but the middle may be explained by the implication of the idea of adoption.

64, 65. These verses show clearly that this son of Apollo was really a phase of Apollo himself. Aristaeos connects Kyrēne with Thebes as according to Hēsiod he married a daughter of Kadmos.

χάρμα ἄγχιστον.] Cf. Pyth. I. 59.

65. καί.] This nearly equals 'or.'

τοῖς δ'.] A *dativus Ethicus* answering to τοῖς μὲν implied before 'Αγρεύς.

καλεῖν.] 'By name.' Lit. 'so that they called him.'—Expletory

ὡς ἄρ' εἰπὼν ἔντυεν τερπνὰν γάμου κραίνειν τελευτάν.

Ἐπ. γ'.

ὠκεῖα δ' ἐπειγομένων ἤδη θεῶν
πρᾶξις ὁδοί τε βραχεῖαι. κεῖνο κεῖν' ἆμαρ διαίτασεν·
    θαλάμῳ δὲ μίγεν   120
ἐν πολυχρύσῳ Λιβύας· ἵνα καλλίσταν πόλιν
70 ἀμφέπει κλεινάν τ' ἀέθλοις.   125
    καί νυν ἐν Πυθῶνί νιν ἀγαθέᾳ Καρνειάδα
    υἱὸς εὐθαλεῖ συνέμιξε τύχᾳ·
    ἔνθα νικάσαις ἀνέφανε Κυράναν, ἅ νιν εὔφρων δέξε-
        ται   130
    καλλιγύναικι πάτρᾳ
75 δόξαν ἱμερτὰν ἀγαγόντ' ἀπὸ Δελφῶν.

Στρ. δ'.

ἀρεταὶ δ' αἰεὶ μεγάλαι πολύμυθοι·
βαιὰ δ' ἐν μακροῖσι ποικίλλειν,
ἀκοὰ σοφοῖς· ὁ δὲ καιρὸς ὁμοίως   135
παντὸς ἔχει κορυφάν. ἔγνων ποτὲ καὶ Ἰόλαον
80 οὐκ ἀτιμάσαντά νιν ἑπτάπυλοι Θῆβαι· τόν, Εὐρυσθῆος
    ἐπεὶ κεφαλὰν   140
    ἔπραθε φασγάνου ἀκμᾷ, κρύψαν ἔνερθ' ὑπὸ γᾶν διφρη-
        λάτα Ἀμφιτρύωνος

infinitive. He is called Zeus and Apollo as a delight, &c.; as a tender of sheep, Agreus, &c.

72. συνέμιξε.] Cf. Ol. i. 22.

73. ἀνέφανε.] Lit. 'brought into notice'—i.e. by having it proclaimed as his city by the herald. Cf. ἐξένεπε, Ol. viii. 20.

δέξεται.] Cf. infra v. 89.

77. 'That one makes an exquisite poem short when the theme is vast is said of true poets. For a sense of proportion constitutes supreme excellence in everything alike.'

79, 81. Two stories are told about Iolâos' slaughter of Eurystheus: one that he obtained a brief renewal of vigour just before his death from old age for the purpose of delivering the Hêrakleidae from their oppressor, the other that he got leave to return for a short time from Hades. Any way at a critical moment he gave unexpected aid to Thebes, thus showing that he deserved the praise bestowed on Dâmophilos, Pyth. iv. 286, 287. Pindar passed from one kind of καιρὸς 'the right time to stop' to the more general meaning 'the right time to act,' unless he meant that the conquest of Eurystheus was a great matter and Iolâos made short work of it.

σάματι, πατροπάτωρ ἔνθα οἱ Σπαρτῶν ξένος		145
κεῖτο, λευκίπποισι Καδμείων μετοικήσαις ἀγυιαῖς.
						'Αντ. δ'.

τέκε οἱ καὶ Ζηνὶ μιγεῖσα δαΐφρων
85 ἐν μόναις ὠδῖσιν 'Αλκμήνα
διδύμων κρατησίμαχον σθένος υἱῶν.			150
κωφὸς ἀνήρ τις, ὃς Ἡρακλεῖ στόμα μὴ παραβάλλει,
μηδὲ Διρκαίων ὑδάτων ἀὲ μέμναται, τά νιν θρέψαντο
καὶ Ἰφικλέα·						155
τοῖσι τέλειον ἐπ' εὐχᾷ κωμάσομαί τι παθὼν ἐσλόν.
Χαρίτων κελαδεννᾶν

82. πατροπάτωρ...οἱ.] For the rare possessive dative cf. Ol. ix. 15, Nem. vii. 22.

83. ἀγυιαῖς.] The locative.

84. οἱ.] This refers to the subject of the last clause.

86. Cf. Ol. vi. 22. The compound adjectives κρατησίμαχος, κρατησίπους do not follow the usual analogy of such forms.

87. παραβάλλει.] The preposition means 'from the immediate subject,' and the reading is preferable to περιβάλλει which most of the best mss. give. 'Dullard the man whoso doth not turn aside his voice to Hêrakles.' Cf. φέροις ἄστει γλῶσσαν, Ol. ix. 41.

88. ἀέ.] For this mss. give ἀεί against the metre. 'Ever and anon' suits the context very well, but ἐπι-, ἀνα-, ἅμα have been proposed as corrections.

89. 'For then shall I utter in kômos song somewhat on my own account since I have received a certain blessing granted in full in answer to a prayer *may the clear light of the tuneful graces not desert me.*' Why he should on this occasion pray for inspiration to Hêrakles and Iphikles is not quite clear. Was Telesikrates a regular ξένος of Thebes and therefore an object of

regard to the family of Amphitryon? There may have been some local association between these heroes and the Graces, or again Pindar may about the time of composition have been keeping some festival in their honour. I suspect that Telesikrates had been training at the gymnasium of Iolâos (Pausanias ix. 23).

τοῖσι.] For the construction cf. Nem. ii. 24, κωμάξατε Τιμοδήμῳ, Isth. vi. 20, 21, κώμαξε—Στρεψιάδᾳ. ἐπ' εὐχᾷ.] Cf. ἐπ' ἐλπίδεσσι, Pyth. ii. 49.

τι.] It is generally thought that this is the object of παθών, its position being changed by hyperbaton: but my rendering gives at least as good sense and the construction proposed is more straightforward. The future tense refers to the time of performance not of composition, as there is nothing more said about the Theban heroes; so probably does the future δέξεται, supra v. 73. There is therefore no need to suppose that Telesikrates was not at Kyrênê at the time of recitation. With these futures cf. κελαδησόμεθα, ἀντιάξει, Ol. xi. (x.) 79, 84.

Χαρίτων — φέγγος.] The very words of the εὐχά.

90 μή με λίποι καθαρὸν φέγγος. Αἰγίνᾳ τε γὰρ   160
φαμὶ Νίσου τ' ἐν λόφῳ τρὶς δὴ πόλιν τάνδ' εὐκλεΐξαι,
                                                'Επ. δ'.

σιγαλὸν ἀμαχανίαν ἔργῳ φυγών·
οὕνεκεν, εἰ φίλος ἀστῶν, εἴ τις ἀντάεις, τό γ' ἐν ξυνῷ
    πεπωναμένον εὖ   165
μὴ λόγον βλάπτων ἁλίοιο γέροντος κρυπτέτω.

95 κεῖνος αἰνεῖν καὶ τὸν ἐχθρὸν
παντὶ θυμῷ σύν τε δίκᾳ καλὰ ῥέζοντ' ἔννεπεν.   170
πλεῖστα νικάσαντά σε καὶ τελεταῖς
ὡρίαις ἐν Παλλάδος εἶδον, ἄφωνοί θ' ὡς ἕκαστα φίλ-
        τατον

91. Νίσου τ' ἐν λόφῳ.] At Megara.

πόλιν τάνδ'.] Kyrêne. The above explanation of the tense of δέξεται does away with the awkwardness of having to refer these words and ἀστῶν v. 93 to Thebes. So Aegina is called τάνδ' ἁλιερκέα χώραν, Ol. VIII. 25, when the victor and the poet are at Olympia. Render 'For I affirm that both at Aegina and at the hill of Nisos I have thrice already glorified this city, having escaped lack of power that brings silence by means of her achievement.' From v. 97 we learn that these six victories were gained by Telesikrates who thus furnished the poet with six themes and shed over him χαρίτων κελαδεννῶν καθαρὸν φέγγος, for the duration of which (i.e. for the supply of another theme) he professes to have prayed before these Pythian games. The theme of an Epinikian poet is ἔργον, without a theme he suffers from ἀμαχανία, μαχάνα being two or three times used of poetic power by Pindar; so that though we should naturally expect ἔργῳ to mean something done by the φυγών, yet this is not necessary, cf. Nem. VIII. 49. The general

sense is the same if we translate ἔργῳ 'by employment,' i.e. the employment furnished by the victories.

93. ἐν ξυνῷ.] Pindar several times insists on the common interest which a state has in the victory of a citizen, cf. Ol. VII. 92—95, Pyth. XI. 54, Isth. v. 69, ξυνὸν ἄστει κόσμον ἐῷ προσάγων.

94. '— disparage not, violating the maxim of the old man of the sea,' i.e. of Nêreus. βλάπτειν (√βλαβ, probably for βλαπ) is not connected with √λαβ, but is from the √MAR. Cf. Skt. √mlai, marcere, βλάξ, 'slack.'

κρυπτέτω.] Cf. Ol. II. 107, VII. 92.

96. σύν τε δίκᾳ.] So mss. Böckh, Don. σύν γε.

97, 98. Dissen infers from the use of τελεταί, which are festivals of gods, that the victories at Aegina and Megara were won in games dedicated to Heroes, of which there were Aeakeia at Aegina and Alkathoia and Diokleia at Megara. The yearly festivals of Pallas and the Olympian and Gaian games of vv. 100, 101 must all have been at Kyrêne, as is shown by the πλεῖστα of v. 97, the καὶ πᾶσι of

παρθενικᾷ πόσιν ἦ 175
100 υἱὸν εὔχοντ᾽, ὦ Τελεσίκρατες, ἔμμεν,

Στρ. ε'.

ἐν Ὀλυμπίοισί τε καὶ βαθυκόλπου
Γᾶς ἀέθλοις ἔν τε καὶ πᾶσιν
ἐπιχωρίοις. ἐμὲ δ᾽ ὦν τιν᾽ ἀοιδᾶς
δίψαν ἀκειόμενον πράσσει χρέος αὖτις ἐγεῖραι 180
105 καὶ παλαιὰ δόξα τεῶν προγόνων· οἷοι Λιβύσσας ἀμφὶ
γυναικὸς ἔβαν
Ἴρασα πρὸς πόλιν, Ἀνταίου μετὰ καλλίκομον μνασ-
τῆρες ἀγακλέα κούραν· 185
τὰν μάλα πολλοὶ ἀριστῆες ἀνδρῶν αἴτεον
σύγγονοι, πολλοὶ δὲ καὶ ξείνων. ἐπεὶ θαητὸν εἶδος 190
Ἀντ. ε'.

ἔπλετο· χρυσοστεφάνου δέ οἱ Ἥβας
110 καρπὸν ἀνθήσαντ᾽ ἀποδρέψαι
ἔθελον. πατὴρ δὲ θυγατρὶ φυτεύων

v. 102 and by the presence of women. 'Very often too at the yearly rites of Pallas maidens have seen thee a winner, and in silence each according to her state prayed to have a most dear husband or son such as thou, Telesikrates,' i. e. those who had no lovers wished for a husband like him, those who had, wished for a son like him. For ἔμμεν cf. Goodwin § 15. 2 note 2. The absence of ' such as thou' from the Greek is not harsh. If the sight of Telesikrates inspired a wish for a husband or a son, the implication is that one or other should be like him. It need not be understood with πόσιν, so by suppressing οἷοι ἐσσὶ with υἱὸν Pindar delicately makes it doubtful whether he actually meant εὔχοντό σε ἔμμεν πόσιν or the less florid compliment.

103. τιν᾽ ἀοιδᾶς.] mss. give τις

ἀοιδὰν and v. 105 the best give παλαιὰν δόξαν τεῶν against the metre. Now the transposition of the last letters of my text would be facilitated by the -τις in the next line, and the nominative form τις when established would cause the change of the real subject into the accusative. Render 'Well, I am eager to slake a kind of thirst for song, and a right antient tale told of your forefathers demands that I should revive its due currency.' The Scholl. διψώσῃ τῇ ᾠδῇ κ.τ.λ., ἢ διψῶσαν ᾠδὴν τῷ θέλειν ὑμνεῖν ὑμᾶς κ.τ.λ., support my reading ἀοιδᾶς. For a very similar use of τιν' cf. Ol. vi. 82.

104. πράσσει.] Cf. Ol. iii. 7.

106. ἀγακλέα.] Pindar several times has two adjectives without a conjunction when one is an epithet of dignity, e. g. πότνια, εὐώνυμος. The daughter was Alkêis or Barke.

κλεινότερον γάμον, ἄκουσεν Δαναόν ποτ' ἐν Ἄργει   195
οἷον εὖρεν τεσσαράκοντα καὶ ὀκτὼ παρθένοισι, πρὶν
     μέσον ἆμαρ ἑλεῖν,
ὠκύτατον γάμον· ἔστασεν γὰρ ἅπαντα χορὸν ἐν τέρ-
     μασιν αὐτίκ' ἀγῶνος·   200
115 σὺν δ' ἀέθλοις ἐκέλευσεν διακρῖναι ποδῶν,
ἄντινα σχήσοι τις ἡρώων, ὅσοι γαμβροί σφιν ἦλθον·   205
                                        Ἐπ. ε΄.

οὕτω δ' ἐδίδου Λίβυς ἁρμόζων κόρᾳ
νυμφίον ἄνδρα· ποτὶ γραμμᾷ μὲν αὐτὰν στᾶσε κοσ-
     μήσαις, τέλος ἔμμεν ἄκρον.   210
εἶπε δ' ἐν μέσσοις ἀπάγεσθαι, ὃς ἂν πρῶτος θορὼν
120 ἀμφὶ οἱ ψαύσειε πέπλοις.
ἔνθ' Ἀλεξίδαμος, ἐπεὶ φύγε λαιψηρὸν δρόμον,   215
παρθένον κεδνὰν χερὶ χειρὸς ἑλὼν
ἆγεν ἱππευτᾶν Νομάδων δι' ὅμιλον. πολλὰ μὲν κεῖνοι
     δίκον
φύλλ' ἔπι καὶ στεφάνους·
125 πολλὰ δὲ πρόσθεν πτερὰ δέξατο Νίκας.   220

---

112. Δαναόν.] Cf. Ol. xiv. 20.
114. χορόν.] The last syllable scans as long.
117. ἁρμόζων.] Cf. supra v. 13.
118. γραμμᾷ.] The line that marked the end of the race.
τέλος ἄκρον.] 'The first prize.' Cf. Ol. xi. (x.) 67.
120. πέπλοις.] For dat. cf. Pyth. x. 28.

121. φύγε.] 'When he had sped lightly over the course.'
123. Νομάδων.] The tribes in the neighbourhood of Barke.
124. This sportive ceremony of congratulation was called φυλλοβολία. Hence the metaphor, Pyth. viii. 57. Join ἐπί-δικον.
125. πτερά.] 'Leaves,' cf. Ol. xiv. 22.

PYTHIA X.

INTRODUCTION.

HIPPOKLES or Hippokleas, who won the victory celebrated in this
ode B.C. 502, was a member of the dynastic family of the Aleuadae,
one of the three Thessalian families which claimed to be Hêrakleidae,
the others being the Skopadae of Krannon (formerly Ephyra) and the
Kreondae of the same place [if they were really distinct, as Theokritos
makes them (XVI. 36—39)]. The Thessalian Hêrakleidae appear to
have united in doing honour to their young kinsman; for though
Hippokles is said to have been of Pelinna or Pelinnaeon the ode was
sung at Larissa (v. 56), and the poet was commissioned by Thôrax,
the head of the Aleuad family, while the Skopadae seem to have fur-
nished the chorus for the κῶμος (vv. 55, 56). In my notes on vv. 16—18
I have given reasons for accepting Hermann's suggestion that Phrikias
(v. 16) was not Hippokles' father, but a race-horse, so that Hippokles'
father, though so highly praised (vv. 22—29), is apparently not
named. This is somewhat strange, as is also the general designation
Thessalos in the inscription of the ode, instead of an adjective indi-
cating the victor's native town or city. Both these peculiarities
vanish if we suppose Hippokles to have been Thôrax' son. The
mention of τὸ Πελινναῖον (v. 4) is not by any means conclusive as to
Pelinna being the victor's town. The Aleuadae may have had special
associations with that town, and again τὸ Πελινναῖον may have been
a building, or street, or quarter in Larissa. The suppression of the
name Larissa in the ode, as in the inscription, would give the cele-
bration of the victory a national rather than a local character. The
introduction of the myth of Perseus may have been suggested by
Larissa, where Perseus was said to have slain Akrisios. This myth

16—2

may have been especially popular among the Hêrakleidae of Thessaly
at this time (Perseus being great-grandfather to Hêrakles), since
Makedonia was nominally subject to Dareios at this time, and the
Thessalian dynasts may well have been ready to assert their kinship
to Perseus' eastern descendants, the Persian Achaemenidae. The
Persians themselves accepted this mythological connection with
Hellenic dynasties (Herod. VII. 150), at least when it suited their
policy. The ode (Pindar's earliest extant work) was probably sung
in a triumphal procession (*v.* 6), and possibly the feasting of Hyper-
boreans is mentioned in reference to the celebration of the victories
with εὐωχίαι, for which cf. Pyth. IV. 129—131.

The rhythm is Lydian and Aeolian.

ANALYSIS.

vv.

1—3. Lakedaemon and Thessaly have the blessing of a Hêrakleid
dynasty.

4—6. Pytho and τὸ Πελινναῖον and the Aleuadae call for this toast
in their desire to honour Hippokles with a κῶμος of men ;

7, 8. For he has won the victory at Pytho in the δίαυλος δρόμος
of boys.

10, 11. Apollo has managed this,

12—16. While Hippokles' hereditary prowess has emulated his
father's victories.

17—21. Prayer for continuance of their prosperity.

21—26. Only a god is free from care, but for a man Hippokles'
father is to be highly congratulated on his lot.

27—30. He has gone as far towards bliss as man can go; but none
can reach the Hyperboreans.

31—48. Perseus visited them and witnessed their feasting and hap-
piness by Athêne's aid, and slew the Gorgon and turned
the Seriphians to stone.

48—50. Nothing is incredible if the gods work for it.

51—54. The poet terminates and excuses in metaphorical language
his digression.

55—59. The poet hopes that the Kômos will have to sing yet other
Epinikia by him in honour of Hippokles, and that the vic-
tor may find favour with maidens.

59—63. Men's desires vary. Attainment thereof makes the immediate future delightful, but no one can tell what a year will bring forth.

64—66. Thôrax' liberality in providing the Kômos is set forth.

67, 68. Gold and rectitude are proved by trial.

69—72. Praise of Thôrax' brothers and of their dynasty.

Στρ. α'.

Ὀλβία Λακεδαίμον·
μάκαιρα Θεσσαλία· πατρὸς δ' ἀμφοτέραις ἐξ ἑνὸς
ἀριστομάχου γένος Ἡρακλέος βασιλεύει.
τί κομπέω; κατὰ καιρὸν ἀλλά με Πυθώ τε καὶ τὸ
    Πελινναῖον ἀπύει   5

5 Ἀλεύα τε παῖδες, Ἱπποκλέα θέλοντες
ἀγαγεῖν ἐπικωμίαν ἀνδρῶν κλυτὰν ὄπα.   10

Ἀντ. α'.

γεύεται γὰρ ἀέθλων·
στρατῷ τ' ἀμφικτιόνων ὁ Παρνάσιος αὐτὸν μυχὸς
διαυλοδρομᾶν ὕπατον παίδων ἀνέειπεν.

10 Ἄπολλον, γλυκὺ δ' ἀνθρώπων τέλος ἀρχά τε δαίμονος
    ὀρνύντος αὔξεται·   15
ὁ μέν που τεοῖς γε μήδεσι τοῦτ' ἔπραξεν,
τὸ δὲ συγγενὲς ἐμβέβακεν ἴχνεσιν πατρὸς   20

1. To associate the Aleuadae with Sparta was a high compliment.

5. τε.] For τε after καί cf. Pyth. I. 42.

6. 'To bring in honour of Hippokles the loud voices of a kômos of men.' The epithet ἐπικωμίαν is definitive, κλυτὰν descriptive, cf. Pyth. IX. 8, infra v. 72.

7. γεύεται.] Cf. πόνων ἐγεύσαντο, Nem. VI. 25, κέαρ ὕμνων γεύεται, Isth. IV. 20.

8. ἀμφικτιόνων.] MSS. ἀμφικτυόνων, cf. Pyth. IV. 66. Hermann reads περικτιόνων as the syllable corresponding to ἀμφ- is elsewhere short.

10. 'Since it is when a god speeds it that men's work in the start and end alike waxeth pleasant.' This is the reason for the statement in the next line. It is immaterial whether we call it a parenthesis or not.

αὔξεται.] Our use of 'wax' for 'become' is exactly analogous, cf. ὅτου ἔτυχεν ὁ υἱὸς εὐφυέστατος γενόμενος εἰς αὔθησιν, οὗτος ἂν ἐλλόγιμος ηὐξήθη, ὅτου δὲ ἀφυής, ἀκλεής, Plat. Protag. p. 327 c, Rep. IV. p. 424 E. For the sing. cf. Ol. V. 15.

12. 'His inborn genius hath trodden in the footsteps of his father.' Dissen makes τὸ συγγενὲς

Ἐπ. α΄.

Ὀλυμπιονίκα δὶς ἐν πολεμαδόκοις
Ἄρεος ὅπλοις·
15 ἔθηκε καὶ βαθυλείμων' ὑπὸ Κίρρας ἀγὼν
πέτραν κρατησίποδα Φρικίαν.　　　　　25
ἔσποιτο μοῖρα καὶ ὑστέραισιν
ἐν ἀμέραις ἀγάνορα πλοῦτον ἀνθεῖν σφίσιν·

Στρ. β΄.

τῶν δ' ἐν Ἑλλάδι τερπνῶν
20 λαχόντες οὐκ ὀλίγαν δόσιν, μὴ φθονεραῖς ἐκ θεῶν　　30
μετατροπίαις ἐπικύρσαιεν. θεὸς εἴη
ἀπήμων κέαρ. εὐδαίμων δὲ καὶ ὑμνητὸς οὗτος ἀνὴρ
γίνεται σοφοῖς,　　　　　35
ὃς ἂν χερσὶν ἢ ποδῶν ἀρετᾷ κρατήσαις
τὰ μέγιστ' ἀέθλων ἕλῃ τόλμᾳ τε καὶ σθένει,

Ἀντ. β΄.

25 καὶ ζώων ἔτι νεαρὸν
κατ' αἶσαν υἱὸν ἴδῃ τυχόντα στεφάνων Πυθίων.　　40
ὁ χάλκεος οὐρανὸς οὔ ποτ' ἀμβατὸς αὐτοῖς·
ὅσαις δὲ βροτὸν ἔθνος ἀγλαΐαις ἀπτόμεσθα, περαίνει
πρὸς ἔσχατον　　　　　45

•

acc. absolute. For abstract instead
of concrete cf. Ol. XIII. 15.
14. Cf. Pyth. IX. 1.
15. βαθυλείμων'.] 'Rising from
rich meadows.'
16. 'Probably the name of a
horse belonging to the victor's
father' (Prof. Paley). Eustathios
gives κρατησίποδα ἵππον from Pin-
dar, probably in reference to this
passage.
17, 18. 'May even in later days
the hap that their lordly wealth
bloom (with victory in a horse-race)
attend them.' Best MSS. ἔποιτο.
ἀγάν. πλ. ἀνθ. is in apposition to
μοῖρα. Dissen compares Herod.
I. 32, εἰ μή οἱ τύχη ἐπίσποιτο, πάντα

καλὰ ἔχοντα τελευτῆσαι εὖ τὸν βίον.
The Schol. explains ὥστε ἀνθεῖν but
I doubt μοῖρα standing by itself for
'good luck.'
20. μή, κ.τ.λ.] 'May they meet
with no envious reverses from the
gods.'
21. θεὸς εἴη.] For omission of
ἂν cf. Pyth. IV. 118. I render 'A
god would of course be free from
care,' Mommsen and Bergk, 'one
free from care would surely be a
god.' For the sentiment cf. Pyth.
V. 50. The following passage of
course refers to the victor's father.
28. For dat. cf. Pyth. IX. 120,
also the dat. with θιγεῖν. For
βρότ. ἔθν. ἀπτ. cf. Nem. III. 74.

πλόον. ναυσὶ δ' οὔτε πεζὸς ἰὼν τάχ' εὔροις
30 ἐς Ὑπερβορέων ἀγῶνα θαυματὰν ὁδόν.

'Επ. β'.

παρ' οἷς ποτε Περσεὺς ἐδαίσατο λαγέτας,   50
δώματ' ἐσελθών,
κλειτὰς ὄνων ἑκατόμβας ἐπιτόσσαις θεῷ
ῥέζοντας· ὧν θαλίαις ἔμπεδον
35 εὐφαμίαις τε μάλιστ' Ἀπόλλων
χαίρει, γελᾷ θ' ὁρῶν ὕβριν ὀρθίαν κνωδάλων.   55

Στρ. γ'.

Μοῖσα δ' οὐκ ἀποδαμεῖ
τρόποις ἐπὶ σφετέροισι· παντᾷ δὲ χοροὶ παρθένων
λυρᾶν τε βοαὶ καναχαί τ' αὐλῶν δονέονται·   60
40 δάφνᾳ τε χρυσέᾳ κόμας ἀναδήσαντες εἰλαπινάζοισιν
εὐφρόνως.
νόσοι δ' οὔτε γῆρας οὐλόμενον κέκραται   65
ἱερᾷ γενεᾷ· πόνων δὲ καὶ μαχᾶν ἄτερ

'Αντ. γ'.

οἰκέοισι φυγόντες
ὑπέρδικον Νέμεσιν. θρασείᾳ δὲ πνέων καρδίᾳ

ἔσχατον πλόον.] Cf. ἐσχατιὰς ἤδη
πρὸς ὄλβου | βάλλετ' ἄγκυραν θεό-
τιμος ἐών, Isth. v. [vi.] 12, Ol. iii.
43.
29. For omission of first οὔτε
cf. Pyth. vi. 48, infra v. 41, Pyth.
iv. 78.
30. ἀγῶνα.] 'Concourse' or
'place of assembly.' This last is
the original meaning of the word,
lit. 'place of bringings' as Πυθὼν
'place of enquiries,' or 'of putre-
factions.' According to Eustathios
it is Boeôtian for ἀγορά.
33. ἐπιτόσσαις.] Cf. Pyth. iv.
25, iii. 27.
36. ὀρ. ὕβριν ὀρθίαν.] 'Rampant
lewdness' (Prof. Paley). Asses
were sacrificed at the Pythian
festival.

37, 38. 'And besides their pecu-
liar customs the Muse ever dwells
among them.'
40. χρυσέᾳ.] Cf. Ol. viii. 1, x.
13.
41. Cf. supra v. 29 for omission
of the first negative.
κέκραται.] Cf. Ol. xi. 104. For
sentiment cf. Frag. 120 [107],
κεῖνοι γάρ τ' ἄνοσοι καὶ ἀγήραοι | πό-
νων τ' ἄπειροι, βαρυβόαν πορθμὸν
πεφευγότες Ἀχέροντος. Here dis-
eases are less nearly associated
with age than are toils and troubles;
diseases being special inflictions,
age and trouble the natural lot
of mankind.
44. ὑπέρδικον.] 'Exacting,' 'mer-
cilessly severe.'

45 μόλεν Δανάας ποτὲ παῖς, ἀγεῖτο δ᾽ Ἀθάνα,   70
ἐς ἀνδρῶν μακάρων ὅμιλον· ἔπεφνέν τε Γοργόνα, καὶ
   ποικίλον κάρα
δρακόντων φόβαισιν ἦλυθε νασιώταις   75
λίθινον θάνατον φέρων. ἐμοὶ δὲ θαυμάσαι

'Επ. γ'.

θεῶν τελεσάντων οὐδέν ποτε φαίνεται
50 ἔμμεν ἄπιστον.
κώπαν σχάσον, ταχὺ δ᾽ ἄγκυραν ἔρεισον χθονὶ   80
πρώραθε, χοιράδος ἄλκαρ πέτρας.
ἐγκωμίων γὰρ ἄωτος ὕμνων
ἐπ᾽ ἄλλοτ᾽ ἄλλον ὦτε μέλισσα θύνει λόγον.

Στρ. δ'.

55 ἔλπομαι δ᾽ Ἐφυραίων   85
ὅπ᾽ ἀμφὶ Πηνειὸν γλυκεῖαν προχεόντων ἐμὰν
τὸν Ἱπποκλέαν ἔτι καὶ μᾶλλον σὺν ἀοιδαῖς
ἕκατι στεφάνων θαητὸν ἐν ἅλιξι θησέμεν ἐν καὶ παλαι-
   τέροις,   90
νέαισίν τε παρθένοισι μέλημα. καὶ γὰρ
60 ἑτέροις ἑτέρων ἔρως ὑπέκνισε φρένας·

'Αντ. δ'.

τῶν δ᾽ ἕκαστος ὀρούει,   95
τυχών κεν ἁρπαλέαν σχέθοι φροντίδα τὰν πὰρ ποδός·

46. ποικίλον.] Used of the hues
of a snake Pyth. VIII. 48. Render
'gleaming with locks consisting of
many-hued snakes.'
48. θαυμάσαι.] On θαυμάσιος
and ἄπιστος cf. Pyth. I. 27. Tafel
rightly objects to ἄπιστον θαυμάσαι
and says θαυμάσαι is for a substan-
tive: I explain 'with regard to won-
der having been raised no state-
ment seems to me to be incredible
if gods have brought the event
about.'
49, 50. The poet recurs to the
sentiment of v. 10.

51. ταχύ, κ.τ.λ.] 'And quickly
lower an anchor from the prow and
let it get hold of the bottom.'
53. ἄωτος.] Cf. Ol. II. 8, v. 1. In
his maturity Pindar would scarcely
have made 'a blossom' flit like
a bee.
54. θύνει.] Intransitive. L. and
S. are mistaken.
56. ὅπ᾽.] Here means 'song'
or 'music.'
62. τυχών κεν...σχέθοι.] i.e. εἰ
τύχοι...σχέθοι κε. Cf. Goodwin § 42.
3, note 1.
τὰν πὰρ ποδός.] Cf. Pyth. I. 76,

τὰ δ' εἰς ἐνιαυτὸν ἀτέκμαρτον προνοῆσαι.
πέποιθα ξενίᾳ προσανέι Θώρακος, ὅσπερ ἐμὰν ποιπνύων
χάριν   100
65 τόδ' ἔζευξεν ἅρμα Πιερίδων τετράορον,
φιλέων φιλέοντ', ἄγων ἄγοντα προφρόνως.

'Επ. δ'.

πειρῶντι δὲ καὶ χρυσὸς ἐν βασάνῳ πρέπει   105
καὶ νόος ὀρθός.
ἀδελφεοὺς ἐπί τ' αἰνήσομεν ἐσλούς, ὅτι
70 ὑψοῦ φέροντι νόμον Θεσσαλῶν
αὔξοντες· ἐν δ' ἀγαθοῖσι κεῖται   110
πατρώϊαι κεδναὶ πολίων κυβερνάσιες.

III. 60. 'He would find his antici-
pation of the immediate future
ravishingly delightful.'

63. For sentiment cf. Ol. XII.
7—9.

64. This confidence that he
will be employed again shows that
ἐμὰν v. 56 is emphatic, as its posi-
tion suggests.

ἐμὰν ποιπνύων χάριν.] 'Display-
ing zeal in my behoof.' That is
giving my poem every chance of
success by liberality in providing
for its proper performance.

65. Cf. Ol. VI. 22.

66. The strained phraseology
seems due to a juvenile over-eager-
ness for effect.

67. 'As gold showeth its nature
by the touchstone so doth an up-
right mind (on trial).'

69. ἀδελφεούς.] Thôrax of La-
rissa with his brothers Eurypylos

and Thrasydaeos were in atten-
dance on Mardonios before the
battle of Plataea, Herod. IX. 58.

71. κεῖται.] This is an instance
of the Schema Pindaricum, cf. Ol.
X. 5, Frag. 53 [45]. 15, τότε
βάλλεται, τότ' ἐπ' ἀμβρόταν χέρσον,
ἐραταὶ | ἴων φόβαι, ῥόδα τε κόμαισι
μίγνυται, | ἀχεῖταί τ' ὀμφαὶ μελέων
σὺν αὐλοῖς, | ἀχεῖται Σεμέλαν ἑλι-
κάμπυκα χοροί. Cf. Dr Thompson's
note on Plato Gorg. p. 500 D, Prof.
Paley on Eurip. Ion, 1146. The
singular verb precedes the plural
(or dual) noun which I believe
rarely expresses living agents as
in Aesch. Pers. 49, στεῦται (some
MSS. στεῦνται) πελάται. For this
use of κεῖμαι, cf. Pyth. VIII. 76.

72. 'The good hereditary govern-
ment of the cities.' For the meta-
phor cf. Pyth. I. 86.

PYTHIA XI.

ON THE VICTORY OF THRASYDAEOS OF THEBES IN THE SHORT FOOT-RACE OF BOYS.

INTRODUCTION.

THIS victory was won and this ode in its honour composed B.C. 478, not two years after the battle of Plataea, and the downfall of the Mēdizing tyrants of Thebes, Attaginos and Temāgenidas (Thuk. III. 62, Herod. IX. 15, 86—88). The episode of Orestes is supposed to allude to some scandal and crime in Thrasydaeos' family which had recently been avenged. The indirect defence of Klytaemnēstra from the charge of infidelity has been explained by supposing a reference to some Theban dame in whom the victor and his father were interested. Possibly the family had lost their head and been driven into exile during the tyranny, while the widow stayed in Thebes and formed a new connection under circumstances which made her liable to suspicions of criminal complicity in her husband's death, after the due avenging of which the family wished to make the best of her conduct. But it seems strange that a cheerful occasion should be chosen for the revival and perpetuation of such very unsavoury memories. Don. says 'The only conclusion which can be drawn with any degree of safety is that some one of the victor's friends or relatives had been accused by calumnious citizens of adultery with some lady of rank (v. 25 and following), and that this had probably been made an excuse for putting him to death by the then tyrants of Thebes; but that his death had been avenged by the family of Thrasydaeus after the restoration of freedom (v. 35 : χρονίῳ σὺν Ἄρει).' I cannot think this satisfactory. Pindar's point seems to be the aspersion of a woman, not a man, while he does not represent Agamemnon as slain for his own adultery, but for his wife's. I hold that Pindar is merely illustrating by anticipation his dictum μέμφομ' αἶσαν τυραννίδων (v. 53). Priamos, Agamemnon, Aegisthos and Orestes form a compact group of signal examples of most unenviable misery in connection with the highest rank. The suggestion that Klytaemnêstra was calumniated aptly induces some general reflection on the evil that most unceasingly besets the great, and is therefore in harmony with the general spirit of the ode. It is therefore wasted ingenuity to guess at special reasons for its insertion. The last twenty lines of the ode suggest that Thrasydaeos' family had been enjoying uninterrupted prosperity in a modest station, keeping aloof from political turmoil. There are not sufficient grounds for Böckh's inference that this ode was sung on the way to the temple of Apollo Ismênios, and that another was sung in the temple. The rhythm is Aeolian.

ANALYSIS.

vv.

1—8. The Theban Heroines are invoked to come to the temple of Apollo Ismênios,

9—12. To sing of Themis and Delphi as a compliment to Thebes and the Pythian games,

13—16. In which Thrasydaeos has won a third victory for his father's hearth in the land of Pylades, host of Orestes,

17—22. Whom Arsinoe saved from his mother when she slew Agamemnon and Kassandra.

22—25. Was she impelled by resentment at Iphigeneia's slaughter, or by infidelity?

25—27. This is an evil most harmful to young wives and sure to be talked about;

28—30. For the commonalty is calumnious.

31—37. Of the fate of Agamemnon and Kassandra, Aegisthos and Klytaemnêstra.

38—40. The poet declares that he has been borne out of the straight course.

41, 42. If his muse accepts fees the engagement should be fulfilled,

43, 44. As now the engagement to praise Thrasydaeos or his father.

45—50. Their praises.

50—53. Moderation and a middle condition are recommended.

54—58. A prize-winner who lives quietly baffles the envious, dies happily, and leaves his posterity the noblest heritage—a glorious name.

59—64. Such renown makes Iolâos and Kastor and Polydeukes the themes of song.

Στρ. α΄.

Κάδμου κόραι, Σεμέλα μὲν Ὀλυμπιάδων ἀγυιᾶτις,
Ἰνώ τε Λευκοθέα ποντιᾶν ὁμοθάλαμε Νηρηΐδων,   5
ἴτε σὺν Ἡρακλέος ἀριστογόνῳ
ματρὶ πὰρ Μελίαν χρυσέων ἐς ἄδυτον τριπόδων
5 θησαυρόν, ὃν περίαλλ᾽ ἐτίμασε Λοξίας,

Ἀντ. α΄.

Ἰσμήνιον δ᾽ ὀνύμαξεν, ἀλαθέα μαντείων θῶκον,   10
ὦ παῖδες Ἁρμονίας, ἔνθα καὶ νῦν ἐπίνομον ἡρωΐδων
στρατὸν ὁμαγυρέα καλεῖ συνίμεν,
ὄφρα Θέμιν ἱερὰν Πυθῶνά τε καὶ ὀρθοδίκαν   15
10 γᾶς ὀμφαλὸν κελαδήσετ᾽ ἄκρα σὺν ἑσπέρᾳ,

2. τε.] For τε after μὲν cf. Ol. IV. 15.

4. Μελίαν.] Pausanias (x. 10) tells us that this nymph bore Ismēnios and Tēneros to Apollo and that she shared her sons' temple.

6. μαντείων.] So mss. The penultimate syllable is short. Böckh and Don. give μαντίων.

7. ἐπίνομον ἡρ. στρατόν.] This phrase is generally held to mean the company of other national heroines; but I think that the construction of ἡρωΐδων is like that of Νηρηΐδων supra v. 2, and that 'the host that inhabited the land of heroines' means the kōmos. Vv. 9, 10 of course allude to an ode sung by Thebans, and it is best to suppose that the poet asks the heroines to join in the chorus; not to form a chorus themselves.

8. ὁμαγυρέα.] Mommsen reads the Epic -γερέα. Most good mss. give ὁμηγυρέα, but four give ὁμηγερέα. It is an extension of the predicate. The subject to καλεῖ is Λοξίας.

10. κελαδήσετε.] For future tense referring to the time of recitation cf. Pyth. IX. 89. It is needless to assume with Dissen and Don. that a second ode is meant.

ἄκρα σὺν ἑσπέρᾳ.] 'At the turn of eventide.' Authorities differ as to the exact meaning of this phrase. I follow Prof. Jebb. Don. gives 'at the beginning of,' Dissen 'late in the evening.' Prof. Jebb on Soph. Aj. 285 says "ἄκρας νυκτός— 'At dead of night.' In reference to time, ἄκρος appears to have been used with two different notions; (1) 'mid'—when the season is spoken of as being at its acme: e.g. Theocr. XI. 36, τυρὸς δ᾽ οὐ λείπει μ᾽ οὔτ᾽ ἐν θέρει, οὔτ᾽ ἐν ὀπώρᾳ, | οὐ χειμῶνος ἄκρω: and so probably Pind. Pyth. XI. 16, ἄκρᾳ σὺν ἑσπέρᾳ, 'at fall of eventide:' (2) 'incipient' or 'waning,'—i.e. on the edge, the threshold (of night, &c.),—or at its uttermost verge: e.g. Arist. H. A. IX. 23. 1, οὐ πᾶσαν νύκτα, ἀλλὰ τὴν ἀκρέσπερον καὶ περὶ ὄρθρον, at the close of evening and the dawn of day: Theophrastus (circ. 320 B.C.) De Sign. Plur. ἀκρόνυχοι ἀνατολαί, ὅταν ἄμα δυομένῳ ἀνατέλλῃ, the rising (of the star) at nightfall, soon after sunset: Hippocrates (circ. 430 B.C.) Aphor. p. 723, τοῦ μὲν ἦρος καὶ ἄκρου τοῦ θέρους, aestate nova; Bekker Anecd. p. 372, ἀκρόνυξ. οἷον ἀρχὴ τῆς νυκτός."

'Επ. α'.

ἑπταπύλοισι Θήβαις
χάριν ἀγῶνί τε Κίρρας,   20
ἐν τῷ Θρασυδαῖος ἔμνασεν, ἑστίαν
τρίτον ἐπὶ στέφανον πατρῴαν βαλών,
15 ἐν ἀφνεαῖς ἀρούραισι Πυλάδα
νικᾶν ξένου Λάκωνος Ὀρέστα.

Στρ. β'.

τὸν δὴ φονευομένου πατρὸς Ἀρσινόα Κλυταιμνήστρας 25
χειρῶν ὕπο κρατερᾶν κἀκ δόλου τροφὸς ἄνελε δυσπεν-
θέος,
ὁπότε Δαρδανίδα κόραν Πριάμου
20 Κασσάνδραν πολιῷ χαλκῷ σὺν Ἀγαμεμνονίᾳ   30
ψυχᾷ πόρευσ' Ἀχέροντος ἀκτὰν παρ' εὔσκιον

'Αντ. β'.

νηλὴς γυνά. πότερόν νιν ἄρ' Ἰφιγένει' ἐπ' Εὐρίπῳ 35
σφαχθεῖσα τῆλε πάτρας ἔκνισεν βαρυπάλαμον ὄρσαι
χόλον;
ἢ ἑτέρῳ λέχει δαμαζομέναν

13. ἔμνασεν.] Generally render-
ed 'made memorable.' I prefer
'called to remembrance.' I take
it that Thrasydaeos' father had
won two out of the three Pythian
wreaths, cf. v. 43.
14. ἐπί.] Join to βαλών. I think
that perhaps the readings ἑστίαν...
πατρῴαν are a mixture of a lost
correction, ἑστιᾶν...πατρῷᾶν, which
Mommsen adopts, and the right
readings ἑστίᾳ...πατρῴᾳ the remote
object to ἐπιβαλών, as there is no
support either for an accusative
with ἔμνασεν or for a second acc.
with ἐπιβαλών. The best way of
rendering the text would be Momm-
sen's—'reminded folk that it was
a third wreath he had placed on
the paternal hearth' but for the
unsupported accusativus termini.
I propose a slight modification,
taking ἑστίαν as an accusative of

reference,— 'reminded folk with
regard to his father's hearth that
it was a third wreath he had placed
on it'—i.e. reminded folk, by his
victory, of his father's two previous
successes. It is difficult to assent
to the suggestion that the φυλλο-
βολία is alluded to in connection
with ἑστία. We might expect the
future participle, as at the time of
the ἀγών he would not have been
home, but the inevitable ceremony
might easily be spoken of as per-
formed, as soon as the victory was
won.
15. In Phôkis.
18. ὕπο.] 'From under,' cf. Ol.
VI. 43.
22, 23. For construction, cf.
Pyth. IV. 151, VI. 32, 'Did the
slaughter of Iphigeneia, &c.'
24, 25. Generally taken to mean
'or did nightly amours lead her

25 ἔννυχοι πάραγον κοῖται; τὸ δὲ νέαις ἀλόχοις　　40
ἔχθιστον ἀμπλάκιον καλύψαι τ' ἀμάχανον

'Επ. β'.

ἀλλοτρίαισι γλώσσαις·
κακολόγοι δὲ πολῖται.
ἴσχει τε γὰρ ὄλβος οὐ μείονα φθόνον·　　45
30 ὁ δὲ χαμηλὰ πνέων ἄφαντον βρέμει.
θάνεν μὲν αὐτὸς ἥρως 'Ατρείδας
ἵκων χρόνῳ κλυταῖς ἐν 'Αμύκλαις,

Στρ. γ'.

μάντιν τ' ὄλεσσε κόραν, ἐπεὶ ἀμφ' 'Ελένᾳ πυρω-
θέντων　　50
Τρώων ἔλυσε δόμους ἀβρότατος. ὁ δ' ἄρα γέροντα
ξένον
35 Στρόφιον ἐξίκετο, νέα κεφαλά,

astray seduced by the bed of another,' Prof. Paley; but may not v. 24 mean 'humiliated by another connection on Agamemnon's part'? The poet suggests that her infidelity was provoked by her husband's. This interpretation gets rid of the awkwardness of λέχεϊ and κοῖται referring to the same bed, and harmonizes with the prominence given above to Kassandra's slaughter.

25. Cf. Pyth. II. 35. Hermann reads ἐννύχια τ. κοιμήμαθ' ὁ νέαις. He alters to correspond exactly to v. 9 four verses out of eight; i. e. v. 4 παρὰ for πάρ, v. 20 οἰκρότατα for Κασσάνδραν, v. 36 Δελφὸν ὑπὸ for Παρνασοῦ, besides this one. Mommsen reads with the best mss. τὸ δὴ though elsewhere two short syllables stand in place of δή, with which νέαις must scan as a monosyllable. However δὲ introducing a parenthesis is better than δή. Render τὸ δὲ 'now this.'

26. καλύψαι.] Cf. Ol. VII. 25.

29. Cf. Pyth. VII. 19.

30—34. 'For he that breathes

the air of low life grumbles in secret. The hero Atreus on his arrival after a long time was himself slain in renowned Amyklae and brought to destruction the maiden prophetess, when he had consumed the dainty dwellings of the Trojans, visited with fire for Helene's sake.'

30. For sentiment, cf. Pyth. I. 84. For δὲ after τε, cf. Pyth. IV. 80. Elsewhere in Pindar πνέω means 'I form aspirations,' Ol. II. 93, Nem. III. 41, but not simply 'I think,' as Cookesley says.

32. ἐν 'Αμύκλαις.] The ordinary tradition places the scene of the murder at Argos or Mykênae; but Pausanias mentions tombs of Agamemnon and Kassandra at Amyklae. The position is justified by the words applying to ὄλεσσε as well as to θάνεν with which ἵκων is brought into close connection by their beginning consecutive verses, cf. Ol. VII. 15.

34. ἀβρότατος.] Cf. Pyth. IV. 234.

Παρνασοῦ πόδα ναίοντ'· ἀλλὰ χρονίῳ σὺν Ἄρει   55
πέφνεν τε ματέρα θῆκέ τ' Αἴγισθον ἐν φοναῖς.

'Αντ. γ'.

ἦ ῥ', ὦ φίλοι, κατ' ἀμευσίπορον τρίοδον ἐδινάθην,
ὀρθὰν κέλευθον ἰὼν τοπρίν· ἤ μέ τις ἄνεμος ἔξω
πλόου   60
40 ἔβαλεν, ὡς ὅτ' ἄκατον εἰναλίαν;
Μοῖσα, τὸ δὲ τεόν, εἰ μισθῷ γε συνέθευ παρέχειν
φωνὰν ὑπάργυρον, ἄλλοτ' ἄλλᾳ ταρασσέμεν   65

'Επ. γ'.

ἦ πατρὶ Πυθονίκῳ
τό γε νῦν ἢ Θρασυδαίῳ,
45 τῶν εὐφροσύνα τε καὶ δόξ' ἐπιφλέγει.

36. 'But with Ares' help at last he slew his mother and laid Aegisthos' body in its gore. Verily my friends I had been whirled along at the meeting of three roads which causes change of route; though before I was going on the straight path. Or did some wind cast me out of my course, as when (it casteth) a barque upon the sea? My muse, 'tis thine, at least if thou didst bargain to let out thy voice for silver fee, to stir it divers ways at different times—now at any rate either for Thrasydaeos or his father a winner at Pytho. For their hospitality and fame do shine with added lustre.'

38. ἀμευσίπορον τρίοδον.] So MSS. For the metre's sake Hermann reads the plur.; but cf. Pyth. III. 6 for lengthening of -ον before a vowel. The Schol. explains ἀμευσίπορον, ἥν ἀμειβόμεθα καὶ ἀνύομεν; Dissen vias mutans, s. ubi viae se secant et mutantur. It is rather uiam mutans where the road branches into two, so that if the wrong road be chosen the πόρος is changed. Prof. Paley takes the metaphor to be from a labyrinth, but neither τρίο-

δον nor ἐδινάθην is appropriate to this idea. The being 'in a whirl' while passing the triuium would suffice to set the poet on the wrong route.

39. ὀρθάν.] 'Correct,' 'direct,' not physically 'straight' in this place.

41. τὸ δὲ τεόν.] MSS. τὸ δ' ἐτεόν. εἰ μισθῷ γε.] The γε is Schmid's. Hermann reads εἰ μ. παρέχεμεν συνέθευ, Böckh εἰ μ. συνετέθευ παρέχευ. The Scholl. support the aorist.—I propose μισθοῖο συνέθευ παρέχευ, 'if thou didst engage for a fee to render thy voice subject to silver,' i. e. 'to confine yourself to the subject set before you by your employer.' In old uncials μισθῷ was written ΜΙΣΘΟΙ; so I only add ο. The gen. seems to be better Greek than the dat. By ἄλλοτ' ἄλλᾳ ταρ. is meant to accommodate the voice to the requirements of different occasions. After giving the particular obligation in the protasis he states the general duty before the particular duty in the apodosis. Cf. Nem. IV. 79—84.

45. εὐφροσύνα τε καὶ δόξ'.] An

τὰ μὲν ἐν ἅρμασι καλλίνικοι πάλαι 70
Ὀλυμπίᾳ τ' ἀγώνων πολυφάτων
ἔσχον θοὰν ἀκτῖνα σὺν ἵπποις,

Στρ. δ'.

Πυθοῖ τε γυμνὸν ἐπὶ στάδιον καταβάντες ἤλεγξαν
50 Ἑλλανίδα στρατιὰν ὠκύτατι. θεόθεν ἐραίμαν καλῶν, 75
δυνατὰ μαιόμενος ἐν ἁλικίᾳ.
τῶν γὰρ ἀνὰ πόλιν εὑρίσκων τὰ μέσα μάσσονι σὺν
ὄλβῳ τεθαλότα, μέμφομ' αἶσαν τυραννίδων· 80

Ἀντ. δ'.

ξυναῖσι δ' ἀμφ' ἀρεταῖς τέταμαι· φθονεροὶ δ' ἀμύνονται
55 τᾶν εἴ τις ἄκρον ἑλὼν ἁσυχᾷ τε νεμόμενος αἰνὰν
ὕβριν 85

analysis of ἀγλαΐα, hospitable festive celebration of a victory.

ἐπιφλέγει.] Note the force of the preposition. For the metaphor cf. Isth. III. 60, 61, VI. 23, Ol. IX. 24, where it is transitive. So φλέγει is used both transitively and intransitively, cf. Pyth. v. 42.

46. 'These indeed as glorious victors with chariots long ago at Olympia they won, glory (to wit) for speed with horses in the much-celebrated games, and at Pytho having entered the course with naked runners they put to shame in swiftness the Hellenic concourse.'

τὰ μέν.] Cf. Pyth. IV. 154.

47. Ὀλυμπίᾳ.] So mss. but with τ' added. However the hiatus is quite admissible. The change to Ὀλυμπίαν is bad.

48. ἀκτῖνα.] Cf. ἐργμάτων ἀκτὶς καλῶν ἄσβεστος ἀεί, Isth. III. 60. So αἴγλα ποδῶν, Ol. XIII. 36.

49. καταβάντες.] Stadia were always on comparatively low ground.

50. θεόθεν, κ.τ.λ.] 'May the gods grant me desire of noble aims, seeking after what is within my capacities among my compeers.'

For of orders in the state I find that the middle flourish with the more lasting prosperity, and I condemn the lot of tyrants. But I have exerted myself for merits in which all have interest. Now the envious are baffled if any one should have won a foremost place in these, and enjoying it in quiet should have avoided fell arrogance and should have at the last found dark death the fairer for his having left to his most dear family the glory of a good name superior to all possessions.'

51. ἐν ἁλικίᾳ.] Dissen explains dum vires florent; the Schol. ἐν τῇ παρούσῃ μοι ἀεὶ ἡλικίᾳ, τουτέστιν ἑκάστοτε.

52, 53. Cf. Phokylides Frag. 12, πολλὰ μέσοισιν ἄριστα· μέσος θέλω ἐν πόλει εἶναι, Theognis 335, πάντων μέσ' ἄριστα. Others explain the words of a moderate form of constitution comparing Aesch. Eum. 503 (P.), Eurip. Suppl. 244.

54. ξυναῖσι.] Cf. Pyth. IX. 93.

54, 55. mss. give: ἀμύνοντ' ἄτᾳ εἴ τις.

Hermann:

1. ἀμεύονται, | εἰ γάρ τις,

ἀπέφυγεν· μέλανα δ' ἀν' ἐσχατιὰν
καλλίονα θάνατον ἔσχεν γλυκυτάτᾳ γενεᾷ
εὐώνυμον κτεάνων κρατίσταν χάριν πορών·   90

'Επ. δ'.

ἅ τε τὸν 'Ιφικλείδαν
60 διαφέρει 'Ιόλαον
ὑμνητὸν ἐόντα, καὶ Κάστορος βίαν,
σέ τε, ἄναξ Πολύδευκες, υἱοὶ θεῶν,
τὸ μὲν παρ' ἆμαρ ἕδραισι Θεράπνας,   95
τὸ δ' οἰκέοντας ἔνδον 'Ολύμπου.

2. ἀμεύονται, | τᾶν εἴ τις,
3. ἀμύνονται, | ἆται, εἴ τις.
Mommsen :
ἀμύνονται | ἆτᾳ, εἴ τις.
Tafel : ἀμύνονται, | τᾶν εἴ τις,
which I prefer, as most like to de-
generate into the ms. reading. The
loss of ι and confusion of ν and ι
are frequent. In uncials ἆτᾳ was
ΑΤΑΙ. The aorists seem to be
almost equivalent to *futura ex-
acta;* but I regard the apodosis as
specially applying to Thrasydaeos
and his father, the protasis as
general, so I do not propose ἀμύ-
νοντ' ἄν, 'would be being baffled.'
For τᾶν (ἀρετᾶν) ἄκρον, cf. πρὸς
ἄκρον ἀρετᾶς ἦλθον, Nem. vi. 24.
Here however ἄκρον seems to mean
'first prize,' cf. τέλος ἄκρον, Pyth.
ix. 118.
56, 57. mss. give μέλανος δ'.
Thiersch proposed σχήσει for ἔσχεν
of two old mss. and Triclinian (the
rest ἐν). But the -ον can scan as a
long syllable before a vowel. Her-
mann reads μέλανος ἀν' ἐ. | κ. θανά-
του ταύταν γλ.; Mommsen the same
except θάνατον τοῦτον. The read-
ing ἔσχεν is thought to be due to
ἐσχ-ατιὰν above. Those who object
to ἔσχεν had better leave a blank.
Fortunately the general sense of
the passage is clear in spite of the

uncertainty as to the text. For
sentiment cf. Pyth. iv. 187.
58. κτεάνων κρατίσταν.] For this
use of the superlative, cf. Pyth. ii.
59.
59. 'The which carries abroad
as a theme of song Iolâos son of
Iphiklos, and mighty Kastor and
thee, king Polydeukes, ye sons of
Deities, for that ye dwell on al-
ternate days in sepulchres at The-
rapne and again in the halls of
Olympos.'
62. For τε after καὶ cf. Ol. iii.
8, Pyth. i. 42. This instance af-
fords the best support to my view ;
in fact demonstrates its correct-
ness.
63. παρ' ἆμαρ.] Lit. 'during
a day,' 'for a day.' Taking it with
τὸ μὲν...τὸ δὲ we get 'every other
day.' The use in Soph. *Aj.* 475 is
different, see Prof. Jebb's note.
For the subject, cf. Nem. x. 55,
μεταμειβόμενοι δ' ἐναλλὰξ ἀμέραν τὰν
μὲν παρὰ πατρὶ φίλῳ—Δὶ νέμονται,
τὰν δ' ὑπὸ κεύθεσι γαίας ἐν γυάλοις
Θεράπνας. This is mentioned as
suggesting their most distinguish-
ing characteristic, their brotherly
love. The introduction of the twins
is not surprising after the previous
notice of their sister Klytaem-
nêstra.

PYTHIA XII.

ON THE VICTORY OF MIDAS OF AKRAGAS WITH THE
FLUTE.

INTRODUCTION.

MIDAS of Agrigentum won the prize for flute-playing twice at
the Pythian games, B.C. 494, 400, and also at the Panathênaea. But
from *vv.* 30—32, and the absence of any reference to a former suc-
cess, it may be gathered that this ode celebrates the first Pythian
victory. Böckh, however, thinks that it may be referred with equal
probability to the second. The musical contests at the Pythian
games were of great importance. The contest in which Midas won
was with the instrument alone, ψιλὴ αὔλησις, or, ἄχορον αὔλημα.
The competition in the αὐλῳδία, or song to the flute, was put down
in the second Pythiad. The Scholiast tells us that during his per-
formance the mouthpiece of Midas' flute[1] got broken off, but that
he managed to play on, and so surprised the audience that he was
declared the winner. This ode was sung at Agrigentum on the
victor's return. Midas appears from the last words of the ode to
have had some ambition still unsatisfied.

The rhythm is Dorian.

vv.	ANALYSIS.
1—6.	Invocation to Akragas and the synonymous tutelary god-dess to welcome Midas after his victory in the art
6—11.	Which Athêne invented from imitating the wail of the Gorgons uttered when Perseus slew Medusa.
12—18.	Other achievements of Perseus,
18—22.	After bringing him safely through which the goddess, in imitation of Euryale's wail, invented flute music,
22—27.	And disclosed it to men as 'the many-headed tune' issuing from reed of Lake Kêphissis.

[1] The αὐλὸς generally consisted of two connected tubes and a mouth-
piece in which were tongues which vibrated, so that it was partly a reed
instrument like our clarinet. The method of blowing and the sound of
an αὐλὸς with its mouthpiece removed would be those of a syrinx, only
instead of having many tubes the length of the vibrating air-columns
would be altered by the keys.

28—32. All human bliss involves toil, but a god can end it at once, and give one success unexpectedly, but withhold another.

Στρ. α'.

Αἰτέω σε, φιλάγλαε, καλλίστα βροτεᾶν πολίων,
Φερσεφόνας ἕδος, ἅτ' ὄχθαις ἔπι μηλοβότου
ναίεις Ἀκράγαντος εὔδματον κολώναν, ὦ ἄνα,   5
ἵλαος ἀθανάτων ἀνδρῶν τε σὺν εὐμενίᾳ

5 δέξαι στεφάνωμα τόδ' ἐκ Πυθῶνος εὐδόξῳ Μίδᾳ,   10
αὐτόν τέ νιν Ἑλλάδα νικάσαντα τέχνᾳ, τάν ποτε
Παλλὰς ἐφεῦρε θρασειᾶν Γοργόνων
οὔλιον θρῆνον διαπλέξαισ' Ἀθάνα·

Στρ. β'.

τὸν παρθενίοις ὑπό τ' ἀπλάτοις ὀφίων κεφαλαῖς   15
10 ἄϊε λειβόμενον δυσπενθέϊ σὺν καμάτῳ,
Περσεὺς ὁπότε τρίτον ἄνυσσεν κασιγνητᾶν μέρος,   20
εἰναλίᾳ Σερίφῳ λαοῖσί τε μοῖραν ἄγων.
ἤτοι τό τε θεσπέσιον Φόρκοι' ἀμαύρωσεν γένος,
λυγρόν τ' ἔρανον Πολυδέκτᾳ θῆκε ματρός τ' ἔμπεδον   25
15 δουλοσύναν τό τ' ἀναγκαῖον λέχος,
εὐπαράου κρᾶτα συλάσαις Μεδοίσας

Στρ. γ'.

υἱὸς Δανάας· τὸν ἀπὸ χρυσοῦ φαμὲν αὐτορύτου   30
ἔμμεναι. ἀλλ' ἐπεὶ ἐκ τούτων φίλον ἄνδρα πόνων
ἐρρύσατο, παρθένος αὐλῶν τεῦχε πάμφωνον μέλος,

2. ἅτ'.] This is the tutelary heroine or nymph Akragas, cf. Pyth. vi. 6.
5. δέξαι.] For this verb with the dat. cf. Pyth. iv. 23.
8. διαπλέξαισ'.] 'When imitating the variations of the dismal wail '— or does οὔλιον mean here 'varied' 'shifting' akin to varius (cf. οὔλε ὄνειρε) distinct from οὔλιος, 'deadly'?
10. λειβόμενον.] For metaphor, cf. Pyth. iv. 137.

11. τρίτον μέρος.] Cf. Pyth. iv. 64.
12. 'Bringing doom both to seagirt Seriphos and its folk.'
14. 'And made grievous to Polydektes the assembly of gift-bringers and his (Perseus') mother's close slavery and enforced union.'
17. For late position of the subject, cf. Ol. xi. 25.
19. πάμφωνον.] Pindaric epithet of the music of flutes (clarionets, Prof. Paley). Cf. Pyth. iii. 17.

20 ὄφρα τὸν Εὐρυάλας ἐκ καρπαλιμᾶν γενύων   35
χριμφθέντα σὺν ἔντεσι μιμήσαιτ' ἐρικλάγκταν γόον.
εὗρεν θεός· ἀλλά νιν εὑροῖσ' ἀνδράσι θνατοῖς ἔχειν,   40
ὠνόμασεν κεφαλᾶν πολλᾶν νόμον,
εὐκλεᾶ λαοσσόων μναστῆρ' ἀγώνων,

Στρ. δ'.

25 λεπτοῦ διανισόμενον χαλκοῦ θάμα καὶ δονάκων,
τοὶ παρὰ καλλιχόρῳ ναίοισι πόλει Χαρίτων   45
Καφισίδος ἐν τεμένει, πιστοὶ χορευτᾶν μάρτυρες.
εἰ δέ τις ὄλβος ἐν ἀνθρώποισιν, ἄνευ καμάτου   50
οὐ φαίνεται· ἐκ δὲ τελευτάσει νιν ἤτοι σάμερον
30 δαίμων· τό γε μόρσιμον οὐ παρφυκτόν, ἀλλ' ἔσται
χρόνος
οὗτος, ὃ καί τιν' ἀελπτίᾳ βαλὼν
ἔμπαλιν γνώμας τὸ μὲν δώσει, τὸ δ' οὔπω.

20. 'In order that she might imitate with their stops the exceeding shrill groan as it burst from the ravening jaws of Euryale.' Stheno is omitted as the mention of one is enough, but is a variation after Γοργόνων, v. 7.

23. 'She named it the many-headed tune, the glorious reminder of folk-stirring contests.' Don. says 'On this νόμος πολυκέφαλος, see Plutarch. de musica, c. 7: λέγεται γὰρ τὸν προειρημένον Ὄλυμπον αὐλητὴν ὄντα τῶν ἐκ Φρυγίας ποιῆσαι νόμον αὐλητικὸν εἰς Ἀπόλλωνα, τὸν καλούμενον Πολυκέφαλον.— ἄλλοι δὲ Κράτητος εἶναι τὸν Πολυκέφαλον νόμον, γενομένου μαθητοῦ Ὀλύμπου· ὁ δὲ Πρατίνας Ὀλύμπου φησὶν εἶναι τὸν νόμον τοῦτον.' This was probably the tune which Midas had played in the competition.

25. λεπτοῦ χαλκοῦ.] The thin metal mouthpiece.

26. πόλει Χαρίτων.] Orchomenos.
27. 'In their precinct by Lake Kôpais.' See Ol. xiv. Introd. μάρτυρες.] Cf. Pyth. i. 2.
28. For sentiment cf. Pyth. v. 44, Ol. x. [xi.] 4, xi. [x.] 22.
29. 'But a god would bring it (κάματον) to an end, aye, to-day.' For these rare gnômic futures, cf. Ol. vii. 3.
30. ἀλλά, κ.τ.λ.] 'But such a time will come as indeed shall cast one into a state of surprise and shall contrary to his expectation give him one thing, but another shall not give yet.'
31. οὗτος.] Cf. Ol. iv. 24. ἀελπτίᾳ.] For the dativus termini, cf. Soph. Trach. 936, αἰτίᾳ βάλοι κακῇ, Ol. vi. 58.
32. ἔμπαλιν γνώμας.] Cf. Ol. xii. 11. Midas would seem to have failed to win some coveted distinction as yet.

CAMBRIDGE: PRINTED BY C. J. CLAY, M.A. AT THE UNIVERSITY PRESS.

CPSIA information can be obtained at www.ICGtesting.com
Printed in the USA
LVOW091357171111

255439LV00002B/3/P